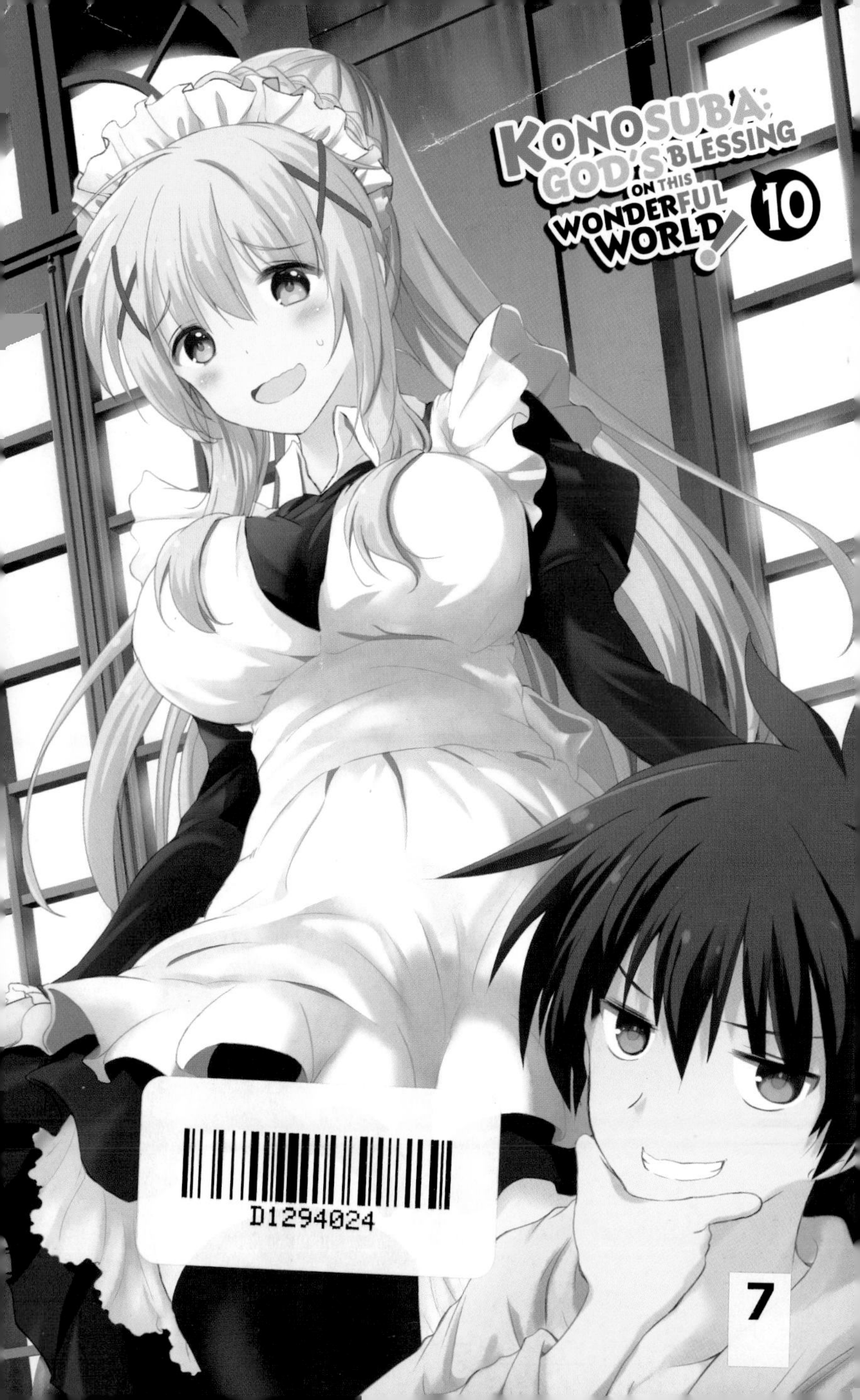
KONOSUBA: GOD'S BLESSING ON THIS WONDERFUL WORLD!
10

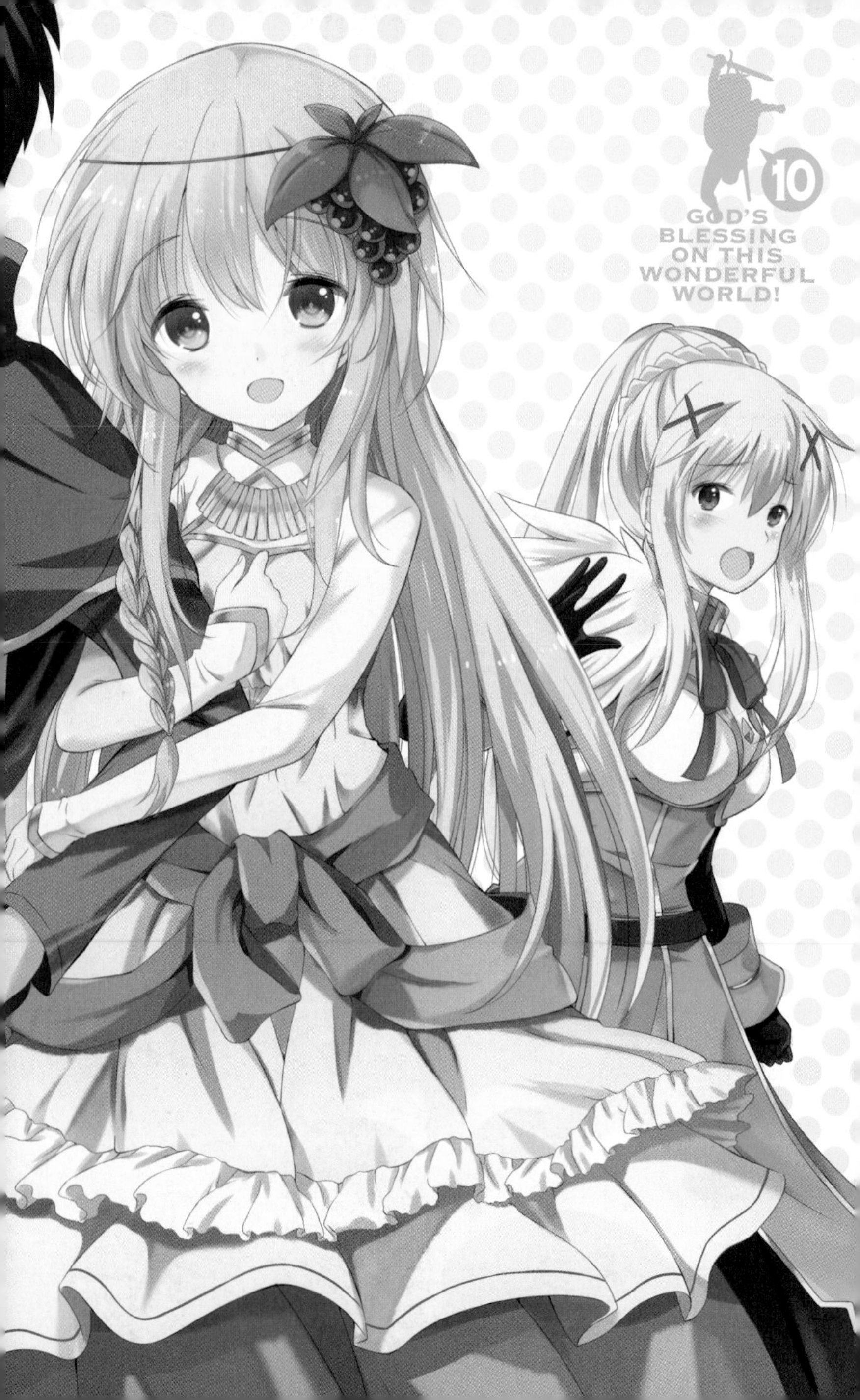
10
GOD'S
BLESSING
ON THIS
WONDERFUL
WORLD!

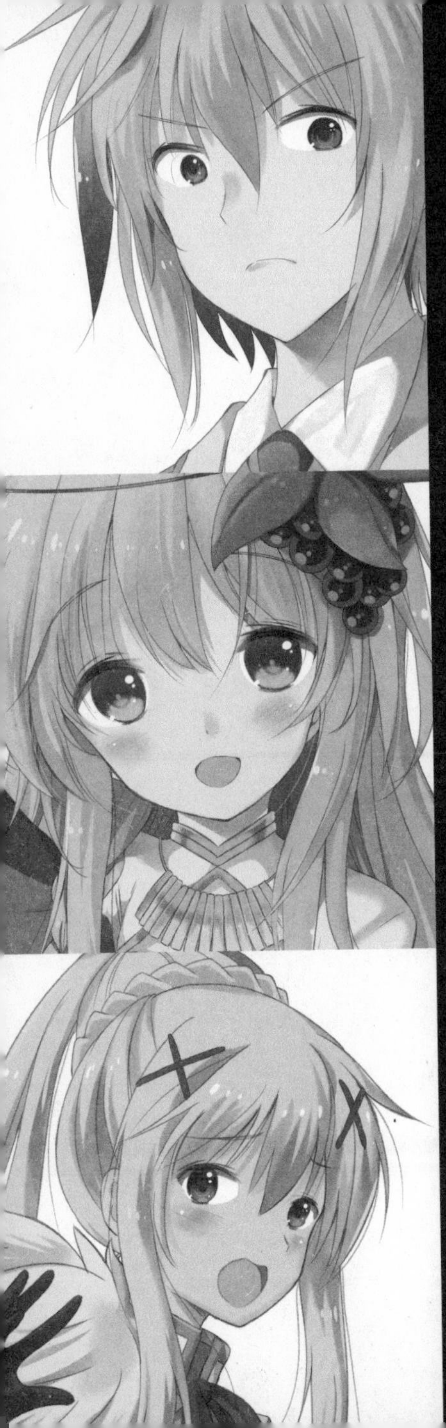

KONOSUBA: GOD'S BLESSING ON THIS WONDERFUL WORLD!

By:

MASAHITO WATARI

Original Work:

NATSUME AKATSUKI

Character Designs:

KURONE MISHIMA

GOD'S BLESSING ON THIS WONDERFUL WORLD!
CONTENTS

Chapter 55 Reeducation for This Clever Girl! 5

Chapter 56 A Playmate for This Innocent Princess! 37

Chapter 57 Retribution on This Handsome Thief! (1) 69

Chapter 58 Retribution on This Handsome Thief! (2) 95

Chapter 59 May Care Be Taken with This Questionable Magic Item! 129

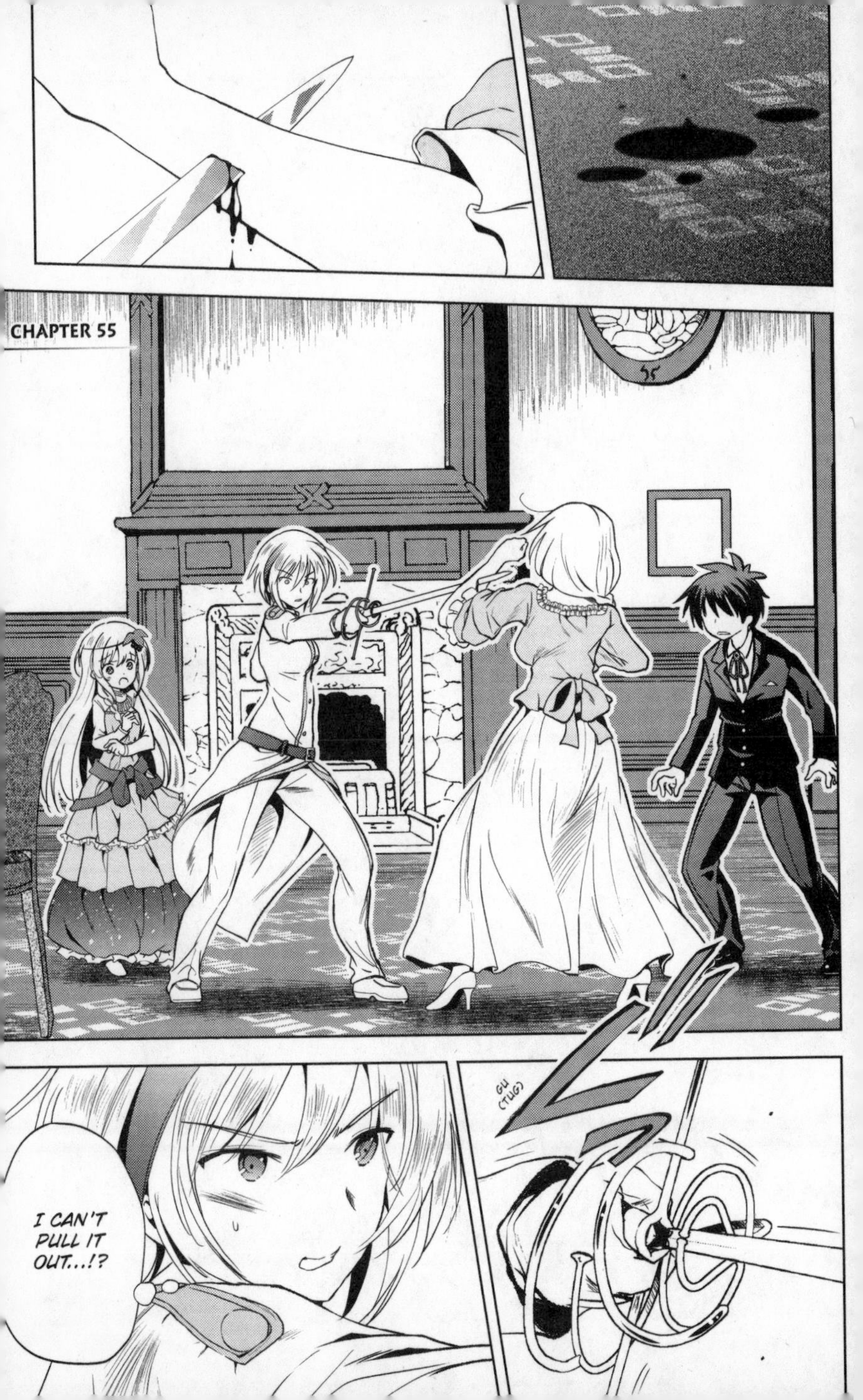
CHAPTER 55
GU (TUG)
I CAN'T PULL IT OUT...!?

CHAPTER 55

REEDUCATION FOR THIS CLEVER GIRL!

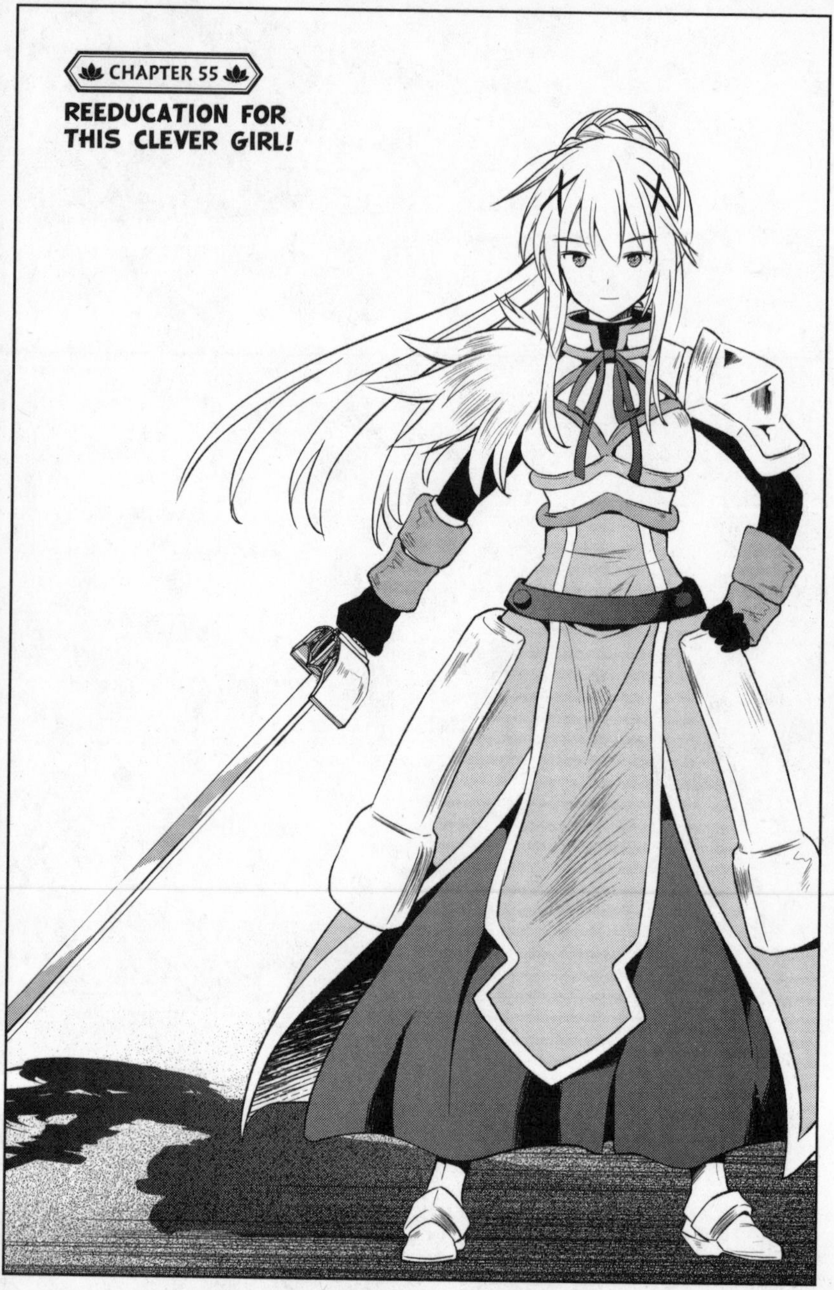

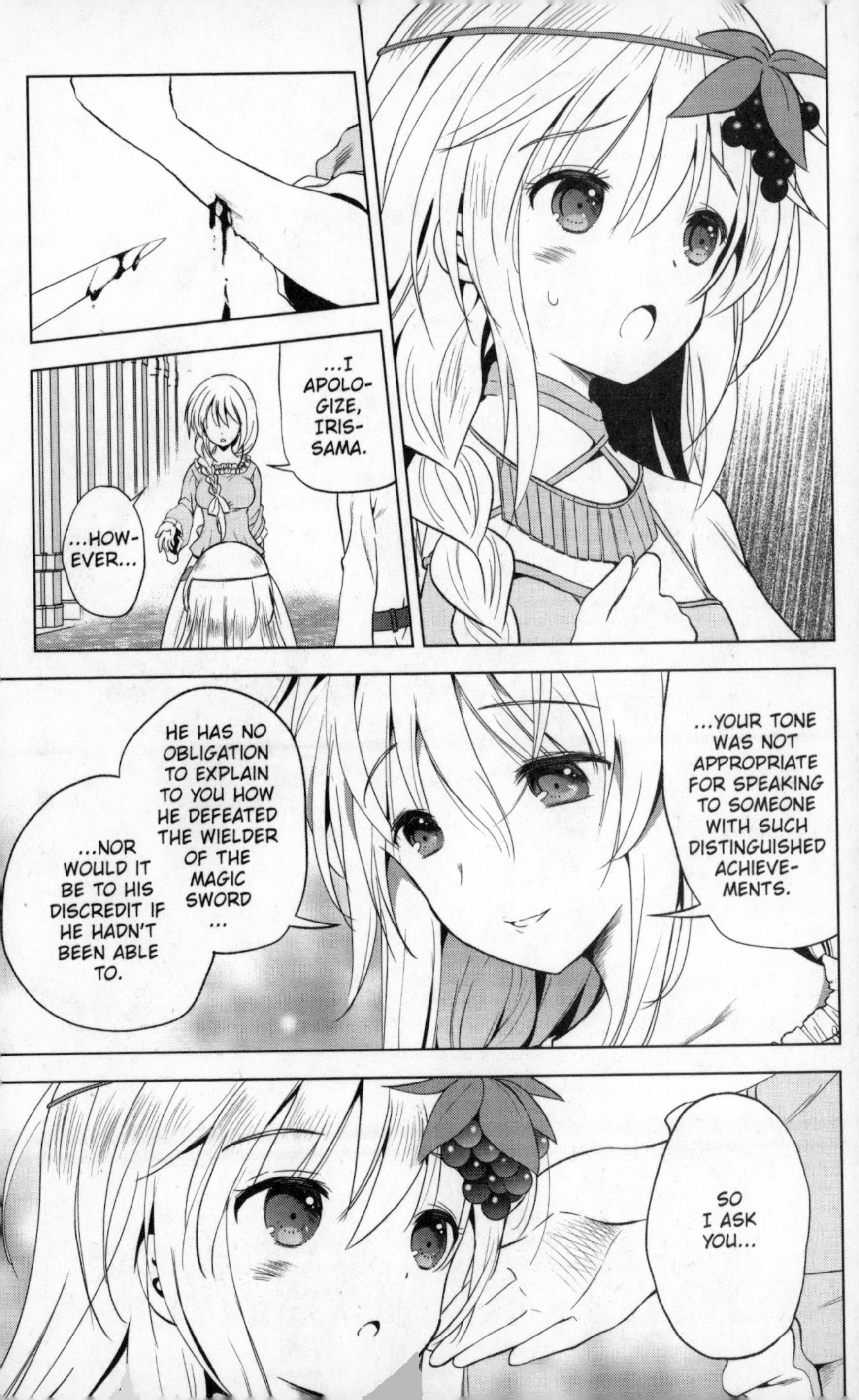
...I APOLOGIZE, IRIS-SAMA.
...HOWEVER...
...YOUR TONE WAS NOT APPROPRIATE FOR SPEAKING TO SOMEONE WITH SUCH DISTINGUISHED ACHIEVEMENTS.
HE HAS NO OBLIGATION TO EXPLAIN TO YOU HOW HE DEFEATED THE WIELDER OF THE MAGIC SWORD...
...NOR WOULD IT BE TO HIS DISCREDIT IF HE HADN'T BEEN ABLE TO.
SO I ASK YOU...

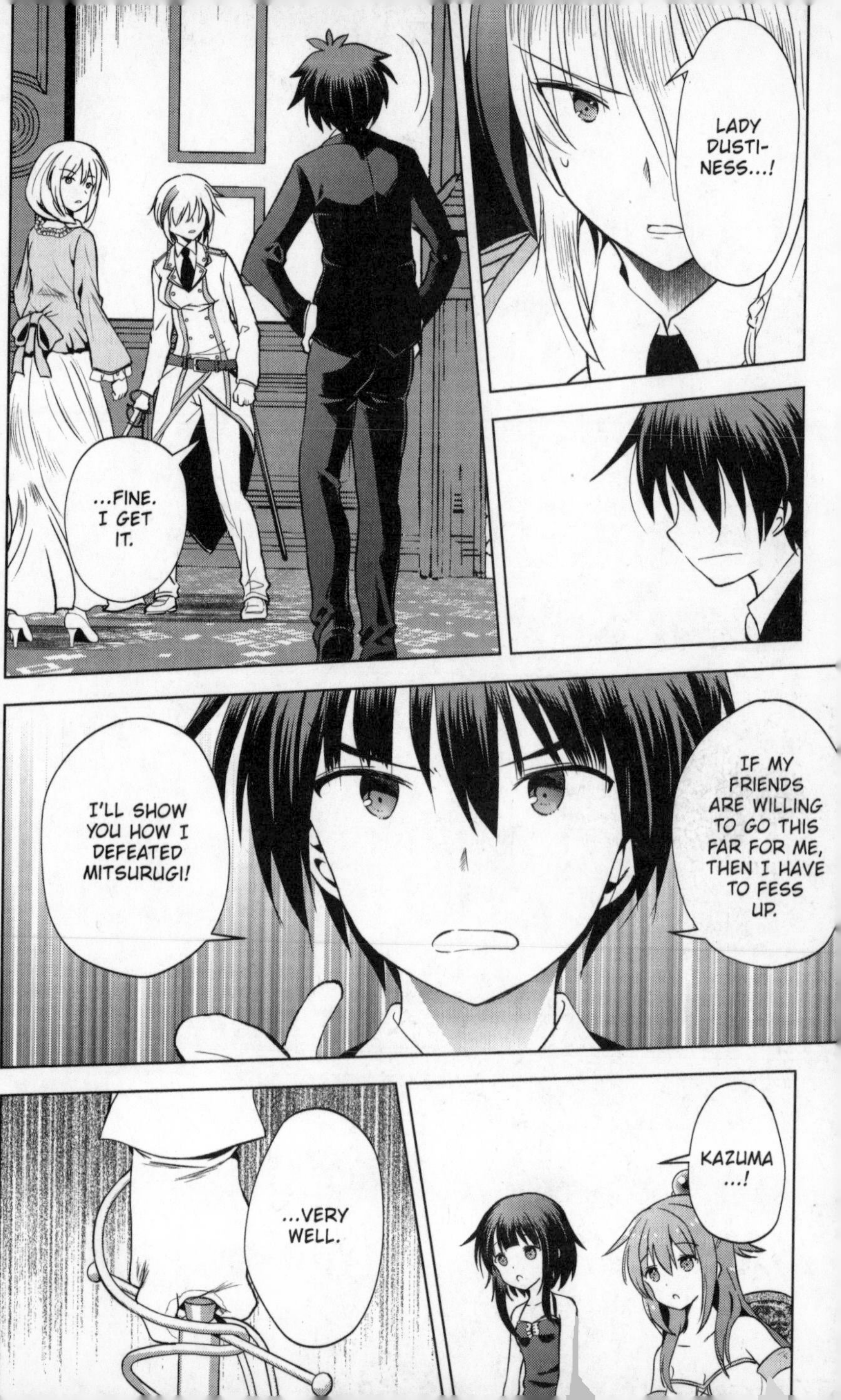
LADY DUSTI-NESS...!
...FINE. I GET IT.
IF MY FRIENDS ARE WILLING TO GO THIS FAR FOR ME, THEN I HAVE TO FESS UP.
I'LL SHOW YOU HOW I DEFEATED MITSURUGI!
KAZUMA...!
...VERY WELL.

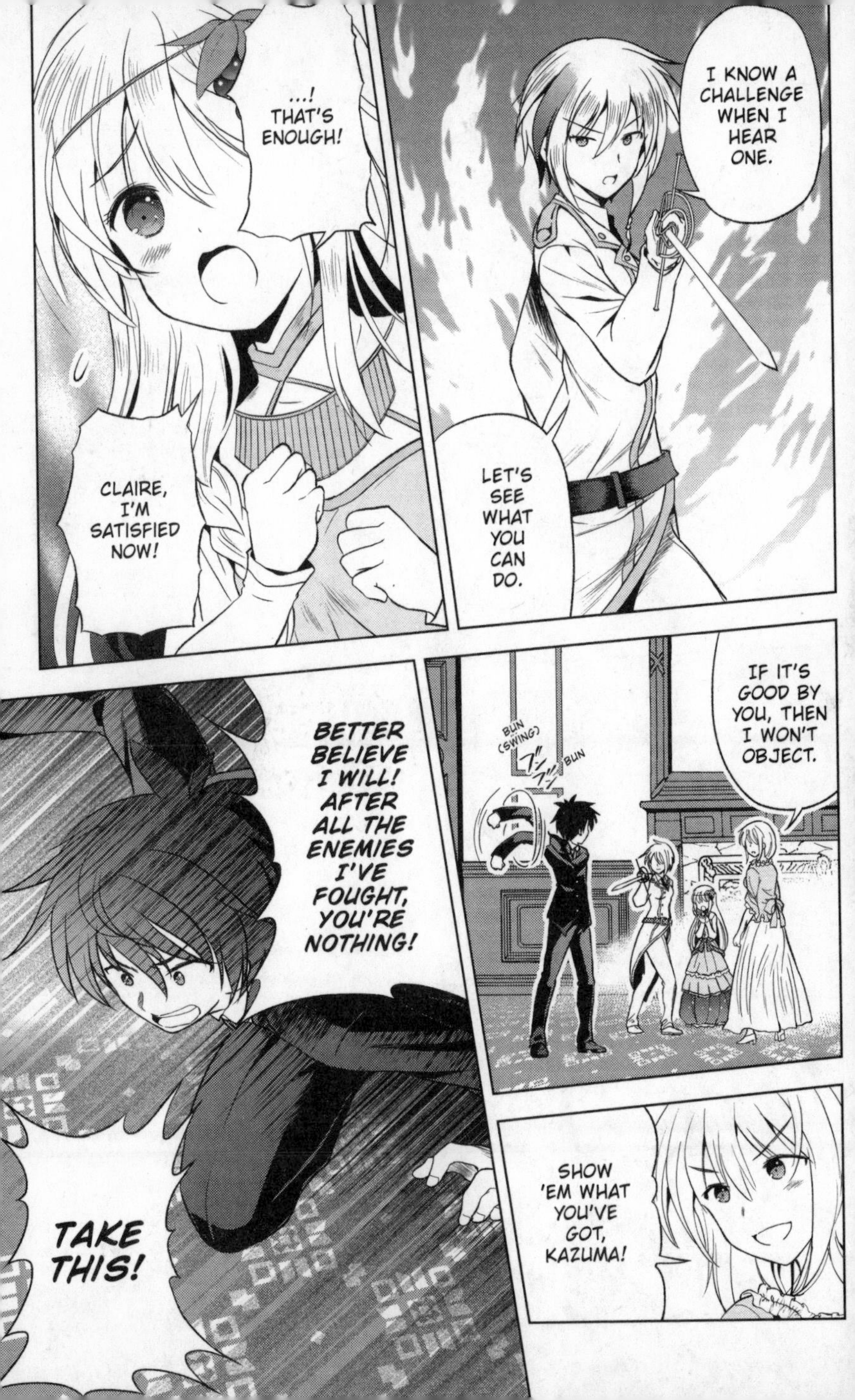
I KNOW A CHALLENGE WHEN I HEAR ONE.
LET'S SEE WHAT YOU CAN DO.
...! THAT'S ENOUGH!
CLAIRE, I'M SATISFIED NOW!
IF IT'S GOOD BY YOU, THEN I WON'T OBJECT.
BUN (SWING)
BUN
SHOW 'EM WHAT YOU'VE GOT, KAZUMA!
BETTER BELIEVE I WILL! AFTER ALL THE ENEMIES I'VE FOUGHT, YOU'RE NOTHING!
TAKE THIS!

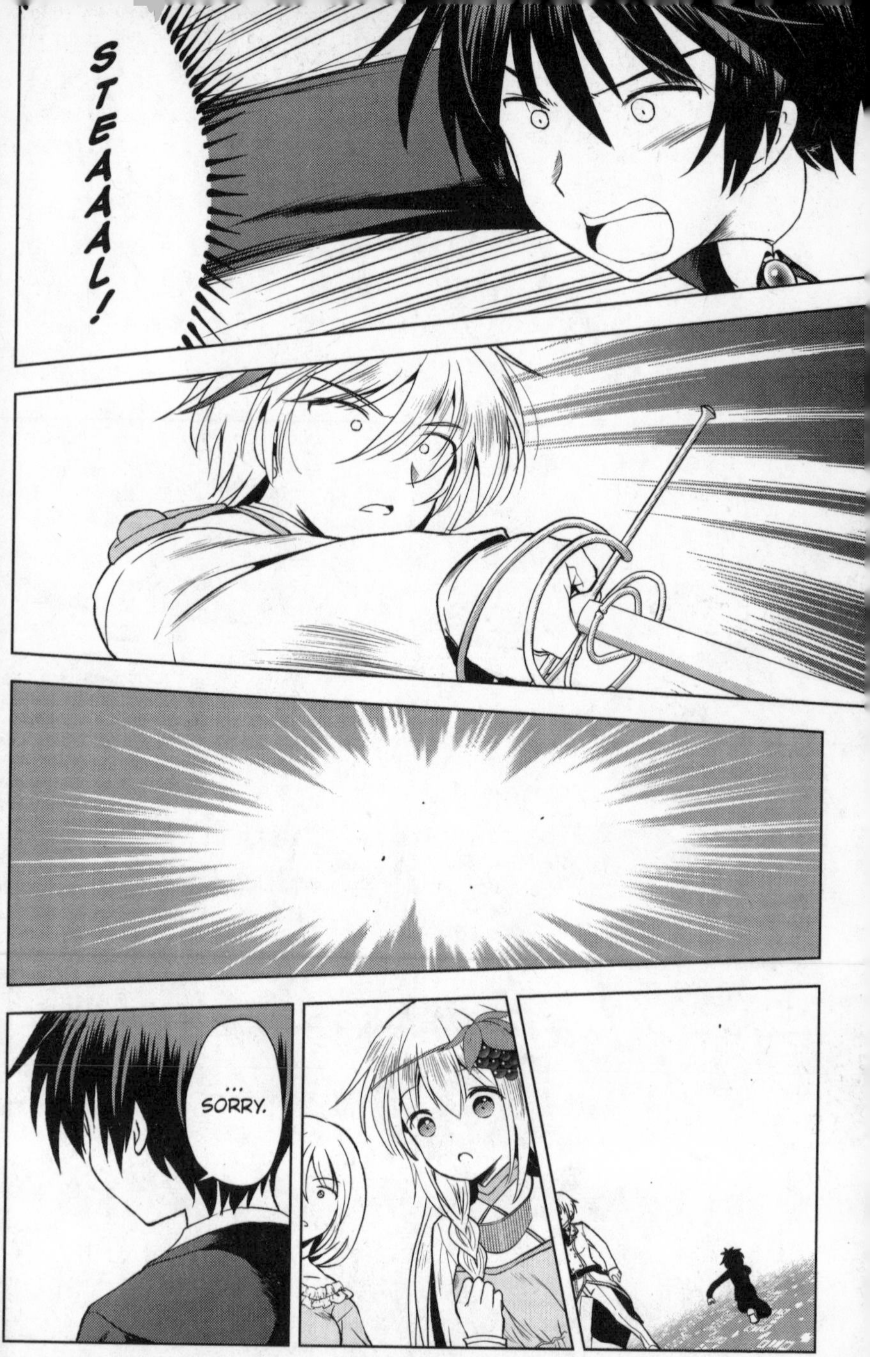
STEAAAL!
... SORRY.

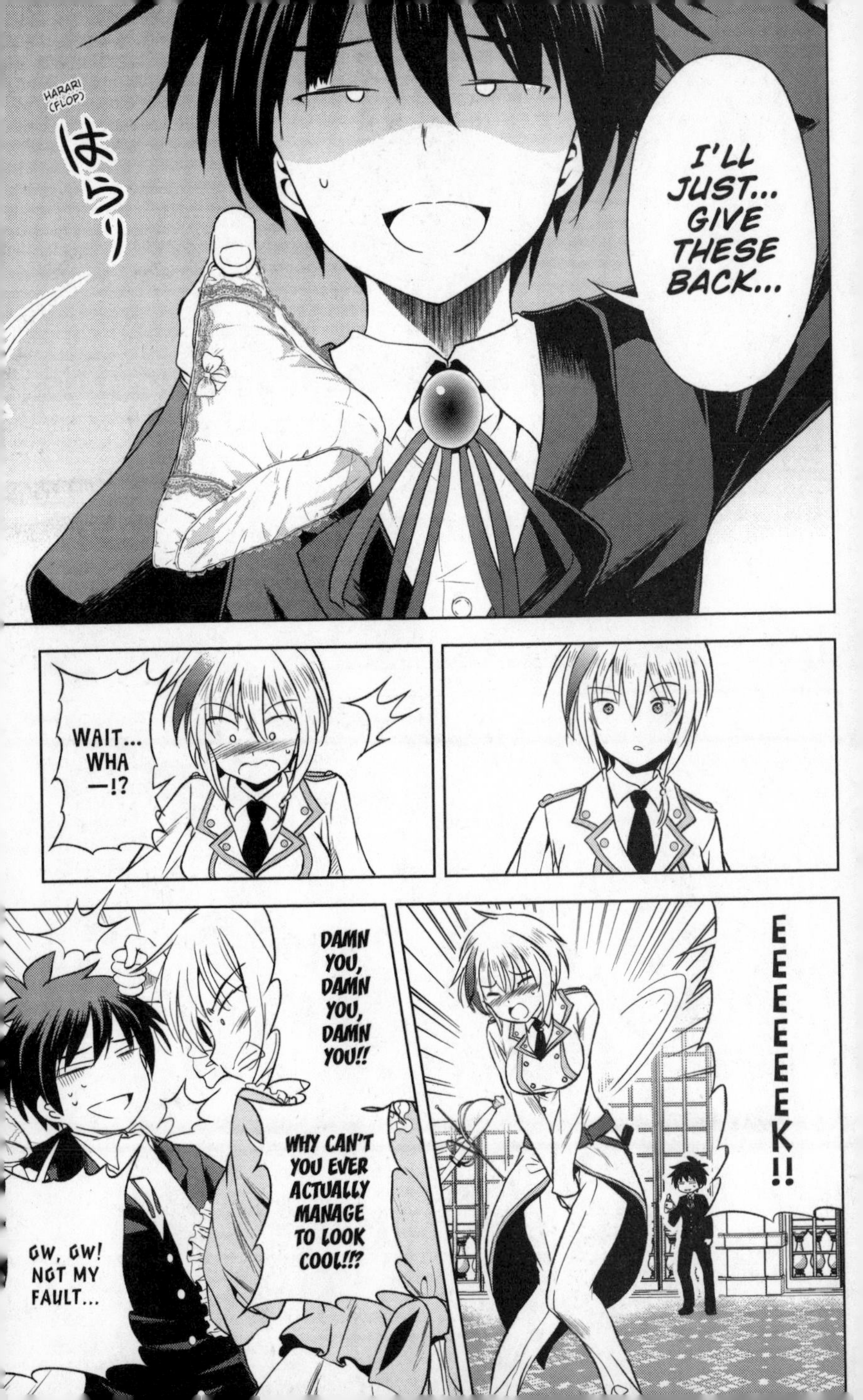
I'LL JUST... GIVE THESE BACK...
HARARI (FLOP)
はらり
WAIT... WHA—!?
EEEEEEEK!!
DAMN YOU, DAMN YOU, DAMN YOU!!
WHY CAN'T YOU EVER ACTUALLY MANAGE TO LOOK COOL!!?
OW, OW! NOT MY FAULT...

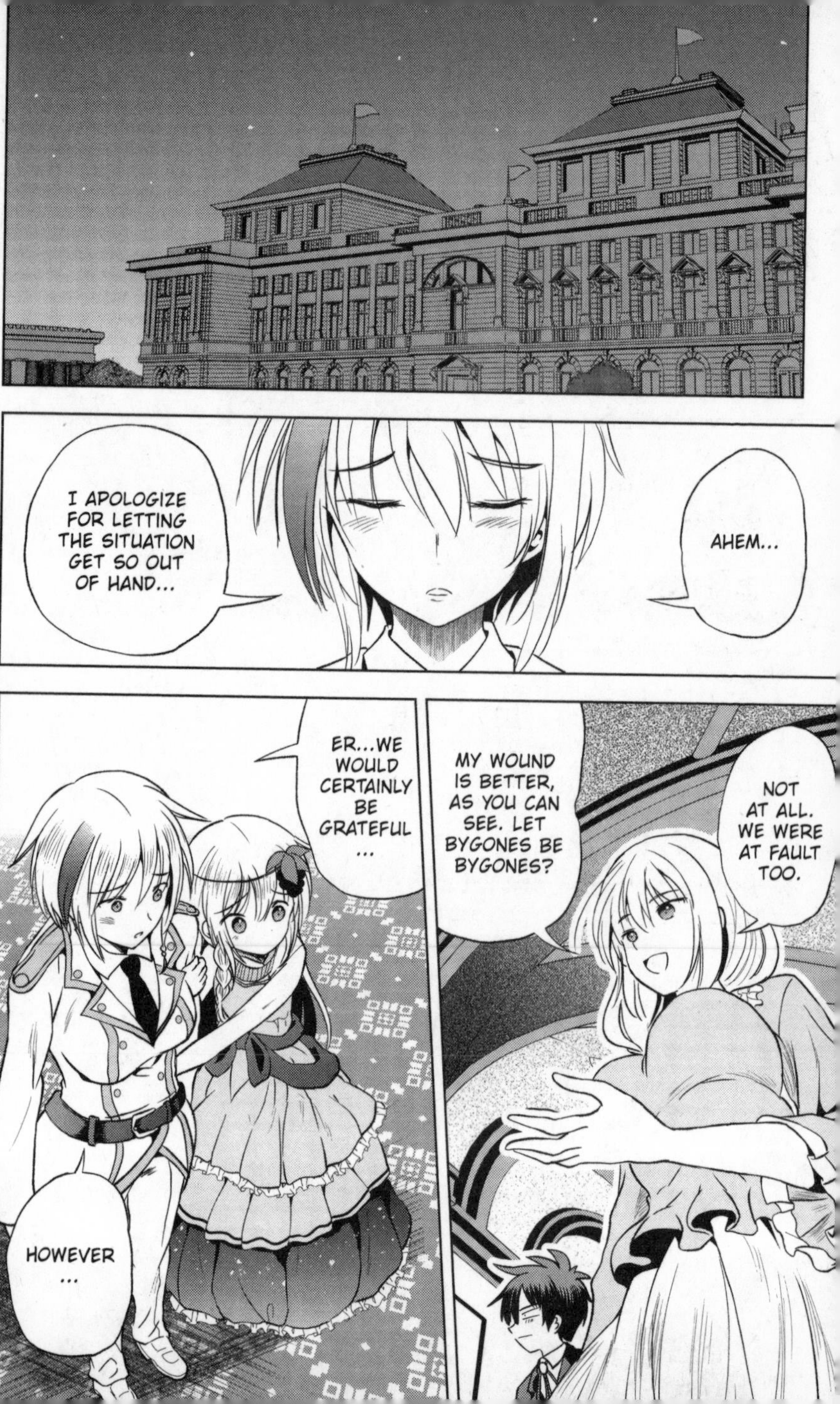
AHEM...
I APOLOGIZE FOR LETTING THE SITUATION GET SO OUT OF HAND...
NOT AT ALL. WE WERE AT FAULT TOO.
MY WOUND IS BETTER, AS YOU CAN SEE. LET BYGONES BE BYGONES?
ER...WE WOULD CERTAINLY BE GRATEFUL ...
HOWEVER ...

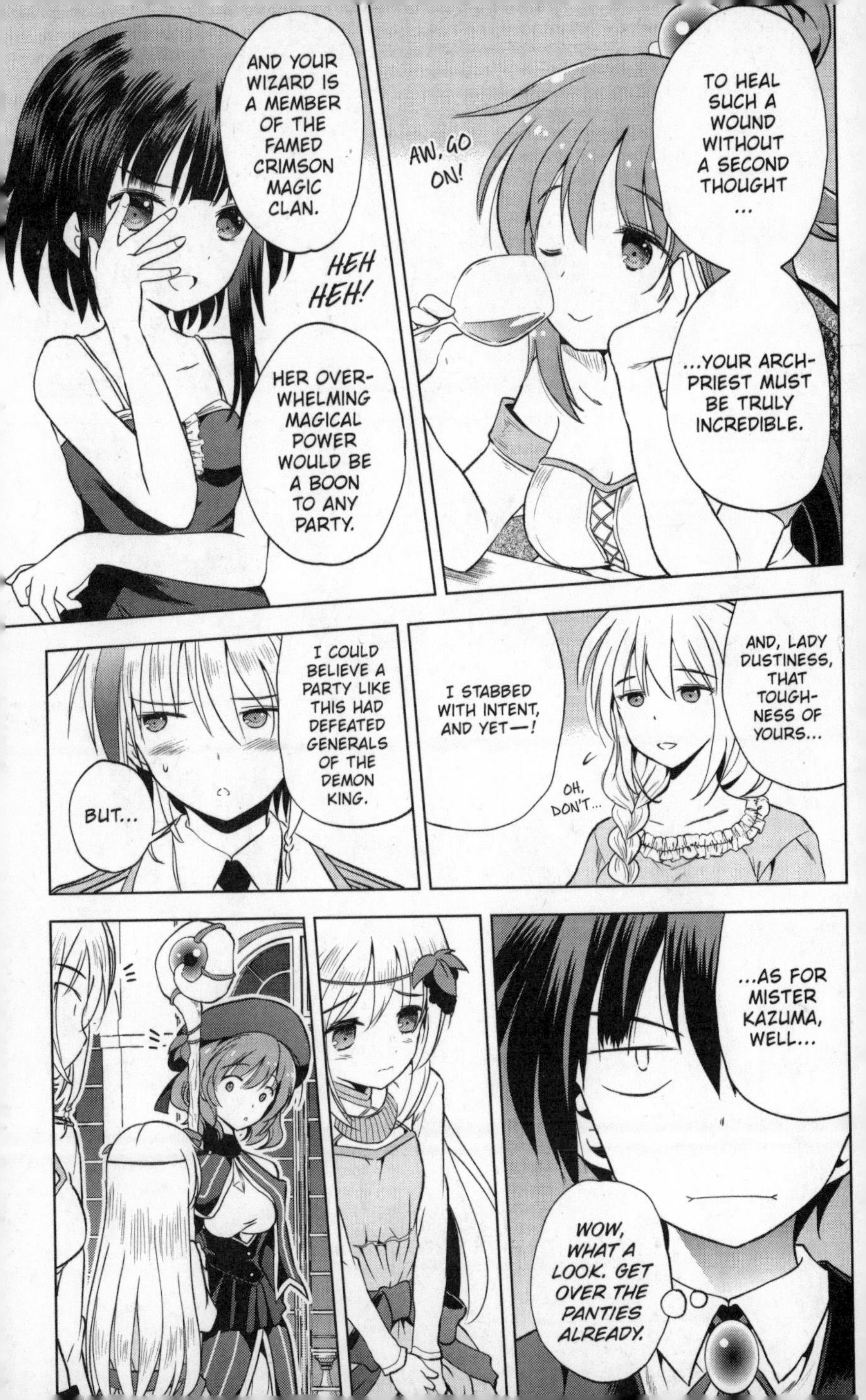
TO HEAL SUCH A WOUND WITHOUT A SECOND THOUGHT ...
AW, GO ON!
...YOUR ARCH-PRIEST MUST BE TRULY INCREDIBLE.
AND YOUR WIZARD IS A MEMBER OF THE FAMED CRIMSON MAGIC CLAN.
HEH HEH!
HER OVER-WHELMING MAGICAL POWER WOULD BE A BOON TO ANY PARTY.
AND, LADY DUSTINESS, THAT TOUGH-NESS OF YOURS...
OH, DON'T...
I STABBED WITH INTENT, AND YET—!
I COULD BELIEVE A PARTY LIKE THIS HAD DEFEATED GENERALS OF THE DEMON KING.
BUT...
...AS FOR MISTER KAZUMA, WELL...
WOW, WHAT A LOOK. GET OVER THE PANTIES ALREADY.

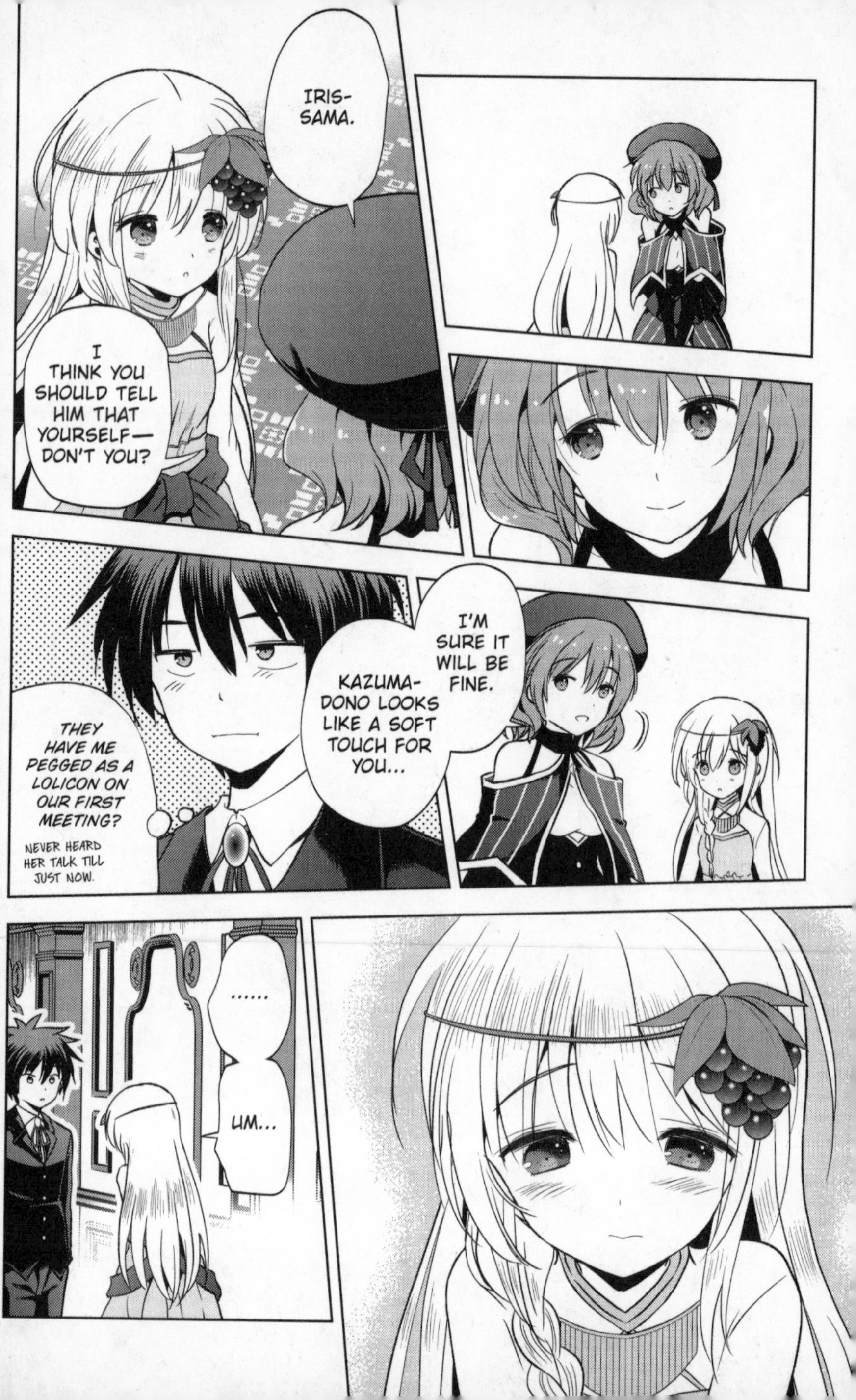
IRIS-SAMA.
I THINK YOU SHOULD TELL HIM THAT YOURSELF— DON'T YOU?
I'M SURE IT WILL BE FINE.
KAZUMA-DONO LOOKS LIKE A SOFT TOUCH FOR YOU...
THEY HAVE ME PEGGED AS A LOLICON ON OUR FIRST MEETING?
NEVER HEARD HER TALK TILL JUST NOW.
......
UM...

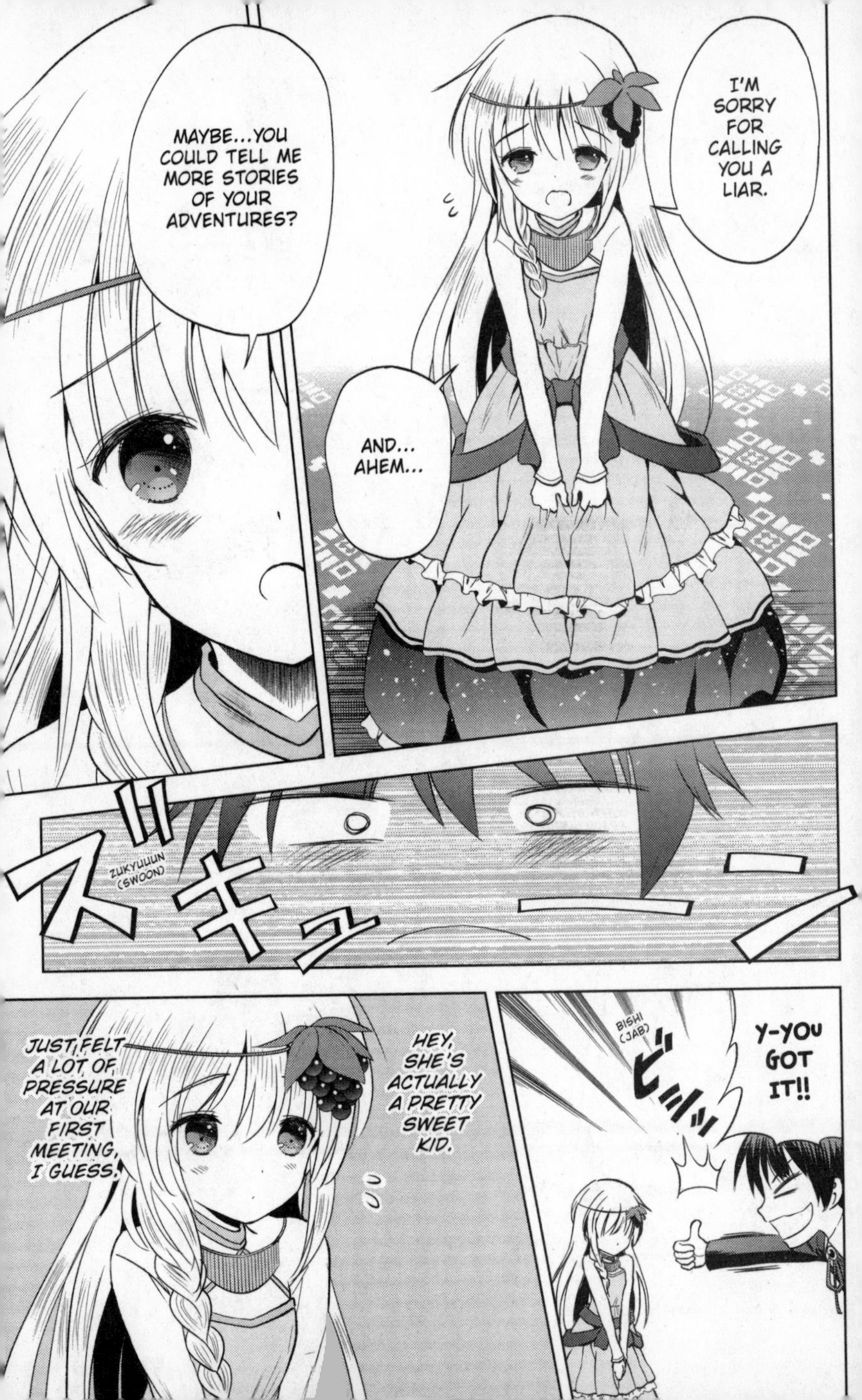
I'M SORRY FOR CALLING YOU A LIAR.
AND... AHEM...
MAYBE...YOU COULD TELL ME MORE STORIES OF YOUR ADVENTURES?
ズキューーン
ZUKYUUUN (SWOON)
Y-YOU GOT IT!!
BISHI (JAB)
HEY, SHE'S ACTUALLY A PRETTY SWEET KID.
JUST FELT A LOT OF PRESSURE AT OUR FIRST MEETING, I GUESS.

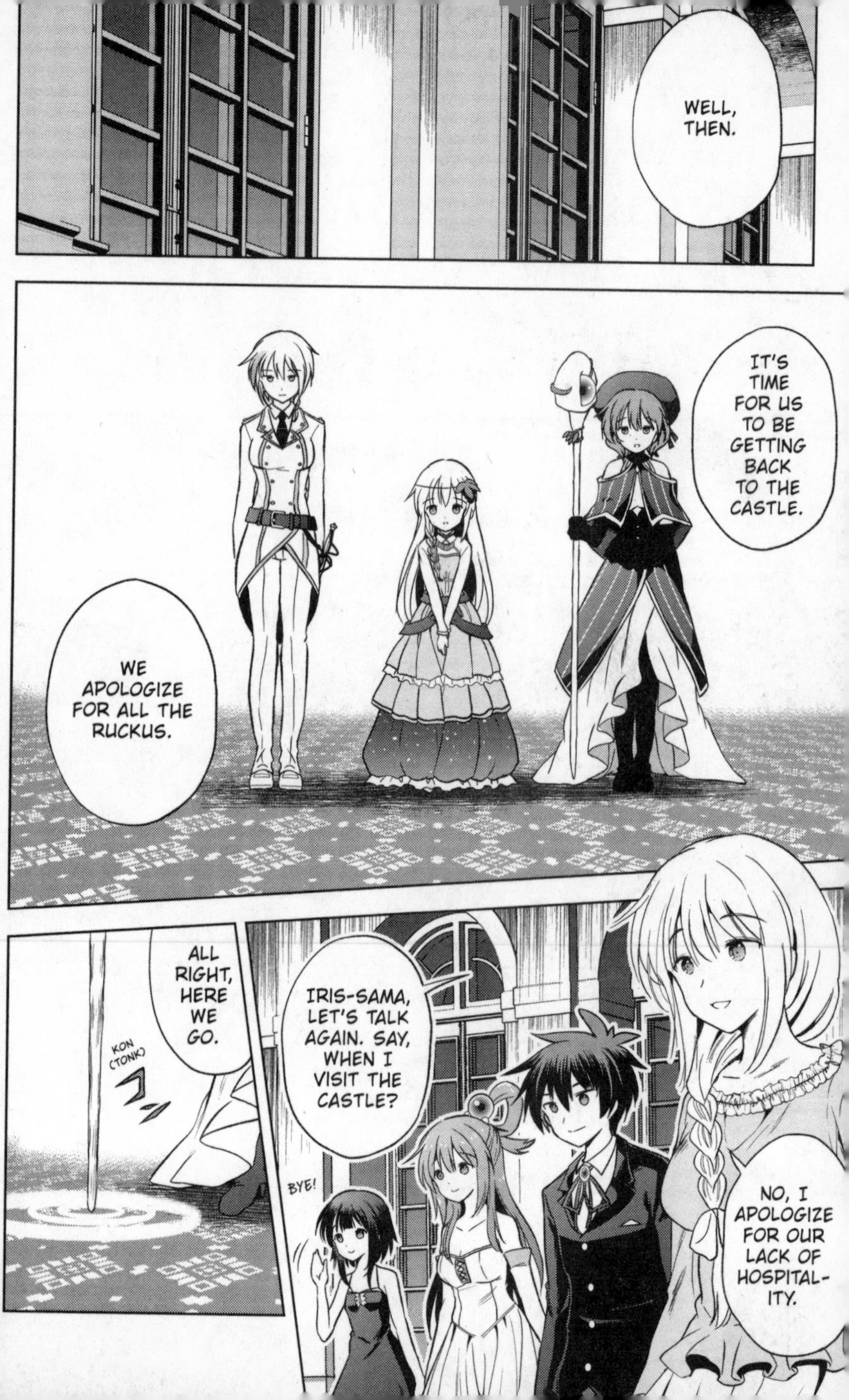
WELL, THEN.
IT'S TIME FOR US TO BE GETTING BACK TO THE CASTLE.
WE APOLOGIZE FOR ALL THE RUCKUS.
NO, I APOLOGIZE FOR OUR LACK OF HOSPITAL-ITY.
IRIS-SAMA, LET'S TALK AGAIN. SAY, WHEN I VISIT THE CASTLE?
BYE!
ALL RIGHT, HERE WE GO.
KON (TONK)

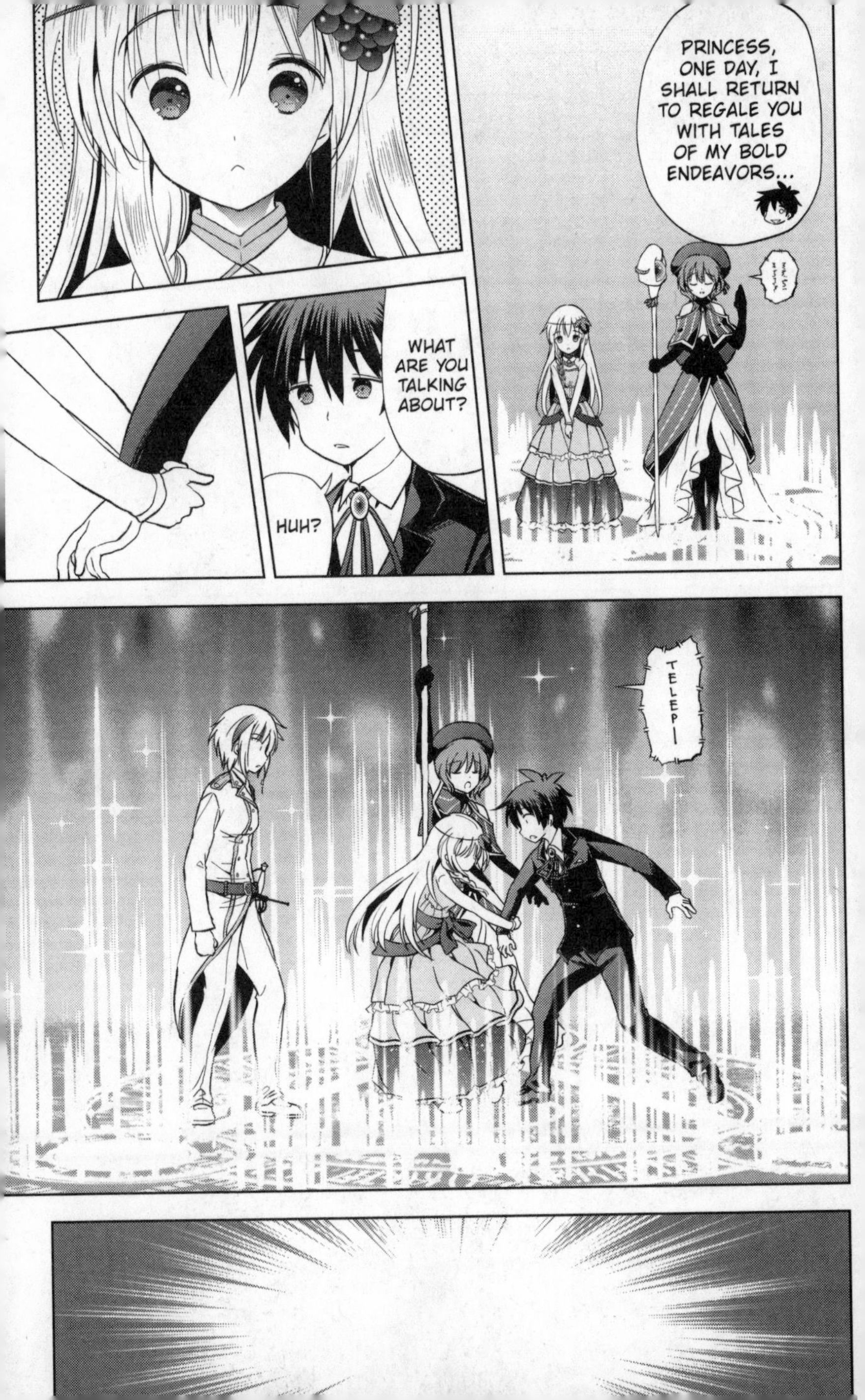
PRINCESS, ONE DAY, I SHALL RETURN TO REGALE YOU WITH TALES OF MY BOLD ENDEAVORS...
WHAT ARE YOU TALKING ABOUT?
HUH?
TELEP—

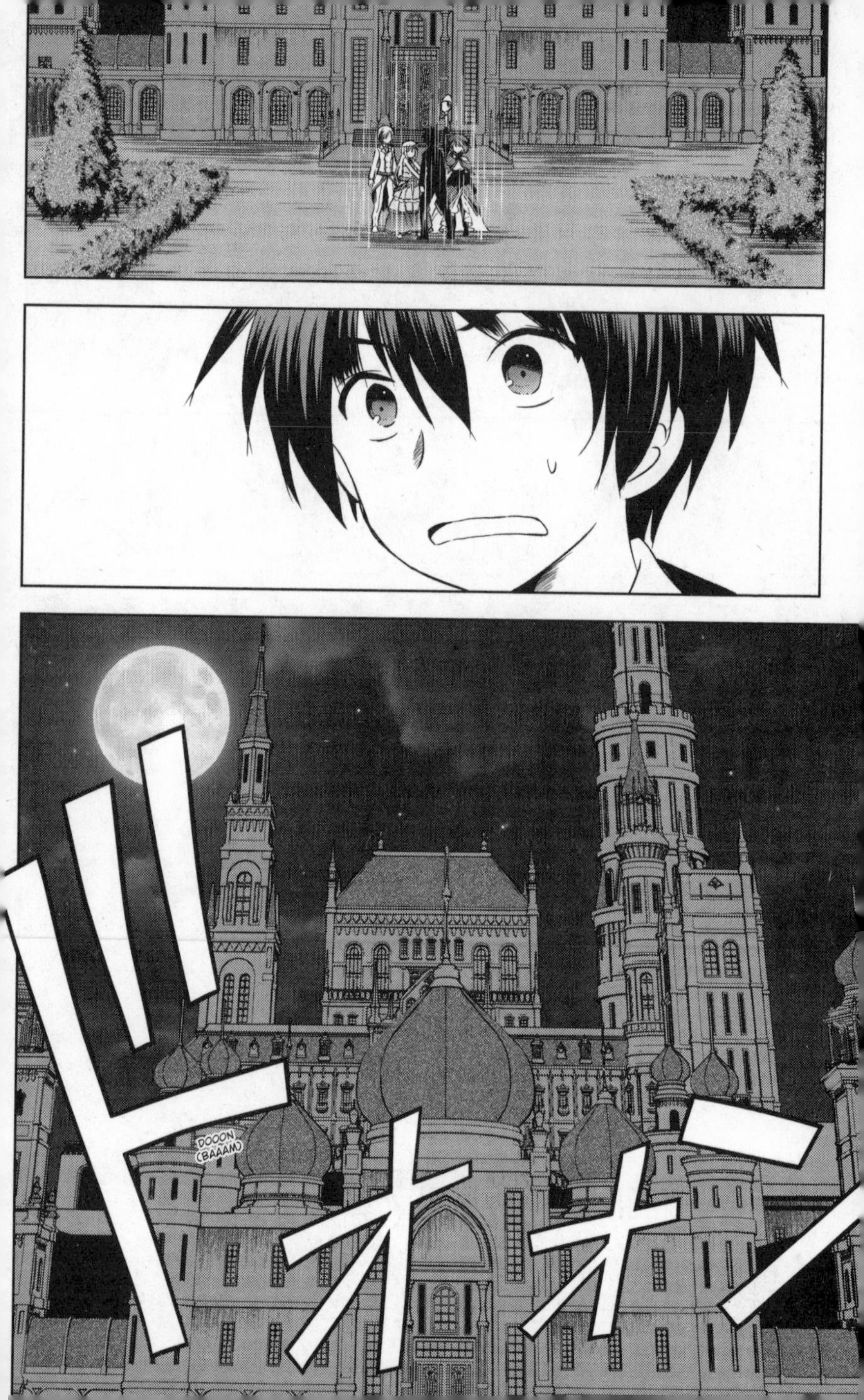
ドオオン
DOOON
(BAAAM)

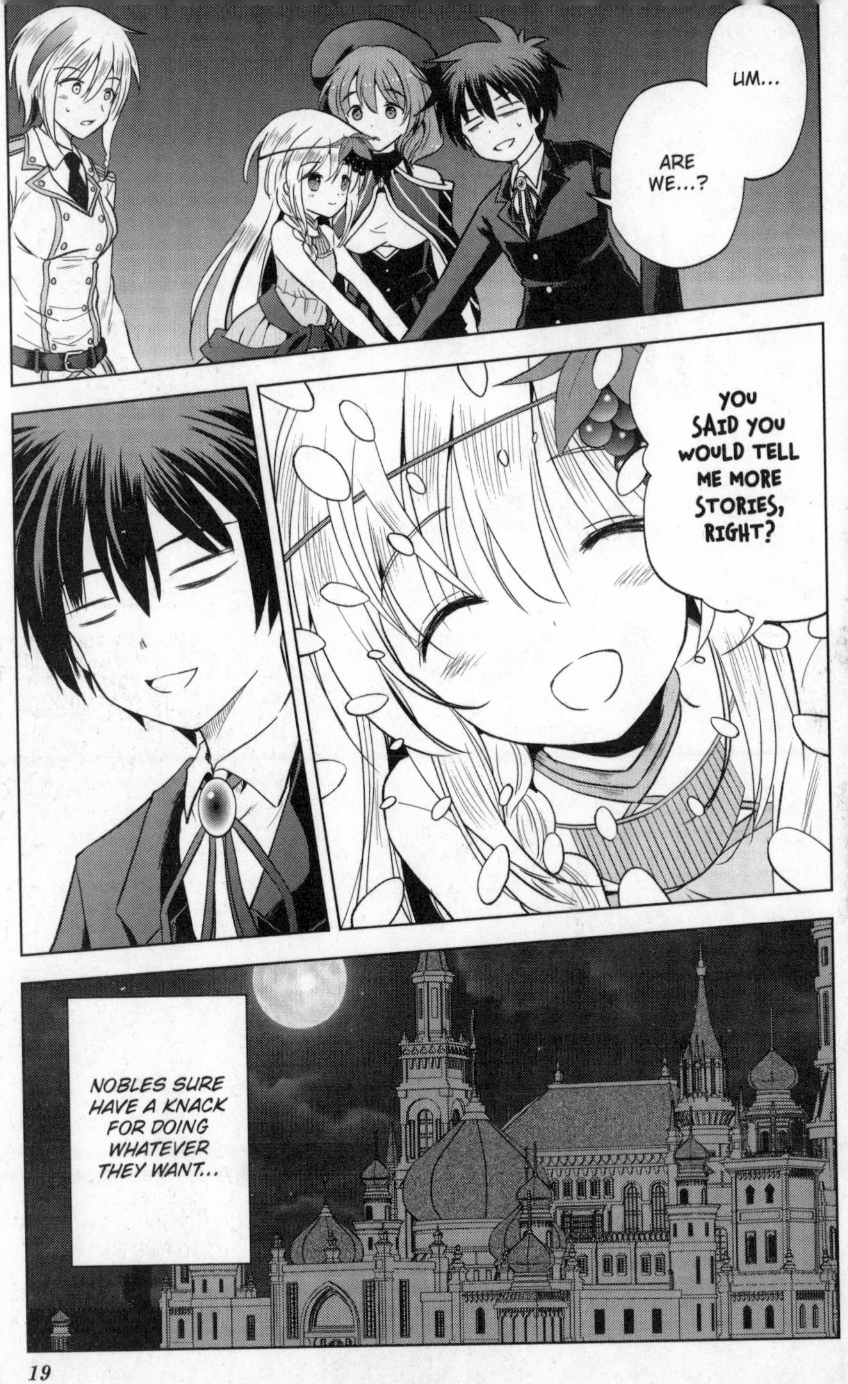
UM...
ARE WE...?
YOU SAID YOU WOULD TELL ME MORE STORIES, RIGHT?
NOBLES SURE HAVE A KNACK FOR DOING WHATEVER THEY WANT...

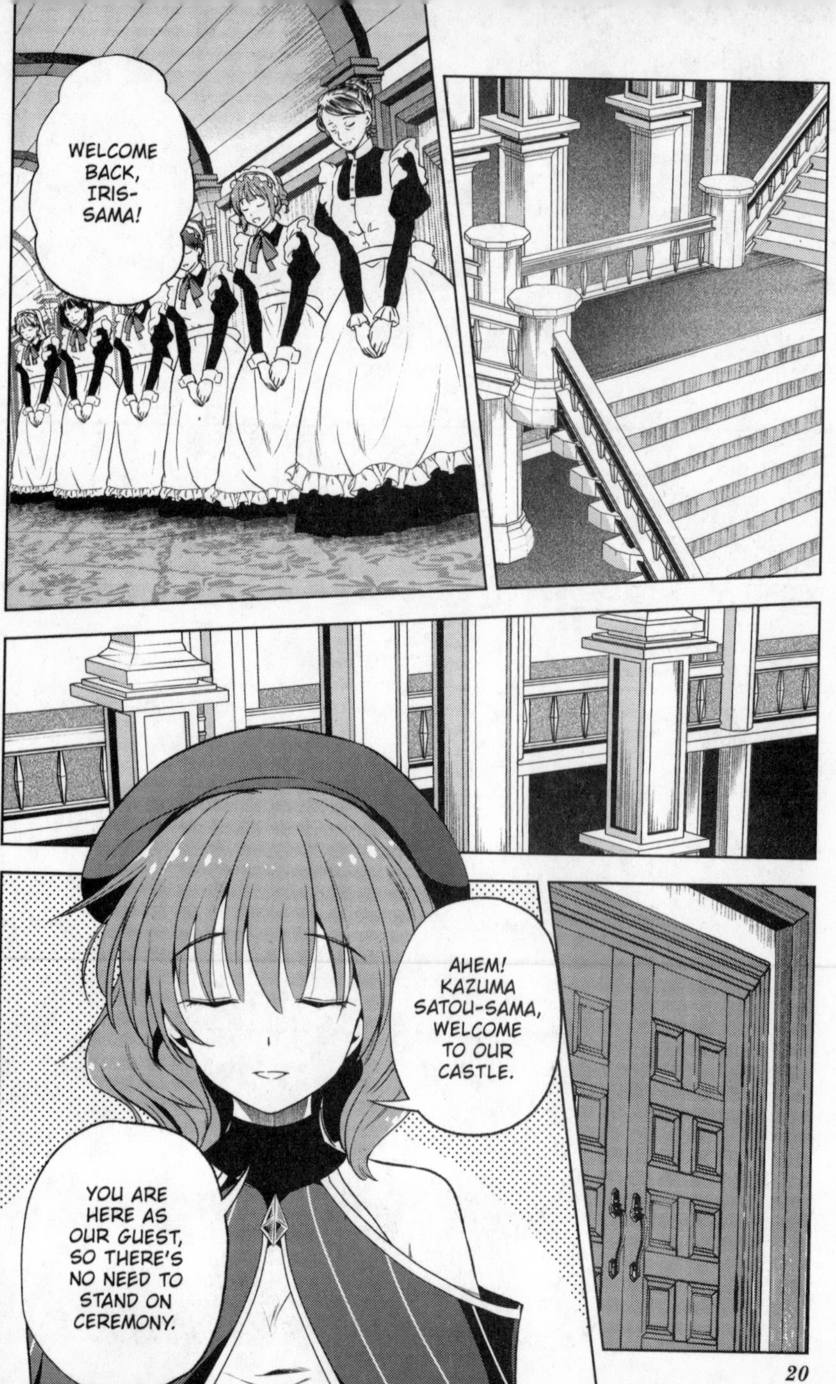
WELCOME BACK, IRIS-SAMA!
AHEM! KAZUMA SATOU-SAMA, WELCOME TO OUR CASTLE.
YOU ARE HERE AS OUR GUEST, SO THERE'S NO NEED TO STAND ON CEREMONY.

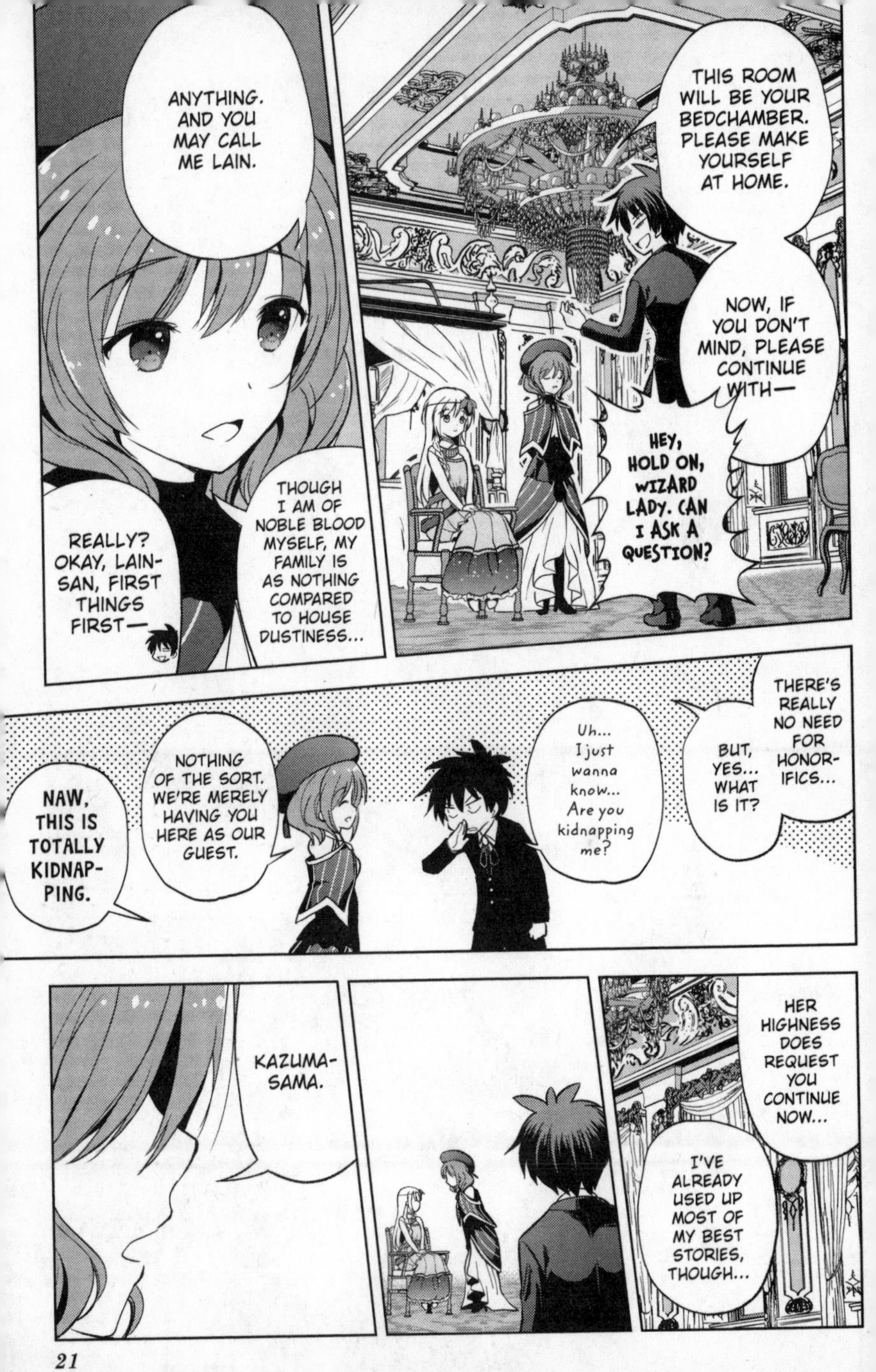
THIS ROOM WILL BE YOUR BEDCHAMBER. PLEASE MAKE YOURSELF AT HOME.
NOW, IF YOU DON'T MIND, PLEASE CONTINUE WITH—
HEY, HOLD ON, WIZARD LADY. CAN I ASK A QUESTION?
ANYTHING. AND YOU MAY CALL ME LAIN.
THOUGH I AM OF NOBLE BLOOD MYSELF, MY FAMILY IS AS NOTHING COMPARED TO HOUSE DUSTINESS...
REALLY? OKAY, LAIN-SAN, FIRST THINGS FIRST—
THERE'S REALLY NO NEED FOR HONORIFICS...
BUT, YES... WHAT IS IT?
Uh... I just wanna know... Are you kidnapping me?
NOTHING OF THE SORT. WE'RE MERELY HAVING YOU HERE AS OUR GUEST.
NAW, THIS IS TOTALLY KIDNAPPING.
HER HIGHNESS DOES REQUEST YOU CONTINUE NOW...
I'VE ALREADY USED UP MOST OF MY BEST STORIES, THOUGH...
KAZUMA-SAMA.

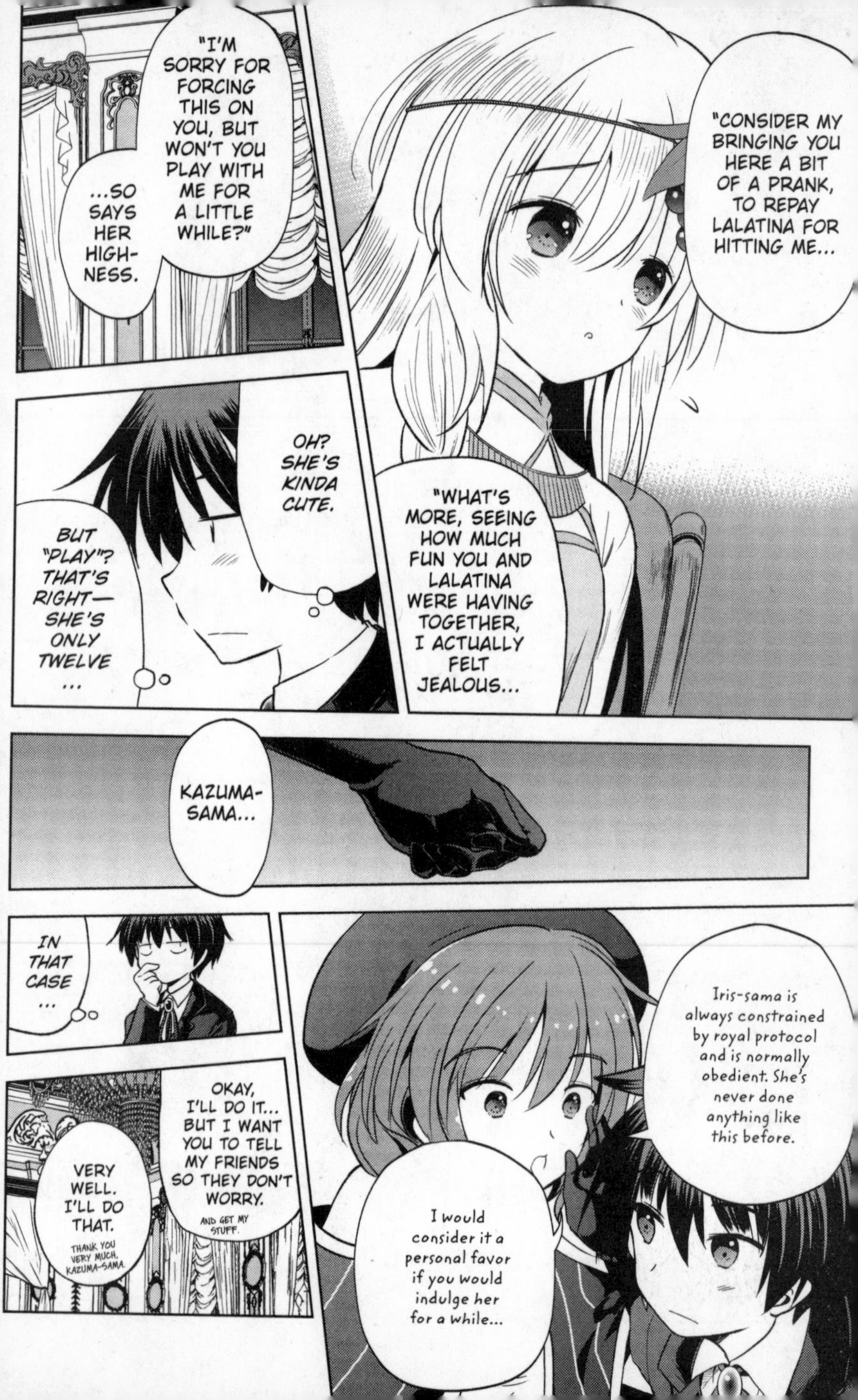
"CONSIDER MY BRINGING YOU HERE A BIT OF A PRANK, TO REPAY LALATINA FOR HITTING ME...
"WHAT'S MORE, SEEING HOW MUCH FUN YOU AND LALATINA WERE HAVING TOGETHER, I ACTUALLY FELT JEALOUS...
"I'M SORRY FOR FORCING THIS ON YOU, BUT WON'T YOU PLAY WITH ME FOR A LITTLE WHILE?"
...SO SAYS HER HIGHNESS.
OH? SHE'S KINDA CUTE.
BUT "PLAY"? THAT'S RIGHT—SHE'S ONLY TWELVE...
KAZUMA-SAMA...
Iris-sama is always constrained by royal protocol and is normally obedient. She's never done anything like this before.
I would consider it a personal favor if you would indulge her for a while...
IN THAT CASE...
OKAY, I'LL DO IT... BUT I WANT YOU TO TELL MY FRIENDS SO THEY DON'T WORRY.
AND GET MY STUFF.
VERY WELL. I'LL DO THAT.
THANK YOU VERY MUCH, KAZUMA-SAMA.

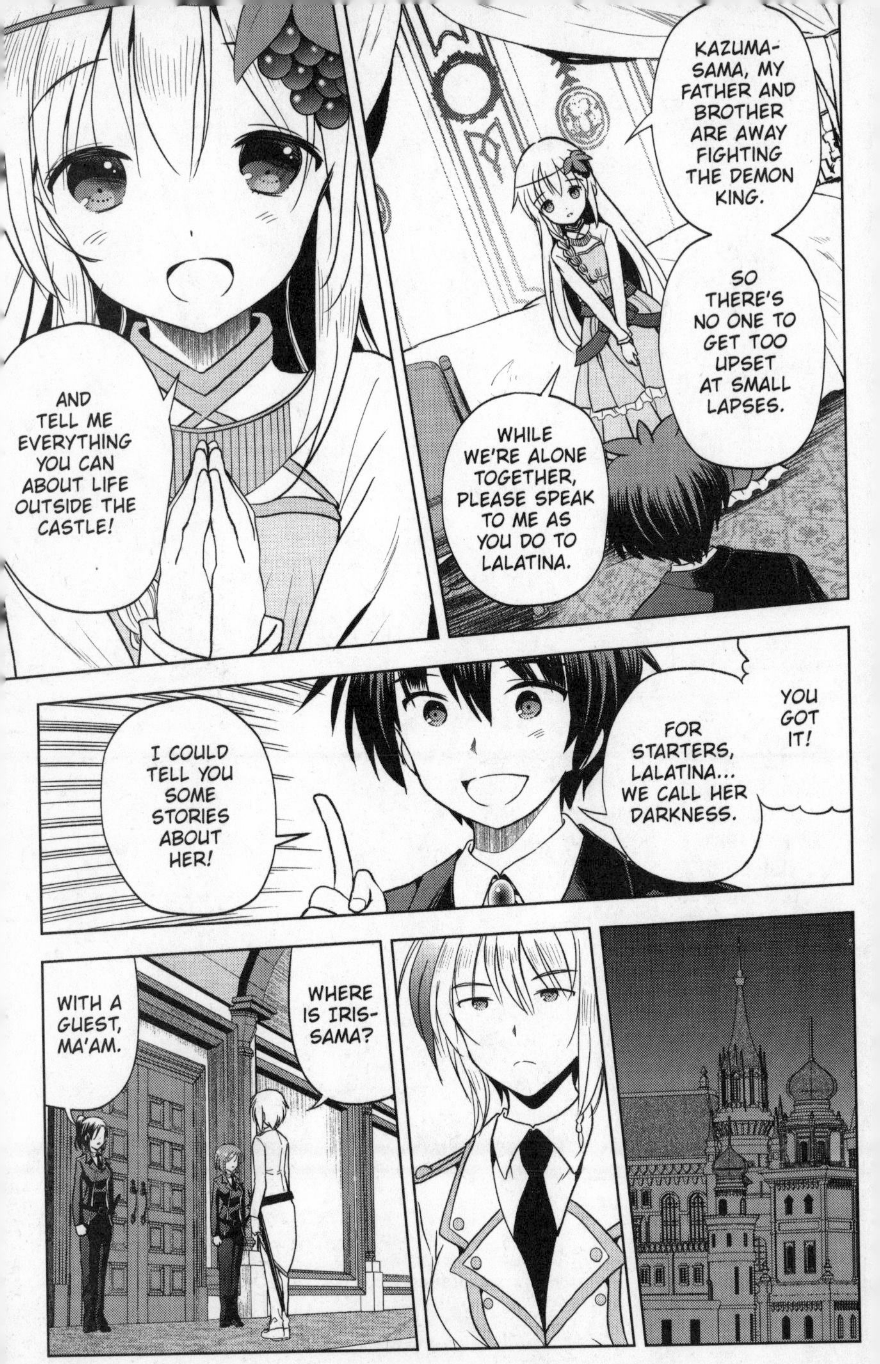
KAZUMA-SAMA, MY FATHER AND BROTHER ARE AWAY FIGHTING THE DEMON KING.
SO THERE'S NO ONE TO GET TOO UPSET AT SMALL LAPSES.
WHILE WE'RE ALONE TOGETHER, PLEASE SPEAK TO ME AS YOU DO TO LALATINA.
AND TELL ME EVERYTHING YOU CAN ABOUT LIFE OUTSIDE THE CASTLE!
YOU GOT IT!
FOR STARTERS, LALATINA... WE CALL HER DARKNESS.
I COULD TELL YOU SOME STORIES ABOUT HER!
WHERE IS IRIS-SAMA?
WITH A GUEST, MA'AM.

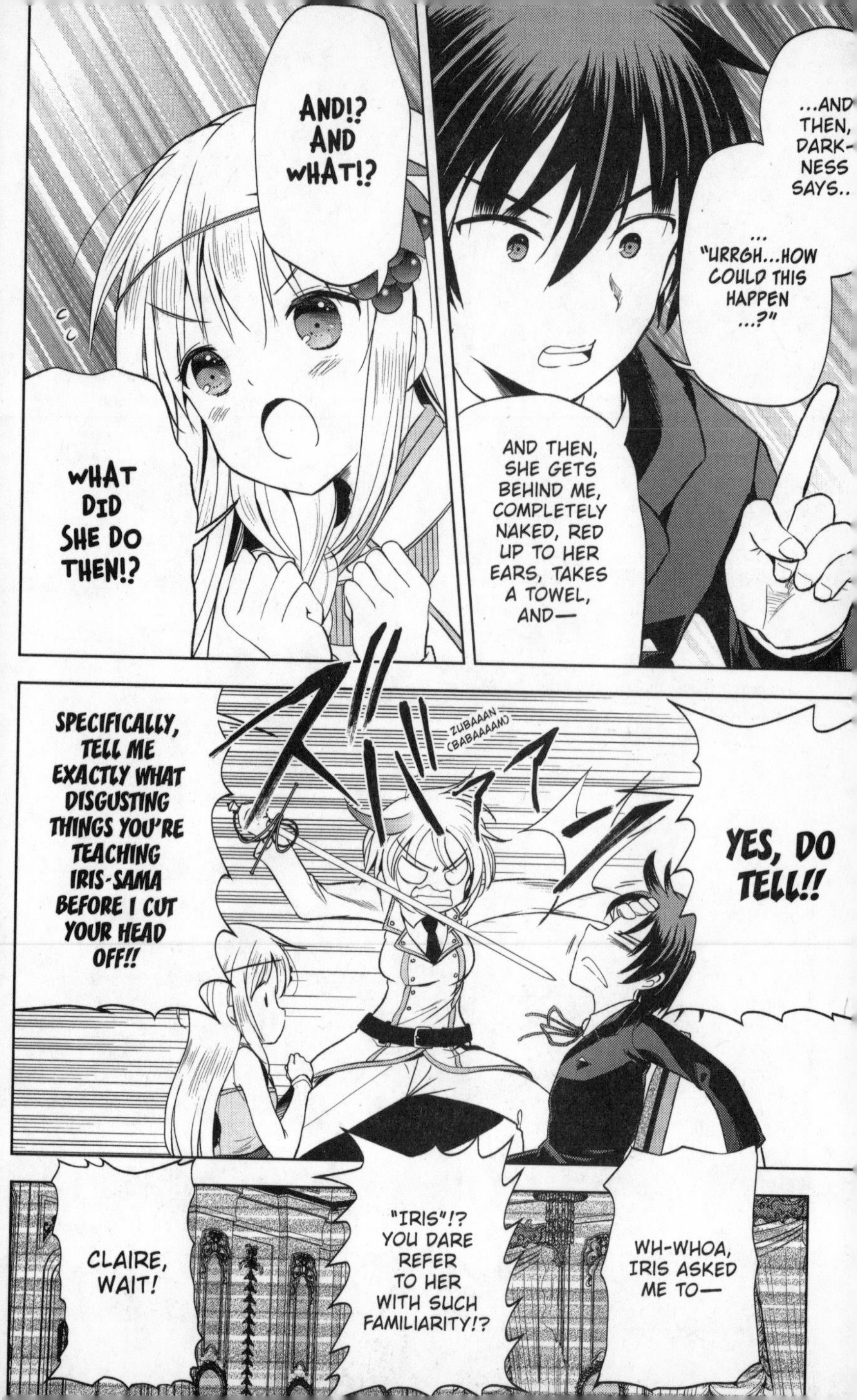
...AND THEN, DARKNESS SAYS..
... "URRGH...HOW COULD THIS HAPPEN ...?"
AND THEN, SHE GETS BEHIND ME, COMPLETELY NAKED, RED UP TO HER EARS, TAKES A TOWEL, AND—
AND!? AND WHAT!?
WHAT DID SHE DO THEN!?
YES, DO TELL!!
ZUBAAAN (BABAAAAM)
SPECIFICALLY, TELL ME EXACTLY WHAT DISGUSTING THINGS YOU'RE TEACHING IRIS-SAMA BEFORE I CUT YOUR HEAD OFF!!
WH-WHOA, IRIS ASKED ME TO—
"IRIS"!? YOU DARE REFER TO HER WITH SUCH FAMILIARITY!?
CLAIRE, WAIT!

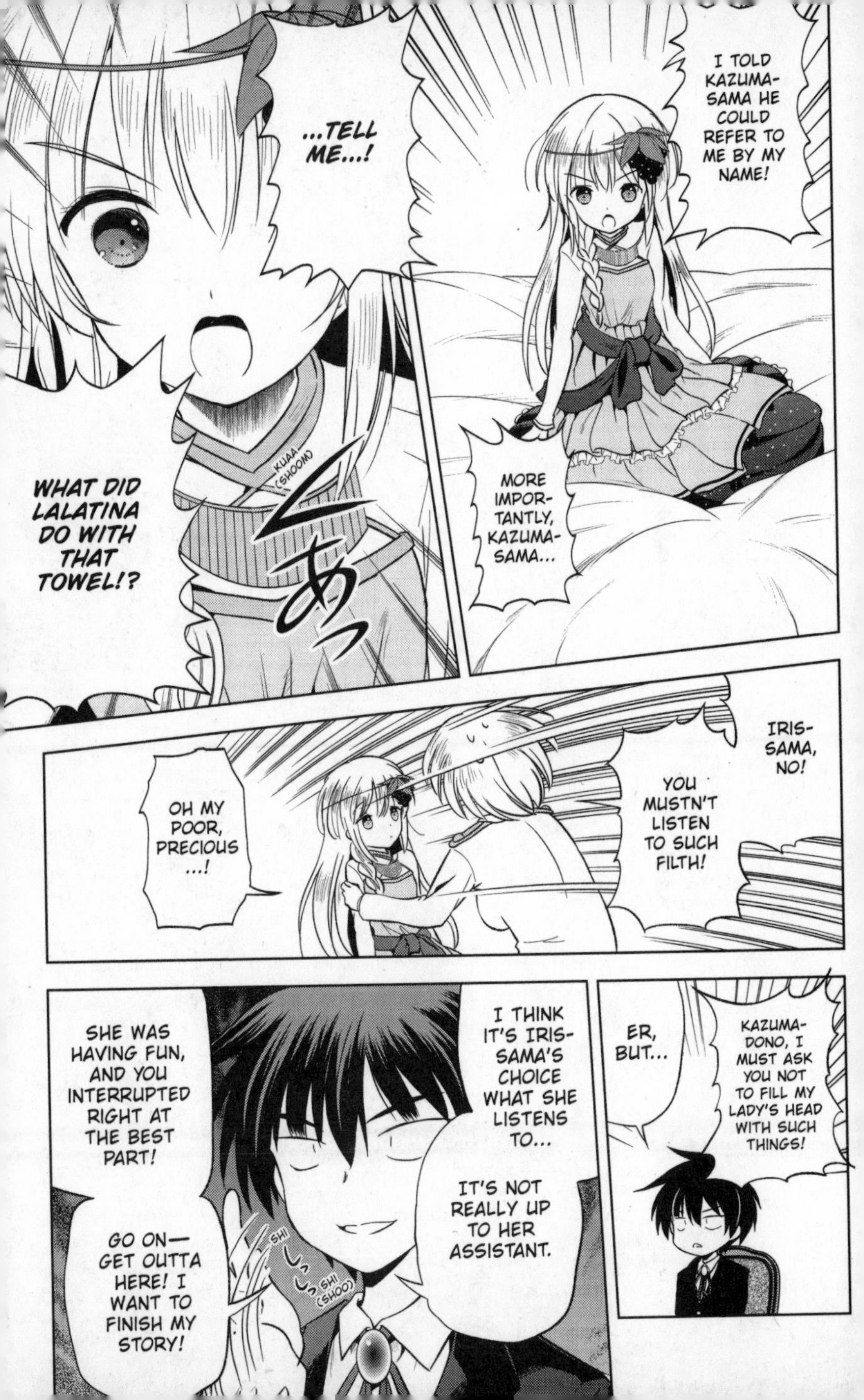
I TOLD KAZUMA-SAMA HE COULD REFER TO ME BY MY NAME!
MORE IMPORTANTLY, KAZUMA-SAMA...
...TELL ME...!
KUAA (SHOOM)
WHAT DID LALATINA DO WITH THAT TOWEL!?
IRIS-SAMA, NO!
YOU MUSTN'T LISTEN TO SUCH FILTH!
OH MY POOR, PRECIOUS ...!
KAZUMA-DONO, I MUST ASK YOU NOT TO FILL MY LADY'S HEAD WITH SUCH THINGS!
ER, BUT...
I THINK IT'S IRIS-SAMA'S CHOICE WHAT SHE LISTENS TO...
IT'S NOT REALLY UP TO HER ASSISTANT.
SHE WAS HAVING FUN, AND YOU INTERRUPTED RIGHT AT THE BEST PART!
GO ON— GET OUTTA HERE! I WANT TO FINISH MY STORY!
SHI SHI (SHOO)

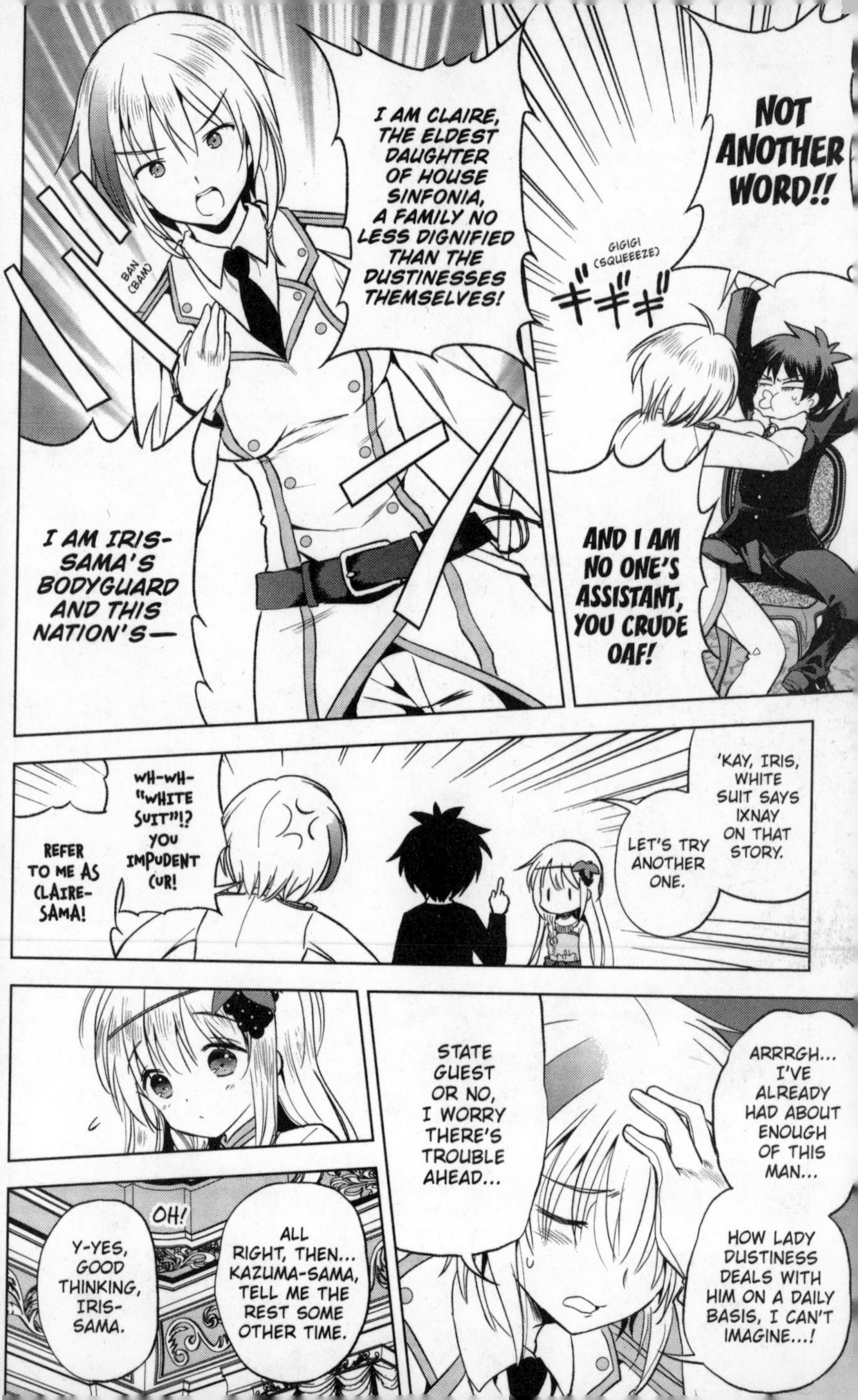
NOT ANOTHER WORD!!
GIGIGI (SQUEEEZE)
AND I AM NO ONE'S ASSISTANT, YOU CRUDE OAF!
I AM CLAIRE, THE ELDEST DAUGHTER OF HOUSE SINFONIA, A FAMILY NO LESS DIGNIFIED THAN THE DUSTINESSES THEMSELVES!
BAN (BAM)
I AM IRIS-SAMA'S BODYGUARD AND THIS NATION'S—
'KAY, IRIS, WHITE SUIT SAYS IXNAY ON THAT STORY.
LET'S TRY ANOTHER ONE.
WH-WH- "WHITE SUIT"!? YOU IMPUDENT CUR!
REFER TO ME AS CLAIRE-SAMA!
ARRRGH... I'VE ALREADY HAD ABOUT ENOUGH OF THIS MAN...
STATE GUEST OR NO, I WORRY THERE'S TROUBLE AHEAD...
HOW LADY DUSTINESS DEALS WITH HIM ON A DAILY BASIS, I CAN'T IMAGINE...!
ALL RIGHT, THEN... KAZUMA-SAMA, TELL ME THE REST SOME OTHER TIME.
OH!
Y-YES, GOOD THINKING, IRIS-SAMA.

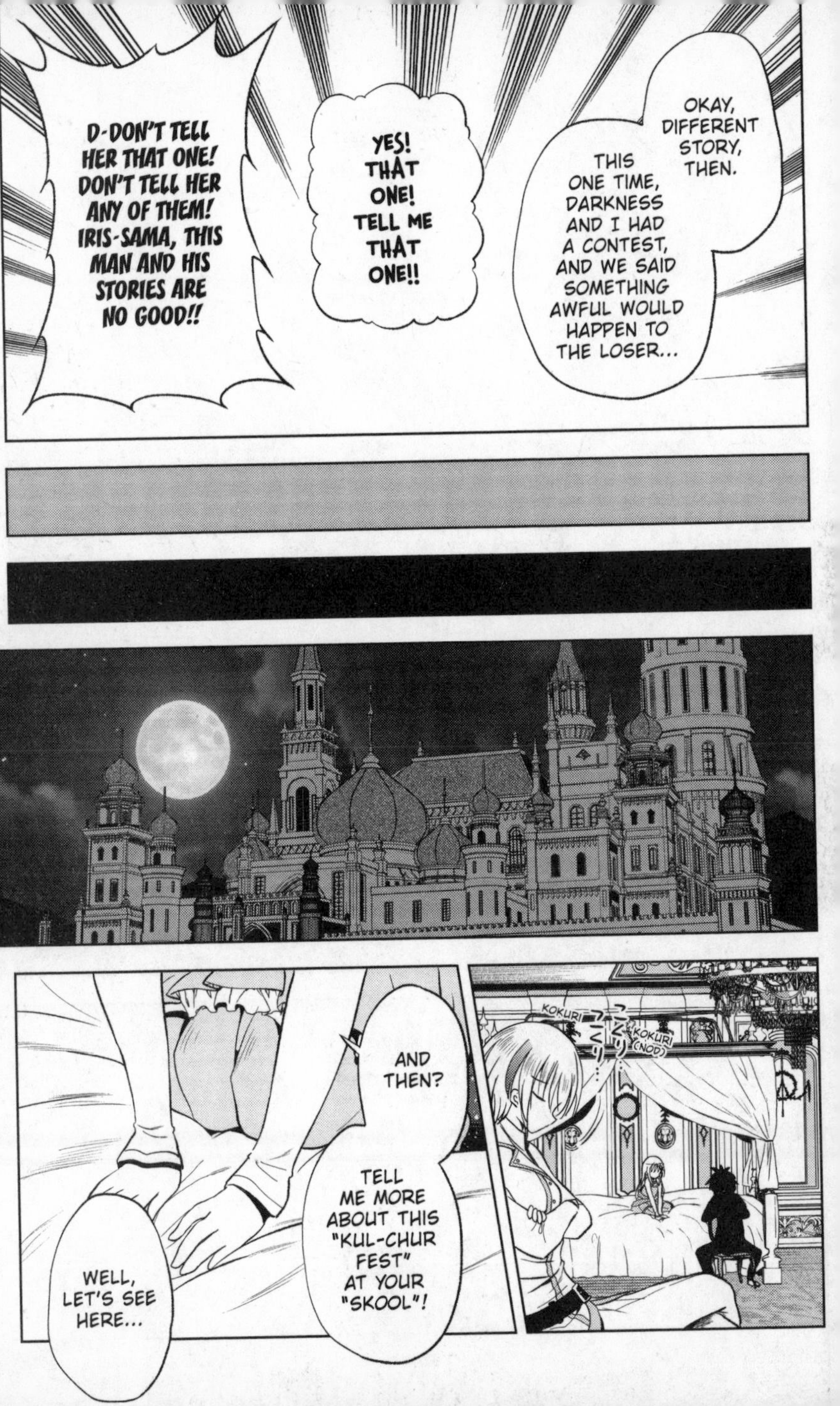
OKAY, DIFFERENT STORY, THEN.
THIS ONE TIME, DARKNESS AND I HAD A CONTEST, AND WE SAID SOMETHING AWFUL WOULD HAPPEN TO THE LOSER...
YES! THAT ONE! TELL ME THAT ONE!!
D-DON'T TELL HER THAT ONE! DON'T TELL HER ANY OF THEM! IRIS-SAMA, THIS MAN AND HIS STORIES ARE NO GOOD!!
KOKURI
KOKURI (NOD)
AND THEN?
TELL ME MORE ABOUT THIS "KUL-CHUR FEST" AT YOUR "SKOOL"!
WELL, LET'S SEE HERE...

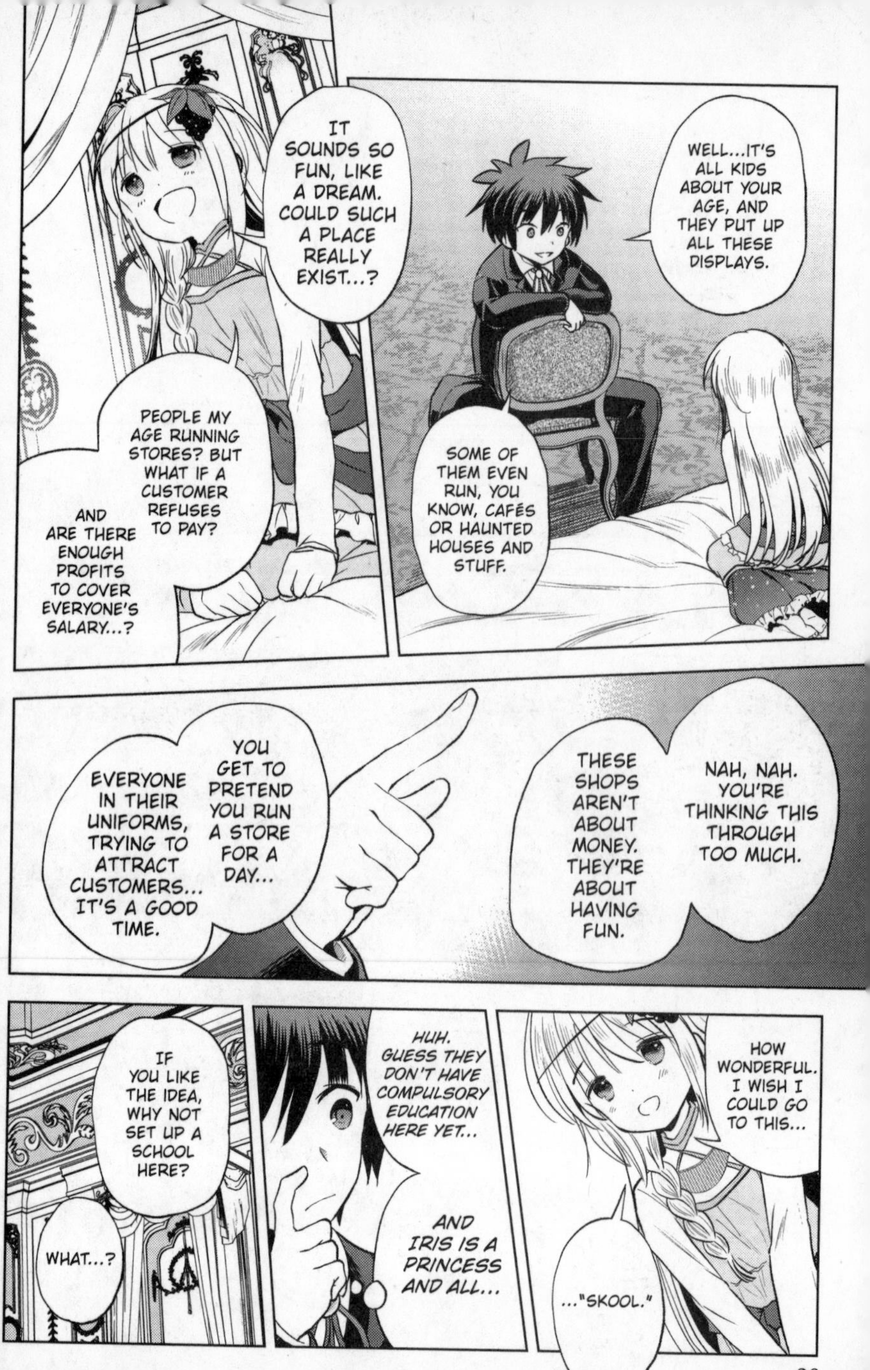
WELL...IT'S ALL KIDS ABOUT YOUR AGE, AND THEY PUT UP ALL THESE DISPLAYS.
SOME OF THEM EVEN RUN, YOU KNOW, CAFÉS OR HAUNTED HOUSES AND STUFF.
IT SOUNDS SO FUN, LIKE A DREAM. COULD SUCH A PLACE REALLY EXIST...?
PEOPLE MY AGE RUNNING STORES? BUT WHAT IF A CUSTOMER REFUSES TO PAY?
AND ARE THERE ENOUGH PROFITS TO COVER EVERYONE'S SALARY...?
NAH, NAH. YOU'RE THINKING THIS THROUGH TOO MUCH.
THESE SHOPS AREN'T ABOUT MONEY. THEY'RE ABOUT HAVING FUN.
YOU GET TO PRETEND YOU RUN A STORE FOR A DAY...
EVERYONE IN THEIR UNIFORMS, TRYING TO ATTRACT CUSTOMERS... IT'S A GOOD TIME.
HOW WONDERFUL. I WISH I COULD GO TO THIS...
..."SKOOL."
HUH. GUESS THEY DON'T HAVE COMPULSORY EDUCATION HERE YET...
AND IRIS IS A PRINCESS AND ALL...
IF YOU LIKE THE IDEA, WHY NOT SET UP A SCHOOL HERE?
WHAT...?

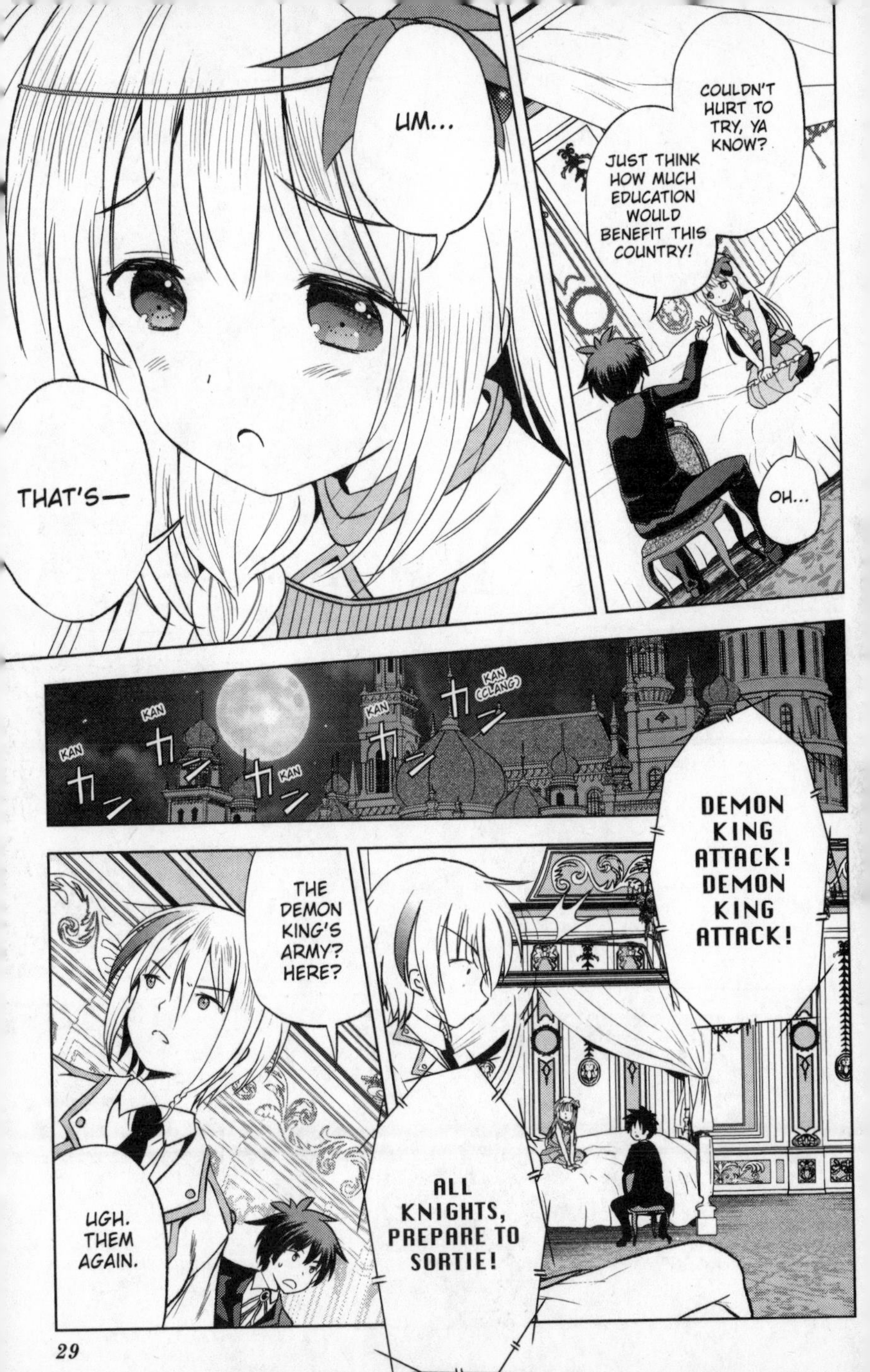

COULDN'T HURT TO TRY, YA KNOW?
JUST THINK HOW MUCH EDUCATION WOULD BENEFIT THIS COUNTRY!
OH...
UM...
THAT'S—
KAN (CLANG)
KAN
KAN
KAN
KAN
DEMON KING ATTACK! DEMON KING ATTACK!
ALL KNIGHTS, PREPARE TO SORTIE!
THE DEMON KING'S ARMY? HERE?
UGH. THEM AGAIN.

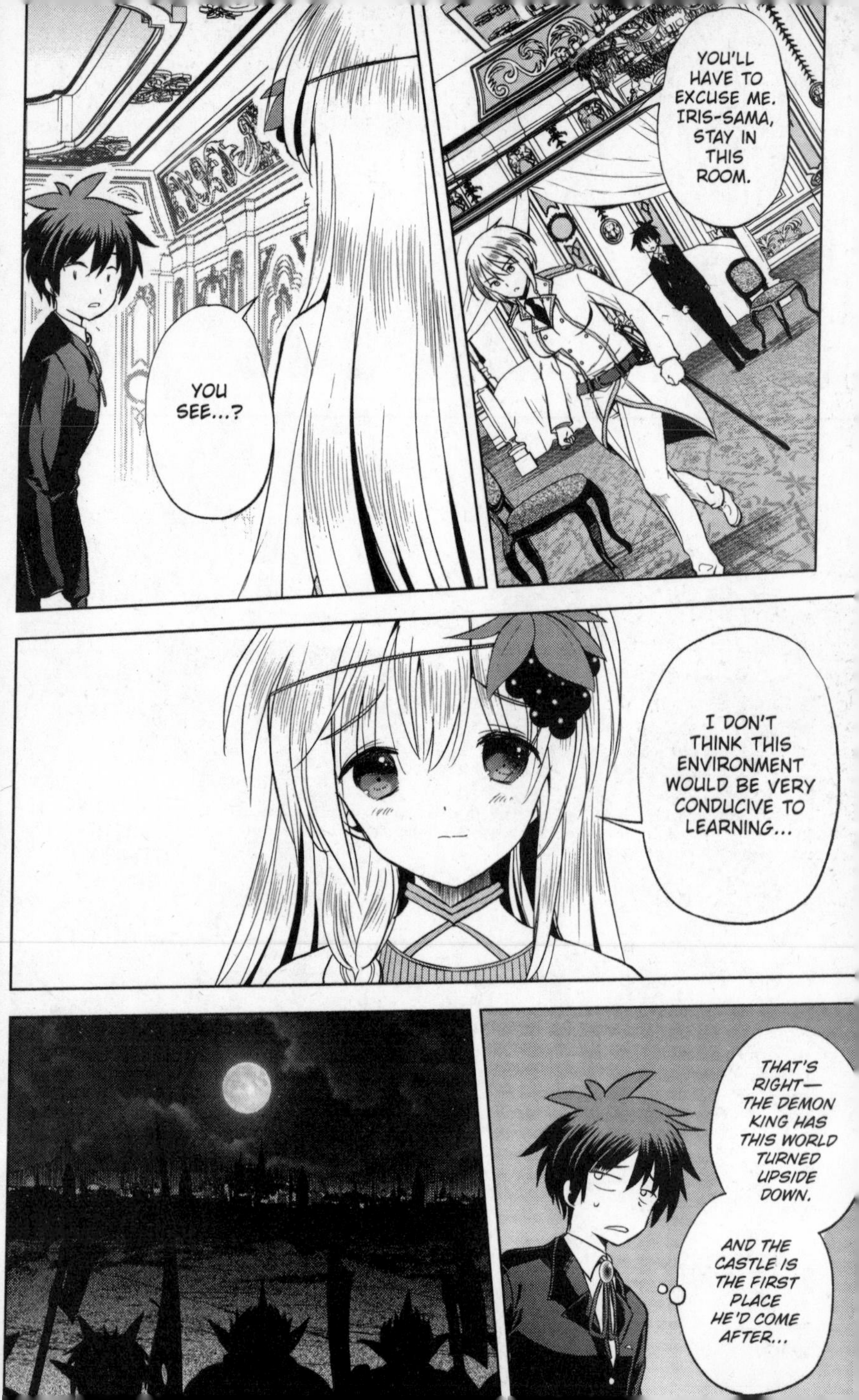
YOU'LL HAVE TO EXCUSE ME. IRIS-SAMA, STAY IN THIS ROOM.
YOU SEE...?
I DON'T THINK THIS ENVIRONMENT WOULD BE VERY CONDUCIVE TO LEARNING...
THAT'S RIGHT— THE DEMON KING HAS THIS WORLD TURNED UPSIDE DOWN.
AND THE CASTLE IS THE FIRST PLACE HE'D COME AFTER...

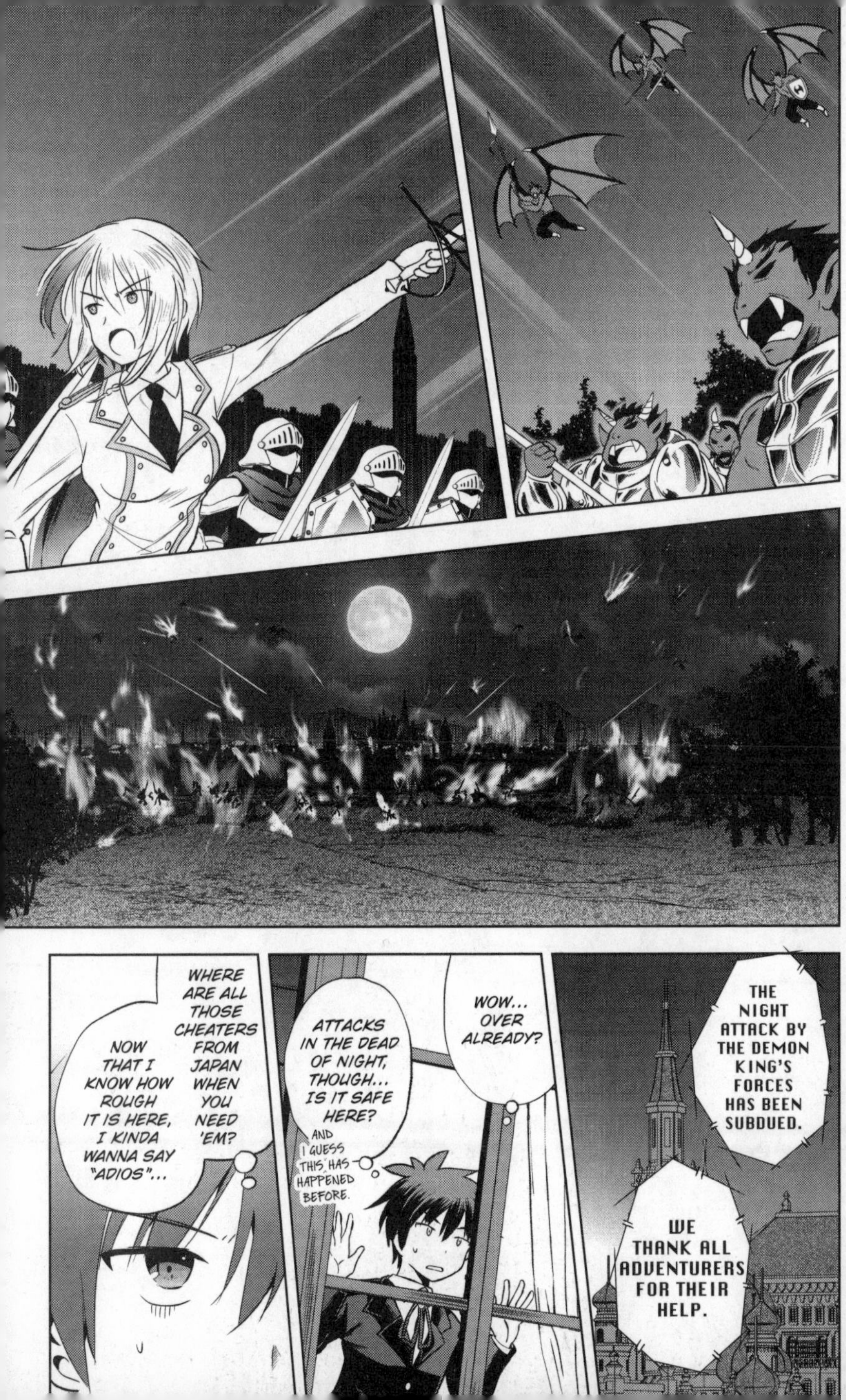
THE NIGHT ATTACK BY THE DEMON KING'S FORCES HAS BEEN SUBDUED.
WE THANK ALL ADVENTURERS FOR THEIR HELP.
WOW... OVER ALREADY?
ATTACKS IN THE DEAD OF NIGHT, THOUGH... IS IT SAFE HERE?
AND I GUESS THIS HAS HAPPENED BEFORE.
WHERE ARE ALL THOSE CHEATERS FROM JAPAN WHEN YOU NEED 'EM?
NOW THAT I KNOW HOW ROUGH IT IS HERE, I KINDA WANNA SAY "ADIOS"...

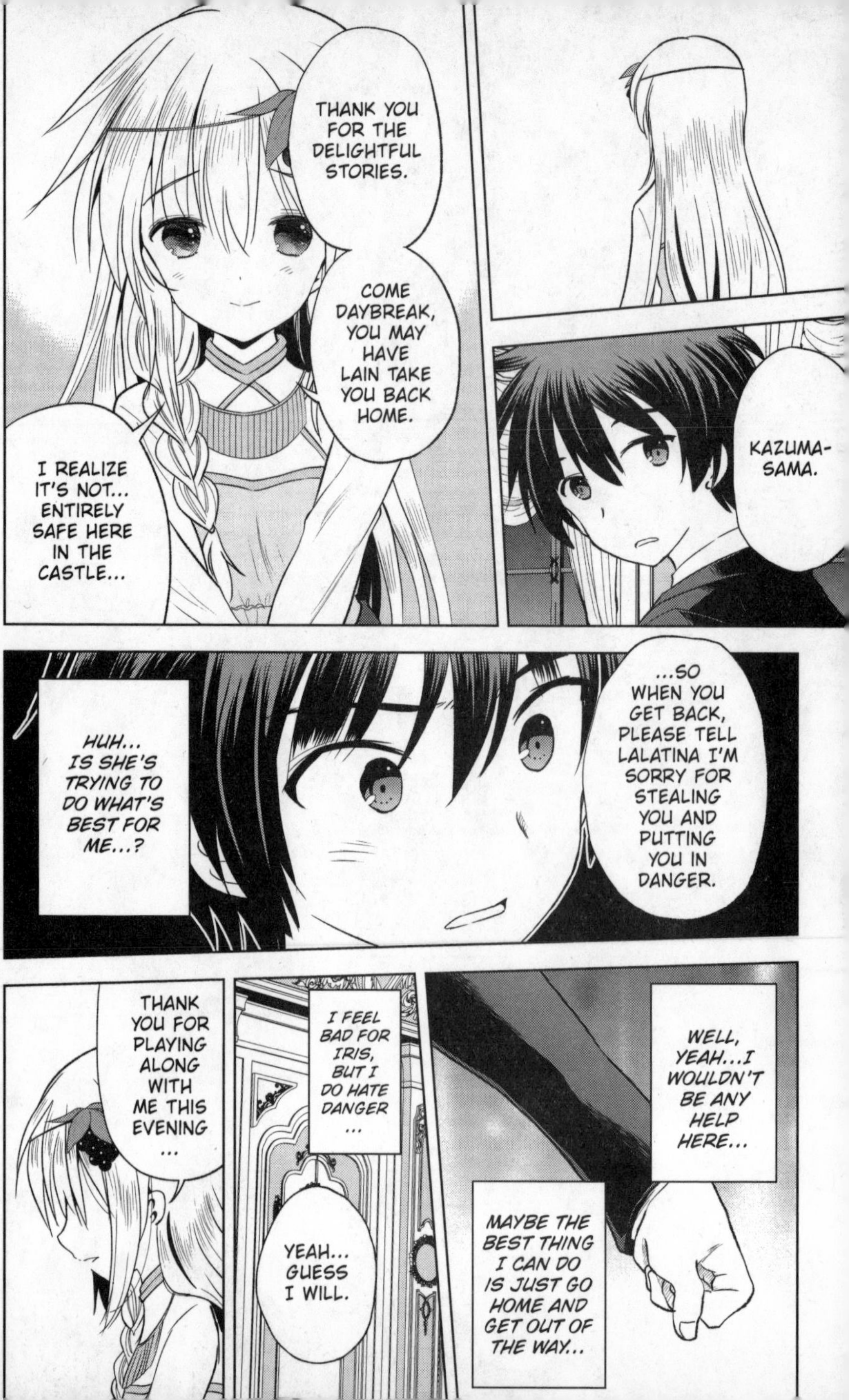
KAZUMA-SAMA.
THANK YOU FOR THE DELIGHTFUL STORIES.
COME DAYBREAK, YOU MAY HAVE LAIN TAKE YOU BACK HOME.
I REALIZE IT'S NOT... ENTIRELY SAFE HERE IN THE CASTLE...
...SO WHEN YOU GET BACK, PLEASE TELL LALATINA I'M SORRY FOR STEALING YOU AND PUTTING YOU IN DANGER.
HUH... IS SHE'S TRYING TO DO WHAT'S BEST FOR ME...?
WELL, YEAH...I WOULDN'T BE ANY HELP HERE...
MAYBE THE BEST THING I CAN DO IS JUST GO HOME AND GET OUT OF THE WAY...
I FEEL BAD FOR IRIS, BUT I DO HATE DANGER...
YEAH... GUESS I WILL.
THANK YOU FOR PLAYING ALONG WITH ME THIS EVENING...

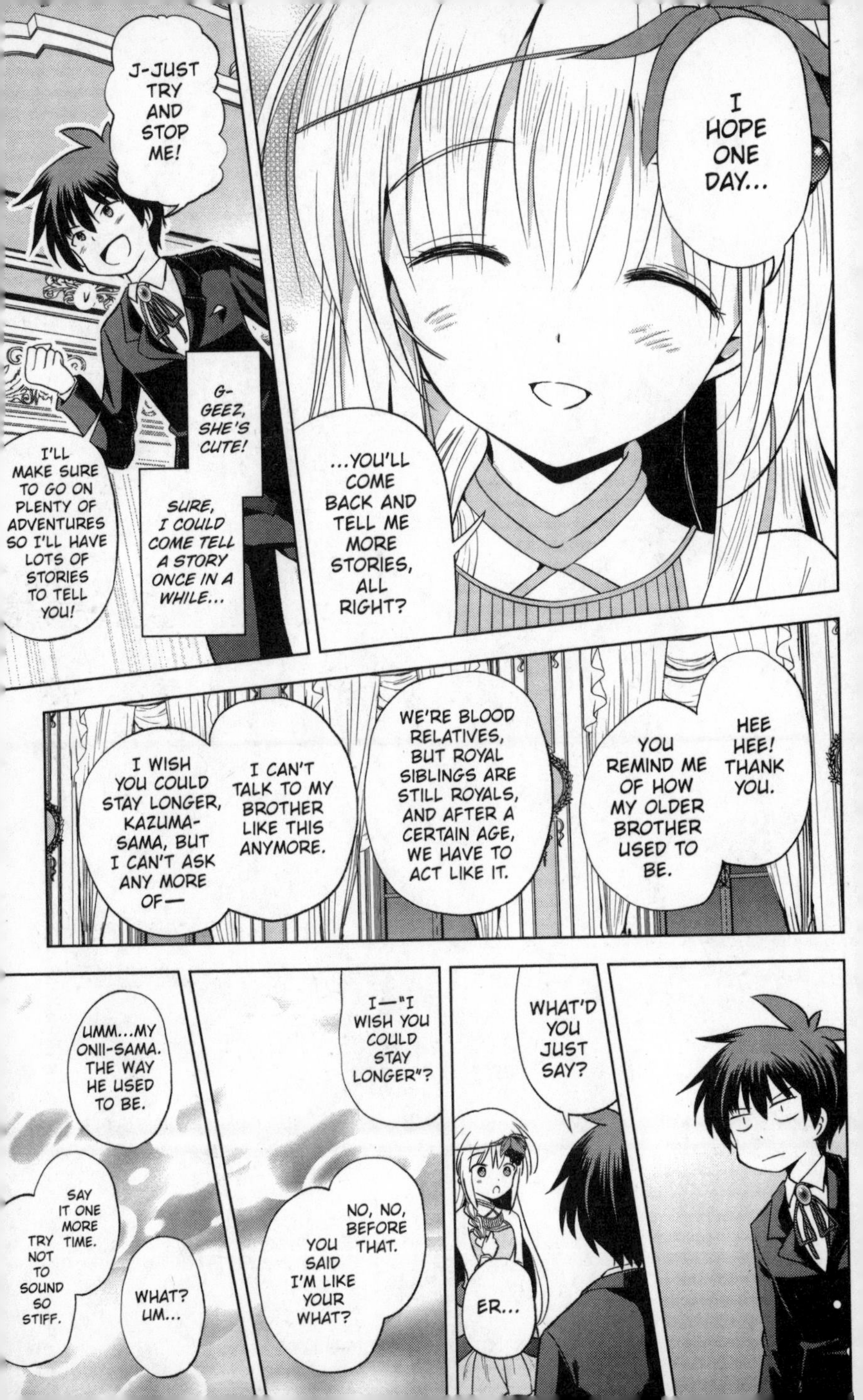
I HOPE ONE DAY...
...YOU'LL COME BACK AND TELL ME MORE STORIES, ALL RIGHT?
G-GEEZ, SHE'S CUTE!
SURE, I COULD COME TELL A STORY ONCE IN A WHILE...
I'LL MAKE SURE TO GO ON PLENTY OF ADVENTURES SO I'LL HAVE LOTS OF STORIES TO TELL YOU!
J-JUST TRY AND STOP ME!
HEE HEE! THANK YOU.
YOU REMIND ME OF HOW MY OLDER BROTHER USED TO BE.
WE'RE BLOOD RELATIVES, BUT ROYAL SIBLINGS ARE STILL ROYALS, AND AFTER A CERTAIN AGE, WE HAVE TO ACT LIKE IT.
I CAN'T TALK TO MY BROTHER LIKE THIS ANYMORE.
I WISH YOU COULD STAY LONGER, KAZUMA-SAMA, BUT I CAN'T ASK ANY MORE OF—
WHAT'D YOU JUST SAY?
ER...
I—"I WISH YOU COULD STAY LONGER"?
NO, NO, BEFORE THAT. YOU SAID I'M LIKE YOUR WHAT?
UMM...MY ONII-SAMA. THE WAY HE USED TO BE.
SAY IT ONE MORE TIME. TRY NOT TO SOUND SO STIFF.
WHAT? UM...

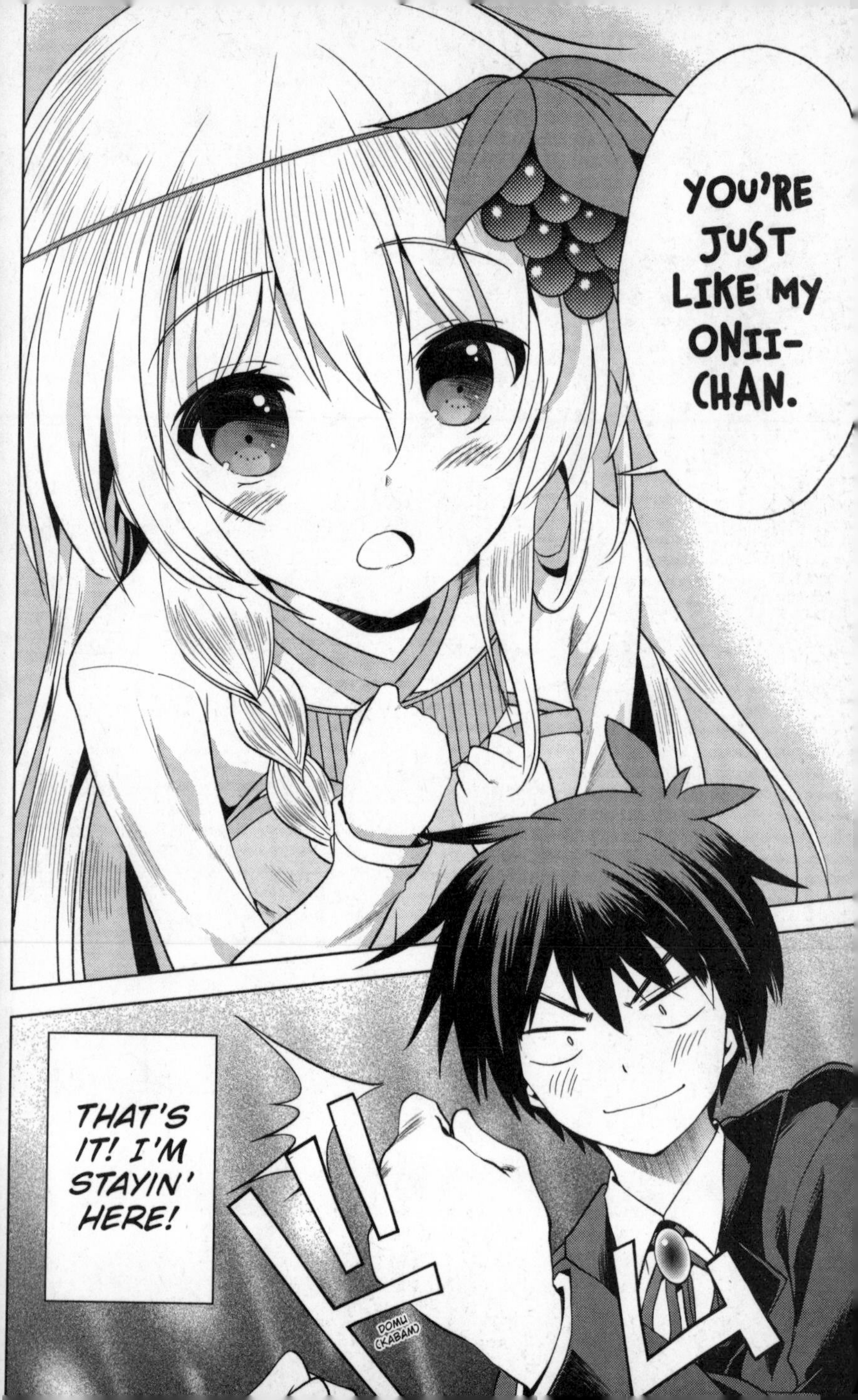
YOU'RE JUST LIKE MY ONII-CHAN.
THAT'S IT! I'M STAYIN' HERE!
DOMU (KABAM)

GOD's BLESSING ON THIS WONDERFUL WORLD! 10

10

GOD'S
BLESSING
ON THIS
WONDERFUL
WORLD!

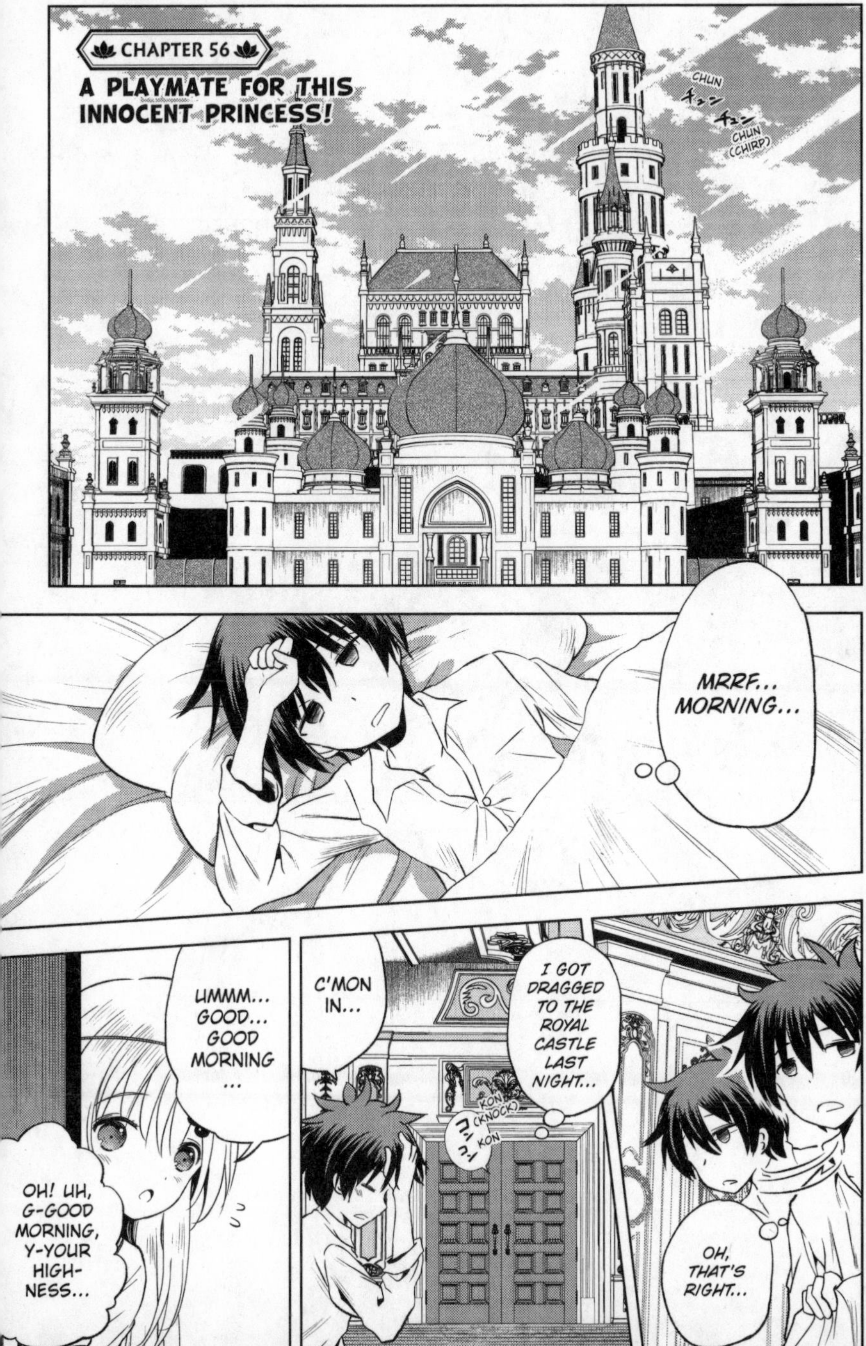
CHAPTER 56
A PLAYMATE FOR THIS INNOCENT PRINCESS!
チュン
CHUN
チュン
CHUN (CHIRP)
MRRF... MORNING...
I GOT DRAGGED TO THE ROYAL CASTLE LAST NIGHT...
OH, THAT'S RIGHT...
コン
KON (KNOCK)
コン
KON
C'MON IN...
UMMM... GOOD... GOOD MORNING...
OH! UH, G-GOOD MORNING, Y-YOUR HIGH-NESS...

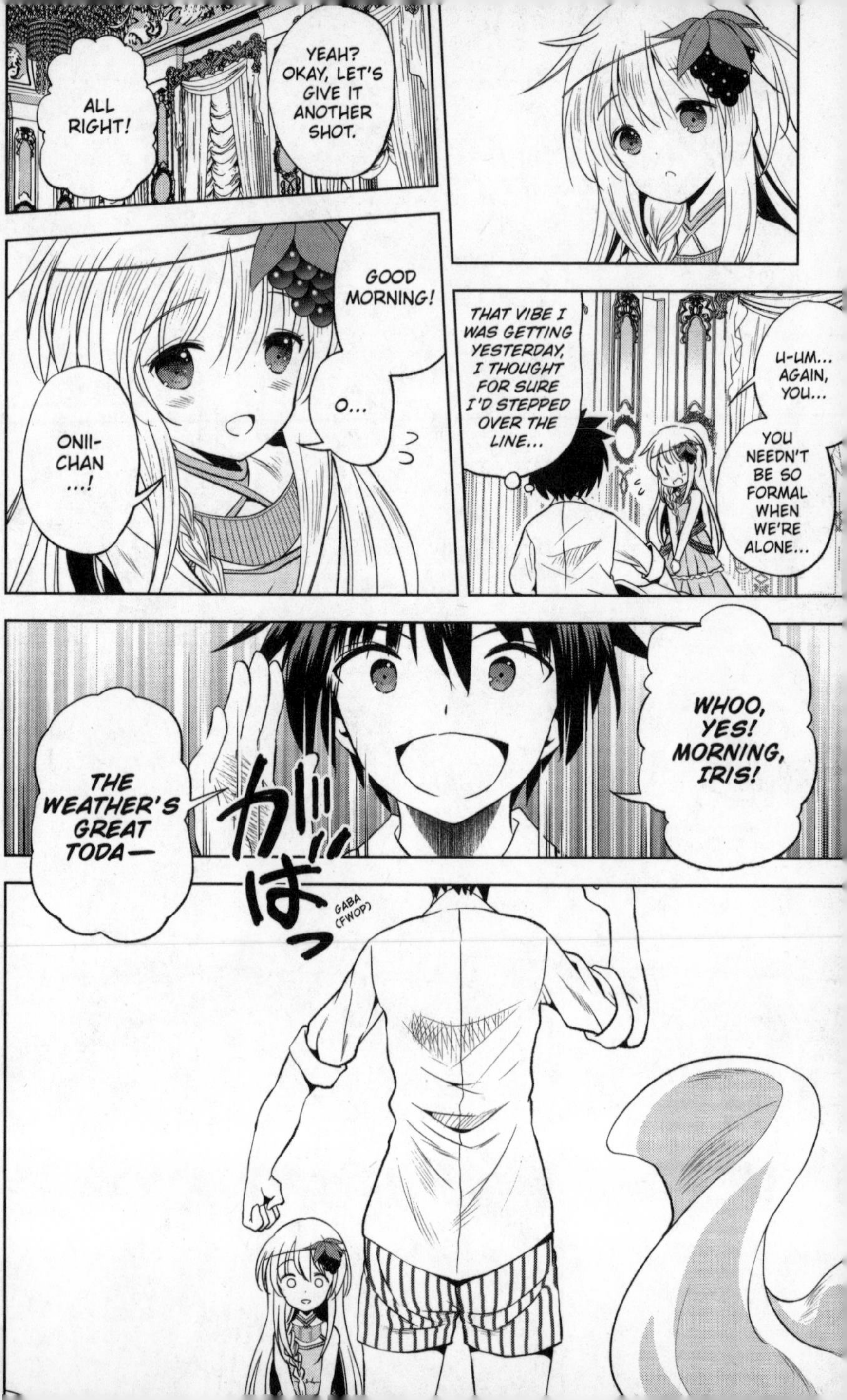
YEAH? OKAY, LET'S GIVE IT ANOTHER SHOT.
ALL RIGHT!
U-UM... AGAIN, YOU...
YOU NEEDN'T BE SO FORMAL WHEN WE'RE ALONE...
THAT VIBE I WAS GETTING YESTERDAY, I THOUGHT FOR SURE I'D STEPPED OVER THE LINE...
GOOD MORNING!
O...
ONII-CHAN ...!
WHOO, YES! MORNING, IRIS!
THE WEATHER'S GREAT TODA—
がばっ
GABA (FWOP)

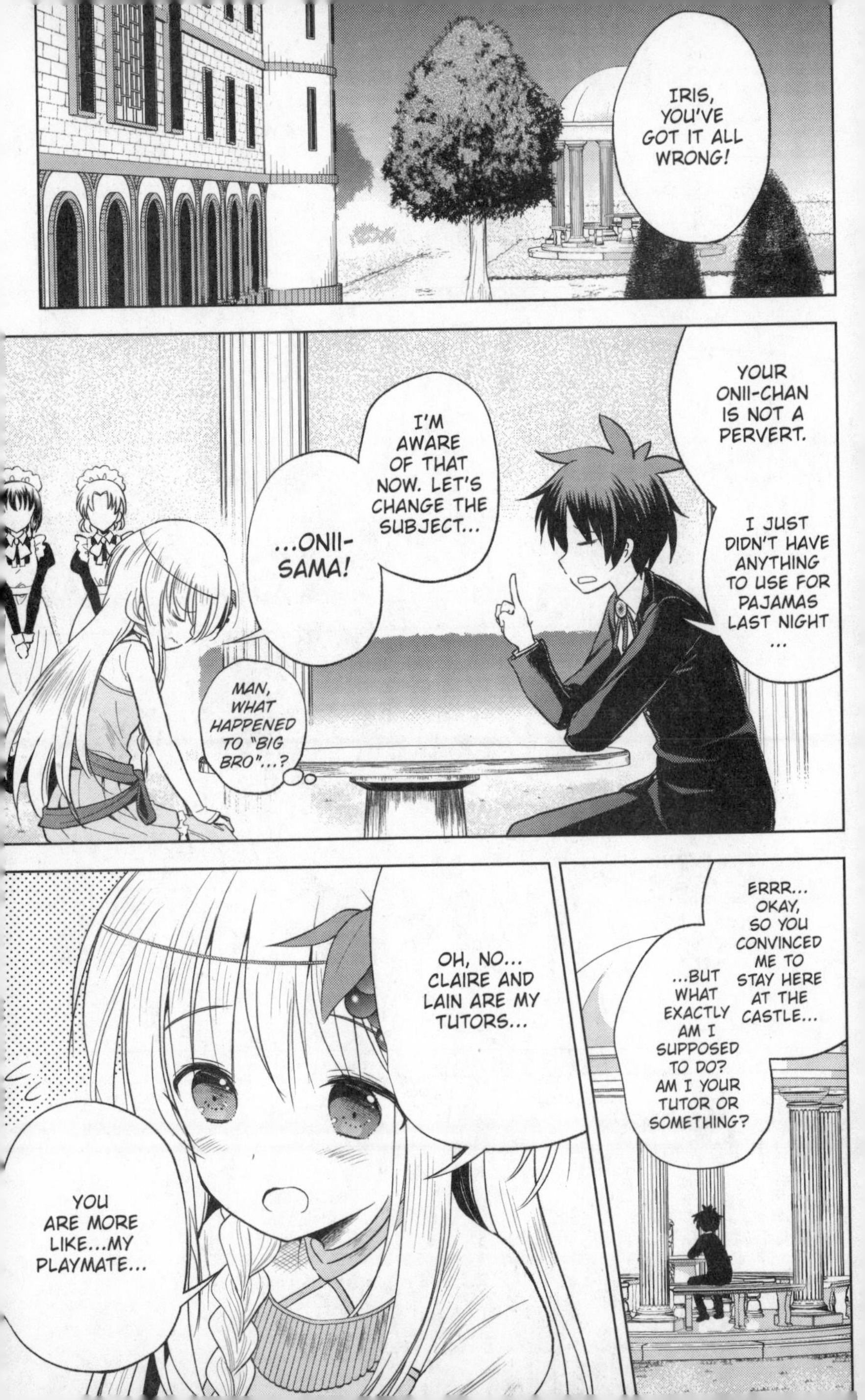
IRIS, YOU'VE GOT IT ALL WRONG!
YOUR ONII-CHAN IS NOT A PERVERT.
I JUST DIDN'T HAVE ANYTHING TO USE FOR PAJAMAS LAST NIGHT...
I'M AWARE OF THAT NOW. LET'S CHANGE THE SUBJECT...
...ONII-SAMA!
MAN, WHAT HAPPENED TO "BIG BRO"...?
ERRR... OKAY, SO YOU CONVINCED ME TO STAY HERE AT THE CASTLE...
...BUT WHAT EXACTLY AM I SUPPOSED TO DO? AM I YOUR TUTOR OR SOMETHING?
OH, NO... CLAIRE AND LAIN ARE MY TUTORS...
YOU ARE MORE LIKE...MY PLAYMATE...

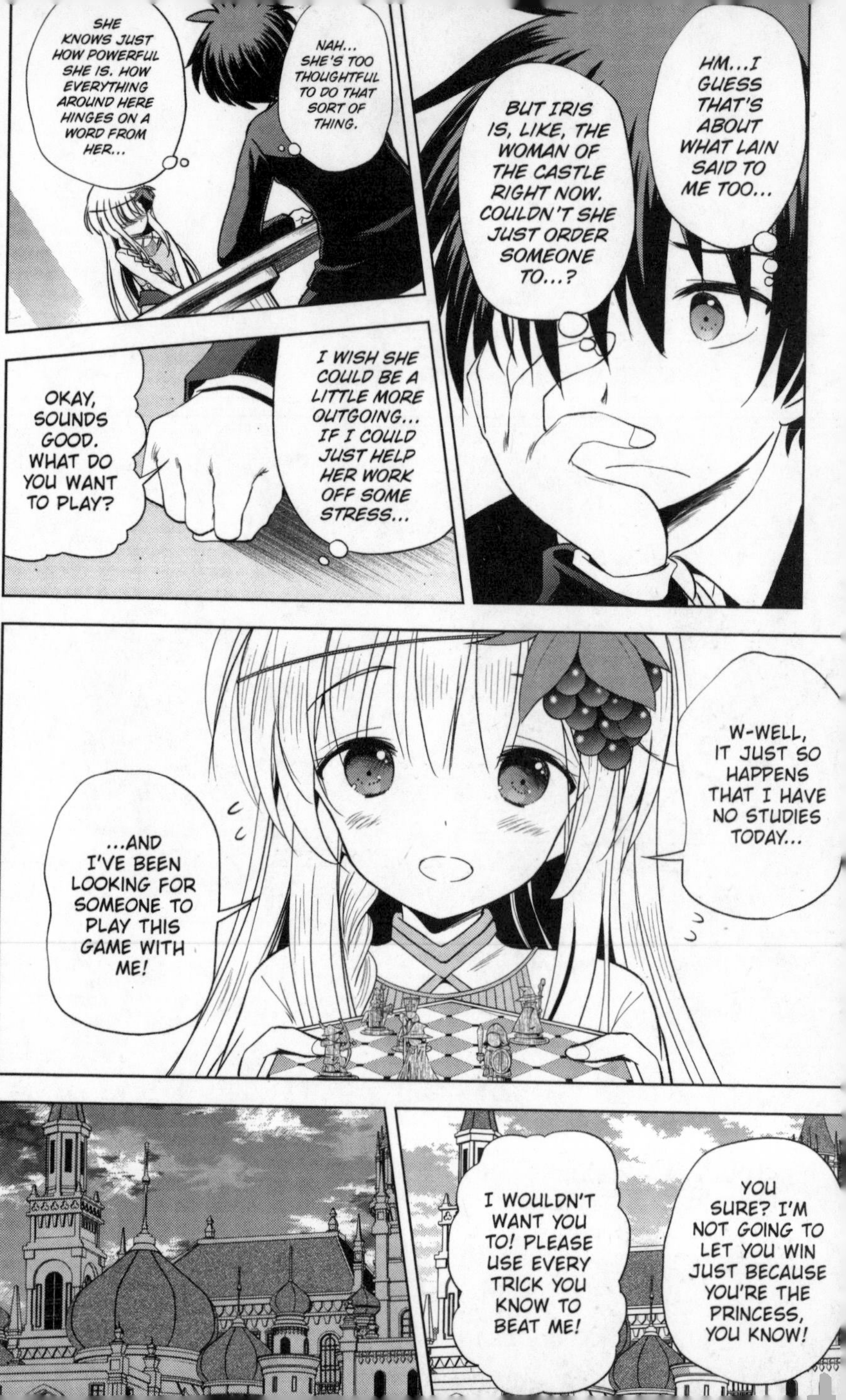
HM...I GUESS THAT'S ABOUT WHAT LAIN SAID TO ME TOO...
BUT IRIS IS, LIKE, THE WOMAN OF THE CASTLE RIGHT NOW. COULDN'T SHE JUST ORDER SOMEONE TO...?
NAH... SHE'S TOO THOUGHTFUL TO DO THAT SORT OF THING.
SHE KNOWS JUST HOW POWERFUL SHE IS. HOW EVERYTHING AROUND HERE HINGES ON A WORD FROM HER...
I WISH SHE COULD BE A LITTLE MORE OUTGOING... IF I COULD JUST HELP HER WORK OFF SOME STRESS...
OKAY, SOUNDS GOOD. WHAT DO YOU WANT TO PLAY?
W-WELL, IT JUST SO HAPPENS THAT I HAVE NO STUDIES TODAY...
...AND I'VE BEEN LOOKING FOR SOMEONE TO PLAY THIS GAME WITH ME!
YOU SURE? I'M NOT GOING TO LET YOU WIN JUST BECAUSE YOU'RE THE PRINCESS, YOU KNOW!
I WOULDN'T WANT YOU TO! PLEASE USE EVERY TRICK YOU KNOW TO BEAT ME!

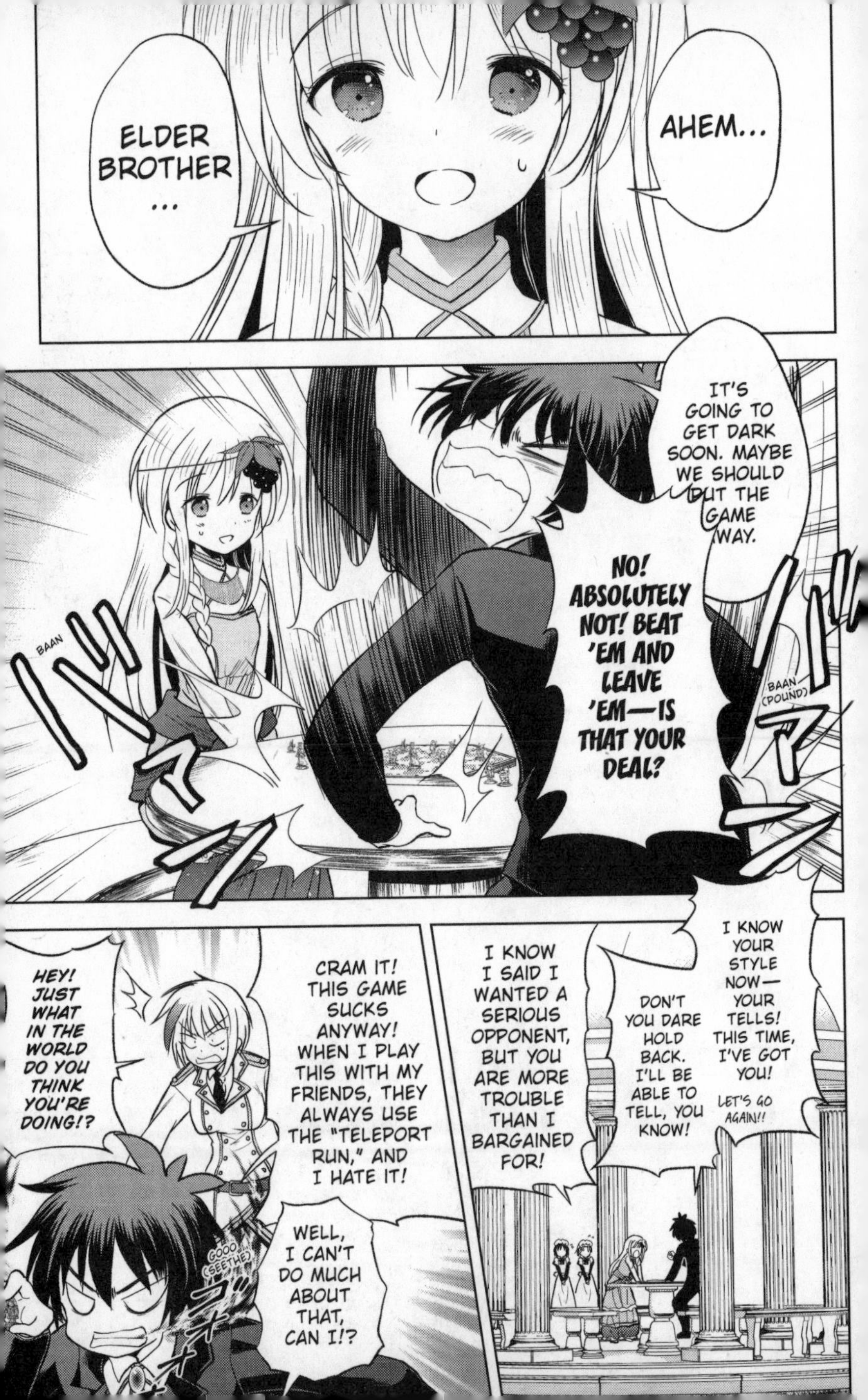
AHEM...
ELDER BROTHER ...
IT'S GOING TO GET DARK SOON. MAYBE WE SHOULD PUT THE GAME AWAY.
NO! ABSOLUTELY NOT! BEAT 'EM AND LEAVE 'EM—IS THAT YOUR DEAL?
BAAN (POUND)
BAAN
I KNOW YOUR STYLE NOW—YOUR TELLS! THIS TIME, I'VE GOT YOU!
LET'S GO AGAIN!!
DON'T YOU DARE HOLD BACK. I'LL BE ABLE TO TELL, YOU KNOW!
I KNOW I SAID I WANTED A SERIOUS OPPONENT, BUT YOU ARE MORE TROUBLE THAN I BARGAINED FOR!
CRAM IT! THIS GAME SUCKS ANYWAY! WHEN I PLAY THIS WITH MY FRIENDS, THEY ALWAYS USE THE "TELEPORT RUN," AND I HATE IT!
HEY! JUST WHAT IN THE WORLD DO YOU THINK YOU'RE DOING!?
GOOO (SEETHE)
WELL, I CAN'T DO MUCH ABOUT THAT, CAN I!?

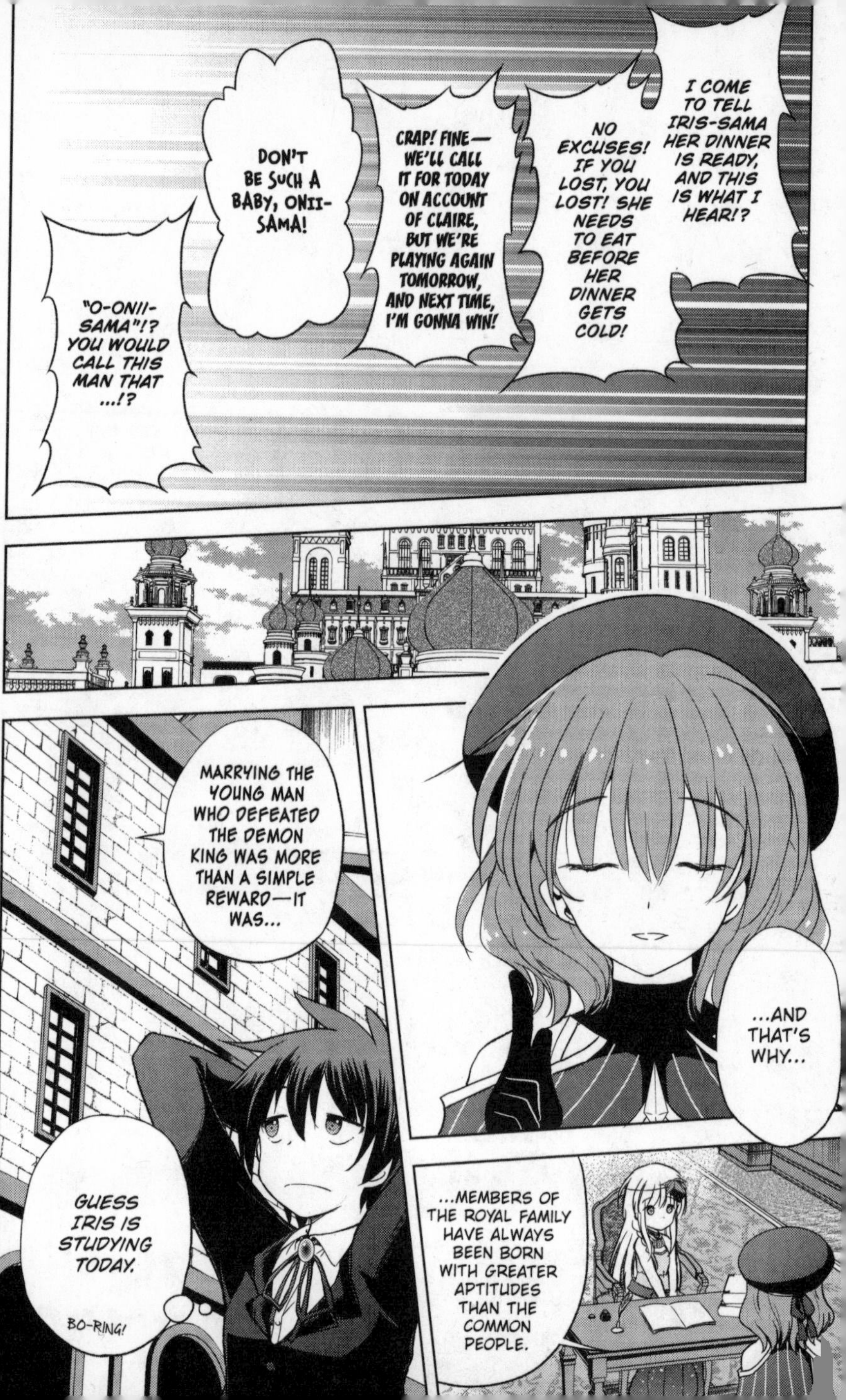

I COME TO TELL IRIS-SAMA HER DINNER IS READY, AND THIS IS WHAT I HEAR!?
NO EXCUSES! IF YOU LOST, YOU LOST! SHE NEEDS TO EAT BEFORE HER DINNER GETS COLD!
CRAP! FINE—WE'LL CALL IT FOR TODAY ON ACCOUNT OF CLAIRE, BUT WE'RE PLAYING AGAIN TOMORROW, AND NEXT TIME, I'M GONNA WIN!
DON'T BE SUCH A BABY, ONII-SAMA!
"O-ONII-SAMA"!? YOU WOULD CALL THIS MAN THAT ...!?
MARRYING THE YOUNG MAN WHO DEFEATED THE DEMON KING WAS MORE THAN A SIMPLE REWARD—IT WAS...
...AND THAT'S WHY...
...MEMBERS OF THE ROYAL FAMILY HAVE ALWAYS BEEN BORN WITH GREATER APTITUDES THAN THE COMMON PEOPLE.
GUESS IRIS IS STUDYING TODAY.
BO-RING!

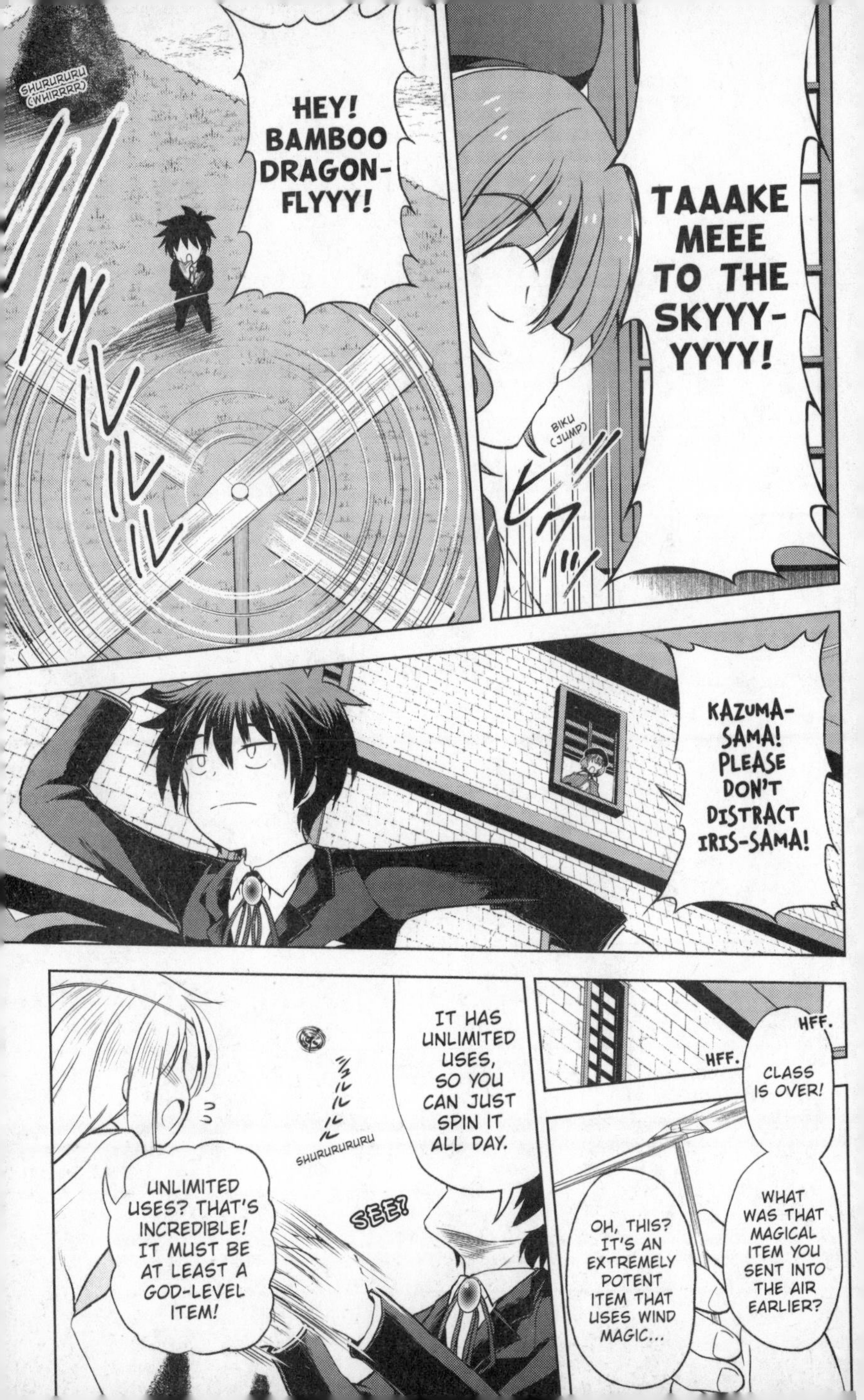
TAAAKE MEEE TO THE SKYYY-YYYY!
BIKU (JUMP)
HEY! BAMBOO DRAGON-FLYYY!
SHURURURU (WHIRRRR)
KAZUMA-SAMA! PLEASE DON'T DISTRACT IRIS-SAMA!
HFF.
HFF.
CLASS IS OVER!
WHAT WAS THAT MAGICAL ITEM YOU SENT INTO THE AIR EARLIER?
OH, THIS? IT'S AN EXTREMELY POTENT ITEM THAT USES WIND MAGIC...
IT HAS UNLIMITED USES, SO YOU CAN JUST SPIN IT ALL DAY.
SHURURURURU
SEE?
UNLIMITED USES? THAT'S INCREDIBLE! IT MUST BE AT LEAST A GOD-LEVEL ITEM!

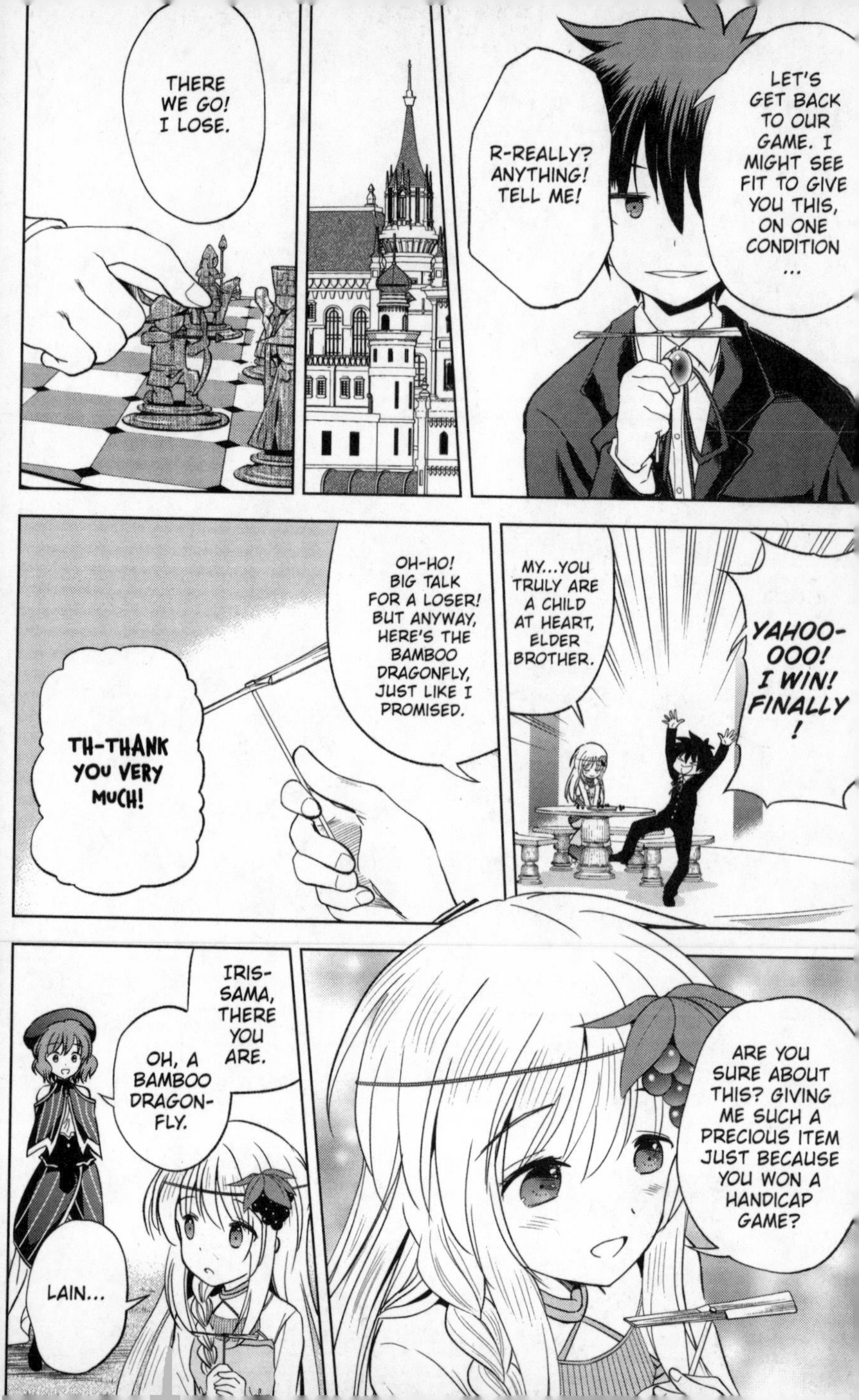
LET'S GET BACK TO OUR GAME. I MIGHT SEE FIT TO GIVE YOU THIS, ON ONE CONDITION ...
R-REALLY? ANYTHING! TELL ME!
THERE WE GO! I LOSE.
YAHOO-OOO! I WIN! FINALLY!
MY...YOU TRULY ARE A CHILD AT HEART, ELDER BROTHER.
OH-HO! BIG TALK FOR A LOSER! BUT ANYWAY, HERE'S THE BAMBOO DRAGONFLY, JUST LIKE I PROMISED.
TH-THANK YOU VERY MUCH!
ARE YOU SURE ABOUT THIS? GIVING ME SUCH A PRECIOUS ITEM JUST BECAUSE YOU WON A HANDICAP GAME?
IRIS-SAMA, THERE YOU ARE.
OH, A BAMBOO DRAGON-FLY.
LAIN...

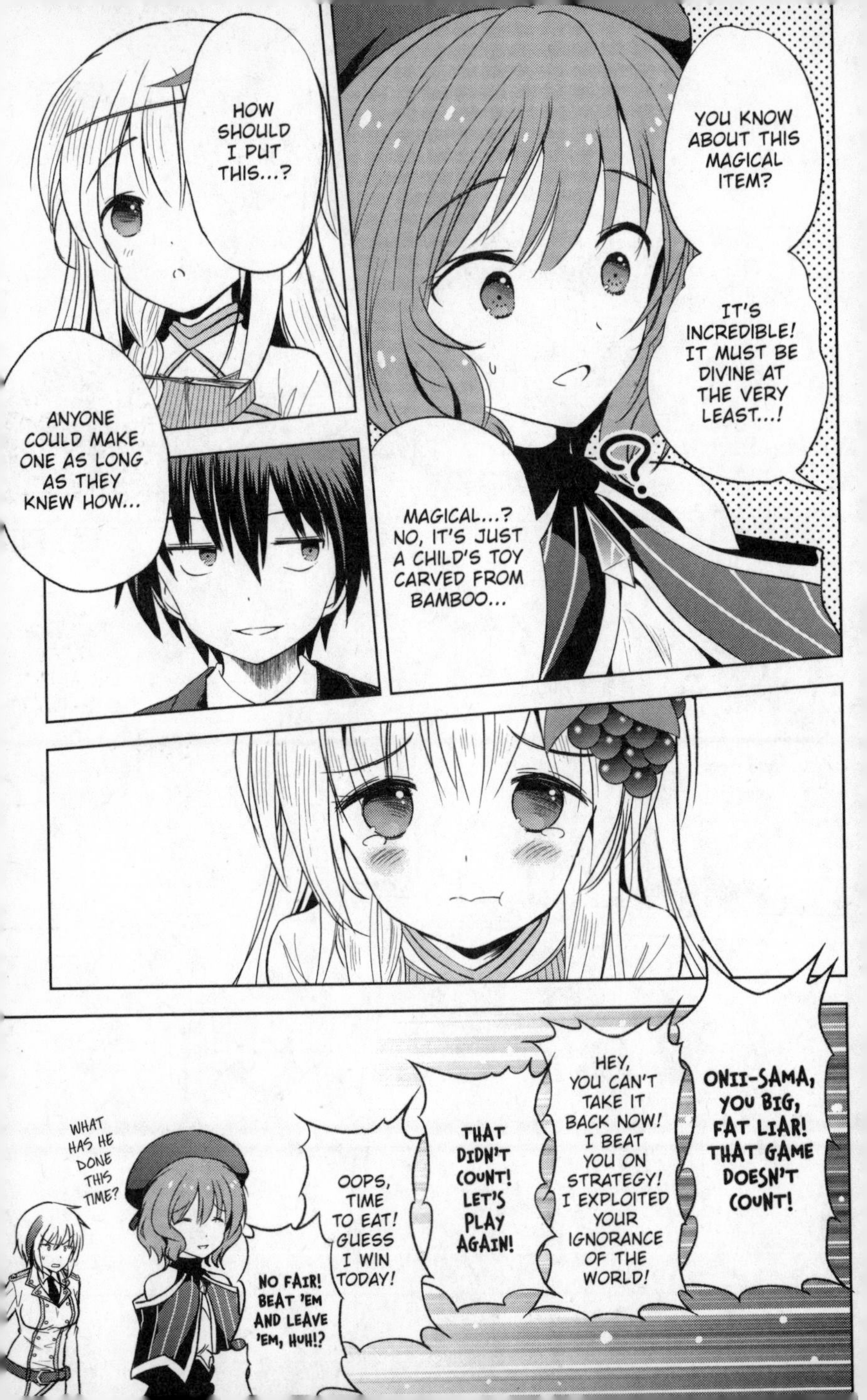
YOU KNOW ABOUT THIS MAGICAL ITEM?
IT'S INCREDIBLE! IT MUST BE DIVINE AT THE VERY LEAST...!
MAGICAL...? NO, IT'S JUST A CHILD'S TOY CARVED FROM BAMBOO...
HOW SHOULD I PUT THIS...?
ANYONE COULD MAKE ONE AS LONG AS THEY KNEW HOW...
ONII-SAMA, YOU BIG, FAT LIAR! THAT GAME DOESN'T COUNT!
HEY, YOU CAN'T TAKE IT BACK NOW! I BEAT YOU ON STRATEGY! I EXPLOITED YOUR IGNORANCE OF THE WORLD!
THAT DIDN'T COUNT! LET'S PLAY AGAIN!
OOPS, TIME TO EAT! GUESS I WIN TODAY!
NO FAIR! BEAT 'EM AND LEAVE 'EM, HUH!?
WHAT HAS HE DONE THIS TIME?

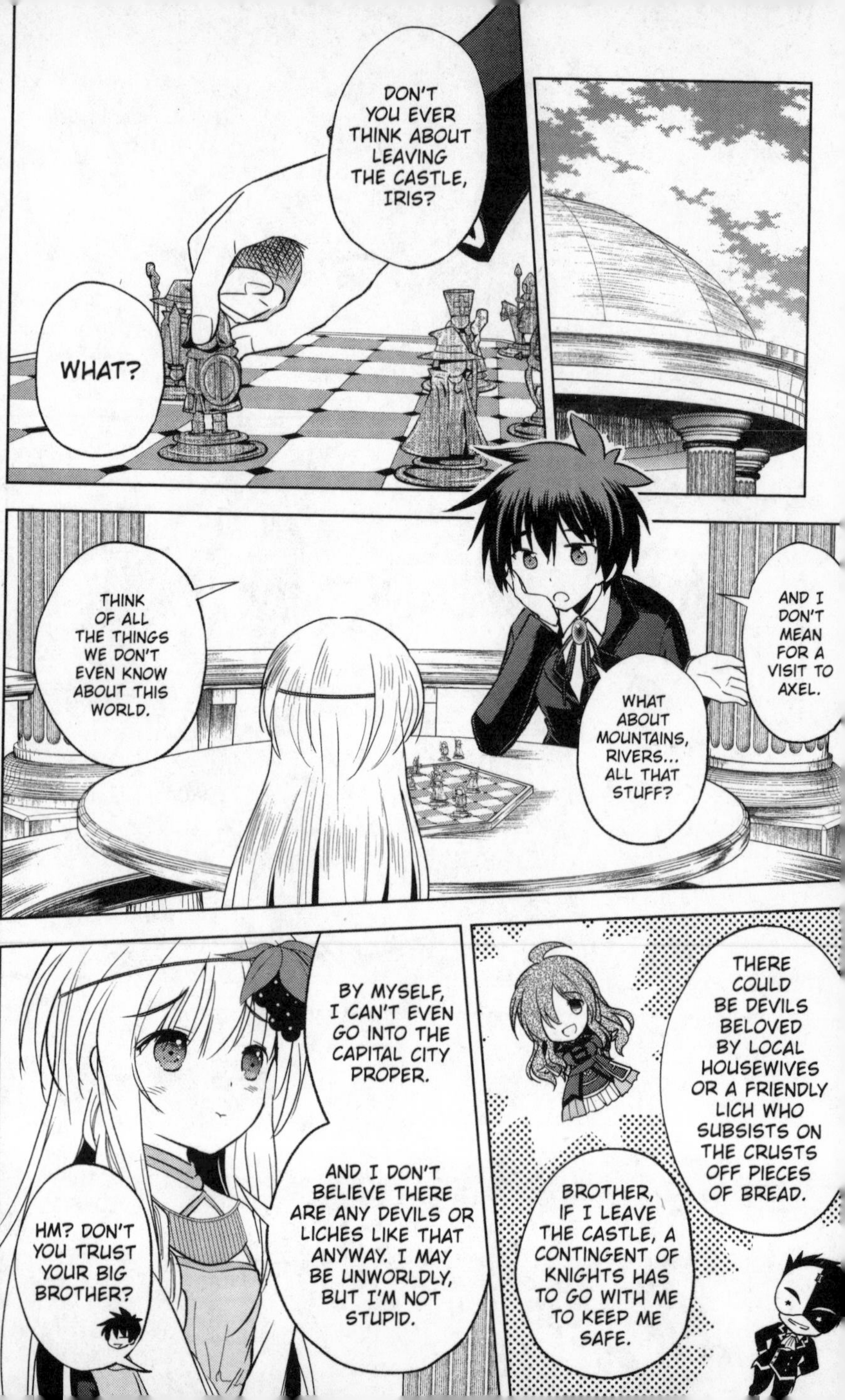
DON'T YOU EVER THINK ABOUT LEAVING THE CASTLE, IRIS?
WHAT?
AND I DON'T MEAN FOR A VISIT TO AXEL.
WHAT ABOUT MOUNTAINS, RIVERS... ALL THAT STUFF?
THINK OF ALL THE THINGS WE DON'T EVEN KNOW ABOUT THIS WORLD.
THERE COULD BE DEVILS BELOVED BY LOCAL HOUSEWIVES OR A FRIENDLY LICH WHO SUBSISTS ON THE CRUSTS OFF PIECES OF BREAD.
BROTHER, IF I LEAVE THE CASTLE, A CONTINGENT OF KNIGHTS HAS TO GO WITH ME TO KEEP ME SAFE.
BY MYSELF, I CAN'T EVEN GO INTO THE CAPITAL CITY PROPER.
AND I DON'T BELIEVE THERE ARE ANY DEVILS OR LICHES LIKE THAT ANYWAY. I MAY BE UNWORLDLY, BUT I'M NOT STUPID.
HM? DON'T YOU TRUST YOUR BIG BROTHER?

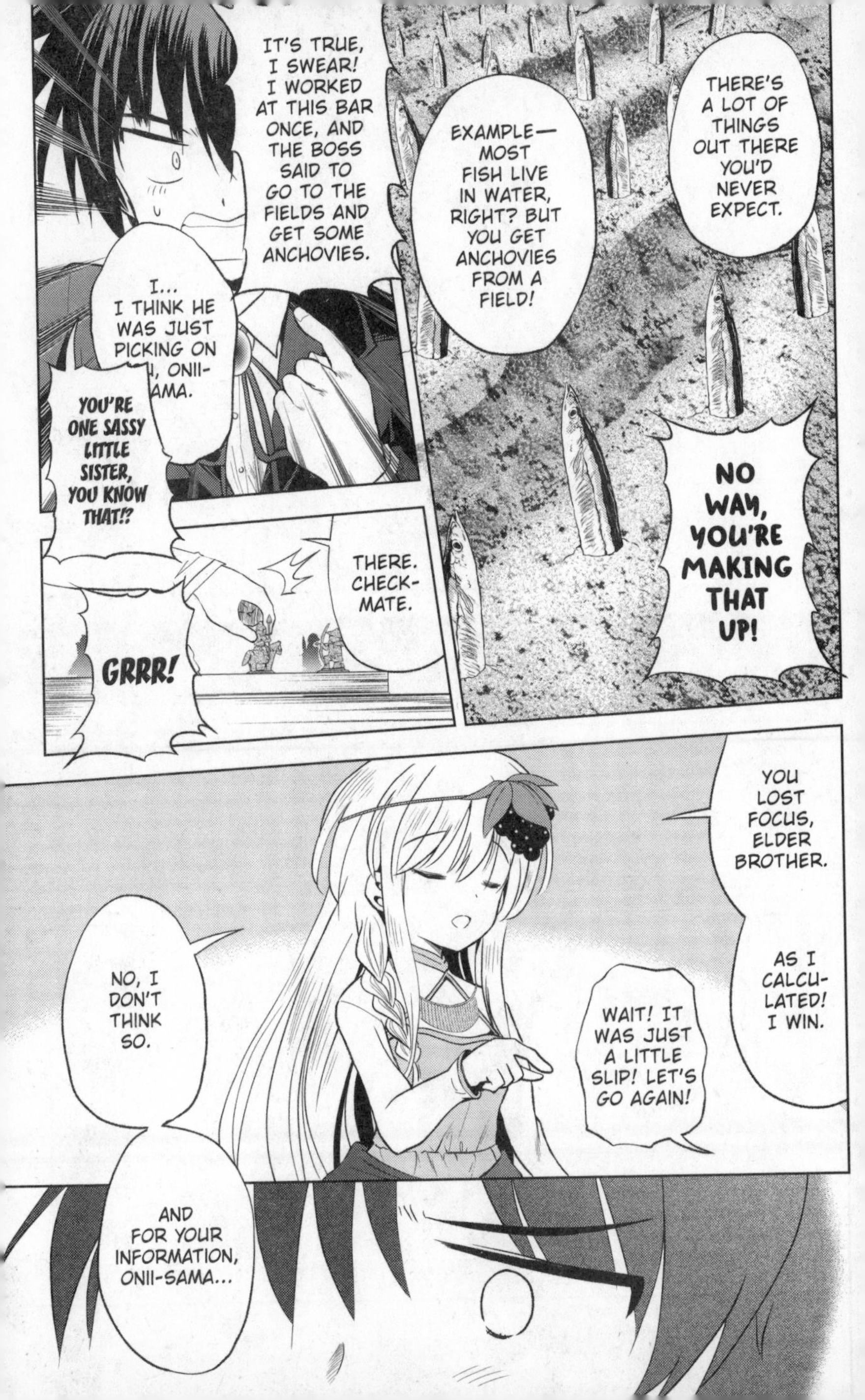

THERE'S A LOT OF THINGS OUT THERE YOU'D NEVER EXPECT.
EXAMPLE— MOST FISH LIVE IN WATER, RIGHT? BUT YOU GET ANCHOVIES FROM A FIELD!
NO WAY, YOU'RE MAKING THAT UP!
IT'S TRUE, I SWEAR! I WORKED AT THIS BAR ONCE, AND THE BOSS SAID TO GO TO THE FIELDS AND GET SOME ANCHOVIES.
I... I THINK HE WAS JUST PICKING ON ...I, ONII-SAMA.
YOU'RE ONE SASSY LITTLE SISTER, YOU KNOW THAT!?
THERE. CHECK-MATE.
GRRR!
YOU LOST FOCUS, ELDER BROTHER.
AS I CALCU-LATED! I WIN.
WAIT! IT WAS JUST A LITTLE SLIP! LET'S GO AGAIN!
NO, I DON'T THINK SO.
AND FOR YOUR INFORMATION, ONII-SAMA...

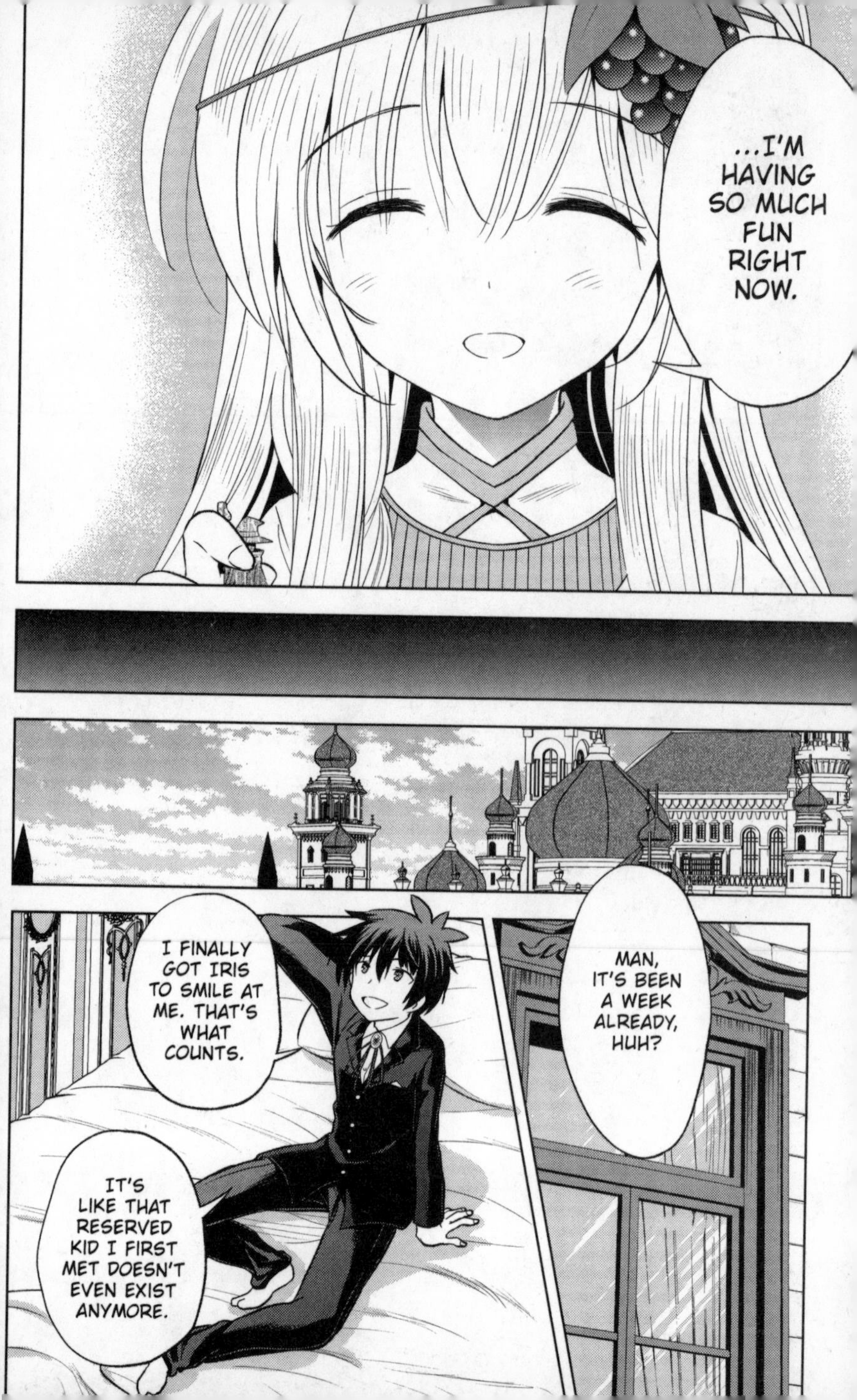
...I'M HAVING SO MUCH FUN RIGHT NOW.
MAN, IT'S BEEN A WEEK ALREADY, HUH?
I FINALLY GOT IRIS TO SMILE AT ME. THAT'S WHAT COUNTS.
IT'S LIKE THAT RESERVED KID I FIRST MET DOESN'T EVEN EXIST ANYMORE.

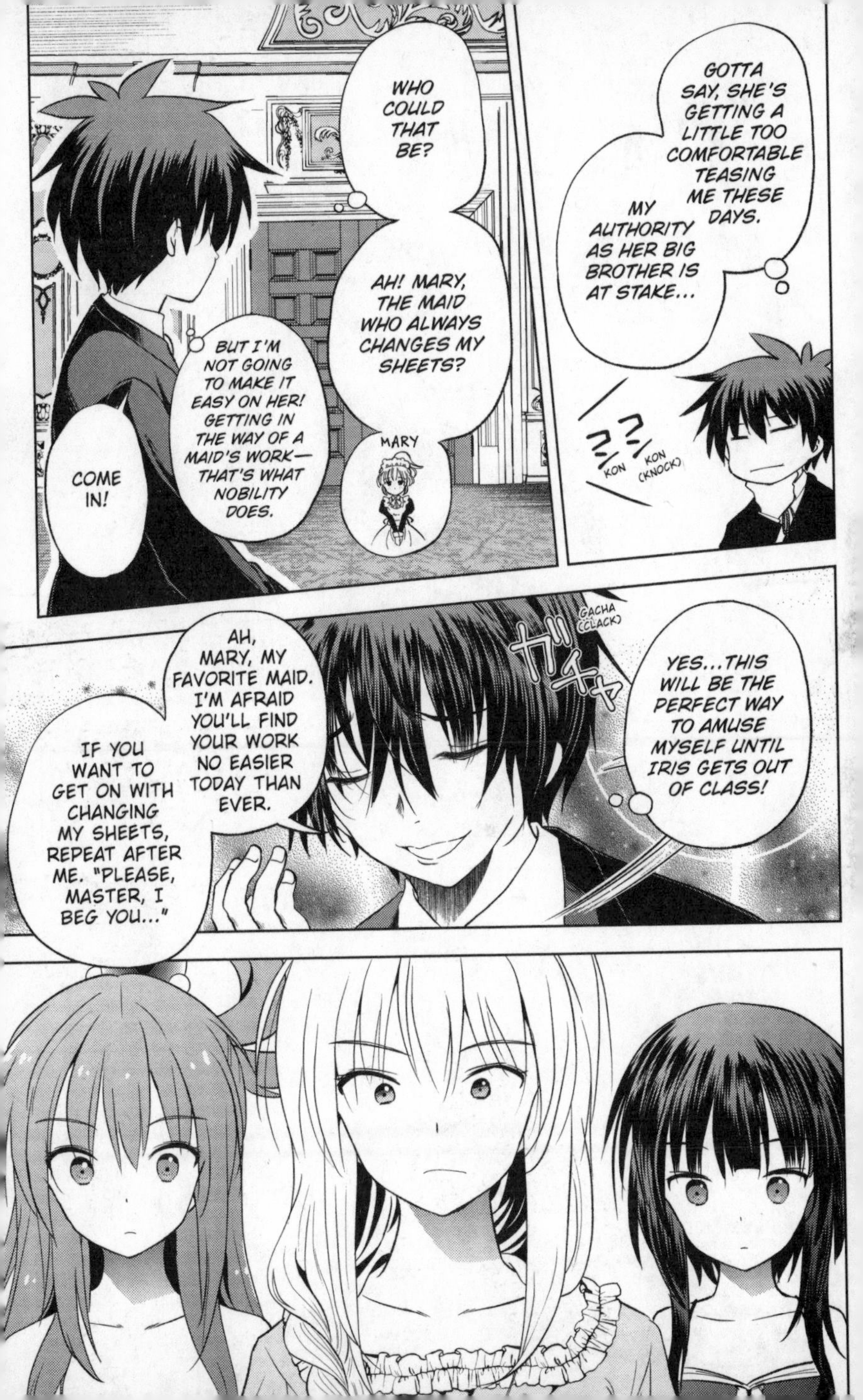
GOTTA SAY, SHE'S GETTING A LITTLE TOO COMFORTABLE TEASING ME THESE DAYS.
MY AUTHORITY AS HER BIG BROTHER IS AT STAKE...
KON KON (KNOCK)
WHO COULD THAT BE?
AH! MARY, THE MAID WHO ALWAYS CHANGES MY SHEETS?
MARY
BUT I'M NOT GOING TO MAKE IT EASY ON HER! GETTING IN THE WAY OF A MAID'S WORK—THAT'S WHAT NOBILITY DOES.
COME IN!
GACHA (CLACK)
YES...THIS WILL BE THE PERFECT WAY TO AMUSE MYSELF UNTIL IRIS GETS OUT OF CLASS!
AH, MARY, MY FAVORITE MAID. I'M AFRAID YOU'LL FIND YOUR WORK NO EASIER TODAY THAN EVER.
IF YOU WANT TO GET ON WITH CHANGING MY SHEETS, REPEAT AFTER ME. "PLEASE, MASTER, I BEG YOU..."

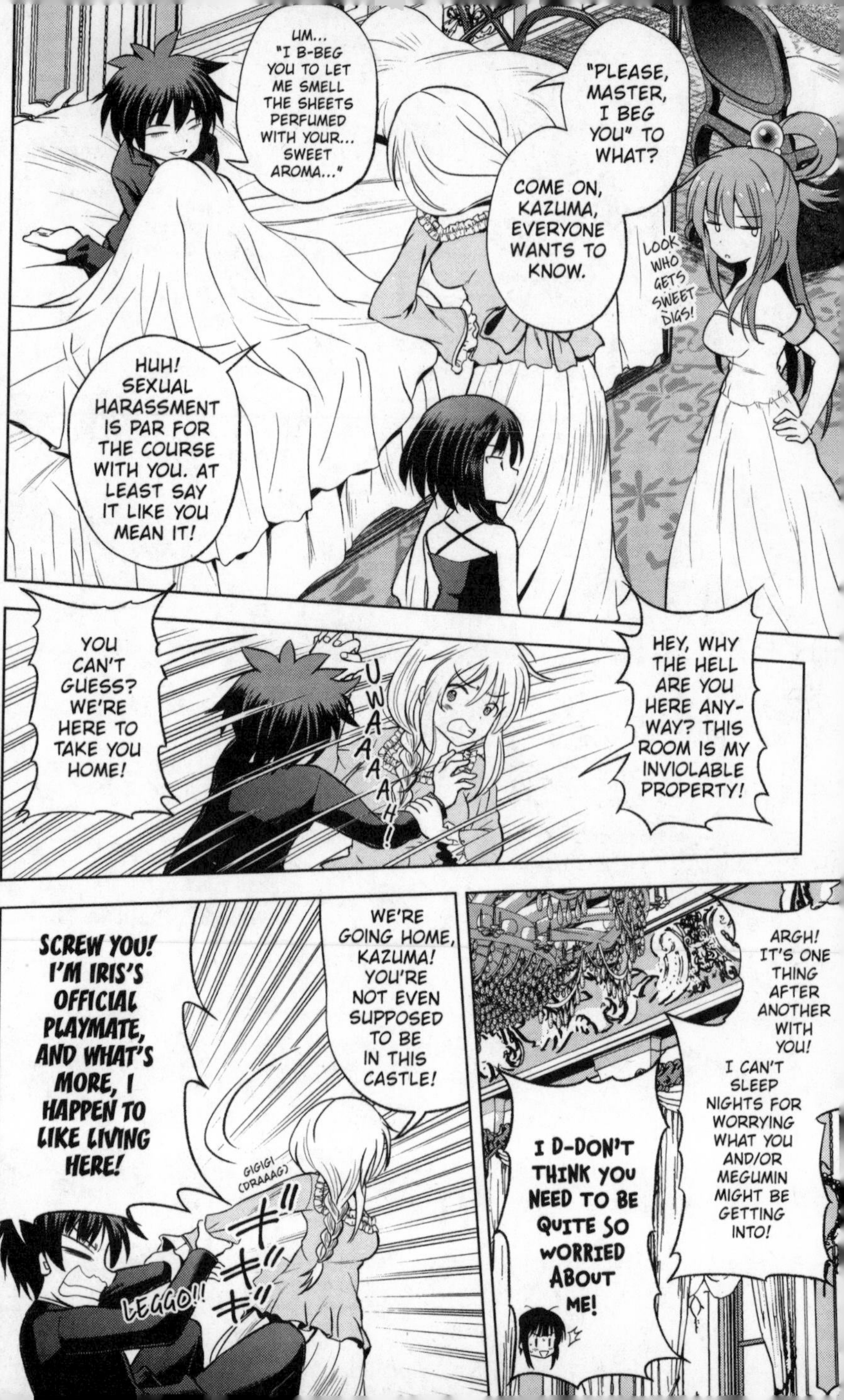
"PLEASE, MASTER, I BEG YOU" TO WHAT?
UM... "I B-BEG YOU TO LET ME SMELL THE SHEETS PERFUMED WITH YOUR... SWEET AROMA..."
COME ON, KAZUMA, EVERYONE WANTS TO KNOW.
LOOK WHO GETS SWEET DIGS!
HUH! SEXUAL HARASSMENT IS PAR FOR THE COURSE WITH YOU. AT LEAST SAY IT LIKE YOU MEAN IT!
HEY, WHY THE HELL ARE YOU HERE ANY-WAY? THIS ROOM IS MY INVIOLABLE PROPERTY!
UWAAAAAH!
YOU CAN'T GUESS? WE'RE HERE TO TAKE YOU HOME!
ARGH! IT'S ONE THING AFTER ANOTHER WITH YOU!
I CAN'T SLEEP NIGHTS FOR WORRYING WHAT YOU AND/OR MEGUMIN MIGHT BE GETTING INTO!
I D-DON'T THINK YOU NEED TO BE QUITE SO WORRIED ABOUT ME!
WE'RE GOING HOME, KAZUMA! YOU'RE NOT EVEN SUPPOSED TO BE IN THIS CASTLE!
SCREW YOU! I'M IRIS'S OFFICIAL PLAYMATE, AND WHAT'S MORE, I HAPPEN TO LIKE LIVING HERE!
GIGIGI (DRAAAG)
LEGGO!!

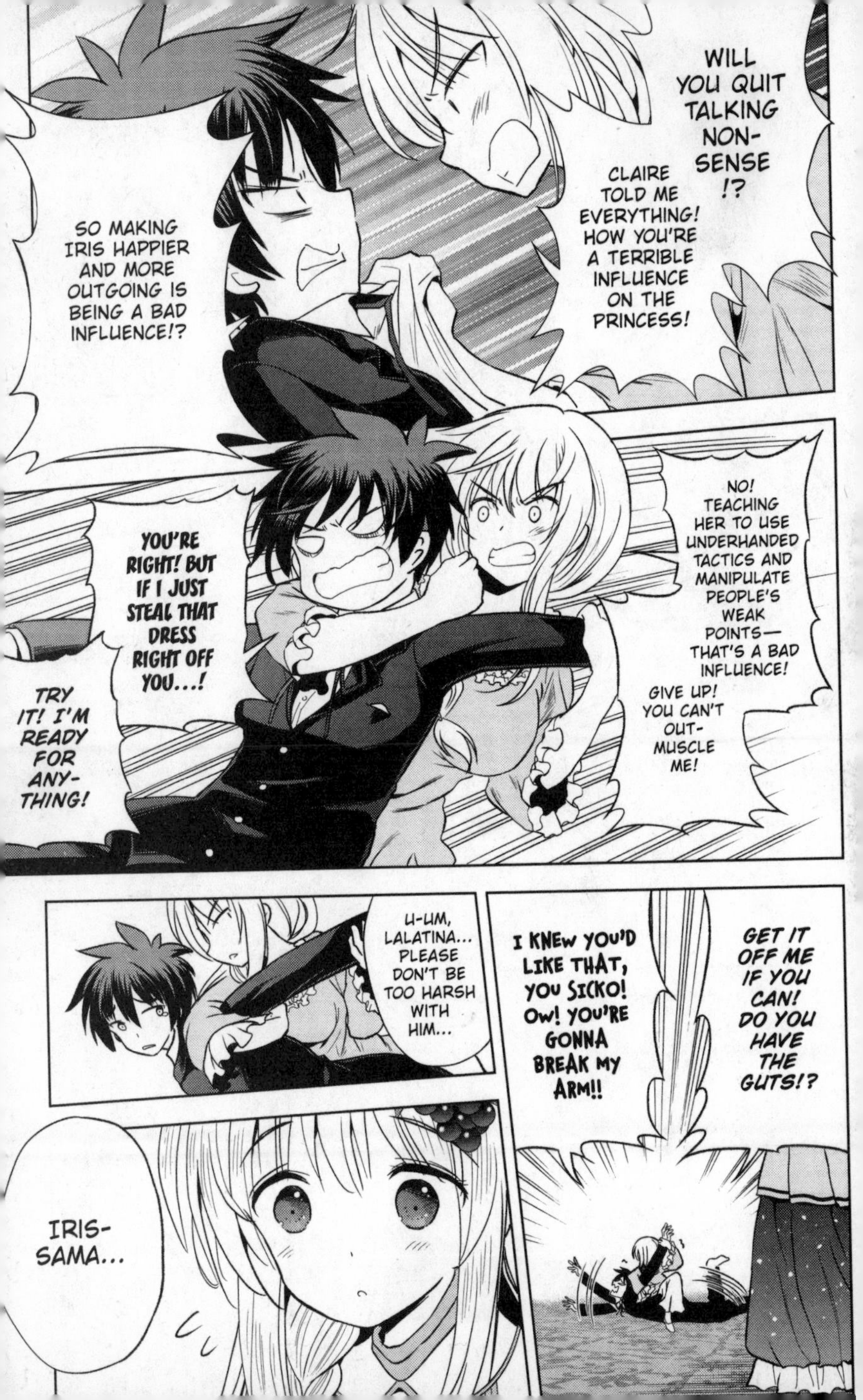
WILL YOU QUIT TALKING NON-SENSE!?
CLAIRE TOLD ME EVERYTHING! HOW YOU'RE A TERRIBLE INFLUENCE ON THE PRINCESS!
SO MAKING IRIS HAPPIER AND MORE OUTGOING IS BEING A BAD INFLUENCE!?
NO! TEACHING HER TO USE UNDERHANDED TACTICS AND MANIPULATE PEOPLE'S WEAK POINTS— THAT'S A BAD INFLUENCE!
YOU'RE RIGHT! BUT IF I JUST STEAL THAT DRESS RIGHT OFF YOU...!
GIVE UP! YOU CAN'T OUT-MUSCLE ME!
TRY IT! I'M READY FOR ANY-THING!
GET IT OFF ME IF YOU CAN! DO YOU HAVE THE GUTS!?
I KNEW YOU'D LIKE THAT, YOU SICKO! OW! YOU'RE GONNA BREAK MY ARM!!
U-UM, LALATINA... PLEASE DON'T BE TOO HARSH WITH HIM...
IRIS-SAMA...

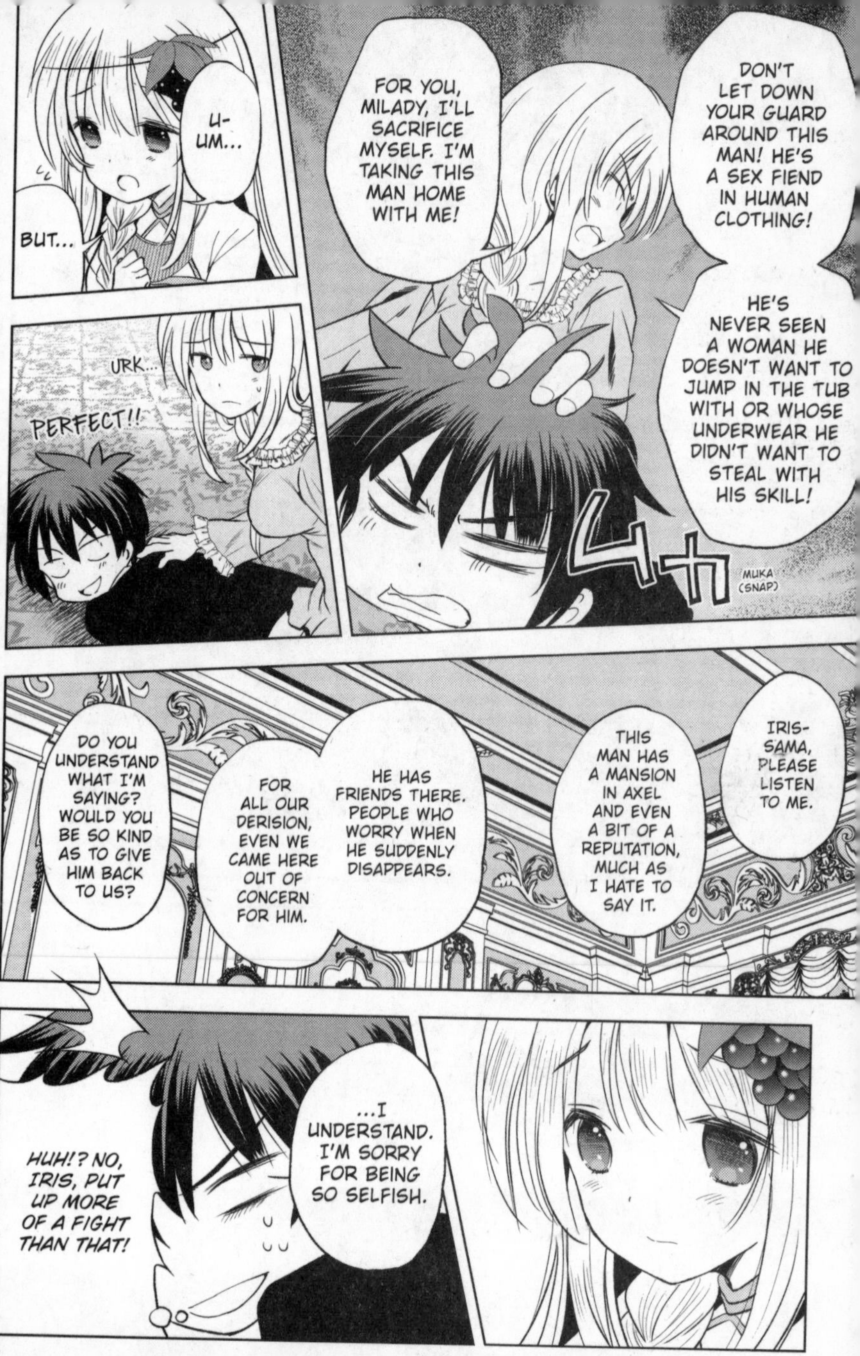
DON'T LET DOWN YOUR GUARD AROUND THIS MAN! HE'S A SEX FIEND IN HUMAN CLOTHING!
HE'S NEVER SEEN A WOMAN HE DOESN'T WANT TO JUMP IN THE TUB WITH OR WHOSE UNDERWEAR HE DIDN'T WANT TO STEAL WITH HIS SKILL!
MUKA (SNAP)
FOR YOU, MILADY, I'LL SACRIFICE MYSELF. I'M TAKING THIS MAN HOME WITH ME!
U-UM...
BUT...
URK...
PERFECT!!
IRIS-SAMA, PLEASE LISTEN TO ME.
THIS MAN HAS A MANSION IN AXEL AND EVEN A BIT OF A REPUTATION, MUCH AS I HATE TO SAY IT.
HE HAS FRIENDS THERE. PEOPLE WHO WORRY WHEN HE SUDDENLY DISAPPEARS.
FOR ALL OUR DERISION, EVEN WE CAME HERE OUT OF CONCERN FOR HIM.
DO YOU UNDERSTAND WHAT I'M SAYING? WOULD YOU BE SO KIND AS TO GIVE HIM BACK TO US?
...I UNDERSTAND. I'M SORRY FOR BEING SO SELFISH.
HUH!? NO, IRIS, PUT UP MORE OF A FIGHT THAN THAT!

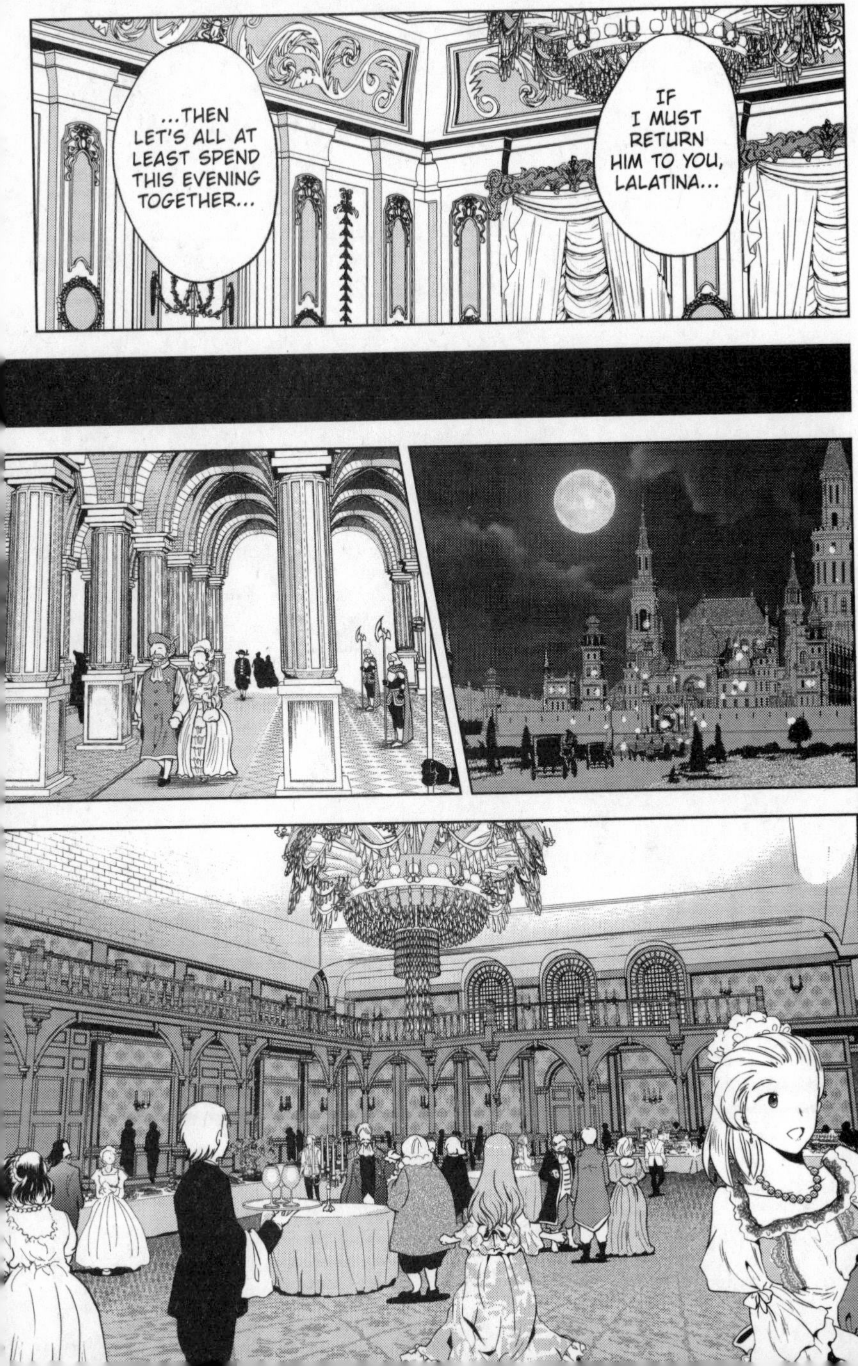
IF I MUST RETURN HIM TO YOU, LALATINA...
...THEN LET'S ALL AT LEAST SPEND THIS EVENING TOGETHER...

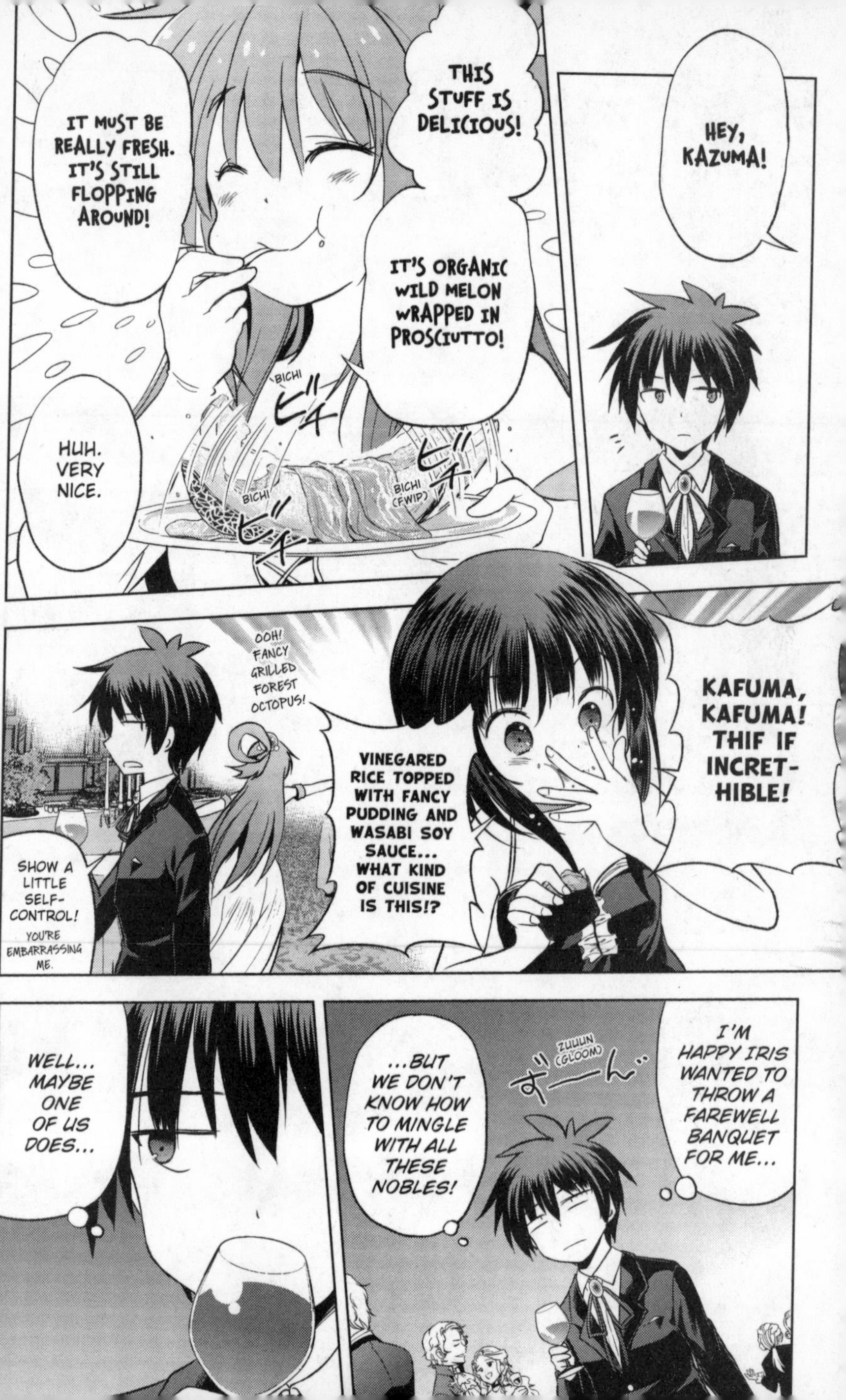
HEY, KAZUMA!
THIS STUFF IS DELICIOUS!
IT MUST BE REALLY FRESH. IT'S STILL FLOPPING AROUND!
IT'S ORGANIC WILD MELON WRAPPED IN PROSCIUTTO!
BICHI
BICHI (FWIP)
BICHI
HUH. VERY NICE.
KAFUMA, KAFUMA! THIF IF INCRET-HIBLE!
OOH! FANCY GRILLED FOREST OCTOPUS!
VINEGARED RICE TOPPED WITH FANCY PUDDING AND WASABI SOY SAUCE... WHAT KIND OF CUISINE IS THIS!?
SHOW A LITTLE SELF-CONTROL!
YOU'RE EMBARRASSING ME.
I'M HAPPY IRIS WANTED TO THROW A FAREWELL BANQUET FOR ME...
ZUUUN (GLOOM)
...BUT WE DON'T KNOW HOW TO MINGLE WITH ALL THESE NOBLES!
WELL... MAYBE ONE OF US DOES...

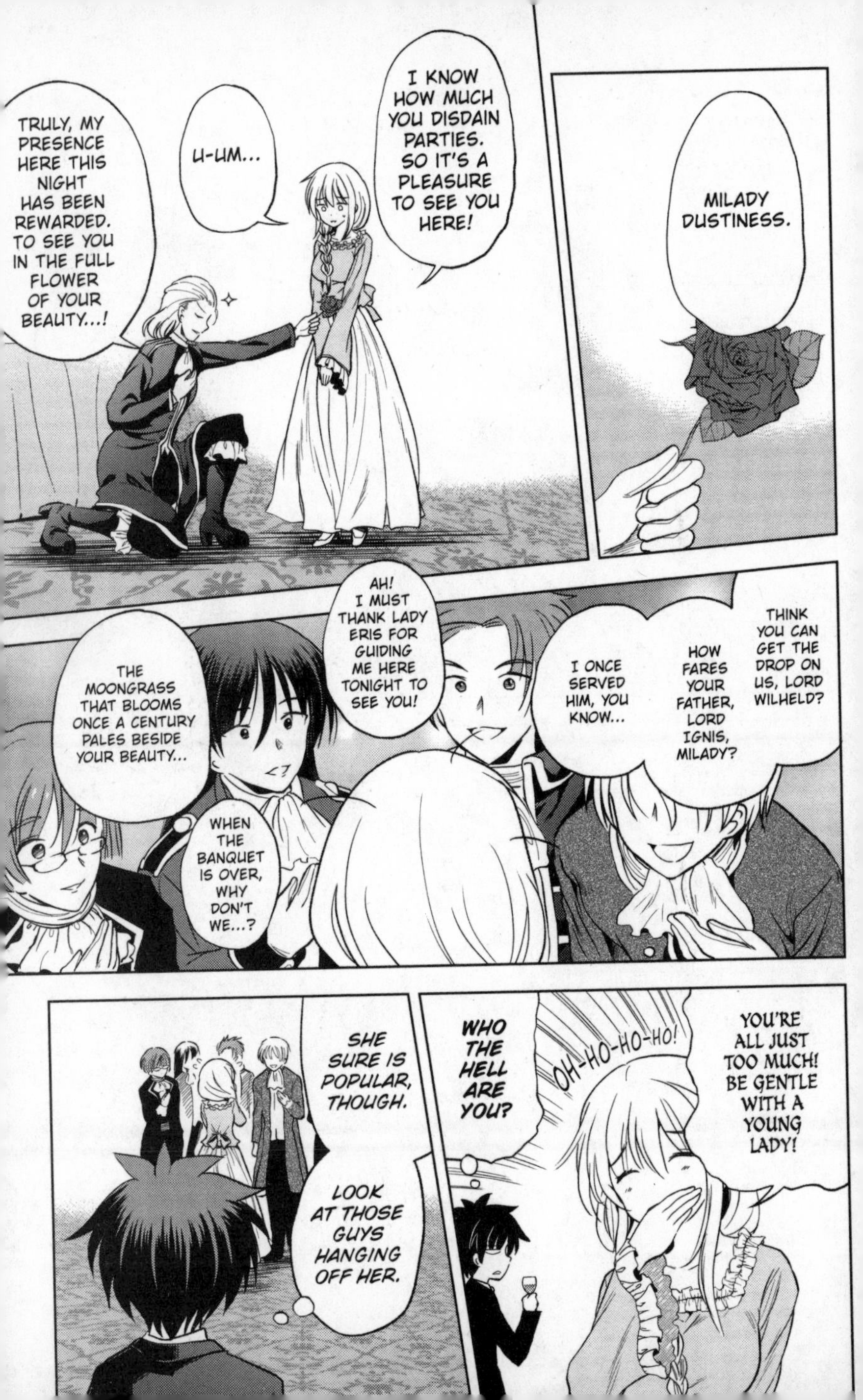
MILADY DUSTINESS.
I KNOW HOW MUCH YOU DISDAIN PARTIES. SO IT'S A PLEASURE TO SEE YOU HERE!
U-UM...
TRULY, MY PRESENCE HERE THIS NIGHT HAS BEEN REWARDED. TO SEE YOU IN THE FULL FLOWER OF YOUR BEAUTY...!
THINK YOU CAN GET THE DROP ON US, LORD WILHELD?
HOW FARES YOUR FATHER, LORD IGNIS, MILADY?
I ONCE SERVED HIM, YOU KNOW...
AH! I MUST THANK LADY ERIS FOR GUIDING ME HERE TONIGHT TO SEE YOU!
THE MOONGRASS THAT BLOOMS ONCE A CENTURY PALES BESIDE YOUR BEAUTY...
WHEN THE BANQUET IS OVER, WHY DON'T WE...?
YOU'RE ALL JUST TOO MUCH! BE GENTLE WITH A YOUNG LADY!
OH-HO-HO-HO!
WHO THE HELL ARE YOU?
SHE SURE IS POPULAR, THOUGH.
LOOK AT THOSE GUYS HANGING OFF HER.

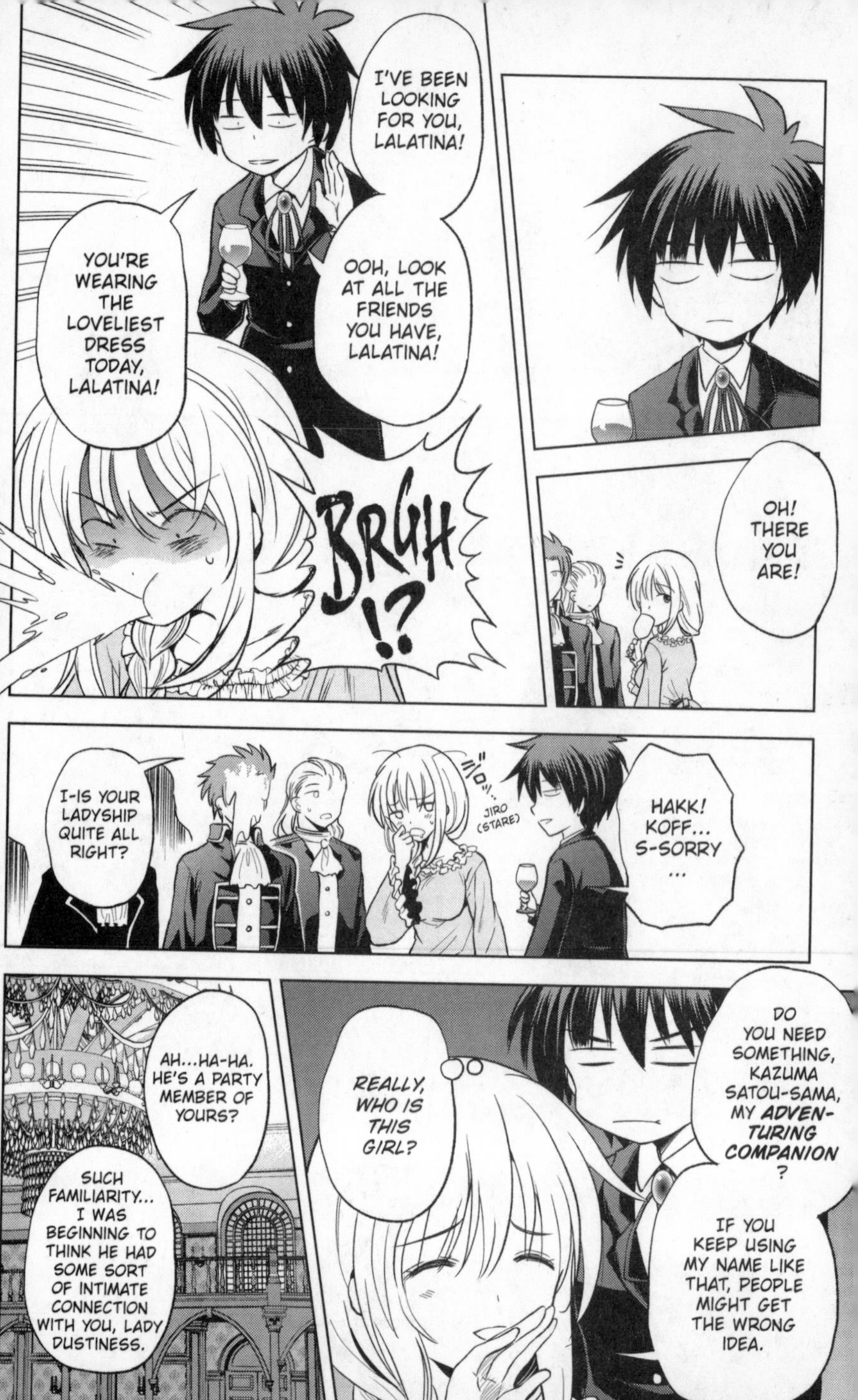
OH! THERE YOU ARE!
I'VE BEEN LOOKING FOR YOU, LALATINA!
OOH, LOOK AT ALL THE FRIENDS YOU HAVE, LALATINA!
YOU'RE WEARING THE LOVELIEST DRESS TODAY, LALATINA!
BRGH !?
HAKK! KOFF... S-SORRY ...
JIRO (STARE)
I-IS YOUR LADYSHIP QUITE ALL RIGHT?
DO YOU NEED SOMETHING, KAZUMA SATOU-SAMA, MY ADVENTURING COMPANION ?
IF YOU KEEP USING MY NAME LIKE THAT, PEOPLE MIGHT GET THE WRONG IDEA.
REALLY, WHO IS THIS GIRL?
AH...HA-HA. HE'S A PARTY MEMBER OF YOURS?
SUCH FAMILIARITY... I WAS BEGINNING TO THINK HE HAD SOME SORT OF INTIMATE CONNECTION WITH YOU, LADY DUSTINESS.

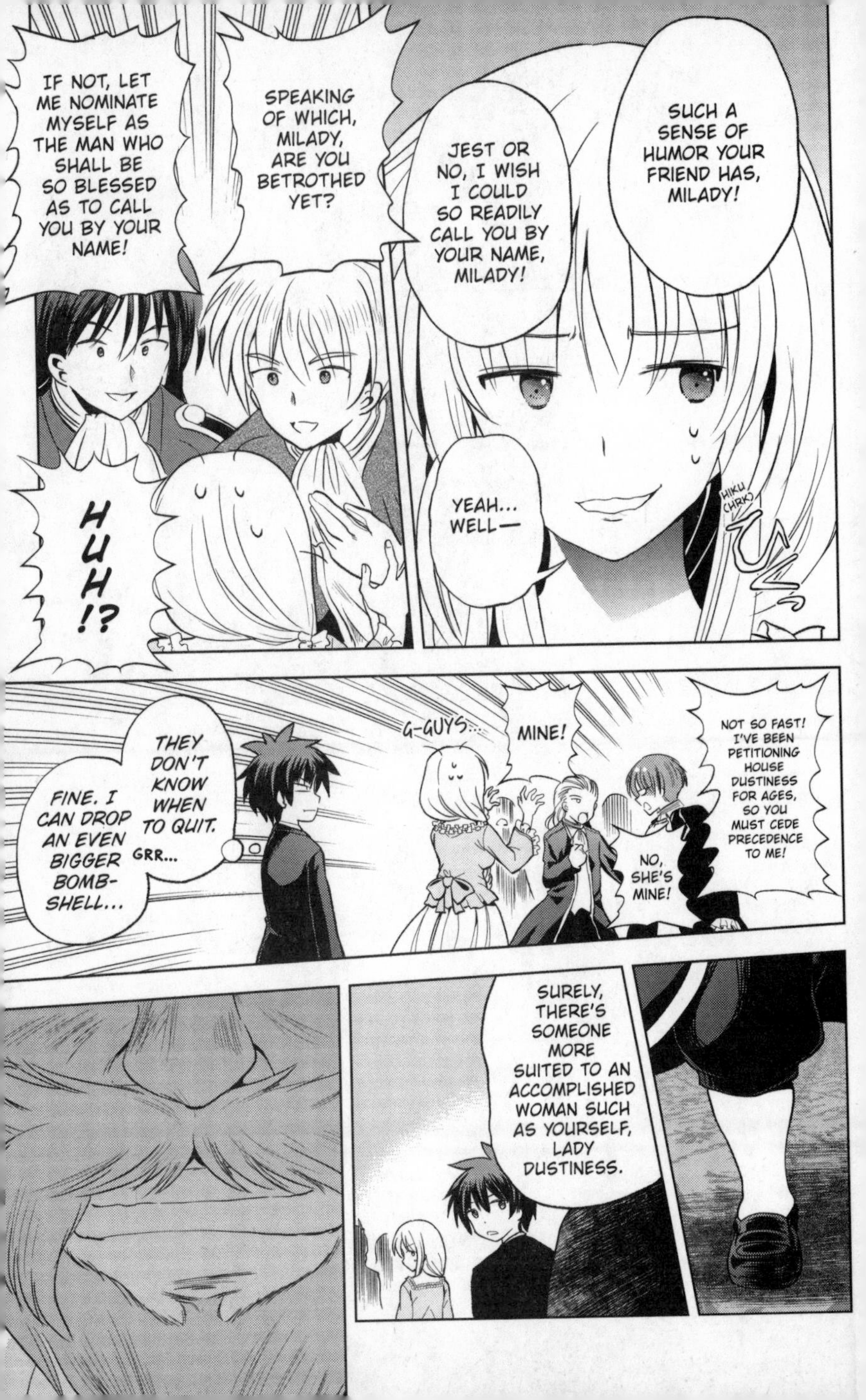
SUCH A SENSE OF HUMOR YOUR FRIEND HAS, MILADY!
JEST OR NO, I WISH I COULD SO READILY CALL YOU BY YOUR NAME, MILADY!
YEAH... WELL—
HIKU (HRK)
SPEAKING OF WHICH, MILADY, ARE YOU BETROTHED YET?
IF NOT, LET ME NOMINATE MYSELF AS THE MAN WHO SHALL BE SO BLESSED AS TO CALL YOU BY YOUR NAME!
HUH!?
NOT SO FAST! I'VE BEEN PETITIONING HOUSE DUSTINESS FOR AGES, SO YOU MUST CEDE PRECEDENCE TO ME!
NO, SHE'S MINE!
MINE!
G-GUYS...
THEY DON'T KNOW WHEN TO QUIT.
GRR...
FINE. I CAN DROP AN EVEN BIGGER BOMB-SHELL...
SURELY, THERE'S SOMEONE MORE SUITED TO AN ACCOMPLISHED WOMAN SUCH AS YOURSELF, LADY DUSTINESS.

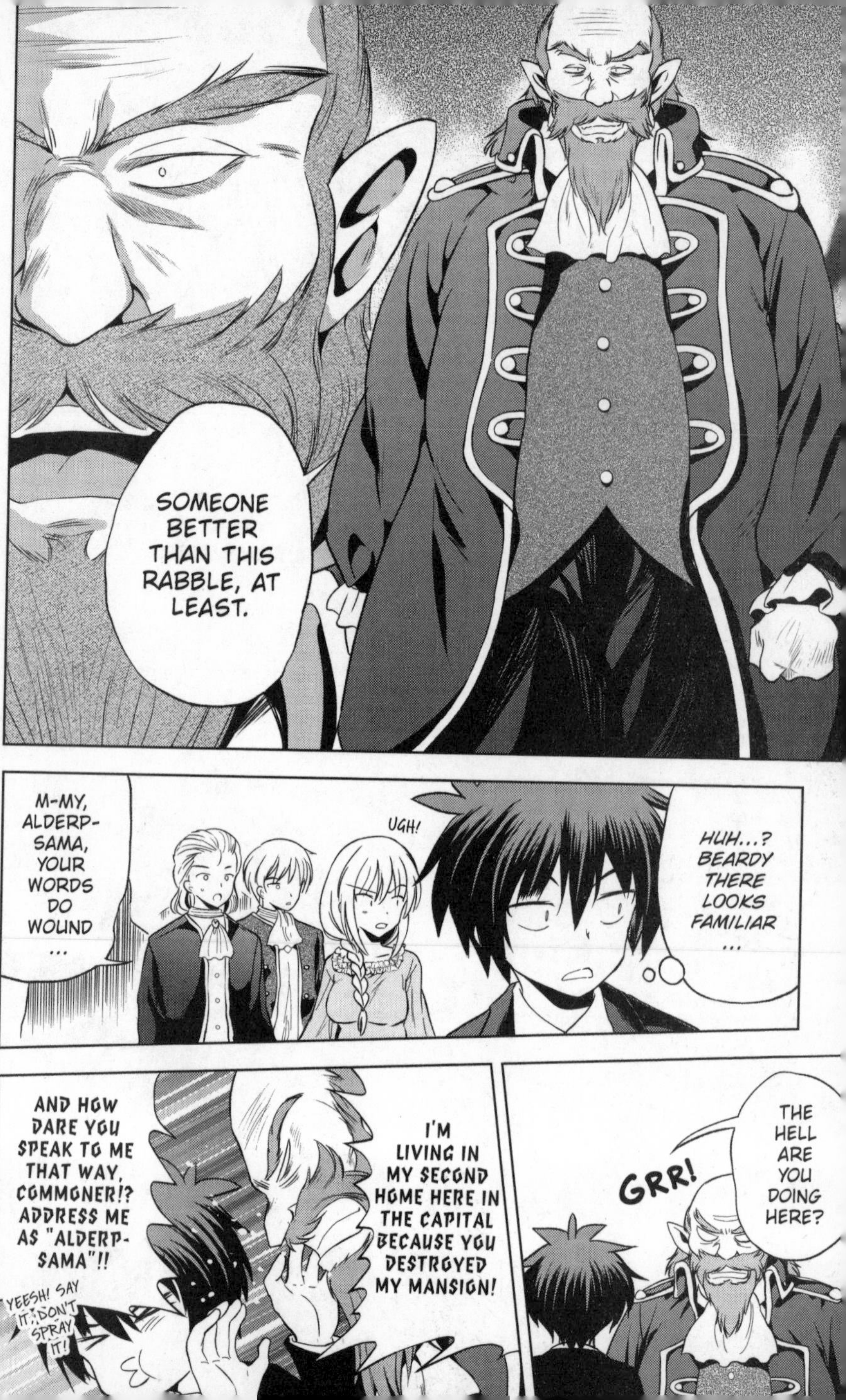
SOMEONE BETTER THAN THIS RABBLE, AT LEAST.
HUH...? BEARDY THERE LOOKS FAMILIAR...
UGH!
M-MY, ALDERP-SAMA, YOUR WORDS DO WOUND...
THE HELL ARE YOU DOING HERE?
GRR!
I'M LIVING IN MY SECOND HOME HERE IN THE CAPITAL BECAUSE YOU DESTROYED MY MANSION!
AND HOW DARE YOU SPEAK TO ME THAT WAY, COMMONER!? ADDRESS ME AS "ALDERP-SAMA"!!
YEESH! SAY IT, DON'T SPRAY IT!

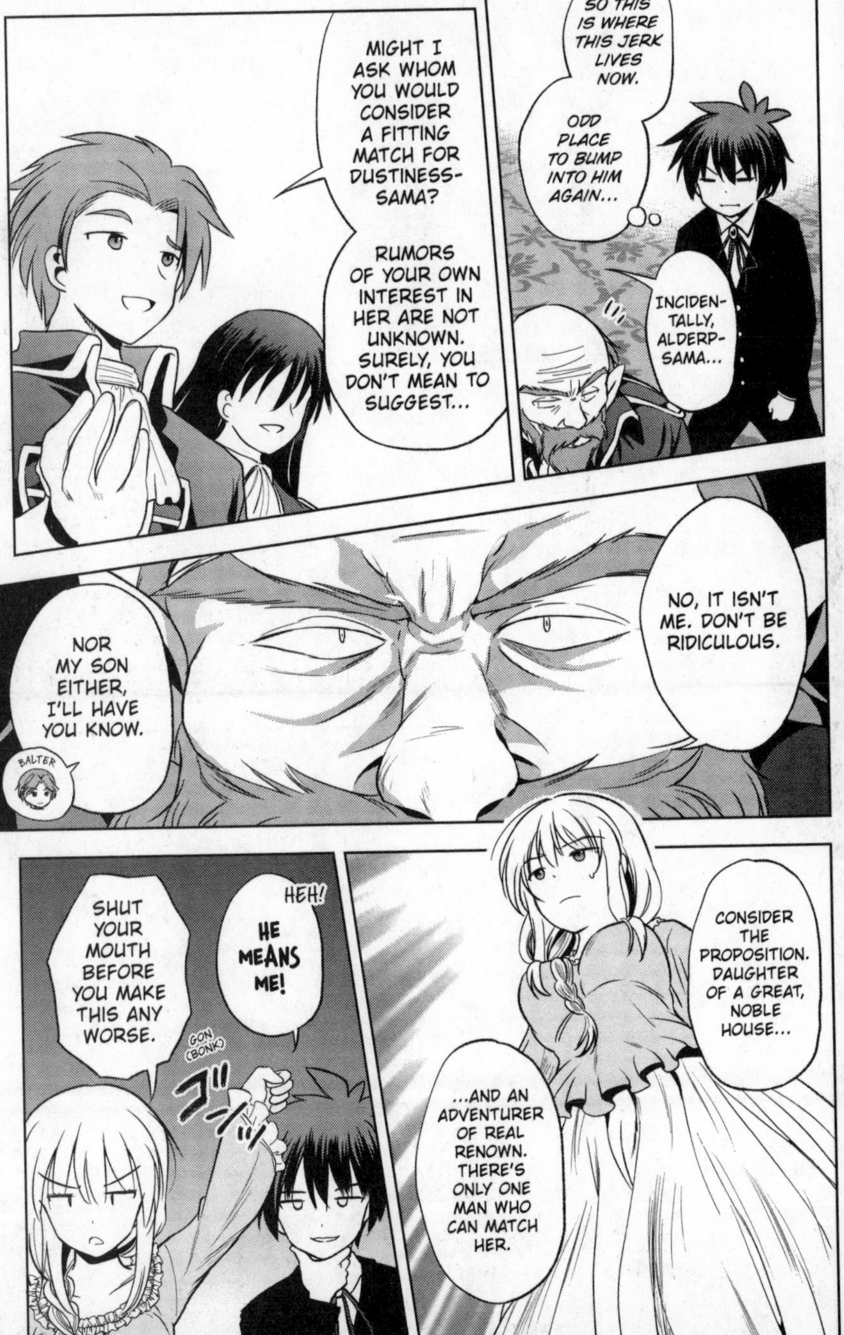
SO THIS IS WHERE THIS JERK LIVES NOW.
ODD PLACE TO BUMP INTO HIM AGAIN...
INCIDENTALLY, ALDERP-SAMA...
MIGHT I ASK WHOM YOU WOULD CONSIDER A FITTING MATCH FOR DUSTINESS-SAMA?
RUMORS OF YOUR OWN INTEREST IN HER ARE NOT UNKNOWN. SURELY, YOU DON'T MEAN TO SUGGEST...
NO, IT ISN'T ME. DON'T BE RIDICULOUS.
NOR MY SON EITHER, I'LL HAVE YOU KNOW.
BALTER
CONSIDER THE PROPOSITION. DAUGHTER OF A GREAT, NOBLE HOUSE...
...AND AN ADVENTURER OF REAL RENOWN. THERE'S ONLY ONE MAN WHO CAN MATCH HER.
HEH!
HE MEANS ME!
SHUT YOUR MOUTH BEFORE YOU MAKE THIS ANY WORSE.
GON (BONK)
ゴッ

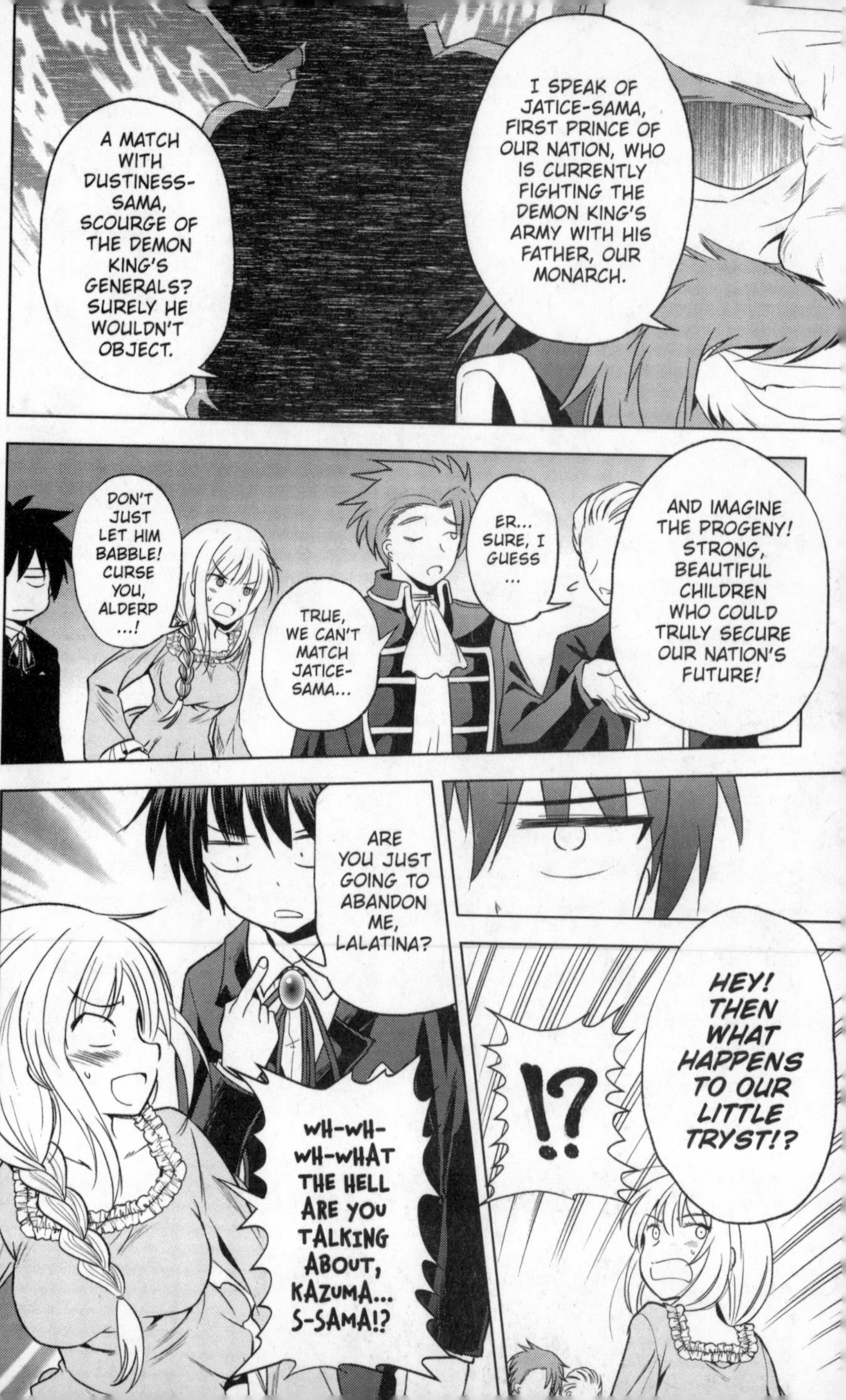
I SPEAK OF JATICE-SAMA, FIRST PRINCE OF OUR NATION, WHO IS CURRENTLY FIGHTING THE DEMON KING'S ARMY WITH HIS FATHER, OUR MONARCH.
A MATCH WITH DUSTINESS-SAMA, SCOURGE OF THE DEMON KING'S GENERALS? SURELY HE WOULDN'T OBJECT.
AND IMAGINE THE PROGENY! STRONG, BEAUTIFUL CHILDREN WHO COULD TRULY SECURE OUR NATION'S FUTURE!
ER... SURE, I GUESS...
TRUE, WE CAN'T MATCH JATICE-SAMA...
DON'T JUST LET HIM BABBLE! CURSE YOU, ALDERP...!
HEY! THEN WHAT HAPPENS TO OUR LITTLE TRYST!?
!?
ARE YOU JUST GOING TO ABANDON ME, LALATINA?
WH-WH-WH-WHAT THE HELL ARE YOU TALKING ABOUT, KAZUMA... S-SAMA!?

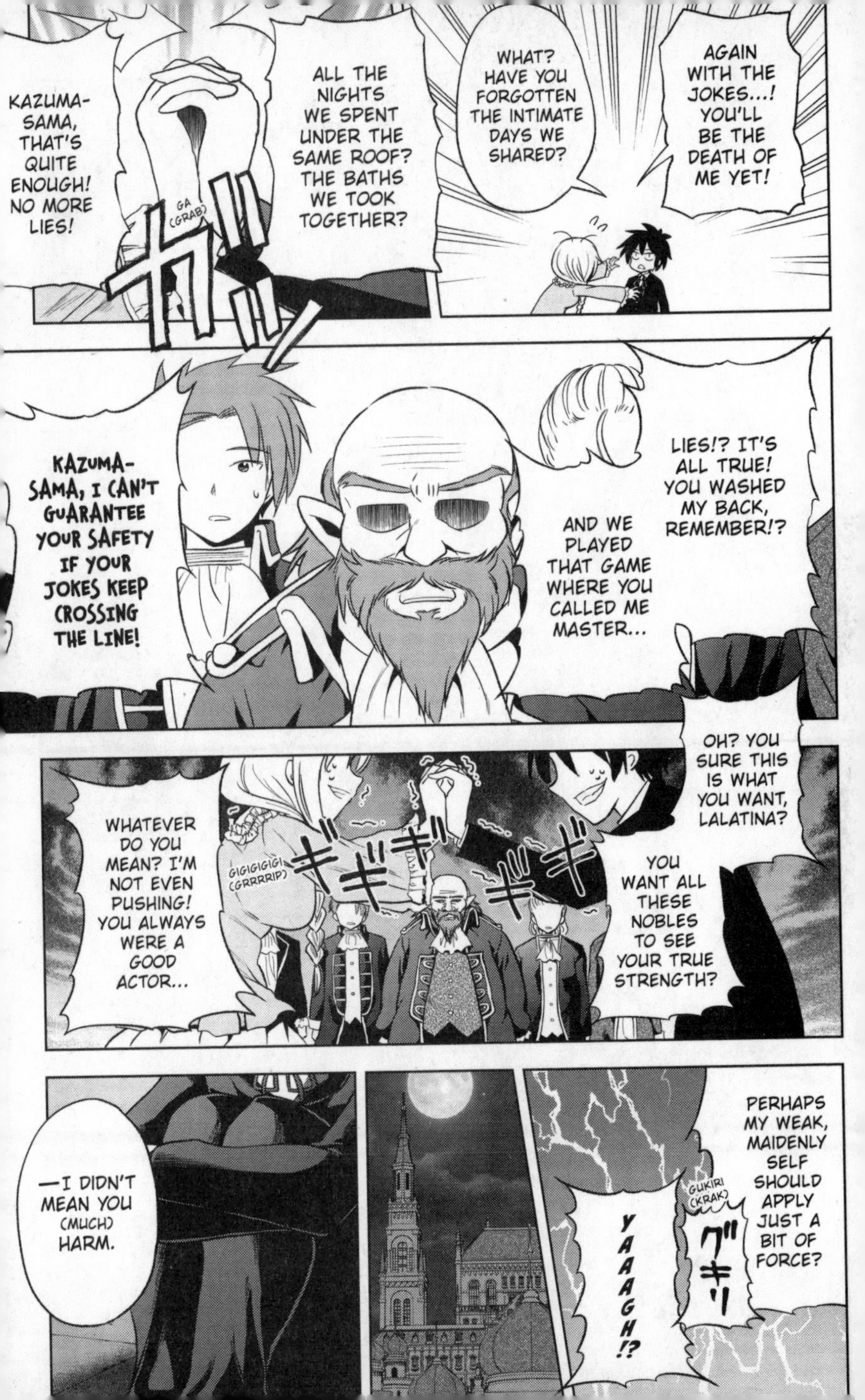
AGAIN WITH THE JOKES...! YOU'LL BE THE DEATH OF ME YET!
WHAT? HAVE YOU FORGOTTEN THE INTIMATE DAYS WE SHARED?
ALL THE NIGHTS WE SPENT UNDER THE SAME ROOF? THE BATHS WE TOOK TOGETHER?
GA (GRAB)
KAZUMA-SAMA, THAT'S QUITE ENOUGH! NO MORE LIES!
LIES!? IT'S ALL TRUE! YOU WASHED MY BACK, REMEMBER!?
AND WE PLAYED THAT GAME WHERE YOU CALLED ME MASTER...
KAZUMA-SAMA, I CAN'T GUARANTEE YOUR SAFETY IF YOUR JOKES KEEP CROSSING THE LINE!
OH? YOU SURE THIS IS WHAT YOU WANT, LALATINA?
YOU WANT ALL THESE NOBLES TO SEE YOUR TRUE STRENGTH?
GIGIGIGIGI (GRRRRIP)
WHATEVER DO YOU MEAN? I'M NOT EVEN PUSHING! YOU ALWAYS WERE A GOOD ACTOR...
PERHAPS MY WEAK, MAIDENLY SELF SHOULD APPLY JUST A BIT OF FORCE?
GUKIRI (KRAK)
YAAAGH!?
—I DIDN'T MEAN YOU (MUCH) HARM.

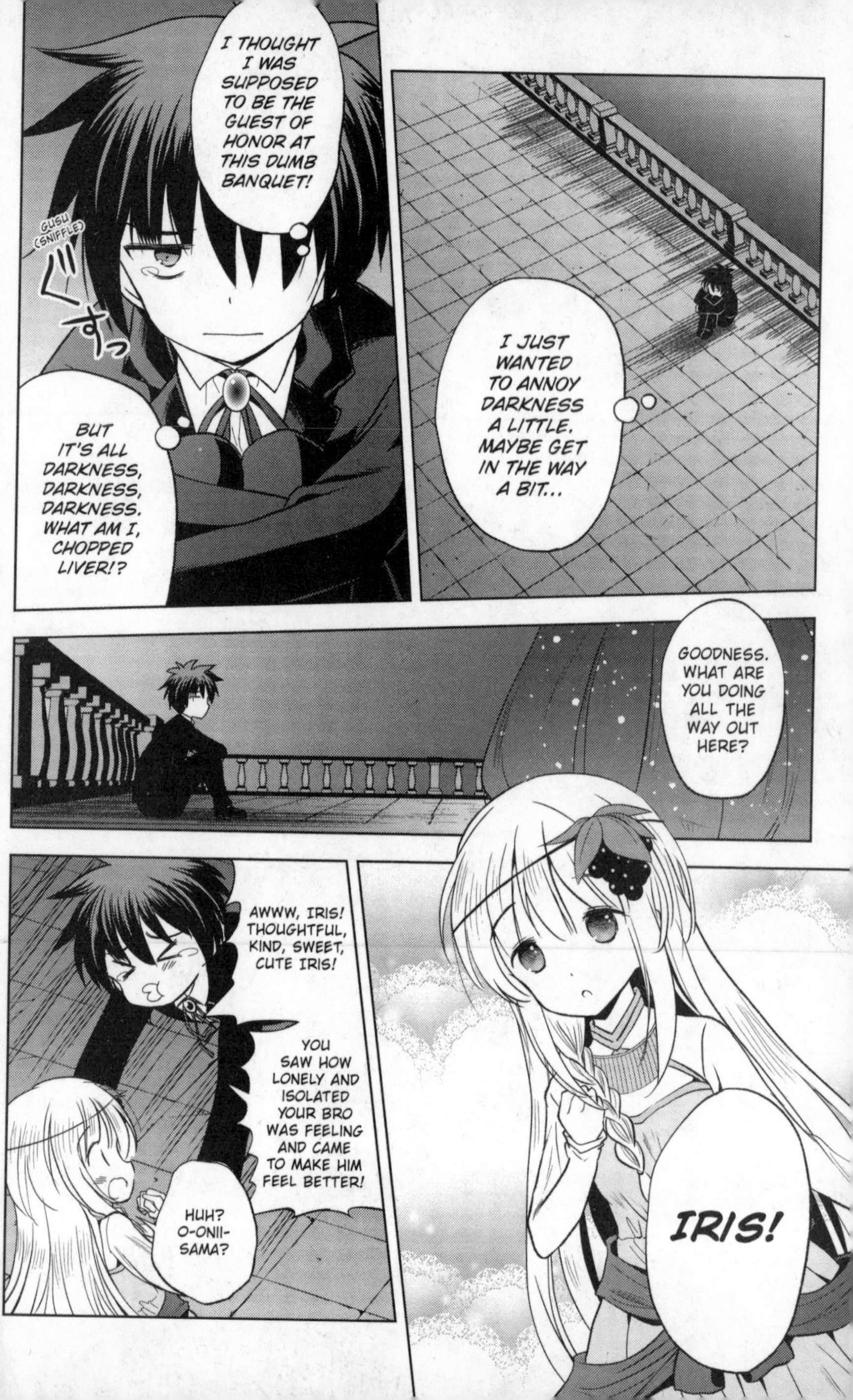
I JUST WANTED TO ANNOY DARKNESS A LITTLE. MAYBE GET IN THE WAY A BIT...
I THOUGHT I WAS SUPPOSED TO BE THE GUEST OF HONOR AT THIS DUMB BANQUET!
GUSU (SNIFFLE)
BUT IT'S ALL DARKNESS, DARKNESS, DARKNESS. WHAT AM I, CHOPPED LIVER!?
GOODNESS. WHAT ARE YOU DOING ALL THE WAY OUT HERE?
IRIS!
AWWW, IRIS! THOUGHTFUL, KIND, SWEET, CUTE IRIS!
YOU SAW HOW LONELY AND ISOLATED YOUR BRO WAS FEELING AND CAME TO MAKE HIM FEEL BETTER!
HUH? O-ONII-SAMA?

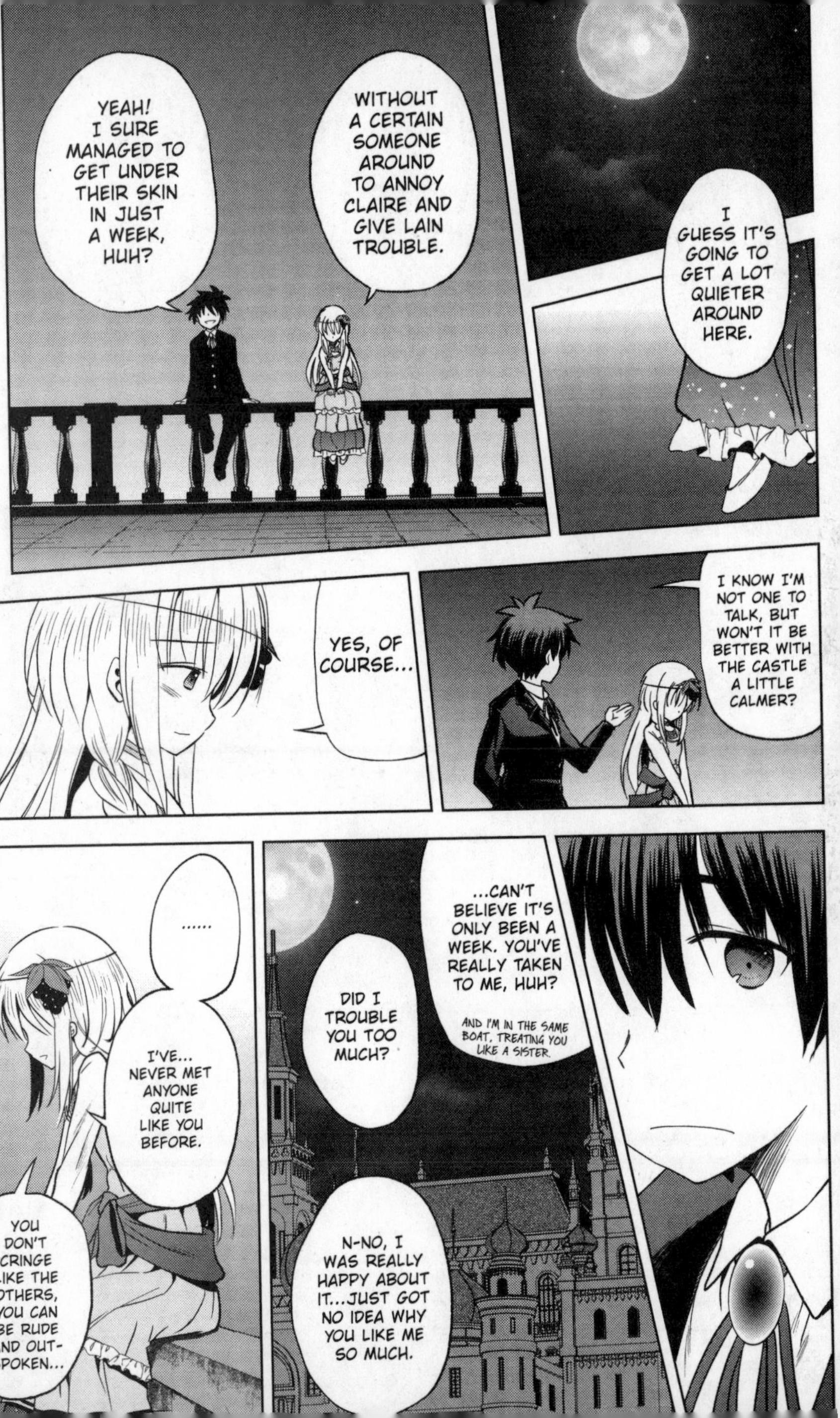
I GUESS IT'S GOING TO GET A LOT QUIETER AROUND HERE.
WITHOUT A CERTAIN SOMEONE AROUND TO ANNOY CLAIRE AND GIVE LAIN TROUBLE.
YEAH! I SURE MANAGED TO GET UNDER THEIR SKIN IN JUST A WEEK, HUH?
I KNOW I'M NOT ONE TO TALK, BUT WON'T IT BE BETTER WITH THE CASTLE A LITTLE CALMER?
YES, OF COURSE...
...CAN'T BELIEVE IT'S ONLY BEEN A WEEK. YOU'VE REALLY TAKEN TO ME, HUH?
AND I'M IN THE SAME BOAT, TREATING YOU LIKE A SISTER.
DID I TROUBLE YOU TOO MUCH?
N-NO, I WAS REALLY HAPPY ABOUT IT...JUST GOT NO IDEA WHY YOU LIKE ME SO MUCH.
......
I'VE... NEVER MET ANYONE QUITE LIKE YOU BEFORE.
YOU DON'T CRINGE LIKE THE OTHERS, YOU CAN BE RUDE AND OUT-SPOKEN...

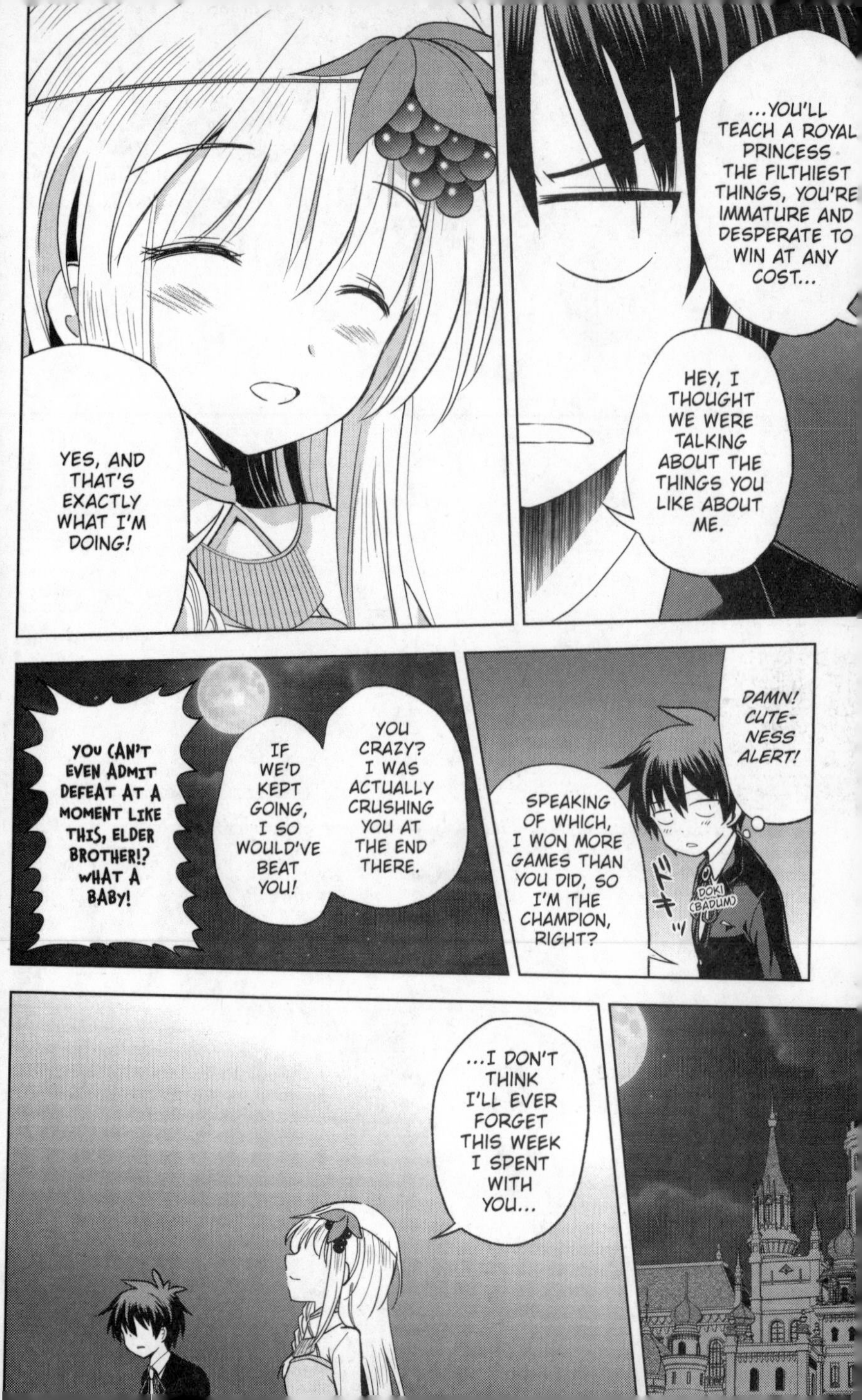

...YOU'LL TEACH A ROYAL PRINCESS THE FILTHIEST THINGS, YOU'RE IMMATURE AND DESPERATE TO WIN AT ANY COST...
HEY, I THOUGHT WE WERE TALKING ABOUT THE THINGS YOU LIKE ABOUT ME.
YES, AND THAT'S EXACTLY WHAT I'M DOING!
DAMN! CUTE-NESS ALERT!
SPEAKING OF WHICH, I WON MORE GAMES THAN YOU DID, SO I'M THE CHAMPION, RIGHT?
DOKI (BADUM)
YOU CRAZY? I WAS ACTUALLY CRUSHING YOU AT THE END THERE.
IF WE'D KEPT GOING, I SO WOULD'VE BEAT YOU!
YOU CAN'T EVEN ADMIT DEFEAT AT A MOMENT LIKE THIS, ELDER BROTHER!? WHAT A BABY!
...I DON'T THINK I'LL EVER FORGET THIS WEEK I SPENT WITH YOU...

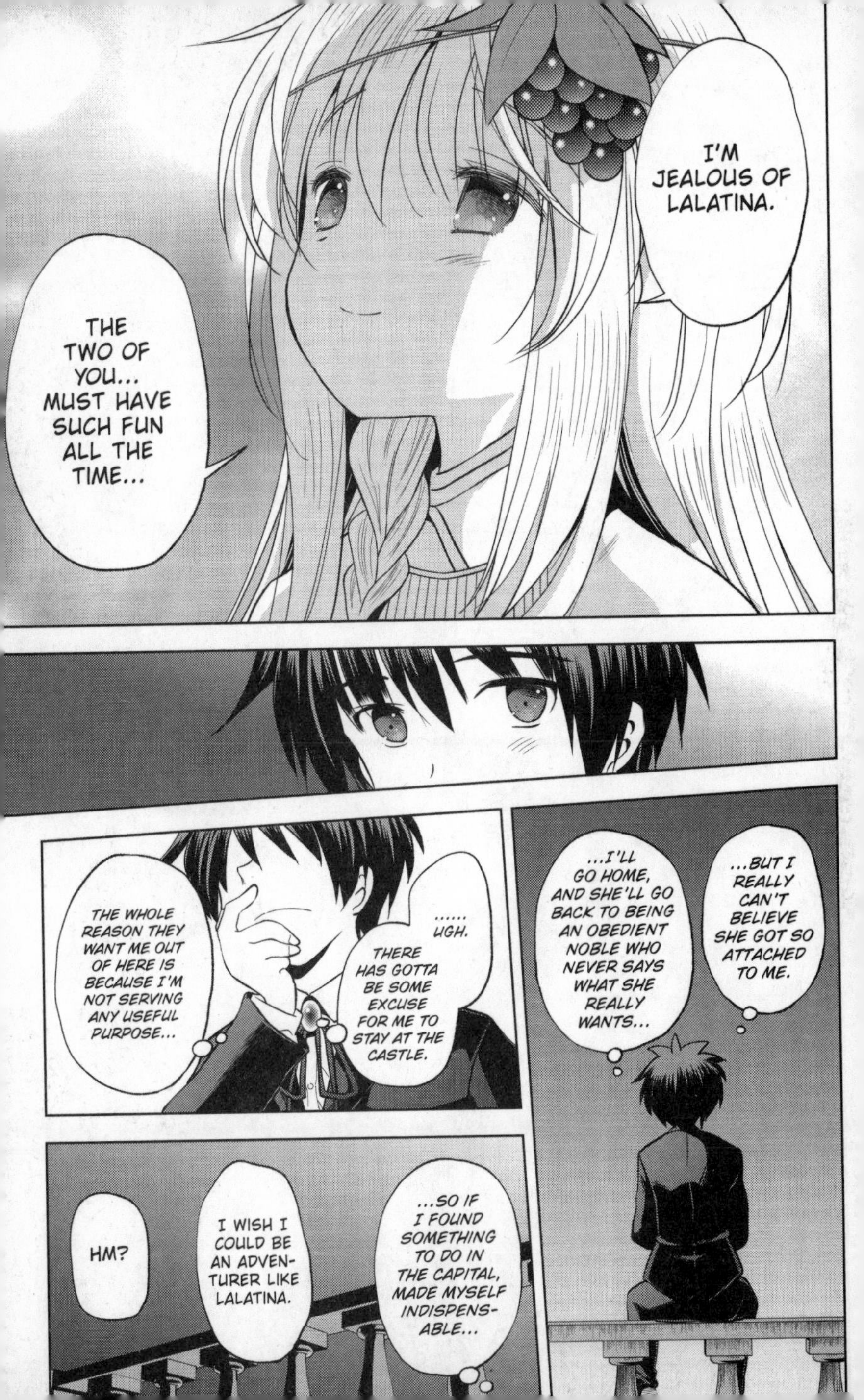
I'M JEALOUS OF LALATINA.
THE TWO OF YOU... MUST HAVE SUCH FUN ALL THE TIME...
...BUT I REALLY CAN'T BELIEVE SHE GOT SO ATTACHED TO ME.
...I'LL GO HOME, AND SHE'LL GO BACK TO BEING AN OBEDIENT NOBLE WHO NEVER SAYS WHAT SHE REALLY WANTS...
......UGH. THERE HAS GOTTA BE SOME EXCUSE FOR ME TO STAY AT THE CASTLE.
THE WHOLE REASON THEY WANT ME OUT OF HERE IS BECAUSE I'M NOT SERVING ANY USEFUL PURPOSE...
...SO IF I FOUND SOMETHING TO DO IN THE CAPITAL, MADE MYSELF INDISPENS-ABLE...
I WISH I COULD BE AN ADVEN-TURER LIKE LALATINA.
HM?

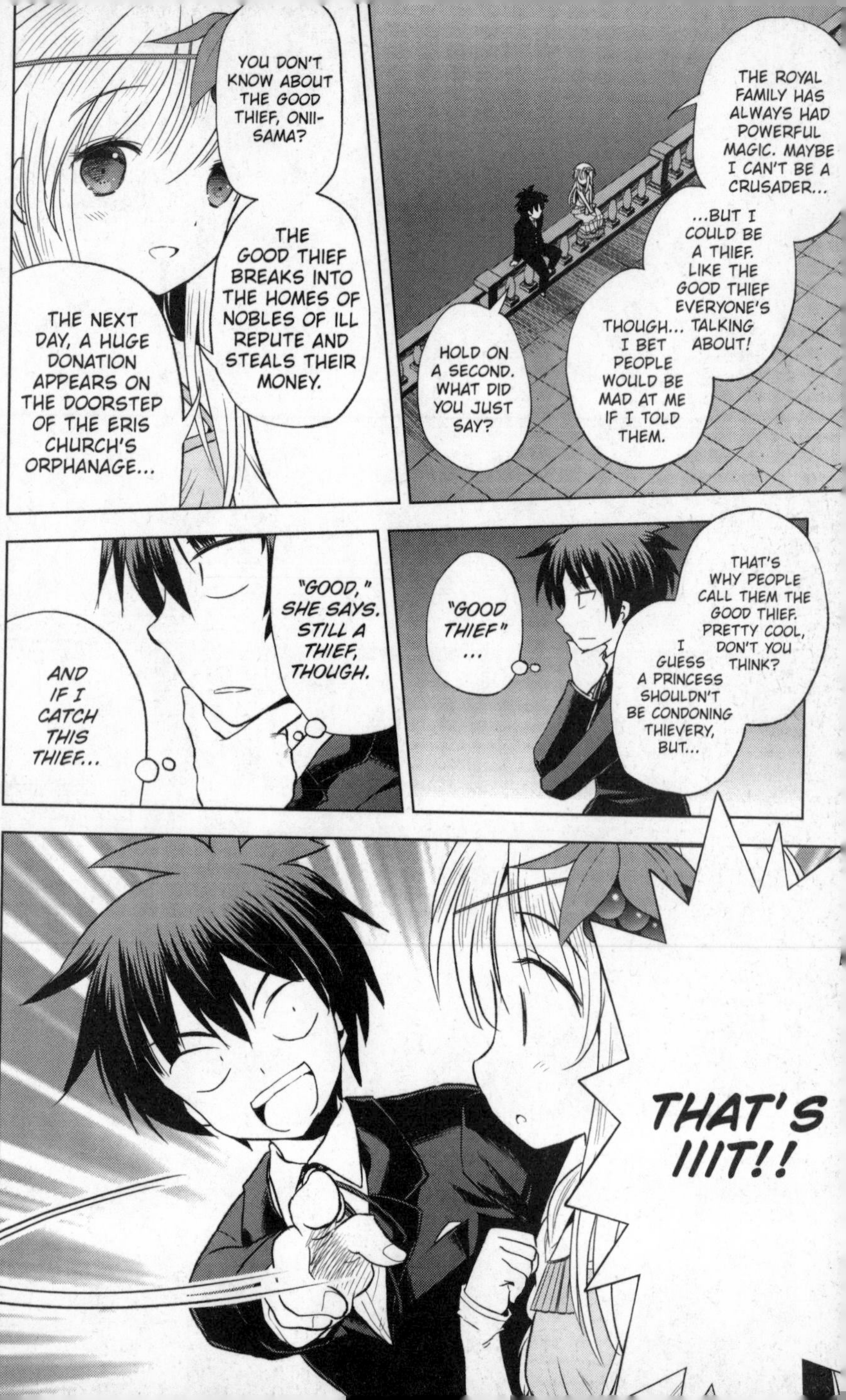
THE ROYAL FAMILY HAS ALWAYS HAD POWERFUL MAGIC. MAYBE I CAN'T BE A CRUSADER...
...BUT I COULD BE A THIEF. LIKE THE GOOD THIEF EVERYONE'S TALKING ABOUT!
THOUGH... I BET PEOPLE WOULD BE MAD AT ME IF I TOLD THEM.
HOLD ON A SECOND. WHAT DID YOU JUST SAY?
YOU DON'T KNOW ABOUT THE GOOD THIEF, ONII-SAMA?
THE GOOD THIEF BREAKS INTO THE HOMES OF NOBLES OF ILL REPUTE AND STEALS THEIR MONEY.
THE NEXT DAY, A HUGE DONATION APPEARS ON THE DOORSTEP OF THE ERIS CHURCH'S ORPHANAGE...
THAT'S WHY PEOPLE CALL THEM THE GOOD THIEF. PRETTY COOL, DON'T YOU THINK?
I GUESS A PRINCESS SHOULDN'T BE CONDONING THIEVERY, BUT...
"GOOD THIEF" ...
"GOOD," SHE SAYS. STILL A THIEF, THOUGH.
AND IF I CATCH THIS THIEF...
THAT'S IIIT!!

GOD'S
BLESSING
ON THIS
WONDERFUL
WORLD!

10

10

GOD'S
BLESSING
ON THIS
WONDERFUL
WORLD!

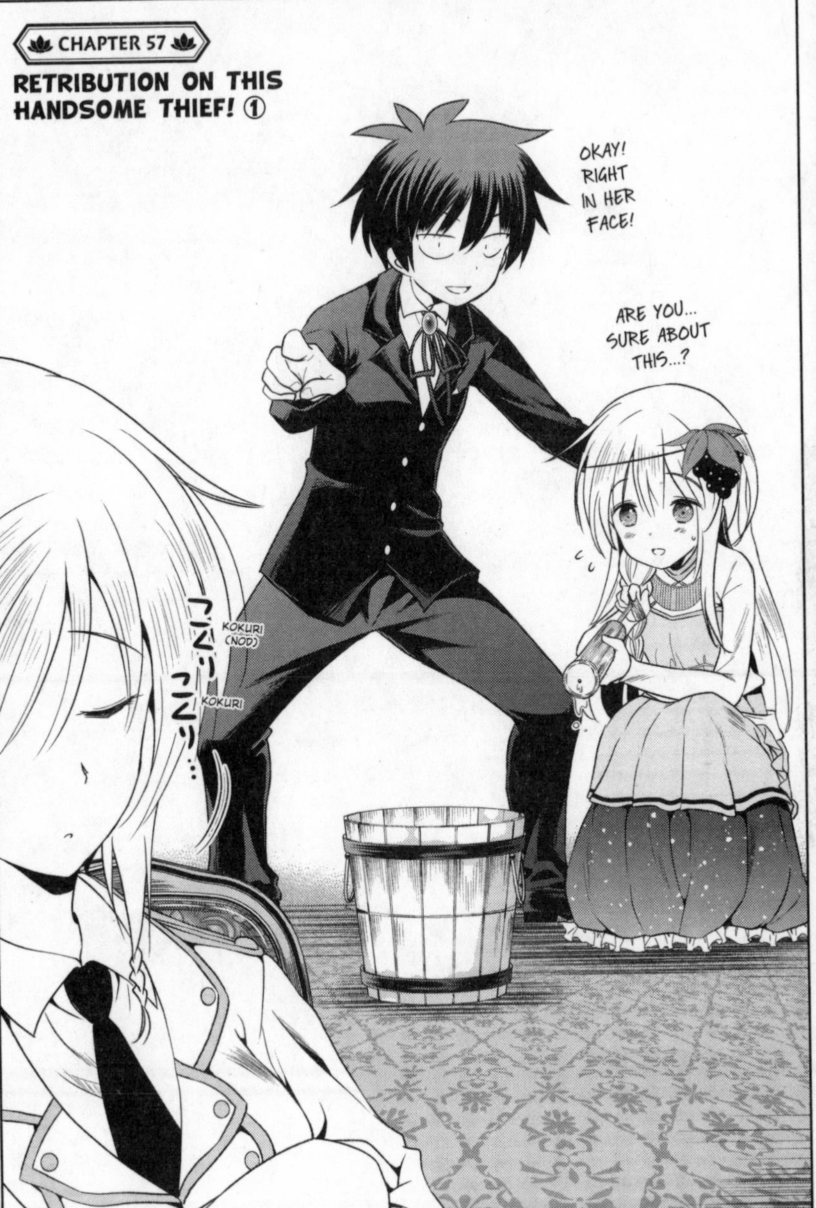
CHAPTER 57
RETRIBUTION ON THIS HANDSOME THIEF! ①
OKAY! RIGHT IN HER FACE!
ARE YOU... SURE ABOUT THIS...?
こくり
KOKURI (NOD)
こくり…
KOKURI

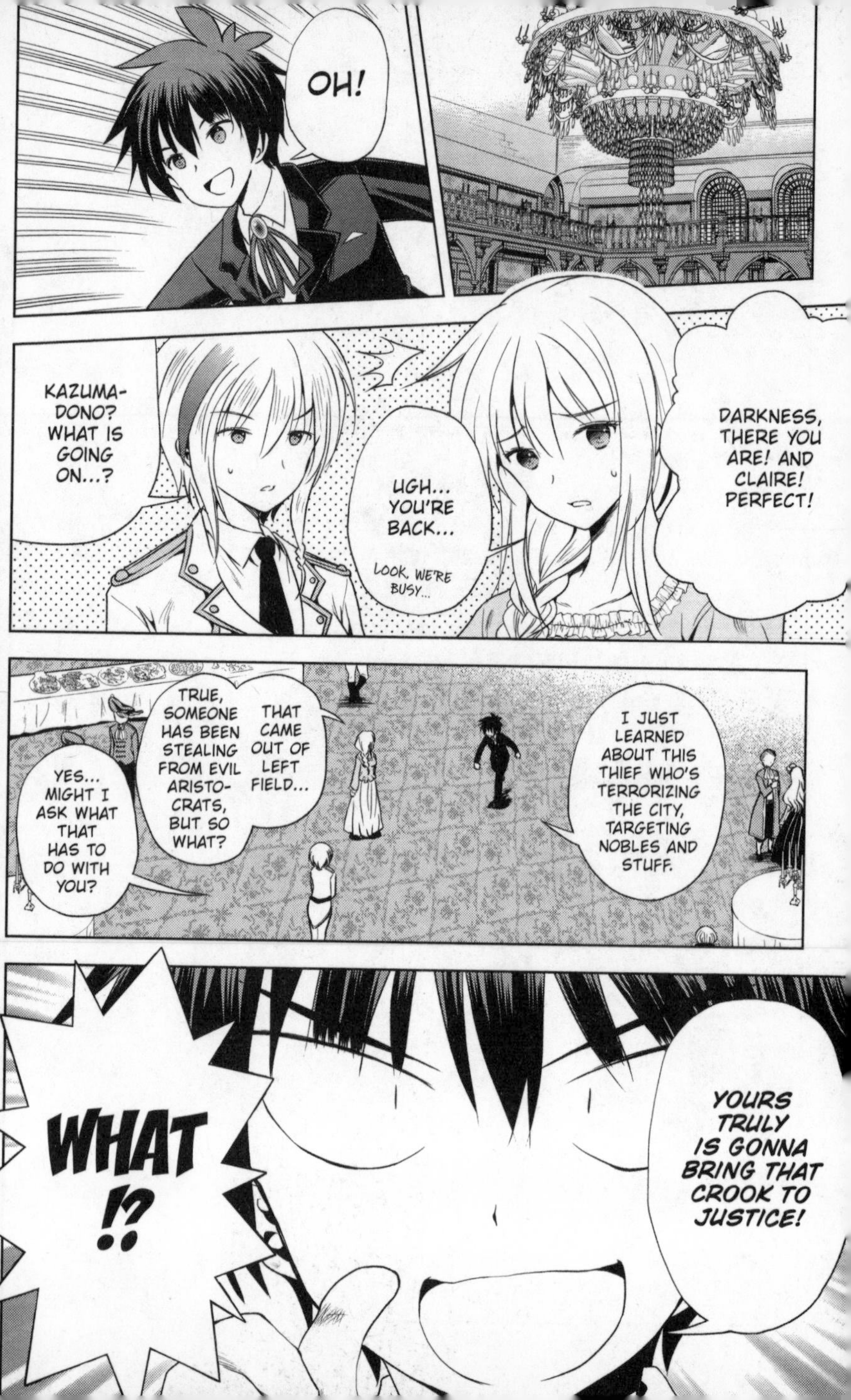
OH!
DARKNESS, THERE YOU ARE! AND CLAIRE! PERFECT!
UGH... YOU'RE BACK...
LOOK, WE'RE BUSY...
KAZUMA-DONO? WHAT IS GOING ON...?
I JUST LEARNED ABOUT THIS THIEF WHO'S TERRORIZING THE CITY, TARGETING NOBLES AND STUFF.
THAT CAME OUT OF LEFT FIELD...
TRUE, SOMEONE HAS BEEN STEALING FROM EVIL ARISTO-CRATS, BUT SO WHAT?
YES... MIGHT I ASK WHAT THAT HAS TO DO WITH YOU?
YOURS TRULY IS GONNA BRING THAT CROOK TO JUSTICE!
WHAT!?

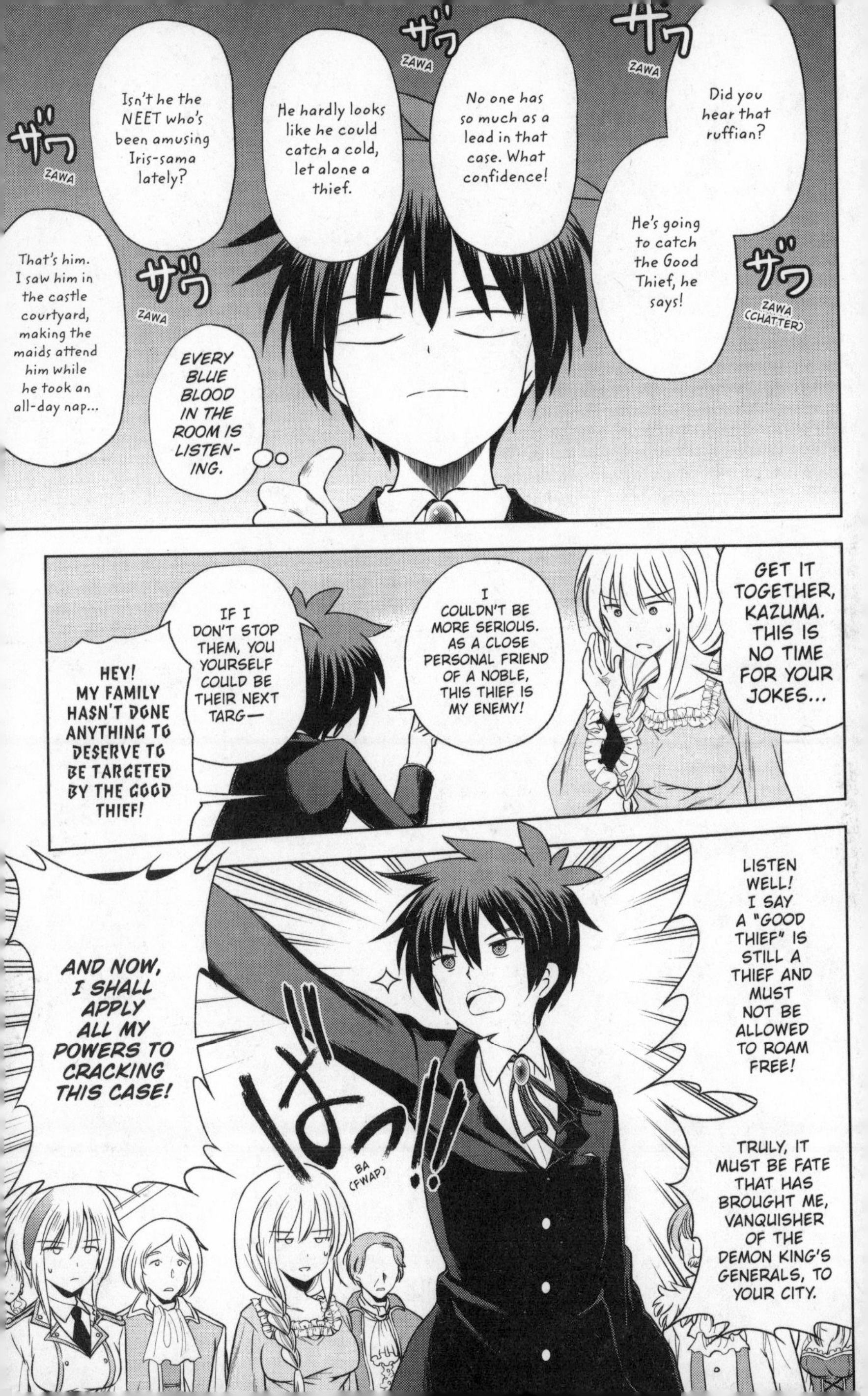
Did you hear that ruffian?
He's going to catch the Good Thief, he says!
ザワ ZAWA (CHATTER)
ザワ ZAWA
No one has so much as a lead in that case. What confidence!
ザワ ZAWA
He hardly looks like he could catch a cold, let alone a thief.
Isn't he the NEET who's been amusing Iris-sama lately?
ザワ ZAWA
That's him. I saw him in the castle courtyard, making the maids attend him while he took an all-day nap...
ザワ ZAWA
EVERY BLUE BLOOD IN THE ROOM IS LISTENING.
GET IT TOGETHER, KAZUMA. THIS IS NO TIME FOR YOUR JOKES...
I COULDN'T BE MORE SERIOUS. AS A CLOSE PERSONAL FRIEND OF A NOBLE, THIS THIEF IS MY ENEMY!
IF I DON'T STOP THEM, YOU YOURSELF COULD BE THEIR NEXT TARG—
HEY! MY FAMILY HASN'T DONE ANYTHING TO DESERVE TO BE TARGETED BY THE GOOD THIEF!
LISTEN WELL! I SAY A "GOOD THIEF" IS STILL A THIEF AND MUST NOT BE ALLOWED TO ROAM FREE!
TRULY, IT MUST BE FATE THAT HAS BROUGHT ME, VANQUISHER OF THE DEMON KING'S GENERALS, TO YOUR CITY.
ばっ!! BA (FWAP)
AND NOW, I SHALL APPLY ALL MY POWERS TO CRACKING THIS CASE!

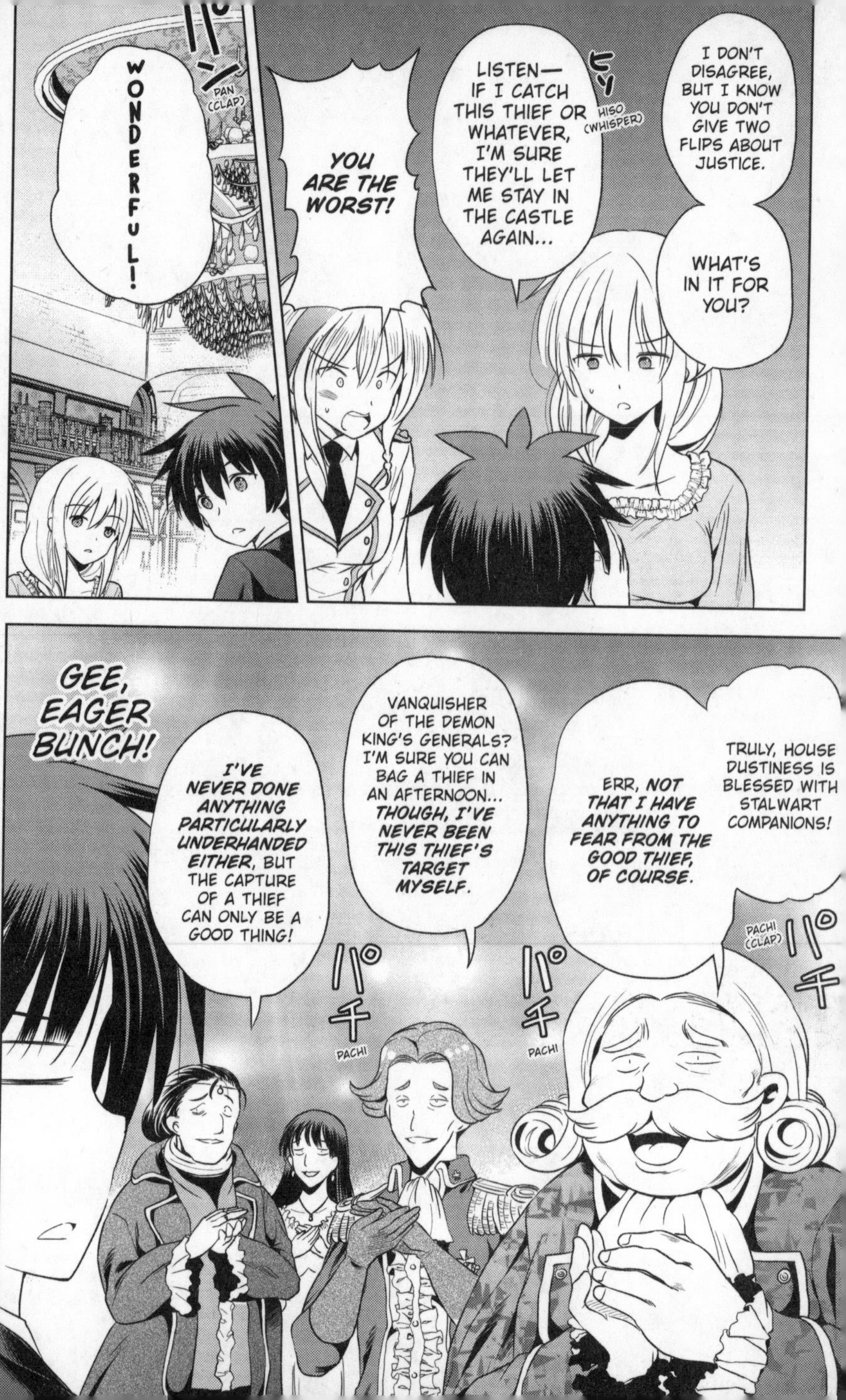
I DON'T DISAGREE, BUT I KNOW YOU DON'T GIVE TWO FLIPS ABOUT JUSTICE.
WHAT'S IN IT FOR YOU?
HISO (WHISPER)
LISTEN— IF I CATCH THIS THIEF OR WHATEVER, I'M SURE THEY'LL LET ME STAY IN THE CASTLE AGAIN...
YOU ARE THE WORST!
WONDERFUL!
PAN (CLAP)
TRULY, HOUSE DUSTINESS IS BLESSED WITH STALWART COMPANIONS!
ERR, NOT THAT I HAVE ANYTHING TO FEAR FROM THE GOOD THIEF, OF COURSE.
PACHI (CLAP)
VANQUISHER OF THE DEMON KING'S GENERALS? I'M SURE YOU CAN BAG A THIEF IN AN AFTERNOON... THOUGH, I'VE NEVER BEEN THIS THIEF'S TARGET MYSELF.
PACHI
I'VE NEVER DONE ANYTHING PARTICULARLY UNDERHANDED EITHER, BUT THE CAPTURE OF A THIEF CAN ONLY BE A GOOD THING!
PACHI
GEE, EAGER BUNCH!

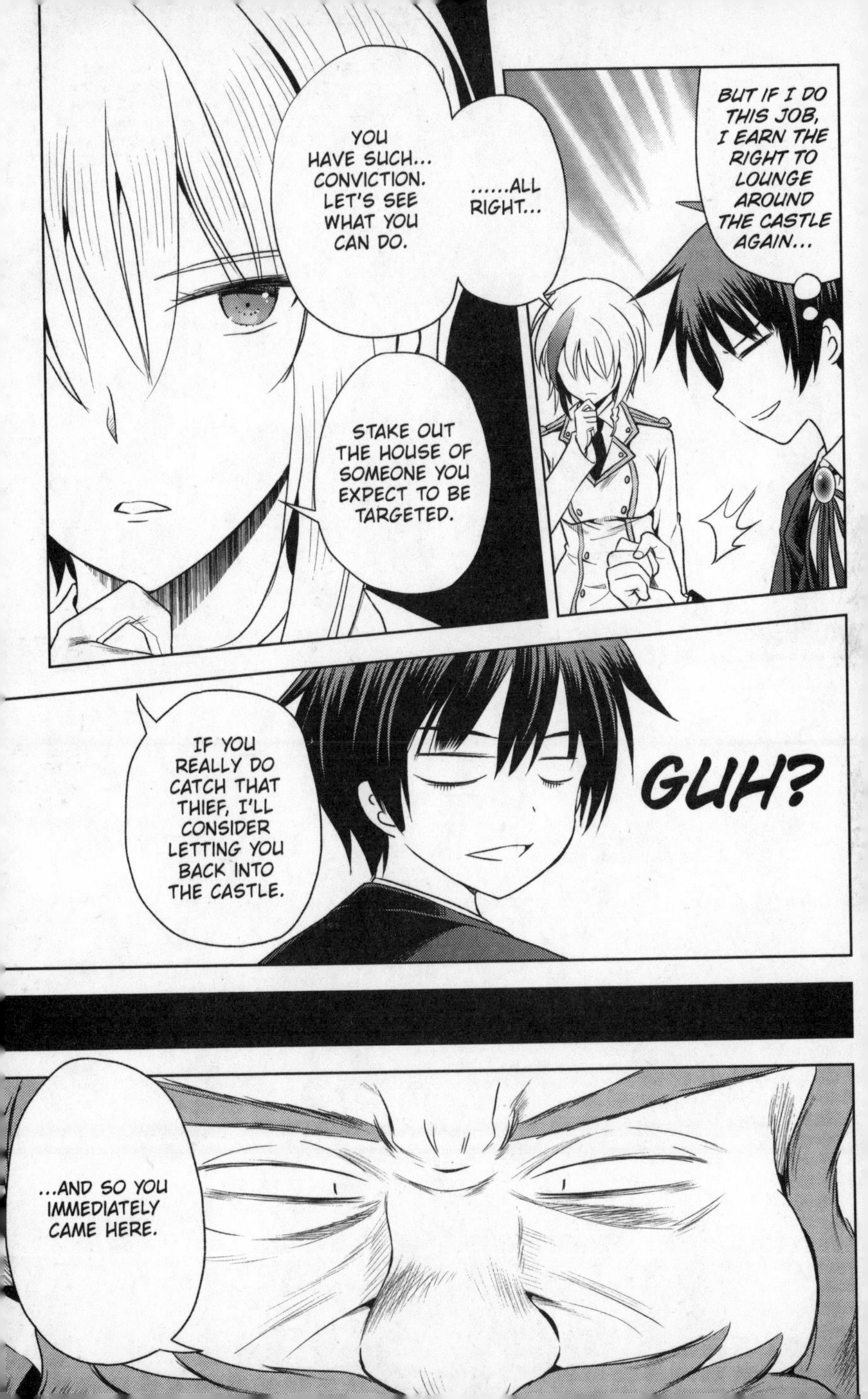
BUT IF I DO THIS JOB, I EARN THE RIGHT TO LOUNGE AROUND THE CASTLE AGAIN...
......ALL RIGHT...
YOU HAVE SUCH... CONVICTION. LET'S SEE WHAT YOU CAN DO.
STAKE OUT THE HOUSE OF SOMEONE YOU EXPECT TO BE TARGETED.
GUH?
IF YOU REALLY DO CATCH THAT THIEF, I'LL CONSIDER LETTING YOU BACK INTO THE CASTLE.
...AND SO YOU IMMEDIATELY CAME HERE.

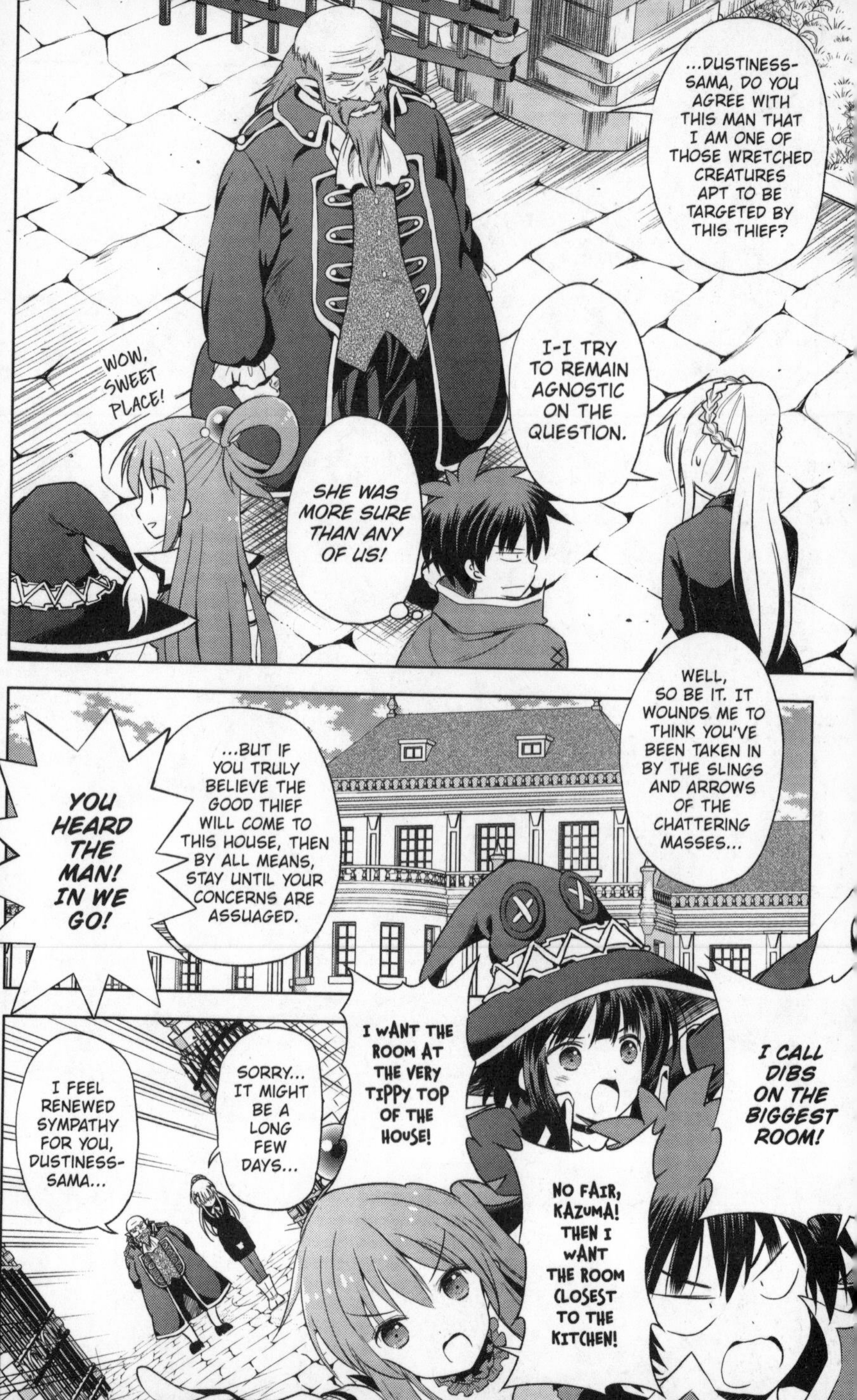
...DUSTINESS-SAMA, DO YOU AGREE WITH THIS MAN THAT I AM ONE OF THOSE WRETCHED CREATURES APT TO BE TARGETED BY THIS THIEF?
I-I TRY TO REMAIN AGNOSTIC ON THE QUESTION.
SHE WAS MORE SURE THAN ANY OF US!
WOW, SWEET PLACE!
WELL, SO BE IT. IT WOUNDS ME TO THINK YOU'VE BEEN TAKEN IN BY THE SLINGS AND ARROWS OF THE CHATTERING MASSES...
...BUT IF YOU TRULY BELIEVE THE GOOD THIEF WILL COME TO THIS HOUSE, THEN BY ALL MEANS, STAY UNTIL YOUR CONCERNS ARE ASSUAGED.
YOU HEARD THE MAN! IN WE GO!
I CALL DIBS ON THE BIGGEST ROOM!
NO FAIR, KAZUMA! THEN I WANT THE ROOM CLOSEST TO THE KITCHEN!
I WANT THE ROOM AT THE VERY TIPPY TOP OF THE HOUSE!
SORRY... IT MIGHT BE A LONG FEW DAYS...
I FEEL RENEWED SYMPATHY FOR YOU, DUSTINESS-SAMA...

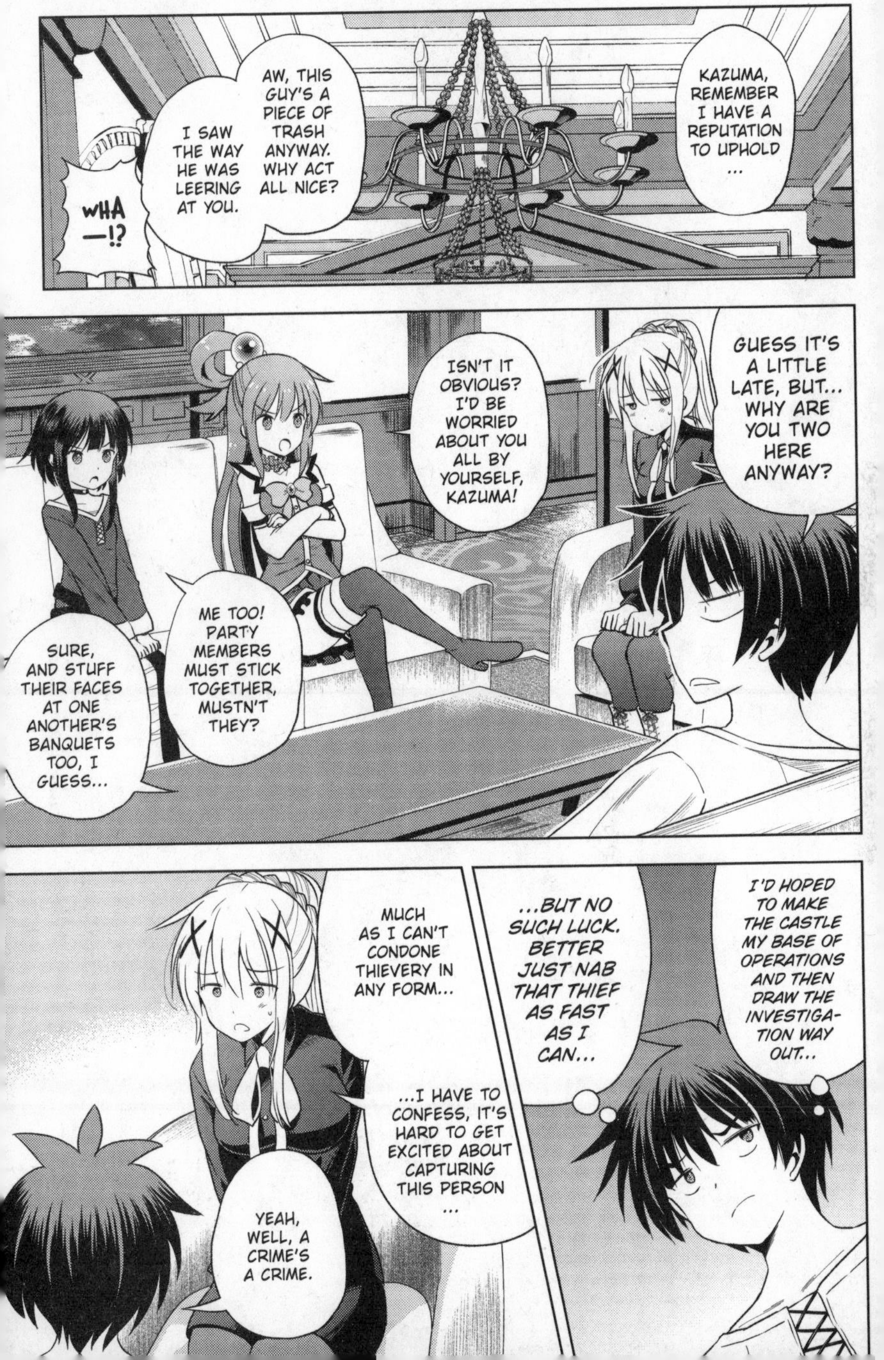
KAZUMA, REMEMBER I HAVE A REPUTATION TO UPHOLD...
AW, THIS GUY'S A PIECE OF TRASH ANYWAY. WHY ACT ALL NICE?
I SAW THE WAY HE WAS LEERING AT YOU.
WHA—!?
GUESS IT'S A LITTLE LATE, BUT... WHY ARE YOU TWO HERE ANYWAY?
ISN'T IT OBVIOUS? I'D BE WORRIED ABOUT YOU ALL BY YOURSELF, KAZUMA!
ME TOO! PARTY MEMBERS MUST STICK TOGETHER, MUSTN'T THEY?
SURE, AND STUFF THEIR FACES AT ONE ANOTHER'S BANQUETS TOO, I GUESS...
I'D HOPED TO MAKE THE CASTLE MY BASE OF OPERATIONS AND THEN DRAW THE INVESTIGATION WAY OUT...
...BUT NO SUCH LUCK. BETTER JUST NAB THAT THIEF AS FAST AS I CAN...
MUCH AS I CAN'T CONDONE THIEVERY IN ANY FORM...
...I HAVE TO CONFESS, IT'S HARD TO GET EXCITED ABOUT CAPTURING THIS PERSON...
YEAH, WELL, A CRIME'S A CRIME.

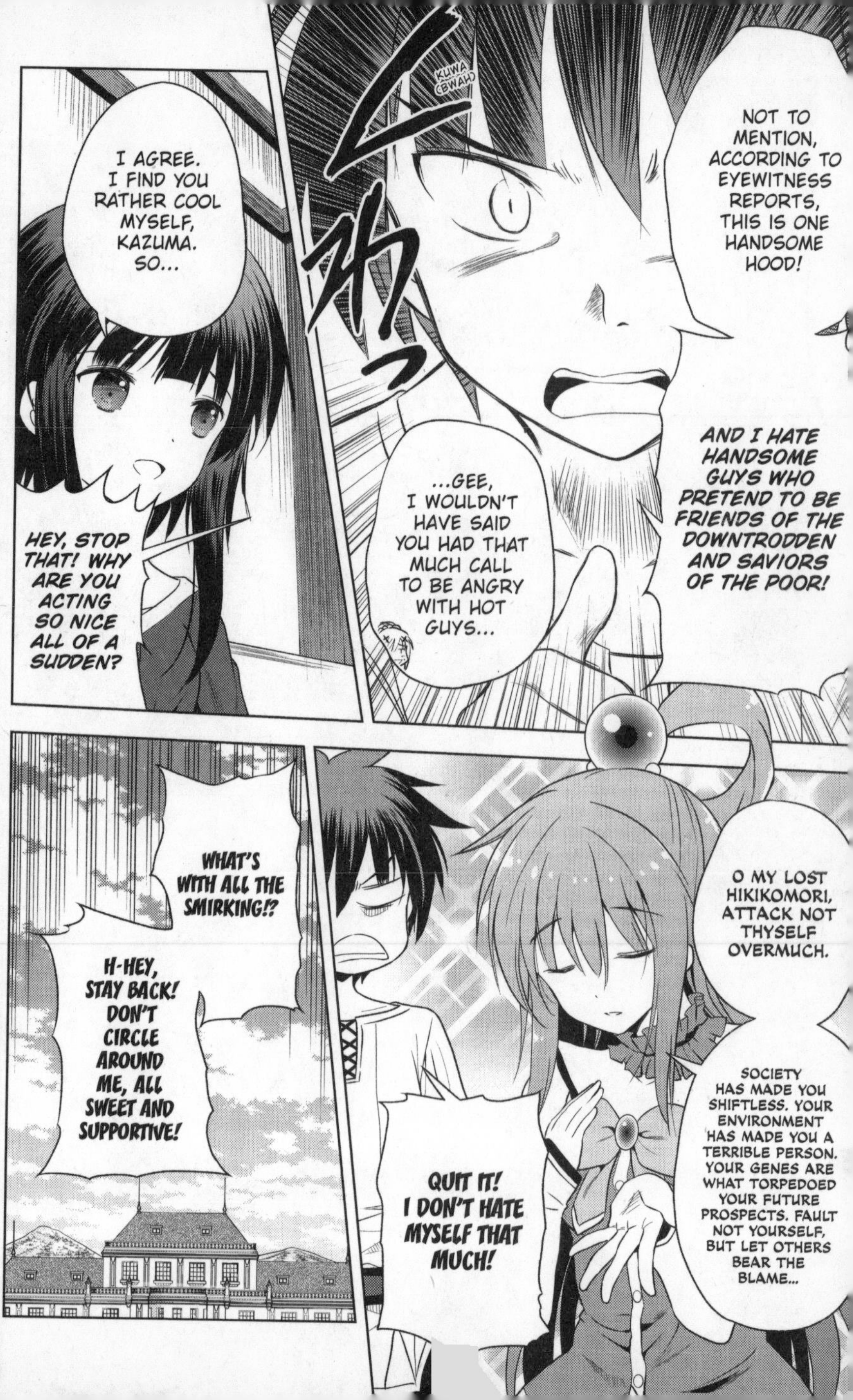
KUWA (BWAH)
NOT TO MENTION, ACCORDING TO EYEWITNESS REPORTS, THIS IS ONE HANDSOME HOOD!
AND I HATE HANDSOME GUYS WHO PRETEND TO BE FRIENDS OF THE DOWNTRODDEN AND SAVIORS OF THE POOR!
...GEE, I WOULDN'T HAVE SAID YOU HAD THAT MUCH CALL TO BE ANGRY WITH HOT GUYS...
I AGREE. I FIND YOU RATHER COOL MYSELF, KAZUMA. SO...
HEY, STOP THAT! WHY ARE YOU ACTING SO NICE ALL OF A SUDDEN?
O MY LOST HIKIKOMORI, ATTACK NOT THYSELF OVERMUCH.
SOCIETY HAS MADE YOU SHIFTLESS. YOUR ENVIRONMENT HAS MADE YOU A TERRIBLE PERSON. YOUR GENES ARE WHAT TORPEDOED YOUR FUTURE PROSPECTS. FAULT NOT YOURSELF, BUT LET OTHERS BEAR THE BLAME...
QUIT IT! I DON'T HATE MYSELF THAT MUCH!
WHAT'S WITH ALL THE SMIRKING!?
H-HEY, STAY BACK! DON'T CIRCLE AROUND ME, ALL SWEET AND SUPPORTIVE!

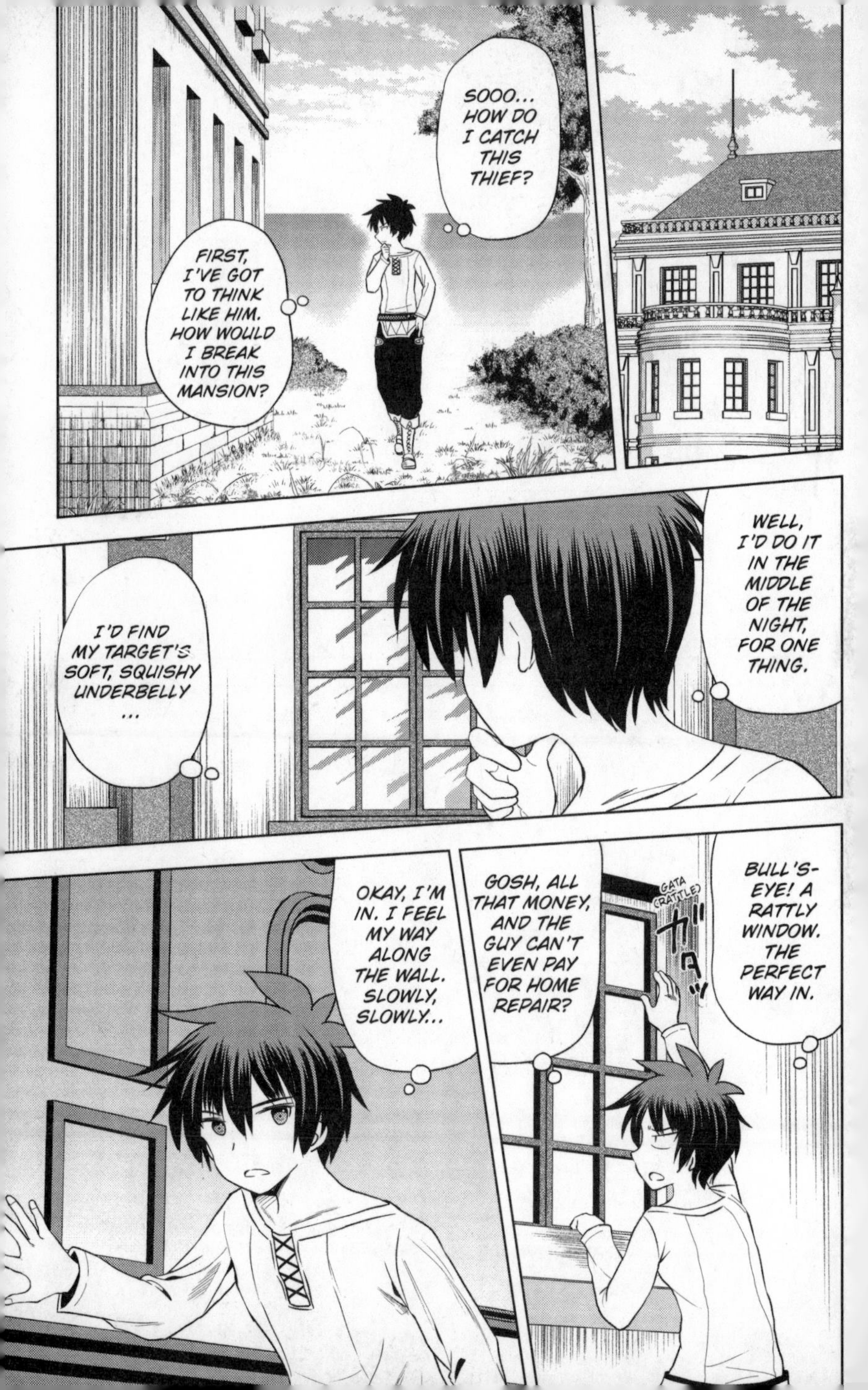
SOOO... HOW DO I CATCH THIS THIEF?
FIRST, I'VE GOT TO THINK LIKE HIM. HOW WOULD I BREAK INTO THIS MANSION?
WELL, I'D DO IT IN THE MIDDLE OF THE NIGHT, FOR ONE THING.
I'D FIND MY TARGET'S SOFT, SQUISHY UNDERBELLY ...
BULL'S-EYE! A RATTLY WINDOW. THE PERFECT WAY IN.
GATA (RATTLE)
GOSH, ALL THAT MONEY, AND THE GUY CAN'T EVEN PAY FOR HOME REPAIR?
OKAY, I'M IN. I FEEL MY WAY ALONG THE WALL. SLOWLY, SLOWLY...

GACHA (CLICK)

DOESN'T LOOK LIKE THE KIND OF PLACE THAT WOULD HAVE ANY LOOT, BUT I MIGHT AS WELL CHECK.

OOH, A DOOR.

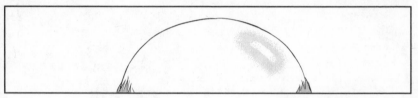

HRM!

A-AND JUST WHAT BUSINESS DO YOU HAVE HERE!?

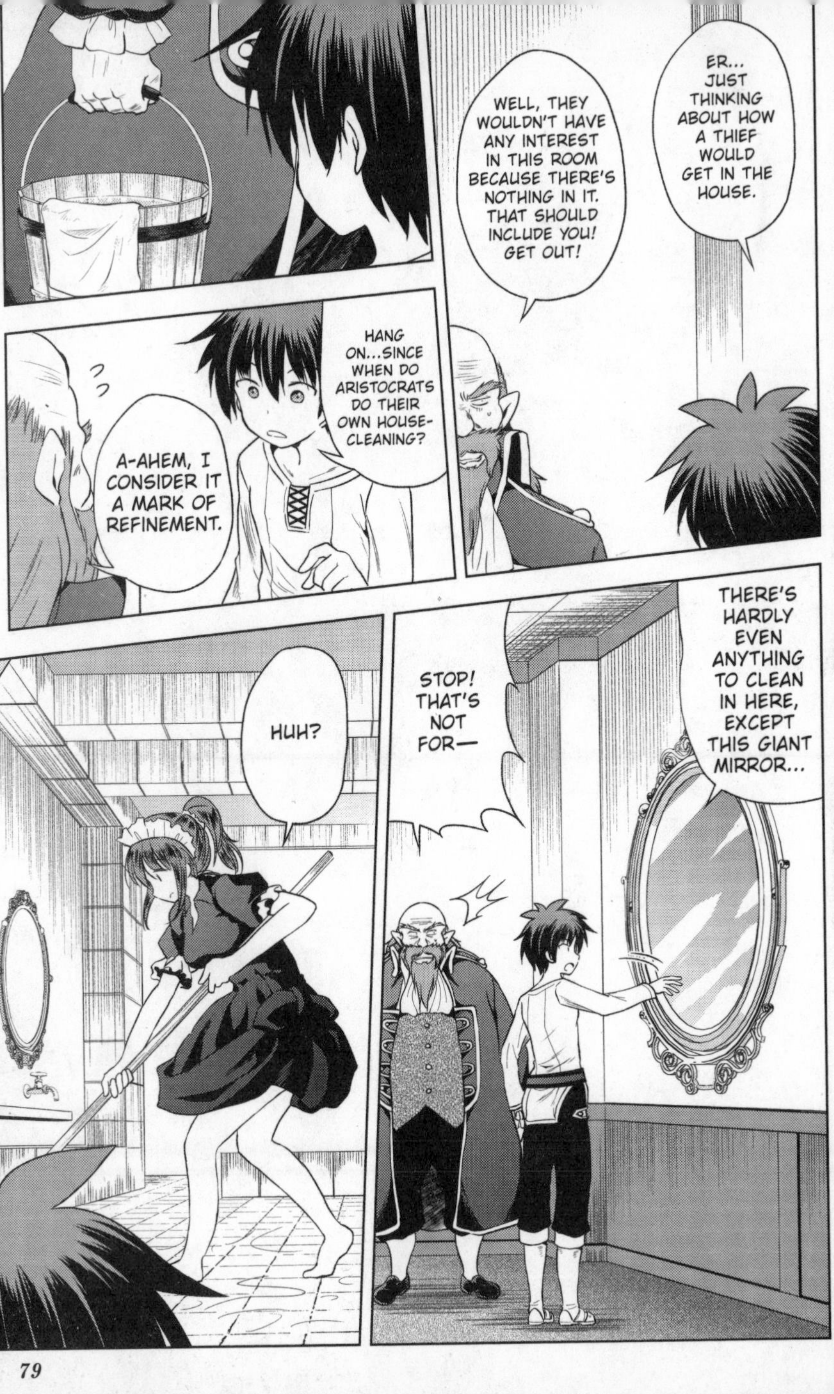
ER... JUST THINKING ABOUT HOW A THIEF WOULD GET IN THE HOUSE.
WELL, THEY WOULDN'T HAVE ANY INTEREST IN THIS ROOM BECAUSE THERE'S NOTHING IN IT. THAT SHOULD INCLUDE YOU! GET OUT!
HANG ON...SINCE WHEN DO ARISTOCRATS DO THEIR OWN HOUSE-CLEANING?
A-AHEM, I CONSIDER IT A MARK OF REFINEMENT.
THERE'S HARDLY EVEN ANYTHING TO CLEAN IN HERE, EXCEPT THIS GIANT MIRROR...
STOP! THAT'S NOT FOR—
HUH?

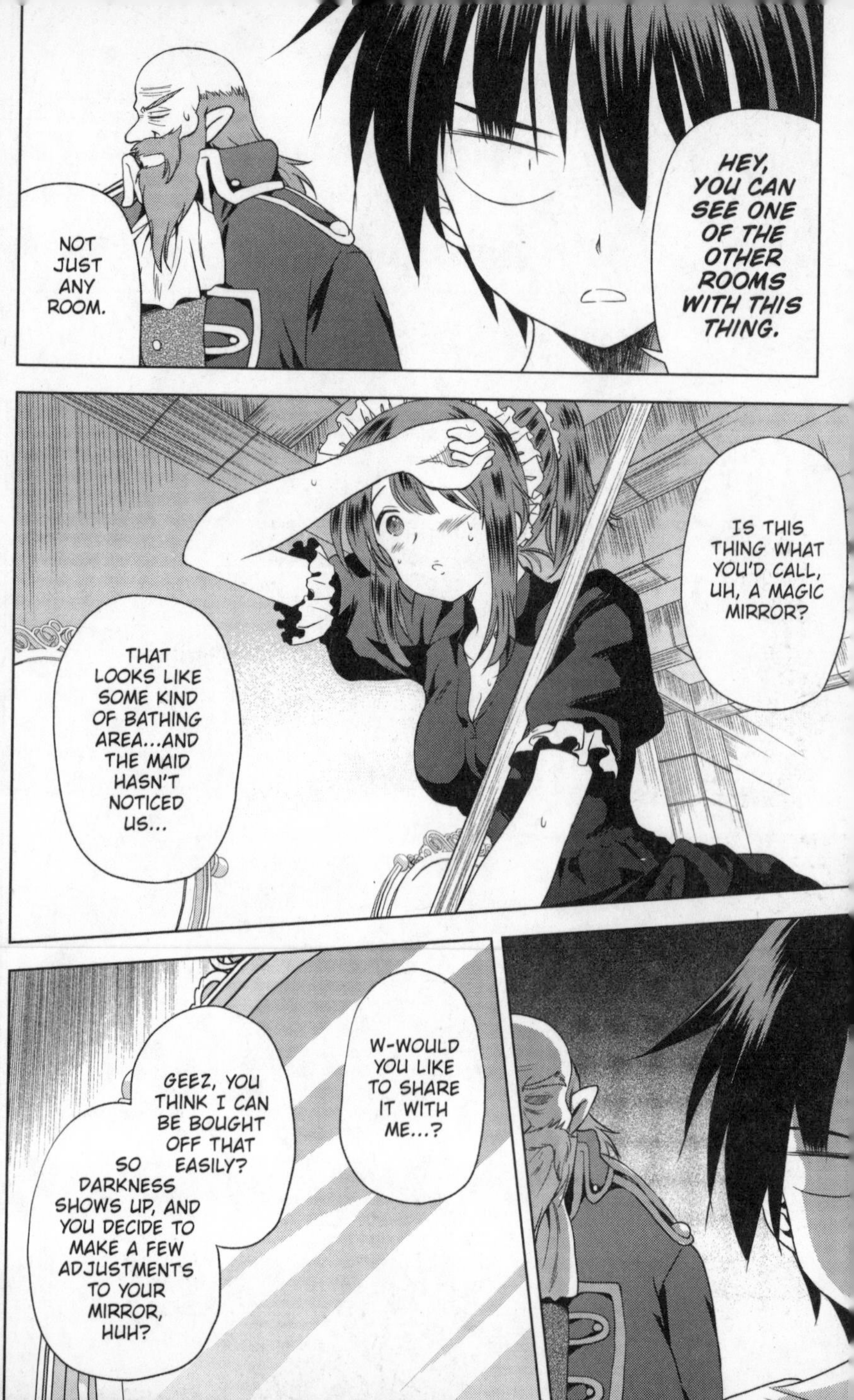
HEY, YOU CAN SEE ONE OF THE OTHER ROOMS WITH THIS THING.
NOT JUST ANY ROOM.
IS THIS THING WHAT YOU'D CALL, UH, A MAGIC MIRROR?
THAT LOOKS LIKE SOME KIND OF BATHING AREA...AND THE MAID HASN'T NOTICED US...
W-WOULD YOU LIKE TO SHARE IT WITH ME...?
GEEZ, YOU THINK I CAN BE BOUGHT OFF THAT EASILY?
SO DARKNESS SHOWS UP, AND YOU DECIDE TO MAKE A FEW ADJUSTMENTS TO YOUR MIRROR, HUH?

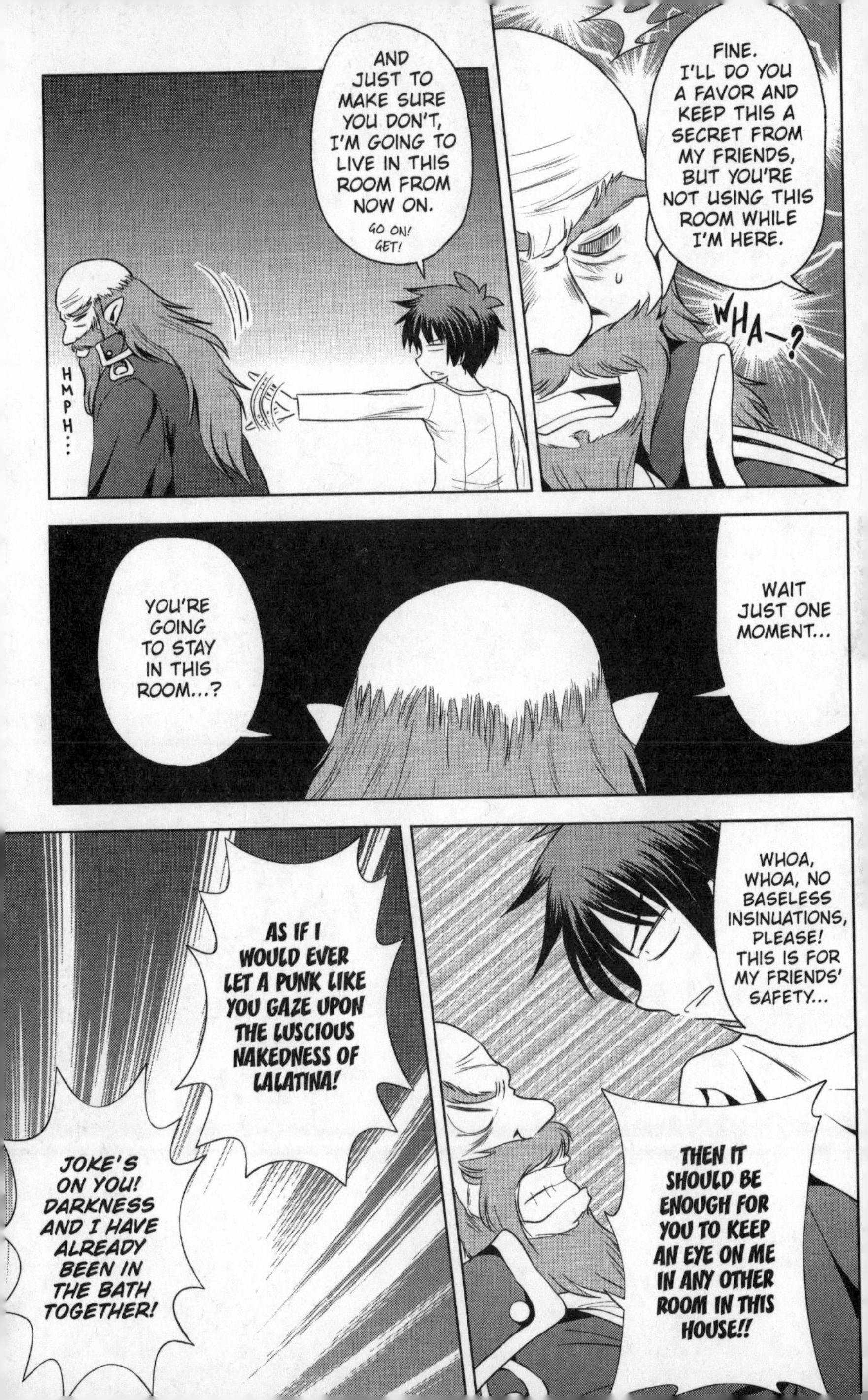
FINE. I'LL DO YOU A FAVOR AND KEEP THIS A SECRET FROM MY FRIENDS, BUT YOU'RE NOT USING THIS ROOM WHILE I'M HERE.
WHA-?
AND JUST TO MAKE SURE YOU DON'T, I'M GOING TO LIVE IN THIS ROOM FROM NOW ON.
GO ON! GET!
HMPH...
WAIT JUST ONE MOMENT...
YOU'RE GOING TO STAY IN THIS ROOM...?
WHOA, WHOA, NO BASELESS INSINUATIONS, PLEASE! THIS IS FOR MY FRIENDS' SAFETY...
THEN IT SHOULD BE ENOUGH FOR YOU TO KEEP AN EYE ON ME IN ANY OTHER ROOM IN THIS HOUSE!!
AS IF I WOULD EVER LET A PUNK LIKE YOU GAZE UPON THE LUSCIOUS NAKEDNESS OF LALATINA!
JOKE'S ON YOU! DARKNESS AND I HAVE ALREADY BEEN IN THE BATH TOGETHER!

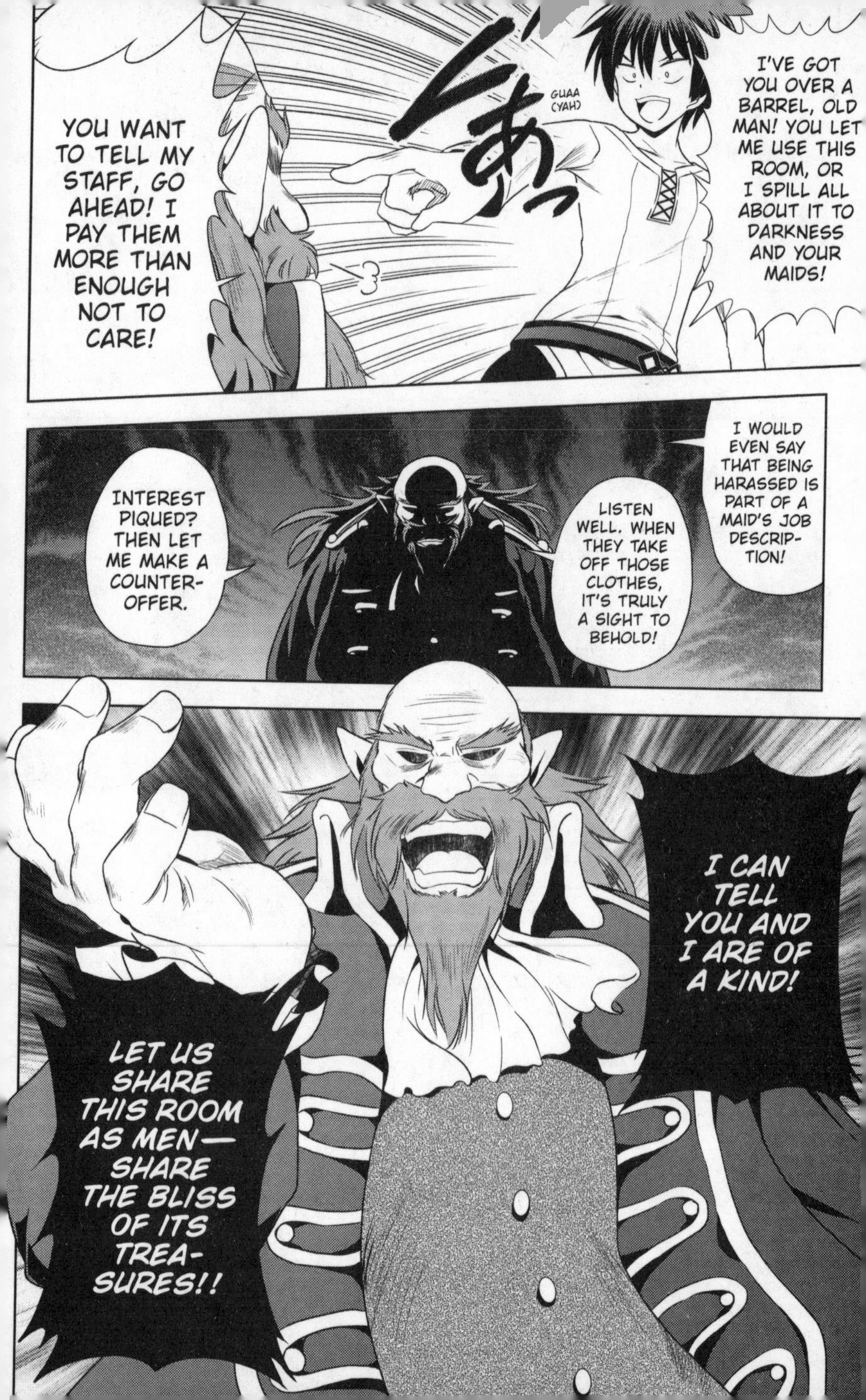
I'VE GOT YOU OVER A BARREL, OLD MAN! YOU LET ME USE THIS ROOM, OR I SPILL ALL ABOUT IT TO DARKNESS AND YOUR MAIDS!
GUAA (YAH)
YOU WANT TO TELL MY STAFF, GO AHEAD! I PAY THEM MORE THAN ENOUGH NOT TO CARE!
I WOULD EVEN SAY THAT BEING HARASSED IS PART OF A MAID'S JOB DESCRIP-TION!
LISTEN WELL. WHEN THEY TAKE OFF THOSE CLOTHES, IT'S TRULY A SIGHT TO BEHOLD!
INTEREST PIQUED? THEN LET ME MAKE A COUNTER-OFFER.
I CAN TELL YOU AND I ARE OF A KIND!
LET US SHARE THIS ROOM AS MEN— SHARE THE BLISS OF ITS TREA-SURES!!

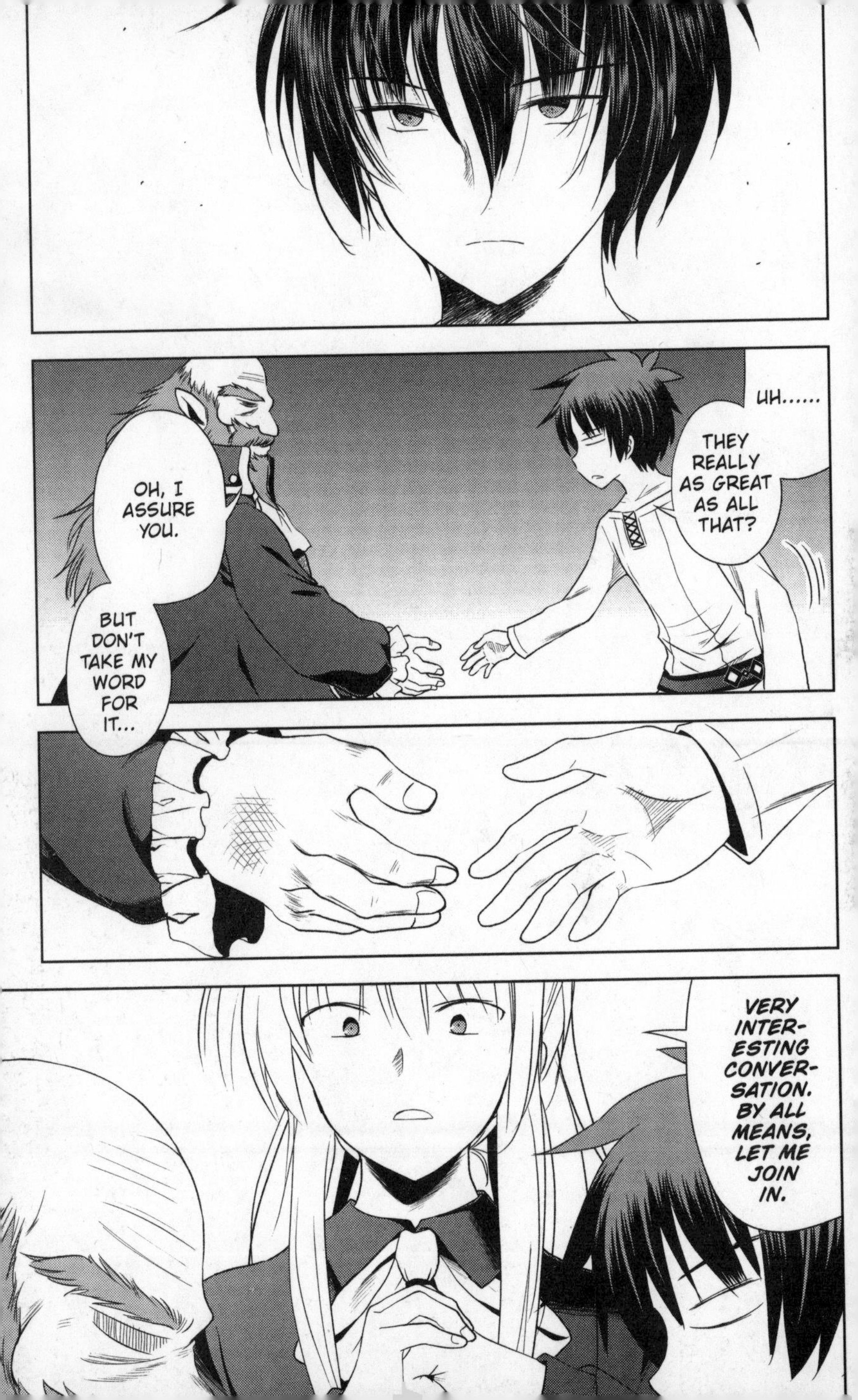
UH......
THEY REALLY AS GREAT AS ALL THAT?
OH, I ASSURE YOU.
BUT DON'T TAKE MY WORD FOR IT...
VERY INTER-ESTING CONVER-SATION. BY ALL MEANS, LET ME JOIN IN.

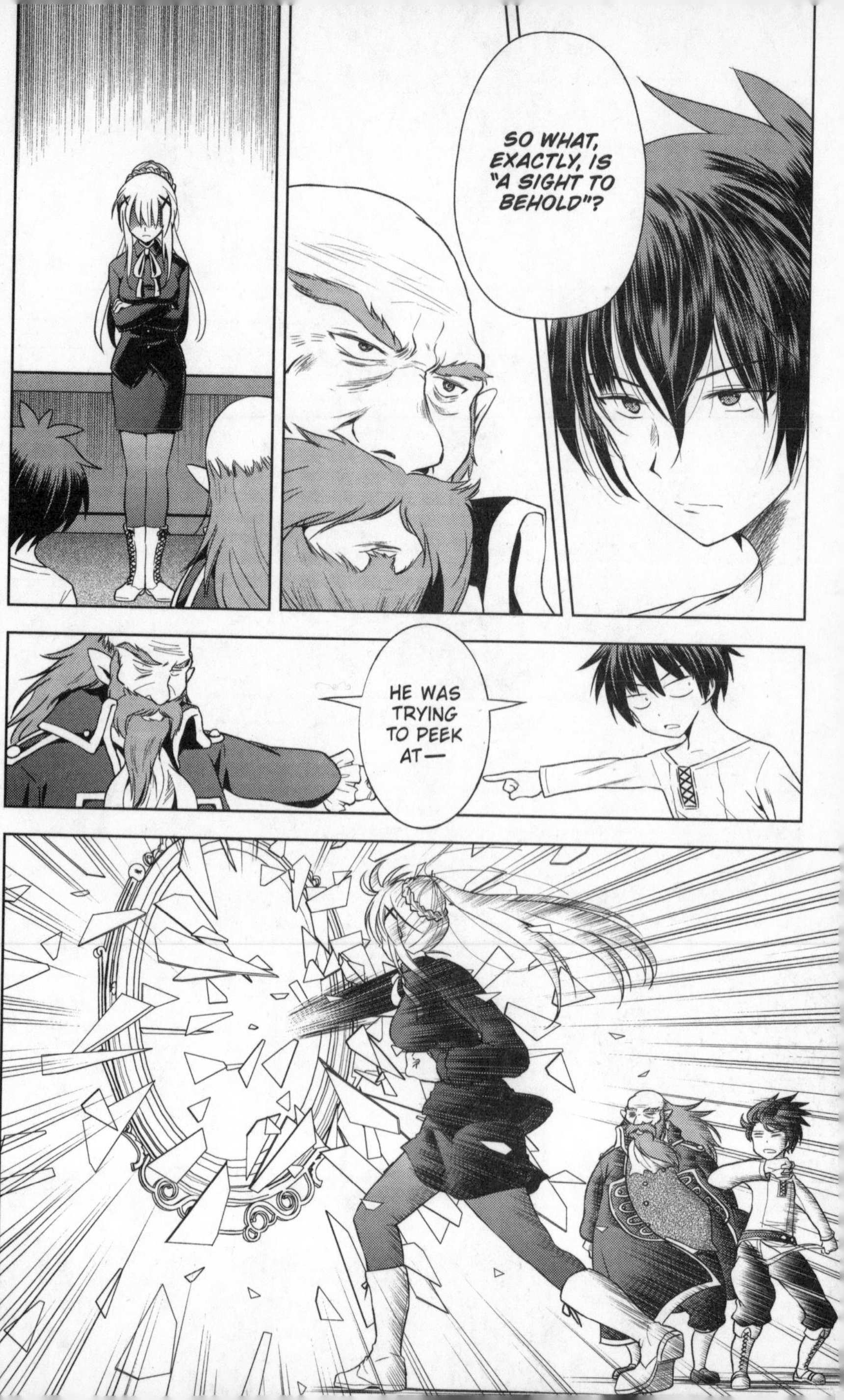
SO WHAT, EXACTLY, IS "A SIGHT TO BEHOLD"?
HE WAS TRYING TO PEEK AT—

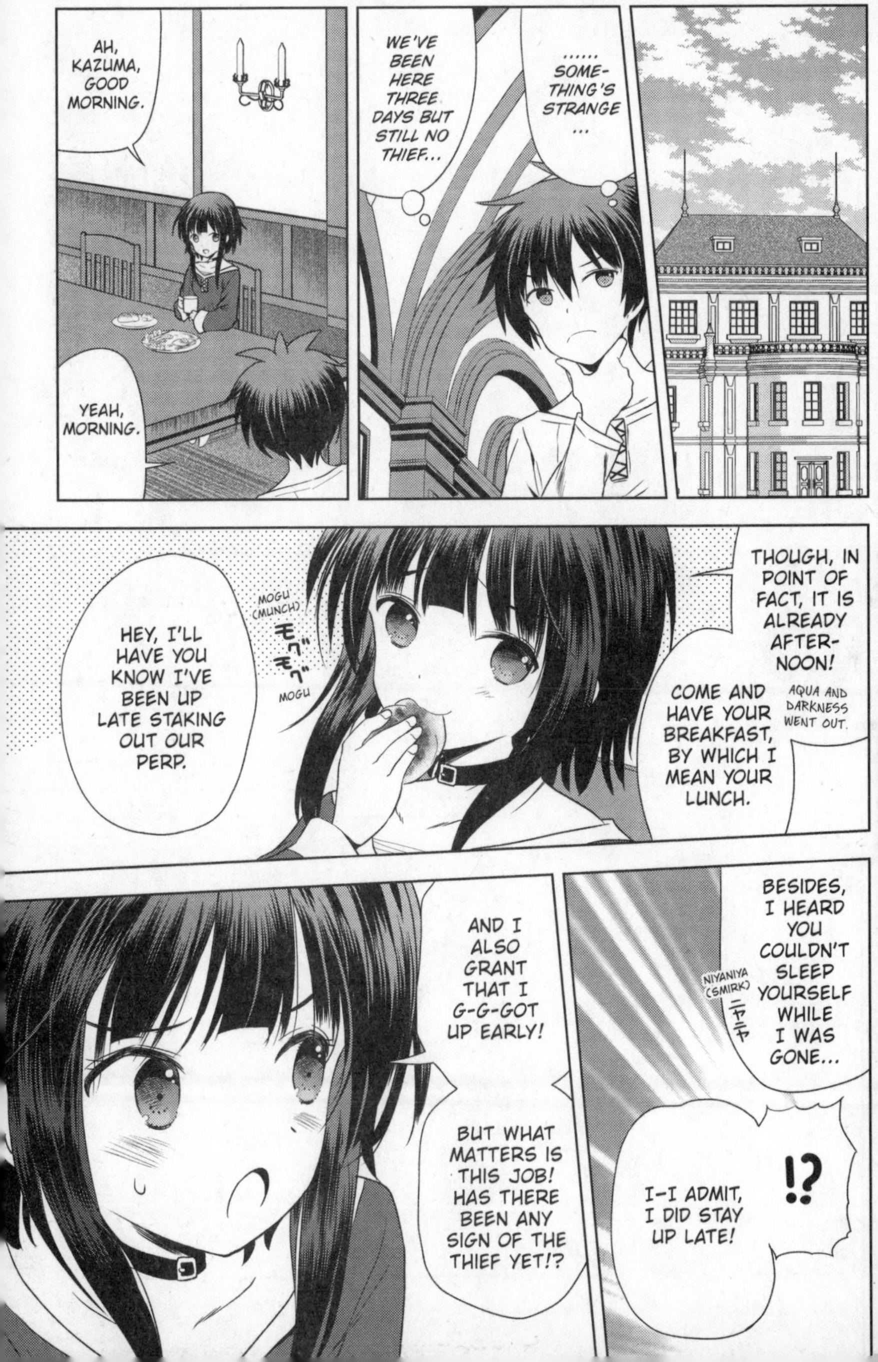

......SOMETHING'S STRANGE...
WE'VE BEEN HERE THREE DAYS BUT STILL NO THIEF...
AH, KAZUMA, GOOD MORNING.
YEAH, MORNING.
THOUGH, IN POINT OF FACT, IT IS ALREADY AFTERNOON!
AQUA AND DARKNESS WENT OUT.
COME AND HAVE YOUR BREAKFAST, BY WHICH I MEAN YOUR LUNCH.
MOGU (MUNCH)
モグモグ
MOGU
HEY, I'LL HAVE YOU KNOW I'VE BEEN UP LATE STAKING OUT OUR PERP.
BESIDES, I HEARD YOU COULDN'T SLEEP YOURSELF WHILE I WAS GONE...
NIYANIYA (SMIRK)
ニヤニヤ
!?
I-I ADMIT, I DID STAY UP LATE!
AND I ALSO GRANT THAT I G-G-GOT UP EARLY!
BUT WHAT MATTERS IS THIS JOB! HAS THERE BEEN ANY SIGN OF THE THIEF YET!?

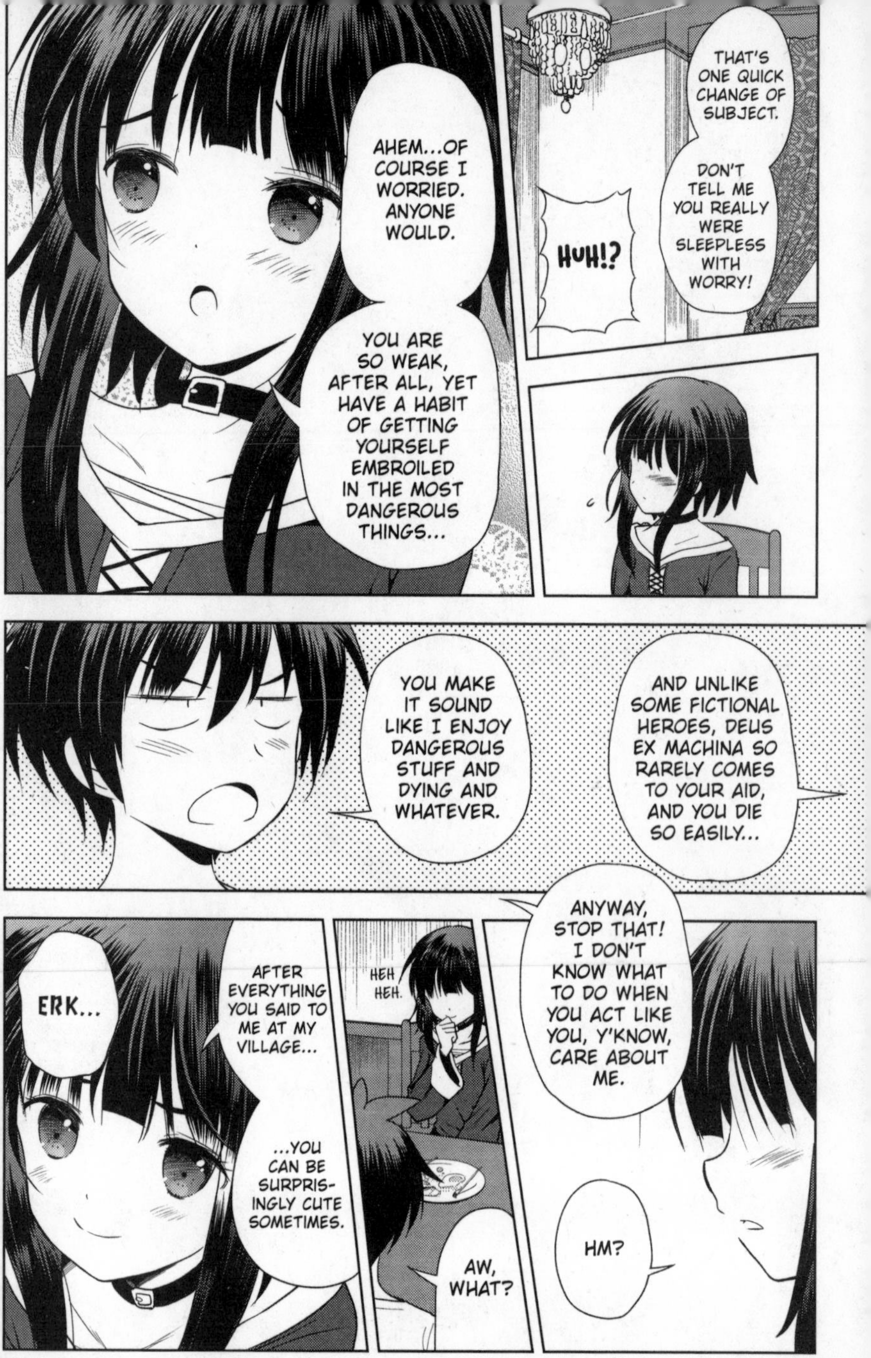
THAT'S ONE QUICK CHANGE OF SUBJECT.
DON'T TELL ME YOU REALLY WERE SLEEPLESS WITH WORRY!
HUH!?
AHEM...OF COURSE I WORRIED. ANYONE WOULD.
YOU ARE SO WEAK, AFTER ALL, YET HAVE A HABIT OF GETTING YOURSELF EMBROILED IN THE MOST DANGEROUS THINGS...
AND UNLIKE SOME FICTIONAL HEROES, DEUS EX MACHINA SO RARELY COMES TO YOUR AID, AND YOU DIE SO EASILY...
YOU MAKE IT SOUND LIKE I ENJOY DANGEROUS STUFF AND DYING AND WHATEVER.
ANYWAY, STOP THAT! I DON'T KNOW WHAT TO DO WHEN YOU ACT LIKE YOU, Y'KNOW, CARE ABOUT ME.
HM?
HEH HEH.
AW, WHAT?
AFTER EVERYTHING YOU SAID TO ME AT MY VILLAGE...
ERK...
...YOU CAN BE SURPRISINGLY CUTE SOMETIMES.

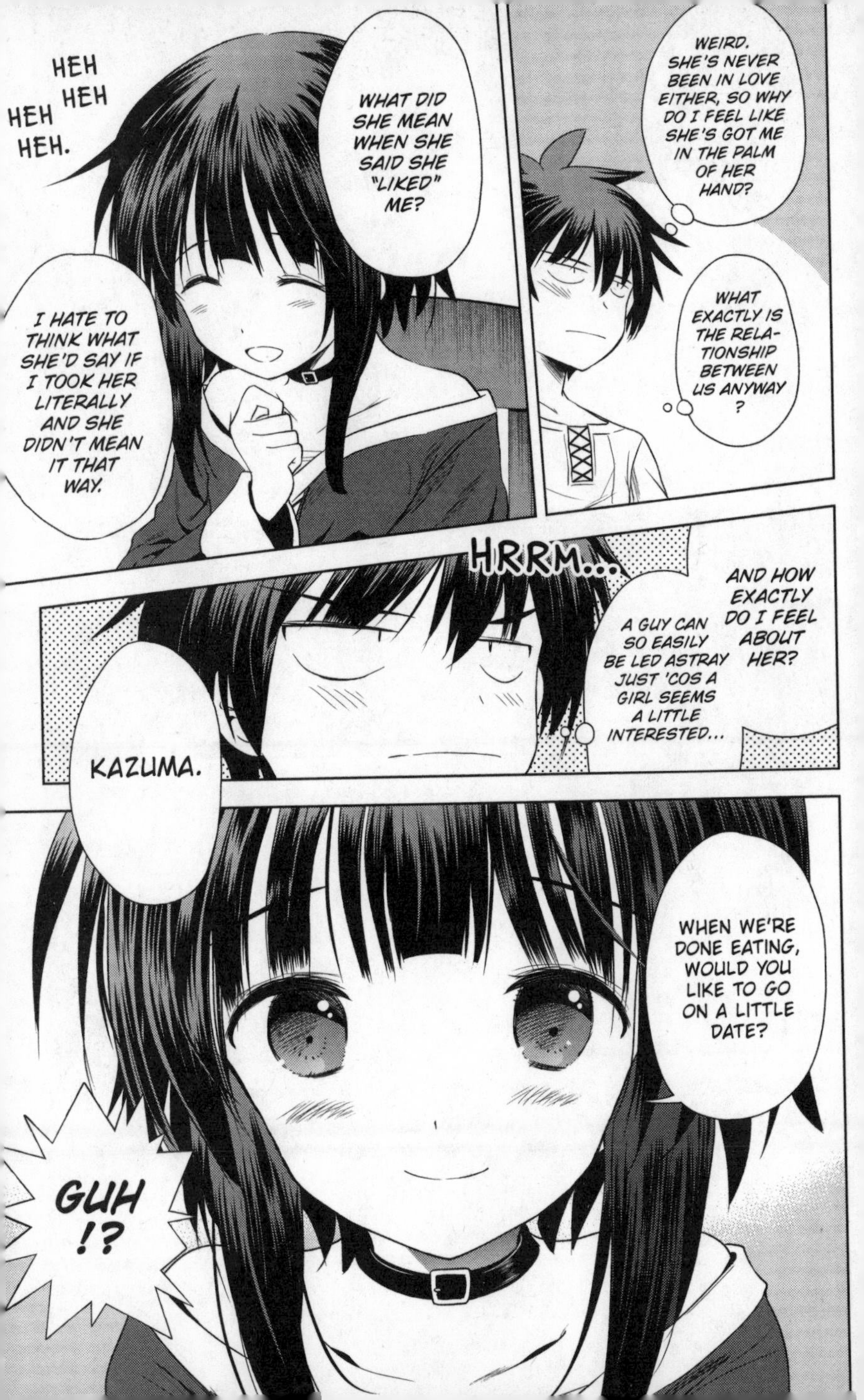
WEIRD. SHE'S NEVER BEEN IN LOVE EITHER, SO WHY DO I FEEL LIKE SHE'S GOT ME IN THE PALM OF HER HAND?
WHAT EXACTLY IS THE RELA- TIONSHIP BETWEEN US ANYWAY ?
WHAT DID SHE MEAN WHEN SHE SAID SHE "LIKED" ME?
HEH HEH HEH HEH.
I HATE TO THINK WHAT SHE'D SAY IF I TOOK HER LITERALLY AND SHE DIDN'T MEAN IT THAT WAY.
HRRM...
AND HOW EXACTLY DO I FEEL ABOUT HER?
A GUY CAN SO EASILY BE LED ASTRAY JUST 'COS A GIRL SEEMS A LITTLE INTERESTED...
KAZUMA.
WHEN WE'RE DONE EATING, WOULD YOU LIKE TO GO ON A LITTLE DATE?
GUH !?

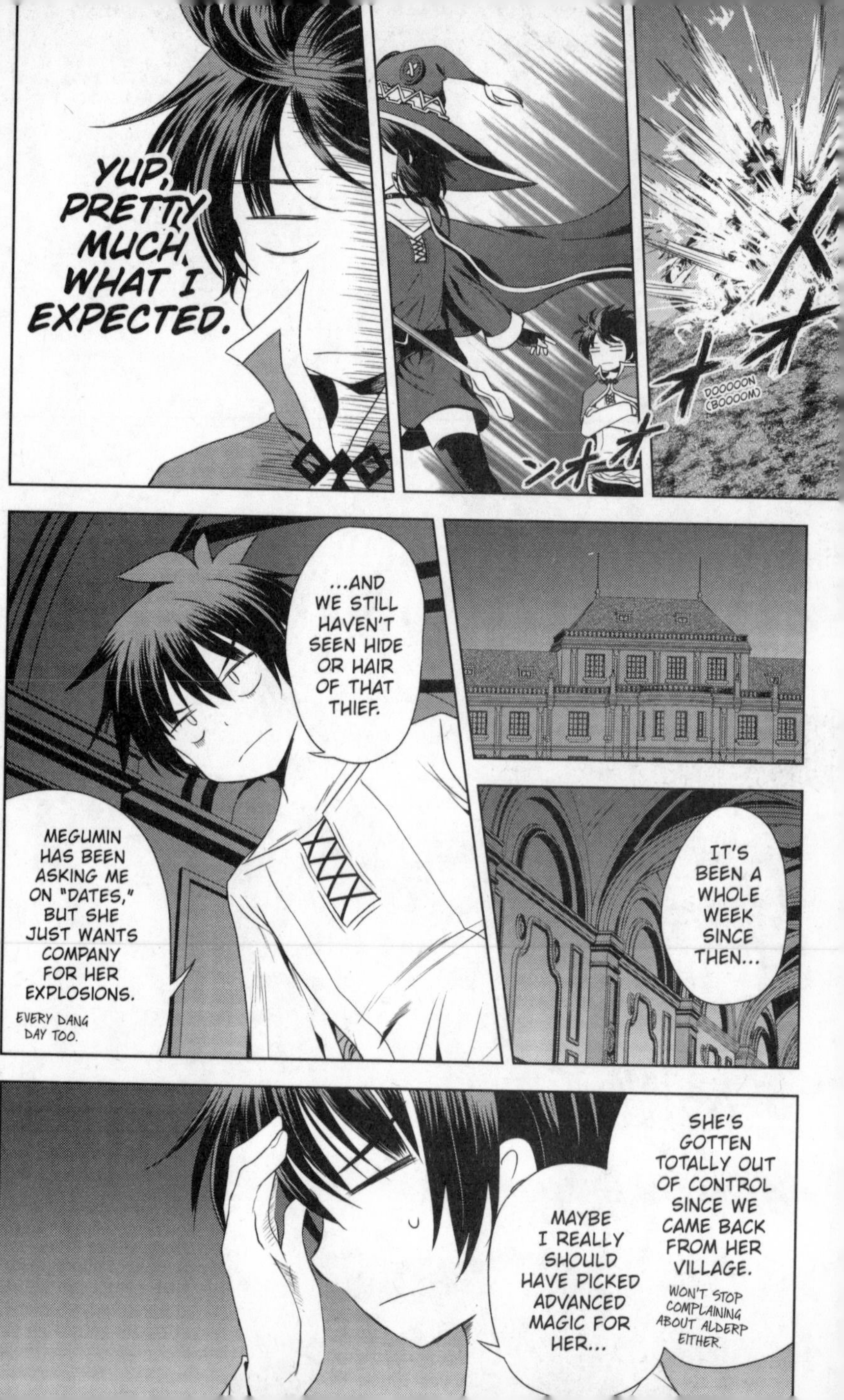
DOOOOON (BOOOOM)
YUP, PRETTY MUCH WHAT I EXPECTED.
IT'S BEEN A WHOLE WEEK SINCE THEN...
...AND WE STILL HAVEN'T SEEN HIDE OR HAIR OF THAT THIEF.
MEGUMIN HAS BEEN ASKING ME ON "DATES," BUT SHE JUST WANTS COMPANY FOR HER EXPLOSIONS.
EVERY DANG DAY TOO.
SHE'S GOTTEN TOTALLY OUT OF CONTROL SINCE WE CAME BACK FROM HER VILLAGE.
WON'T STOP COMPLAINING ABOUT ALDERP EITHER.
MAYBE I REALLY SHOULD HAVE PICKED ADVANCED MAGIC FOR HER...

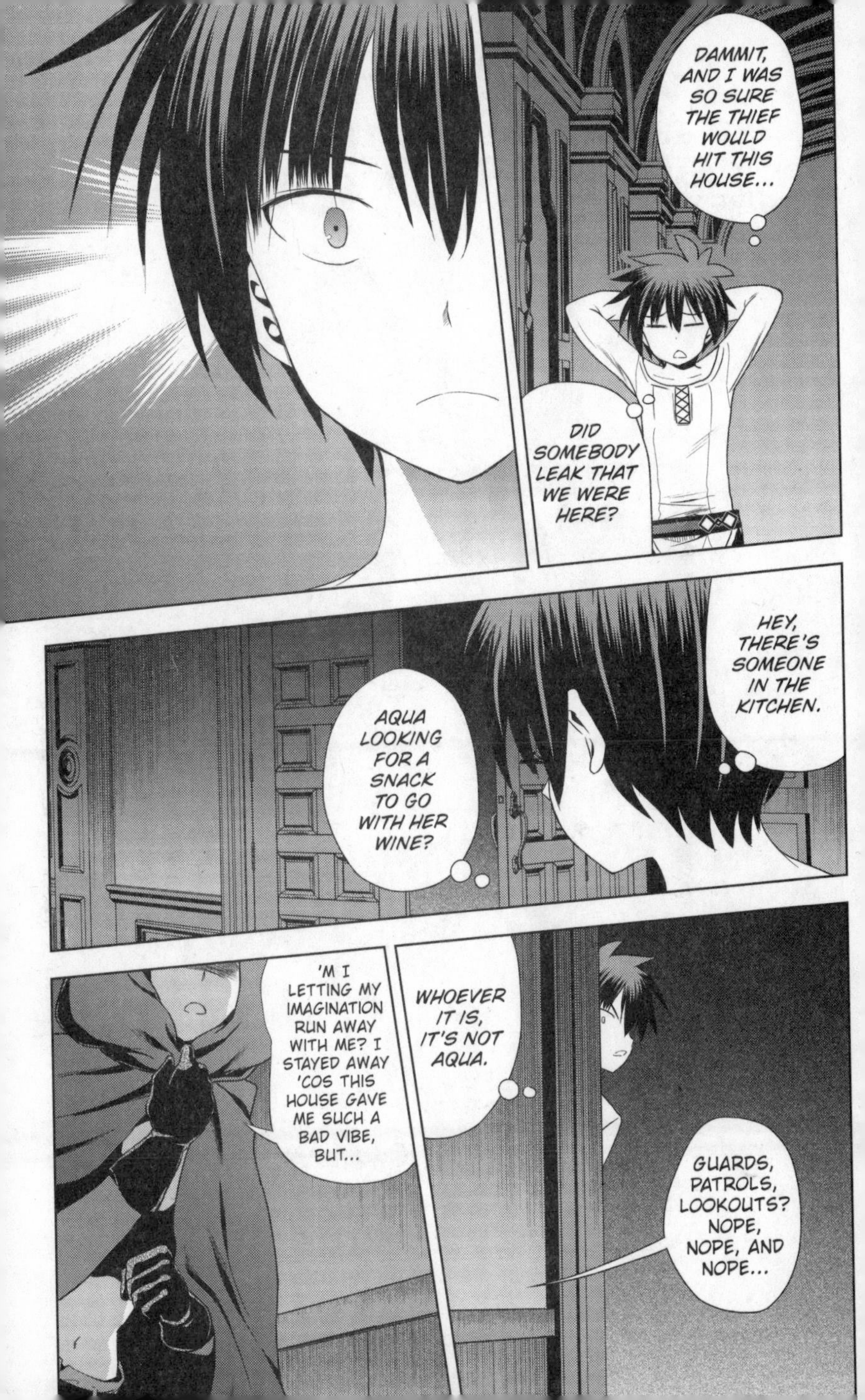
DAMMIT, AND I WAS SO SURE THE THIEF WOULD HIT THIS HOUSE...
DID SOMEBODY LEAK THAT WE WERE HERE?
HEY, THERE'S SOMEONE IN THE KITCHEN.
AQUA LOOKING FOR A SNACK TO GO WITH HER WINE?
WHOEVER IT IS, IT'S NOT AQUA.
GUARDS, PATROLS, LOOKOUTS? NOPE, NOPE, AND NOPE...
'M I LETTING MY IMAGINATION RUN AWAY WITH ME? I STAYED AWAY 'COS THIS HOUSE GAVE ME SUCH A BAD VIBE, BUT...

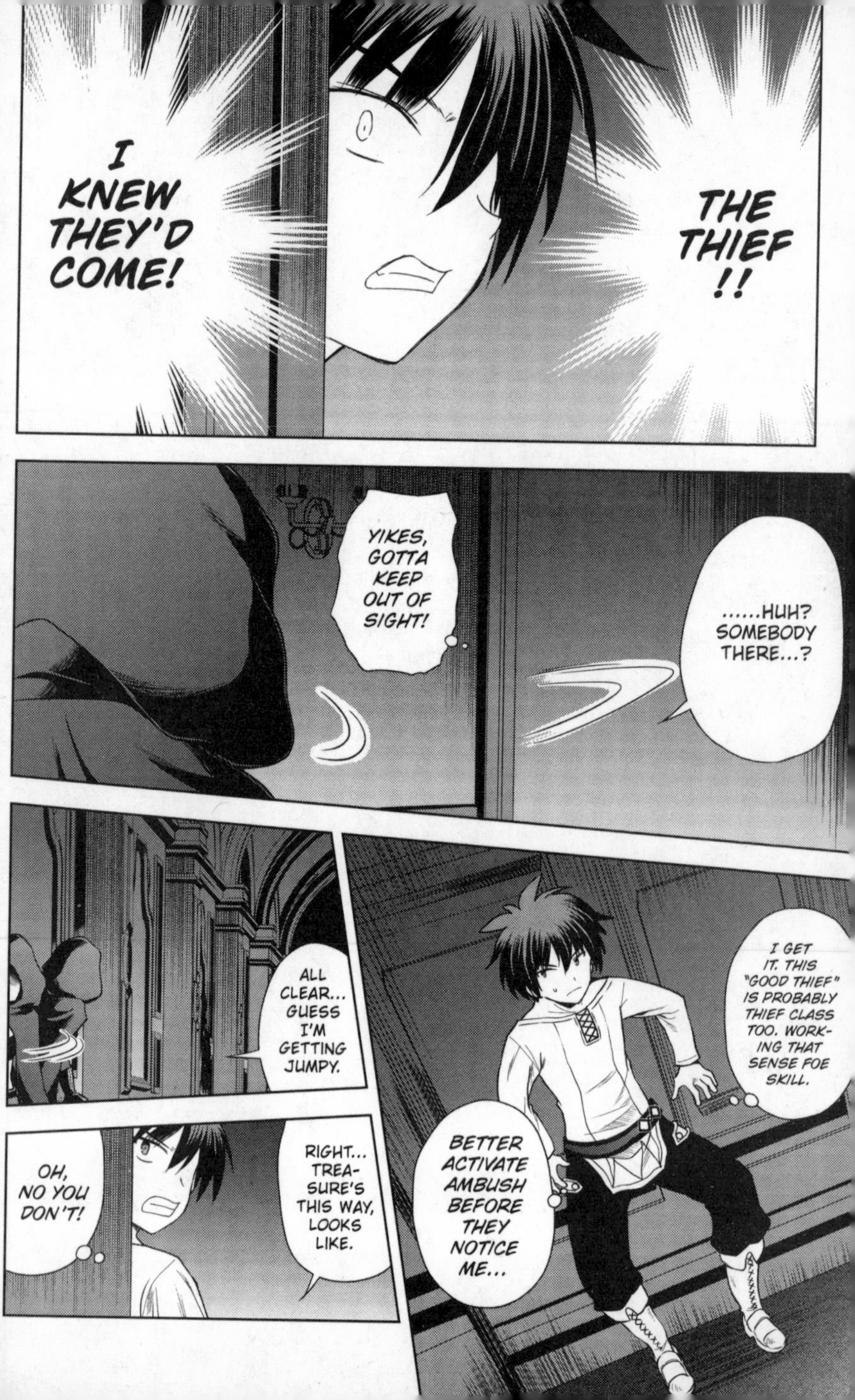
THE THIEF!!
I KNEW THEY'D COME!
......HUH? SOMEBODY THERE...?
YIKES, GOTTA KEEP OUT OF SIGHT!
I GET IT. THIS "GOOD THIEF" IS PROBABLY THIEF CLASS TOO. WORK-ING THAT SENSE FOE SKILL.
BETTER ACTIVATE AMBUSH BEFORE THEY NOTICE ME...
ALL CLEAR... GUESS I'M GETTING JUMPY.
RIGHT... TREA-SURE'S THIS WAY, LOOKS LIKE.
OH, NO YOU DON'T!

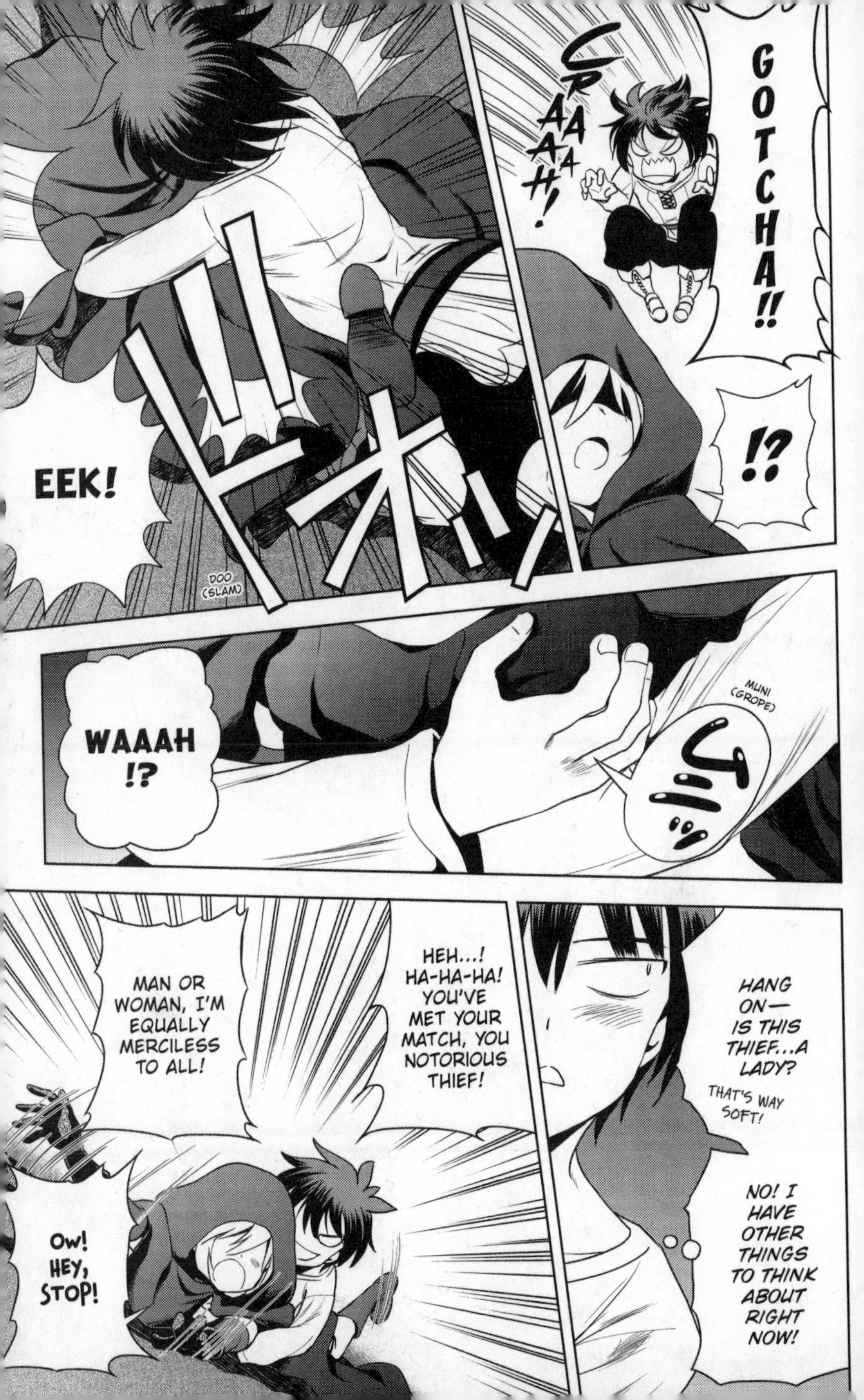
GOTCHA!!
CRAAAAAH!
!?
EEK!
DOO (SLAM)
MUNI (GROPE)
WAAAH !?
HANG ON—IS THIS THIEF...A LADY?
THAT'S WAY SOFT!
NO! I HAVE OTHER THINGS TO THINK ABOUT RIGHT NOW!
HEH...! HA-HA-HA! YOU'VE MET YOUR MATCH, YOU NOTORIOUS THIEF!
MAN OR WOMAN, I'M EQUALLY MERCILESS TO ALL!
OW! HEY, STOP!

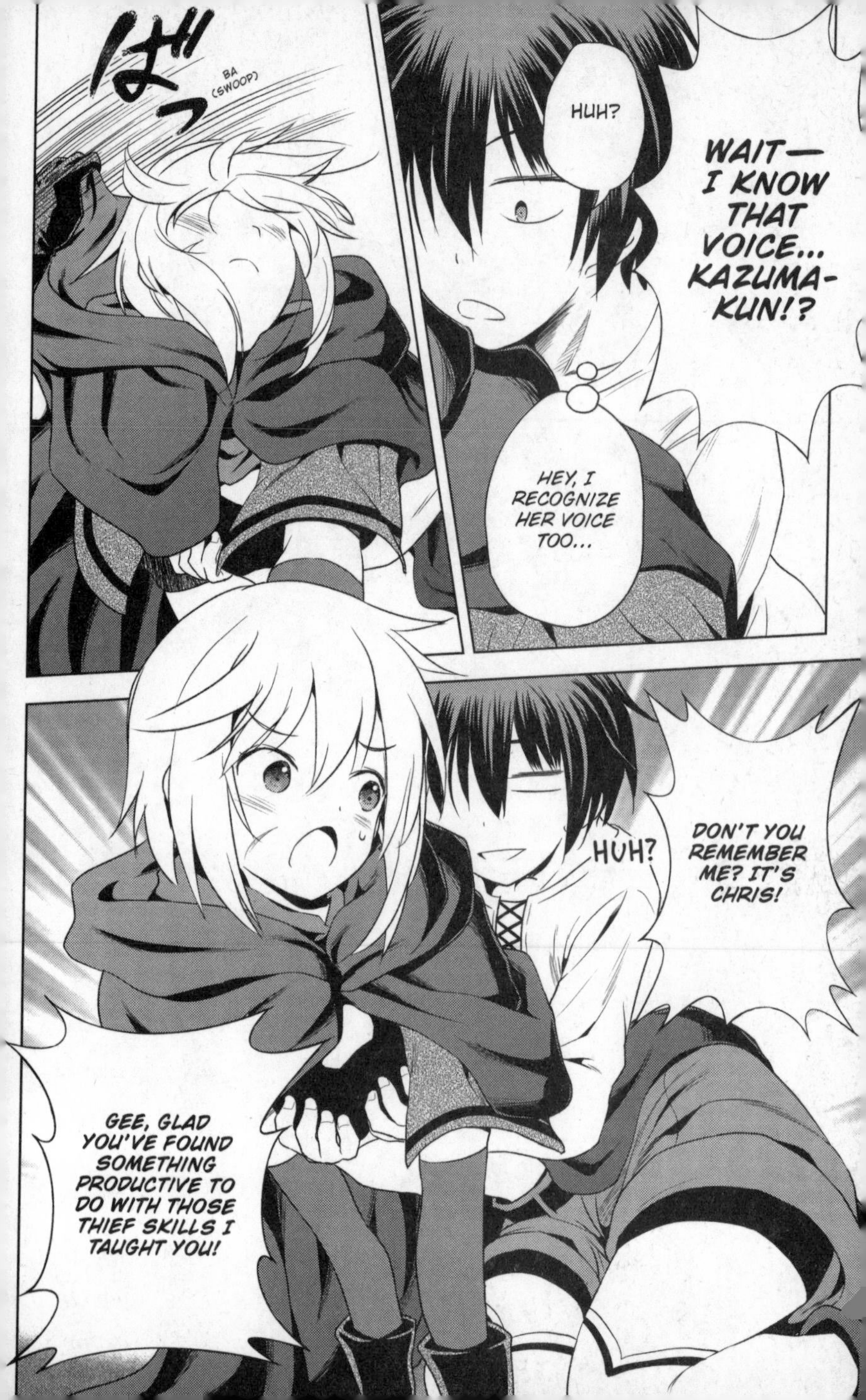
HUH?
WAIT— I KNOW THAT VOICE... KAZUMA-KUN!?
HEY, I RECOGNIZE HER VOICE TOO...
ばっ
BA (SWOOP)
DON'T YOU REMEMBER ME? IT'S CHRIS!
HUH?
GEE, GLAD YOU'VE FOUND SOMETHING PRODUCTIVE TO DO WITH THOSE THIEF SKILLS I TAUGHT YOU!

GOD's
BLESSING
ON THIS
WONDERFUL
WORLD!

10

10

GOD'S
BLESSING
ON THIS
WONDERFUL
WORLD!

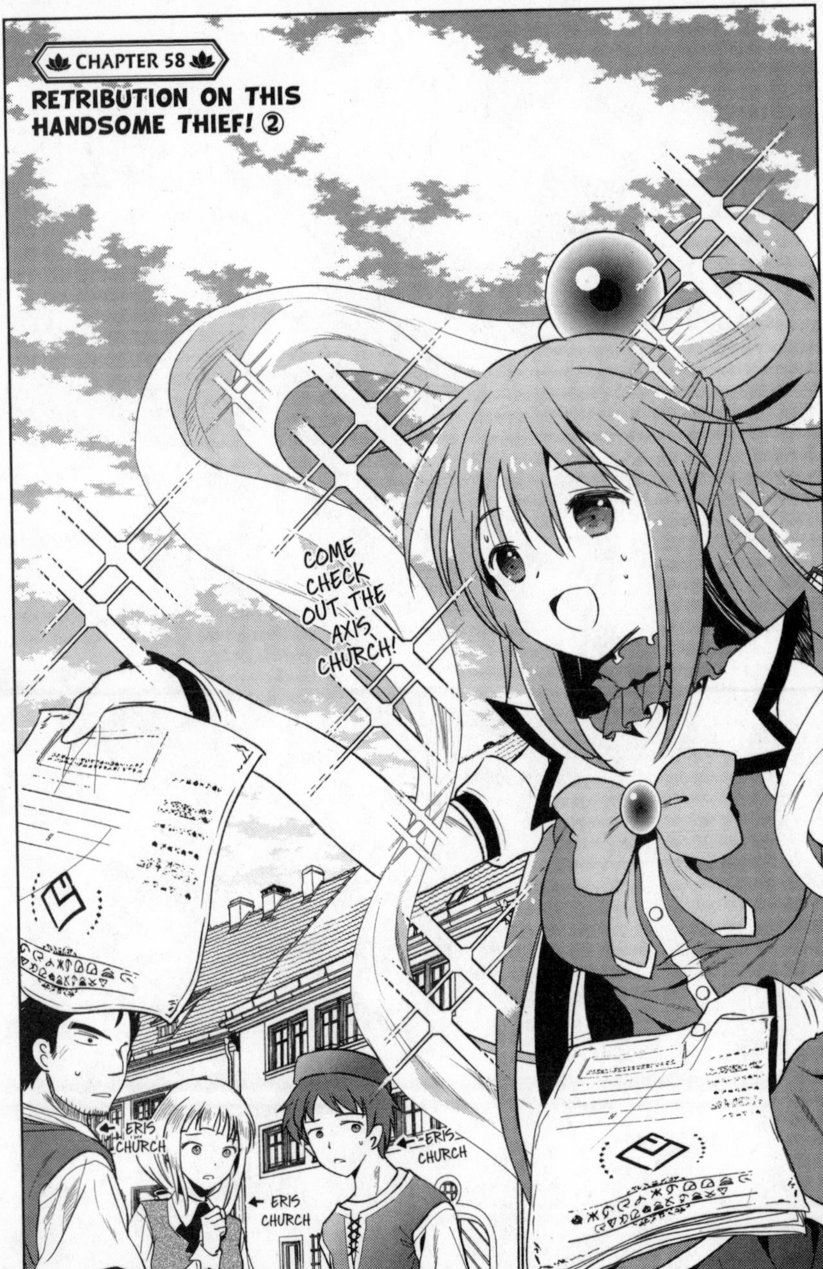
CHAPTER 58
RETRIBUTION ON THIS HANDSOME THIEF! ②
COME CHECK OUT THE AXIS CHURCH!
ERIS CHURCH
ERIS CHURCH
ERIS CHURCH

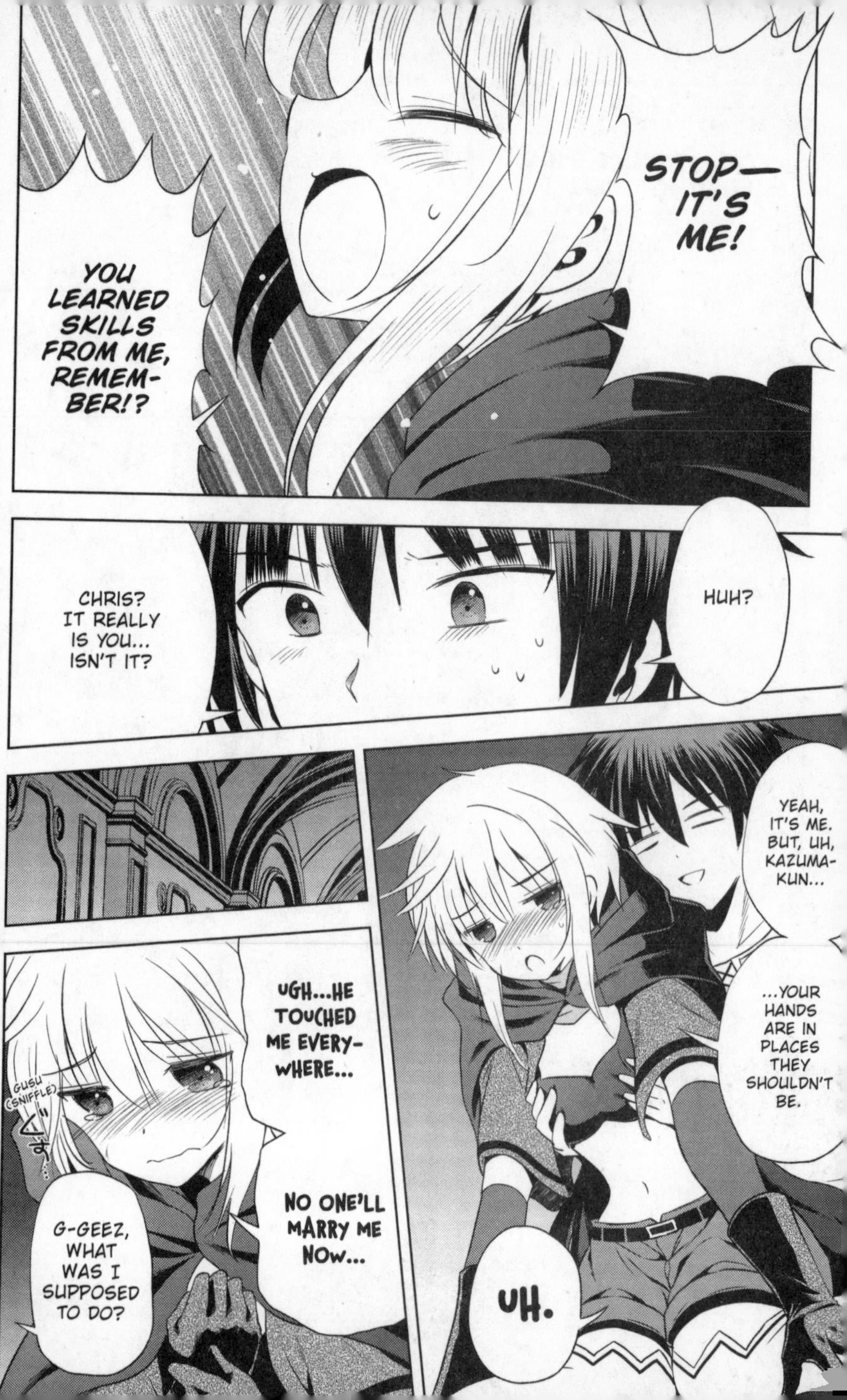
STOP— IT'S ME!
YOU LEARNED SKILLS FROM ME, REMEMBER!?
HUH?
CHRIS? IT REALLY IS YOU... ISN'T IT?
YEAH, IT'S ME. BUT, UH, KAZUMA-KUN...
...YOUR HANDS ARE IN PLACES THEY SHOULDN'T BE.
UH.
UGH...HE TOUCHED ME EVERY-WHERE...
NO ONE'LL MARRY ME NOW...
GUSU (SNIFFLE)
G-GEEZ, WHAT WAS I SUPPOSED TO DO?

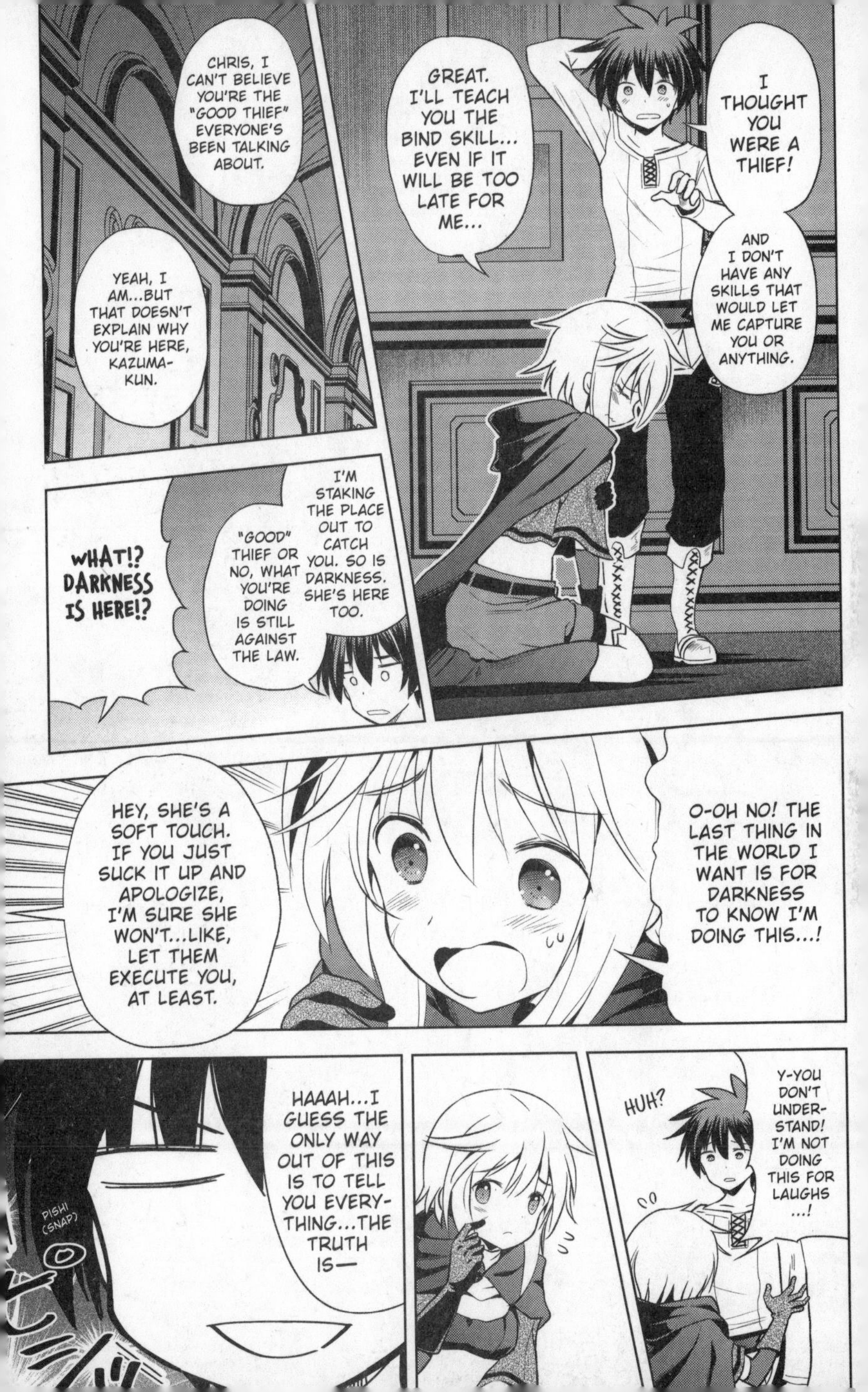
I THOUGHT YOU WERE A THIEF!
AND I DON'T HAVE ANY SKILLS THAT WOULD LET ME CAPTURE YOU OR ANYTHING.
GREAT. I'LL TEACH YOU THE BIND SKILL... EVEN IF IT WILL BE TOO LATE FOR ME...
CHRIS, I CAN'T BELIEVE YOU'RE THE "GOOD THIEF" EVERYONE'S BEEN TALKING ABOUT.
YEAH, I AM...BUT THAT DOESN'T EXPLAIN WHY YOU'RE HERE, KAZUMA-KUN.
I'M STAKING THE PLACE OUT TO CATCH YOU. SO IS DARKNESS. SHE'S HERE TOO.
"GOOD" THIEF OR NO, WHAT YOU'RE DOING IS STILL AGAINST THE LAW.
WHAT!? DARKNESS IS HERE!?
O-OH NO! THE LAST THING IN THE WORLD I WANT IS FOR DARKNESS TO KNOW I'M DOING THIS...!
HEY, SHE'S A SOFT TOUCH. IF YOU JUST SUCK IT UP AND APOLOGIZE, I'M SURE SHE WON'T...LIKE, LET THEM EXECUTE YOU, AT LEAST.
Y-YOU DON'T UNDER-STAND! I'M NOT DOING THIS FOR LAUGHS ...!
HUH?
HAAAH...I GUESS THE ONLY WAY OUT OF THIS IS TO TELL YOU EVERY-THING...THE TRUTH IS—
PISHI (SNAP)

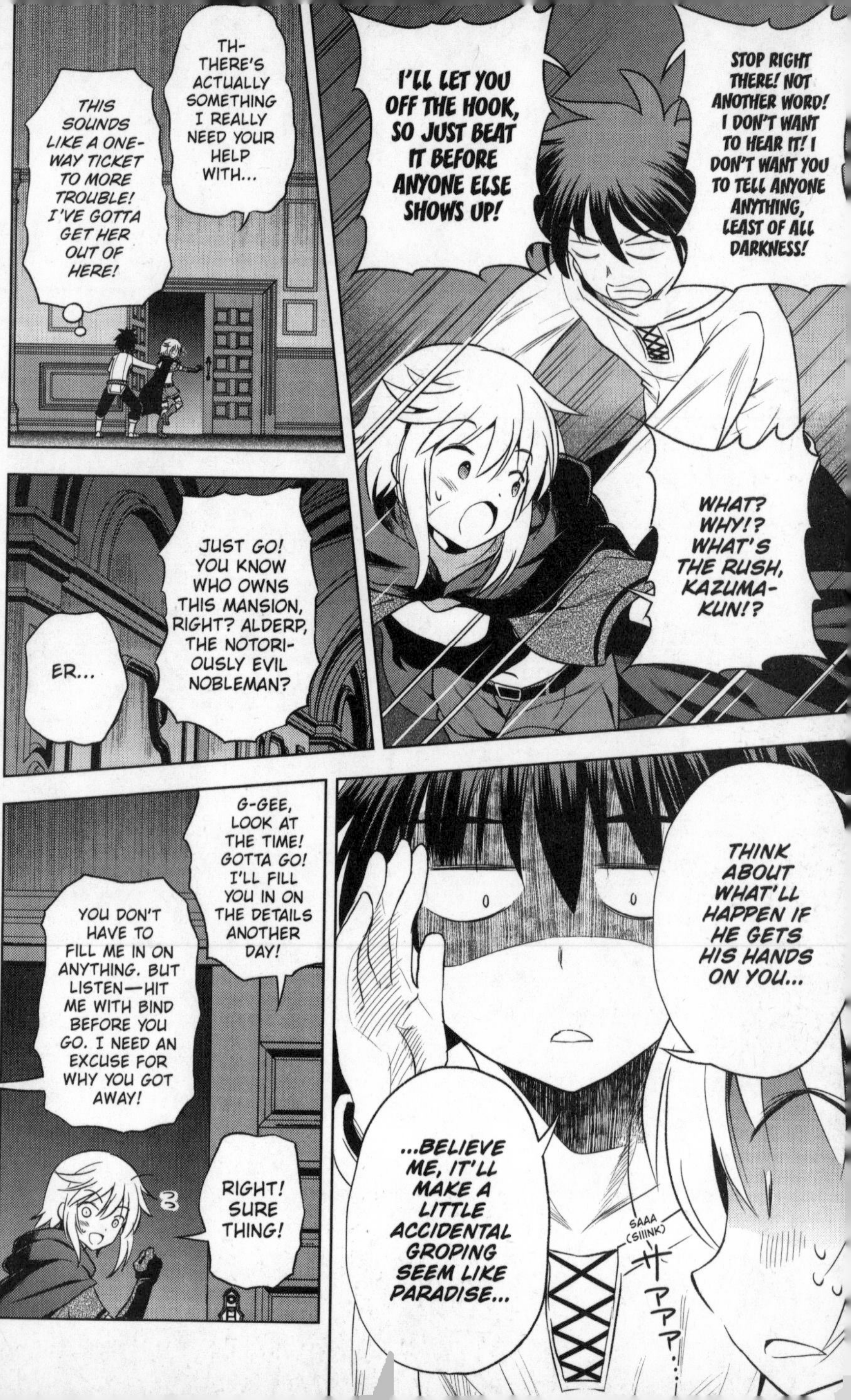
STOP RIGHT THERE! NOT ANOTHER WORD! I DON'T WANT TO HEAR IT! I DON'T WANT YOU TO TELL ANYONE ANYTHING, LEAST OF ALL DARKNESS!
I'LL LET YOU OFF THE HOOK, SO JUST BEAT IT BEFORE ANYONE ELSE SHOWS UP!
WHAT? WHY!? WHAT'S THE RUSH, KAZUMA-KUN!?
TH-THERE'S ACTUALLY SOMETHING I REALLY NEED YOUR HELP WITH...
THIS SOUNDS LIKE A ONE-WAY TICKET TO MORE TROUBLE! I'VE GOTTA GET HER OUT OF HERE!
JUST GO! YOU KNOW WHO OWNS THIS MANSION, RIGHT? ALDERP, THE NOTORIOUSLY EVIL NOBLEMAN?
ER...
THINK ABOUT WHAT'LL HAPPEN IF HE GETS HIS HANDS ON YOU...
...BELIEVE ME, IT'LL MAKE A LITTLE ACCIDENTAL GROPING SEEM LIKE PARADISE...
SAAA (SIIINK)
G-GEE, LOOK AT THE TIME! GOTTA GO! I'LL FILL YOU IN ON THE DETAILS ANOTHER DAY!
YOU DON'T HAVE TO FILL ME IN ON ANYTHING. BUT LISTEN—HIT ME WITH BIND BEFORE YOU GO. I NEED AN EXCUSE FOR WHY YOU GOT AWAY!
RIGHT! SURE THING!

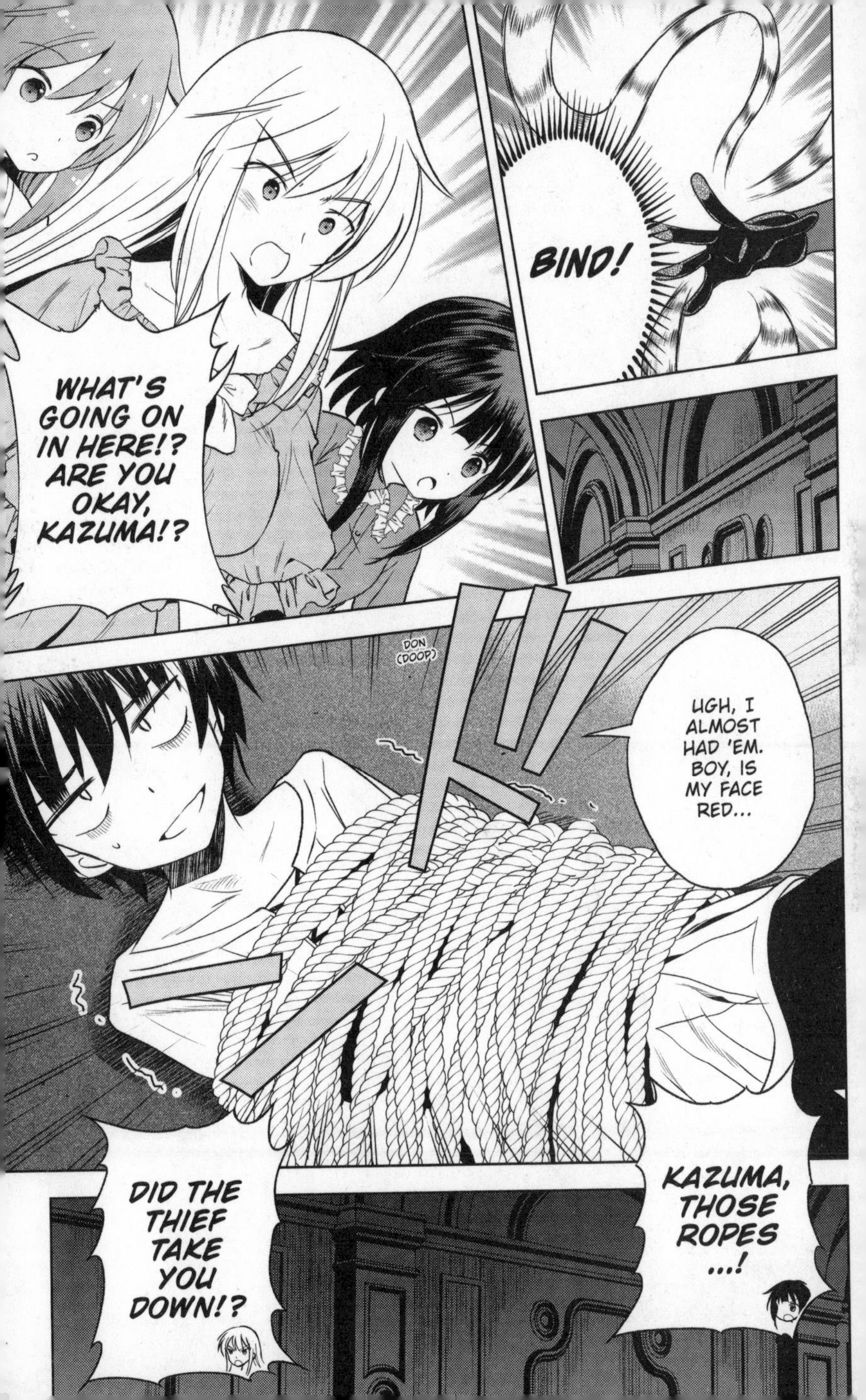
BIND!
WHAT'S GOING ON IN HERE!? ARE YOU OKAY, KAZUMA!?
DON (DOOP)
UGH, I ALMOST HAD 'EM. BOY, IS MY FACE RED...
KAZUMA, THOSE ROPES ...!
DID THE THIEF TAKE YOU DOWN!?

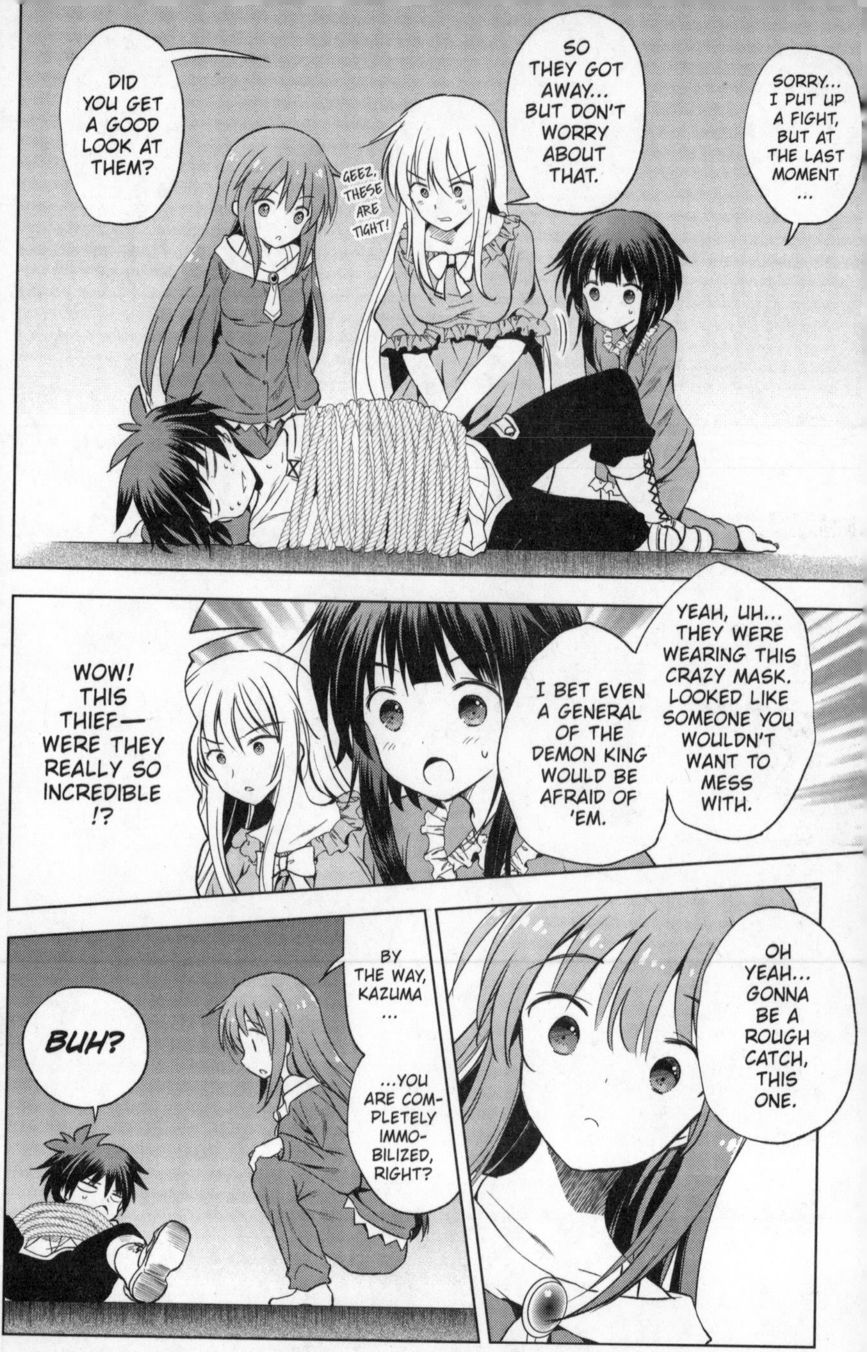
SORRY... I PUT UP A FIGHT, BUT AT THE LAST MOMENT ...
SO THEY GOT AWAY... BUT DON'T WORRY ABOUT THAT.
GEEZ, THESE ARE TIGHT!
DID YOU GET A GOOD LOOK AT THEM?
YEAH, UH... THEY WERE WEARING THIS CRAZY MASK. LOOKED LIKE SOMEONE YOU WOULDN'T WANT TO MESS WITH.
I BET EVEN A GENERAL OF THE DEMON KING WOULD BE AFRAID OF 'EM.
WOW! THIS THIEF— WERE THEY REALLY SO INCREDIBLE !?
OH YEAH... GONNA BE A ROUGH CATCH, THIS ONE.
BY THE WAY, KAZUMA ...
...YOU ARE COMPLETELY IMMOBILIZED, RIGHT?
BUH?

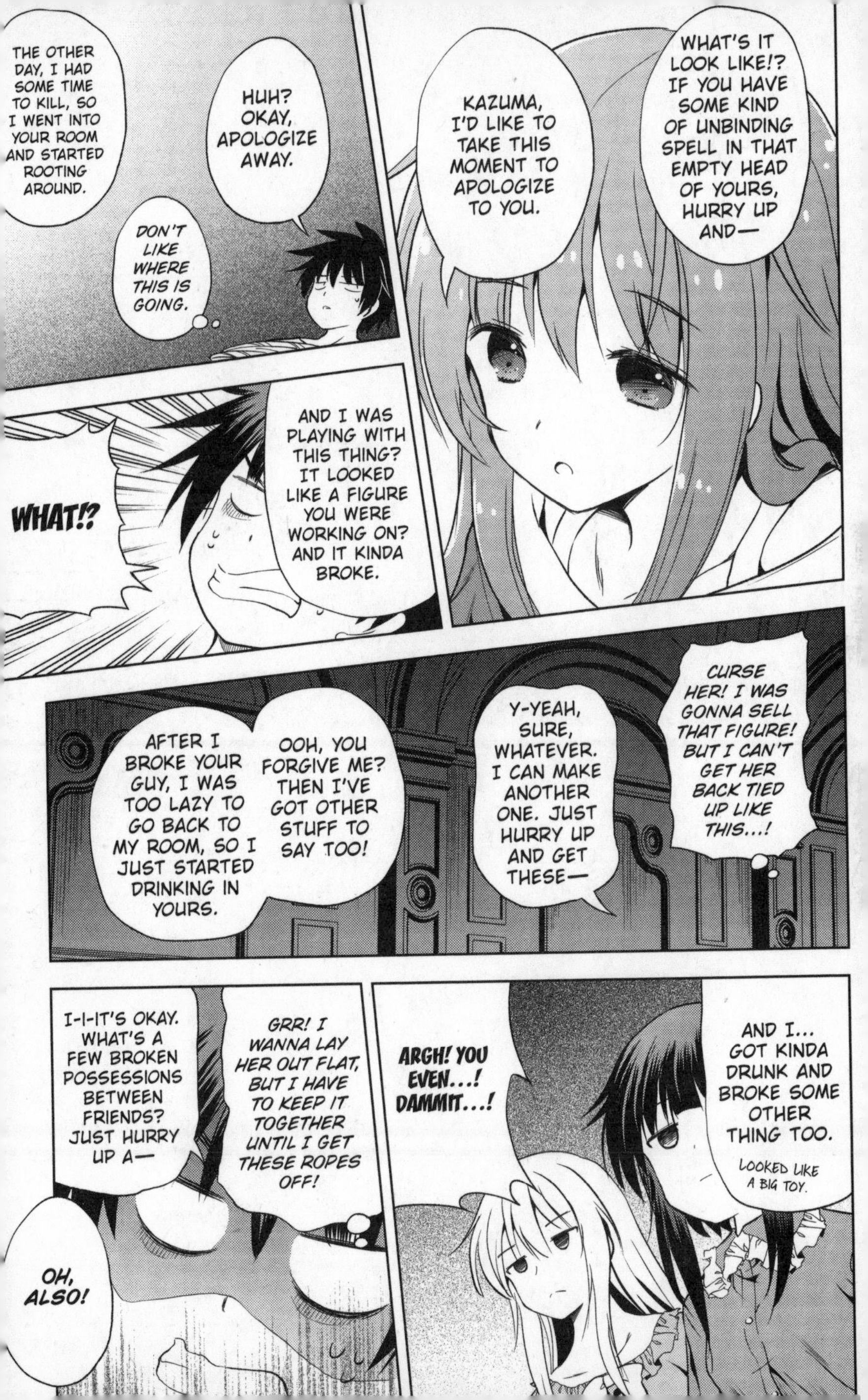
WHAT'S IT LOOK LIKE!? IF YOU HAVE SOME KIND OF UNBINDING SPELL IN THAT EMPTY HEAD OF YOURS, HURRY UP AND—
KAZUMA, I'D LIKE TO TAKE THIS MOMENT TO APOLOGIZE TO YOU.
HUH? OKAY, APOLOGIZE AWAY.
DON'T LIKE WHERE THIS IS GOING.
THE OTHER DAY, I HAD SOME TIME TO KILL, SO I WENT INTO YOUR ROOM AND STARTED ROOTING AROUND.
AND I WAS PLAYING WITH THIS THING? IT LOOKED LIKE A FIGURE YOU WERE WORKING ON? AND IT KINDA BROKE.
WHAT!?
CURSE HER! I WAS GONNA SELL THAT FIGURE! BUT I CAN'T GET HER BACK TIED UP LIKE THIS...!
Y-YEAH, SURE, WHATEVER. I CAN MAKE ANOTHER ONE. JUST HURRY UP AND GET THESE—
OOH, YOU FORGIVE ME? THEN I'VE GOT OTHER STUFF TO SAY TOO!
AFTER I BROKE YOUR GUY, I WAS TOO LAZY TO GO BACK TO MY ROOM, SO I JUST STARTED DRINKING IN YOURS.
AND I... GOT KINDA DRUNK AND BROKE SOME OTHER THING TOO.
LOOKED LIKE A BIG TOY.
ARGH! YOU EVEN...! DAMMIT...!
GRR! I WANNA LAY HER OUT FLAT, BUT I HAVE TO KEEP IT TOGETHER UNTIL I GET THESE ROPES OFF!
I-I-IT'S OKAY. WHAT'S A FEW BROKEN POSSESSIONS BETWEEN FRIENDS? JUST HURRY UP A—
OH, ALSO!

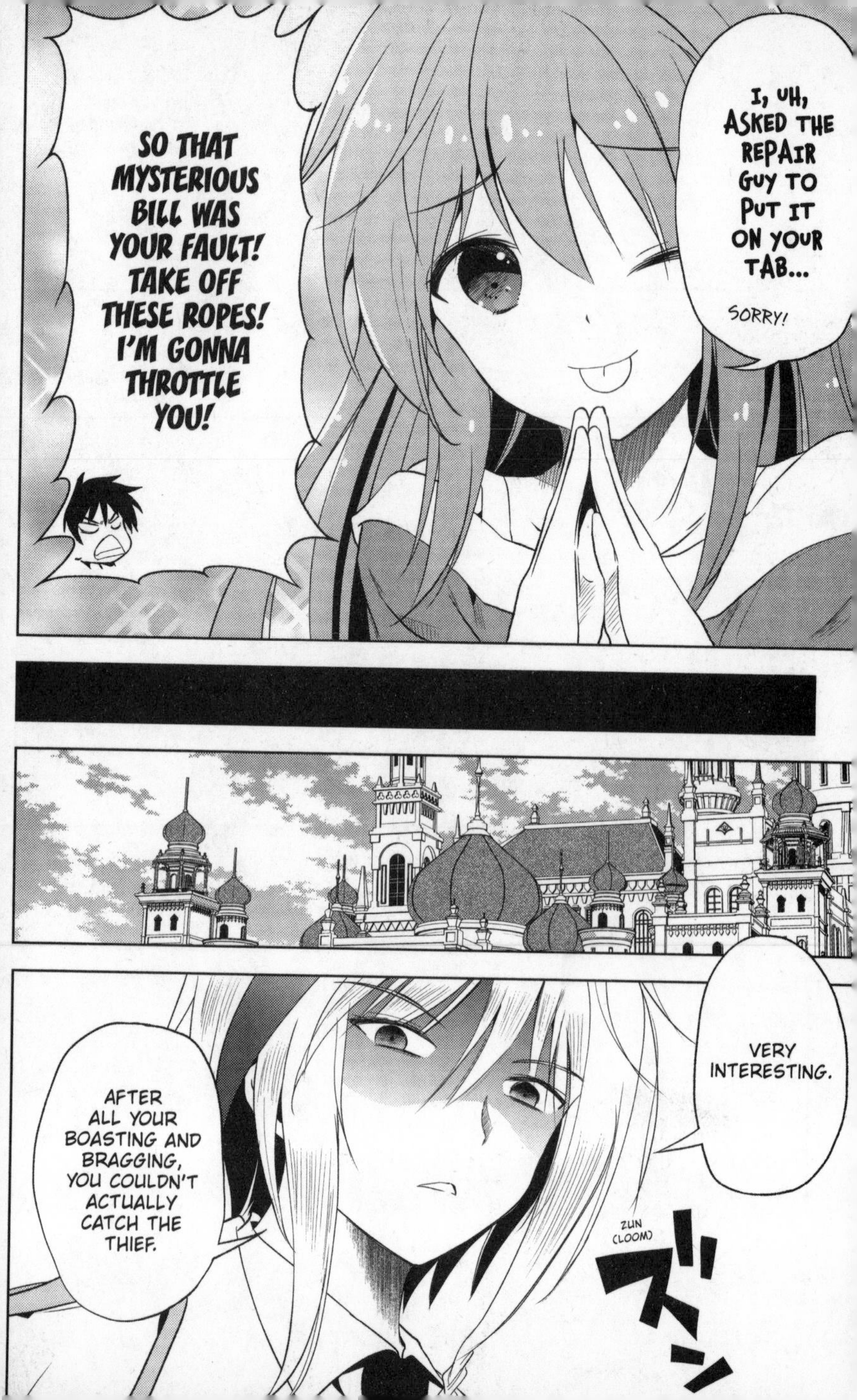
I, UH, ASKED THE REPAIR GUY TO PUT IT ON YOUR TAB...
SORRY!
SO THAT MYSTERIOUS BILL WAS YOUR FAULT! TAKE OFF THESE ROPES! I'M GONNA THROTTLE YOU!
VERY INTERESTING.
AFTER ALL YOUR BOASTING AND BRAGGING, YOU COULDN'T ACTUALLY CATCH THE THIEF.
ZUN (LOOM)

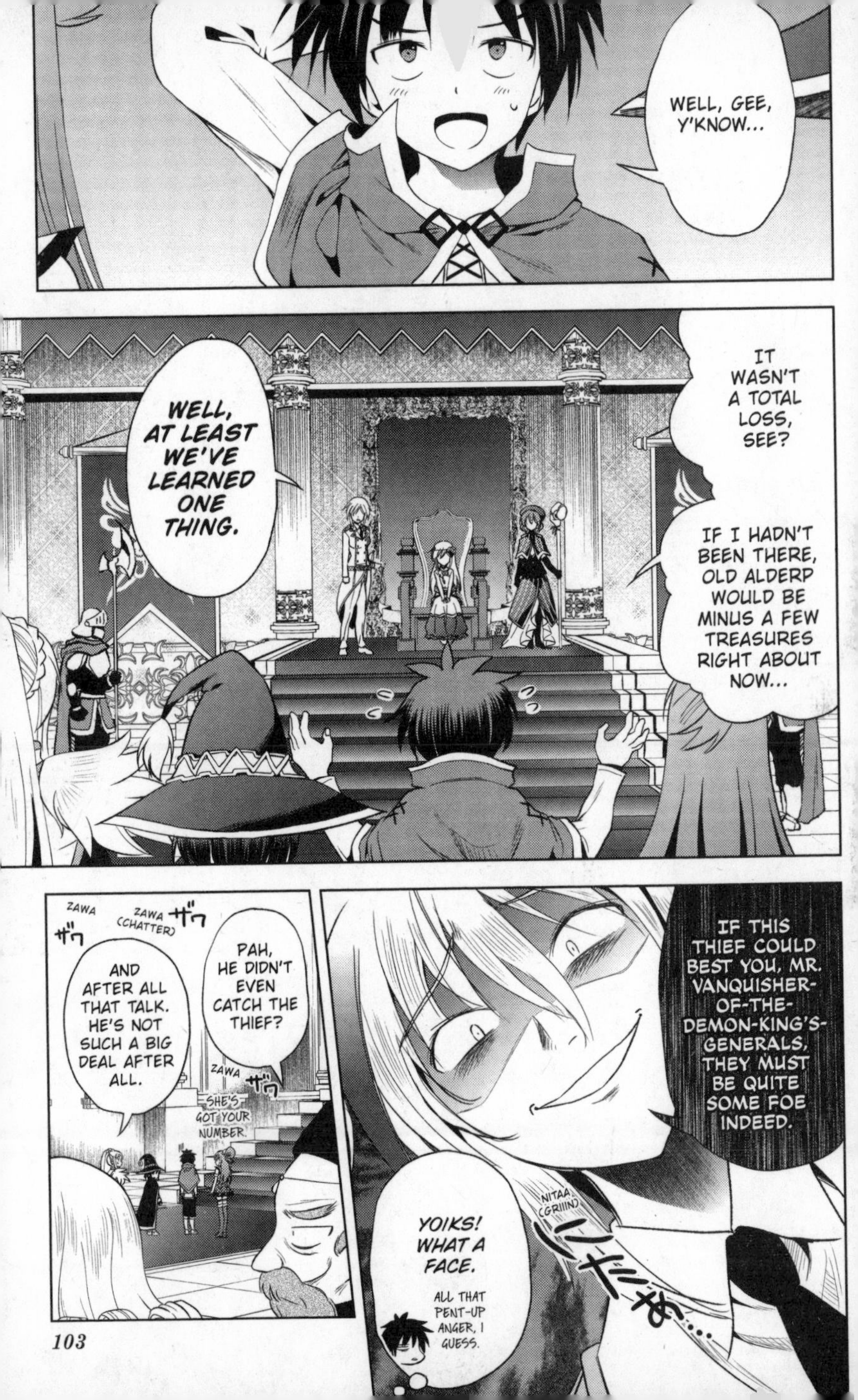
WELL, GEE, Y'KNOW...
IT WASN'T A TOTAL LOSS, SEE?
IF I HADN'T BEEN THERE, OLD ALDERP WOULD BE MINUS A FEW TREASURES RIGHT ABOUT NOW...
WELL, AT LEAST WE'VE LEARNED ONE THING.
IF THIS THIEF COULD BEST YOU, MR. VANQUISHER-OF-THE-DEMON-KING'S-GENERALS, THEY MUST BE QUITE SOME FOE INDEED.
NITAA (GRIIIN)
YOIKS! WHAT A FACE.
ALL THAT PENT-UP ANGER, I GUESS.
ZAWA ZAWA (CHATTER)
PAH, HE DIDN'T EVEN CATCH THE THIEF?
AND AFTER ALL THAT TALK. HE'S NOT SUCH A BIG DEAL AFTER ALL.
ZAWA
SHE'S GOT YOUR NUMBER.

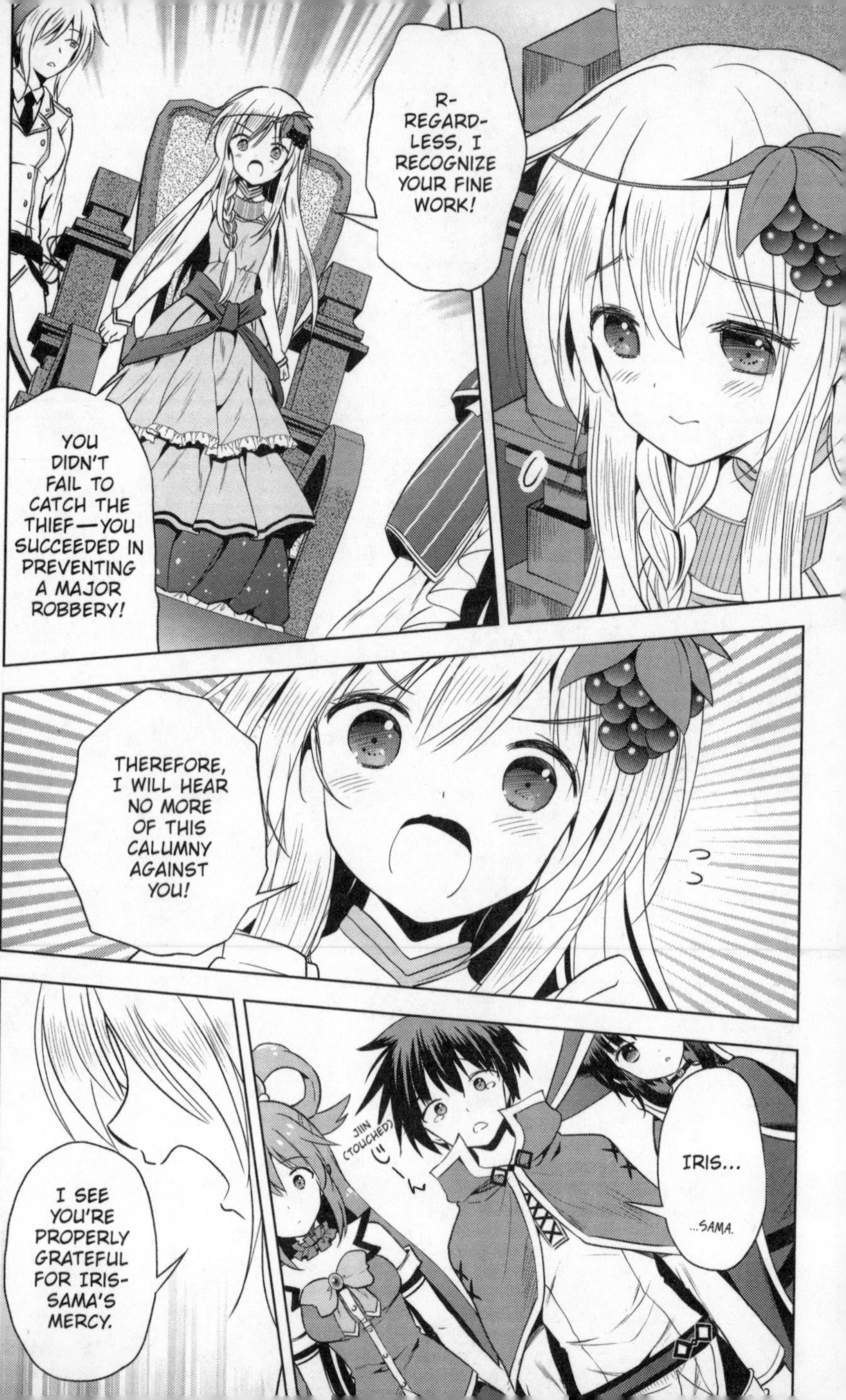
R-REGARDLESS, I RECOGNIZE YOUR FINE WORK!
YOU DIDN'T FAIL TO CATCH THE THIEF—YOU SUCCEEDED IN PREVENTING A MAJOR ROBBERY!
THEREFORE, I WILL HEAR NO MORE OF THIS CALUMNY AGAINST YOU!
IRIS...
...SAMA.
JIIN (TOUCHED)
I SEE YOU'RE PROPERLY GRATEFUL FOR IRIS-SAMA'S MERCY.

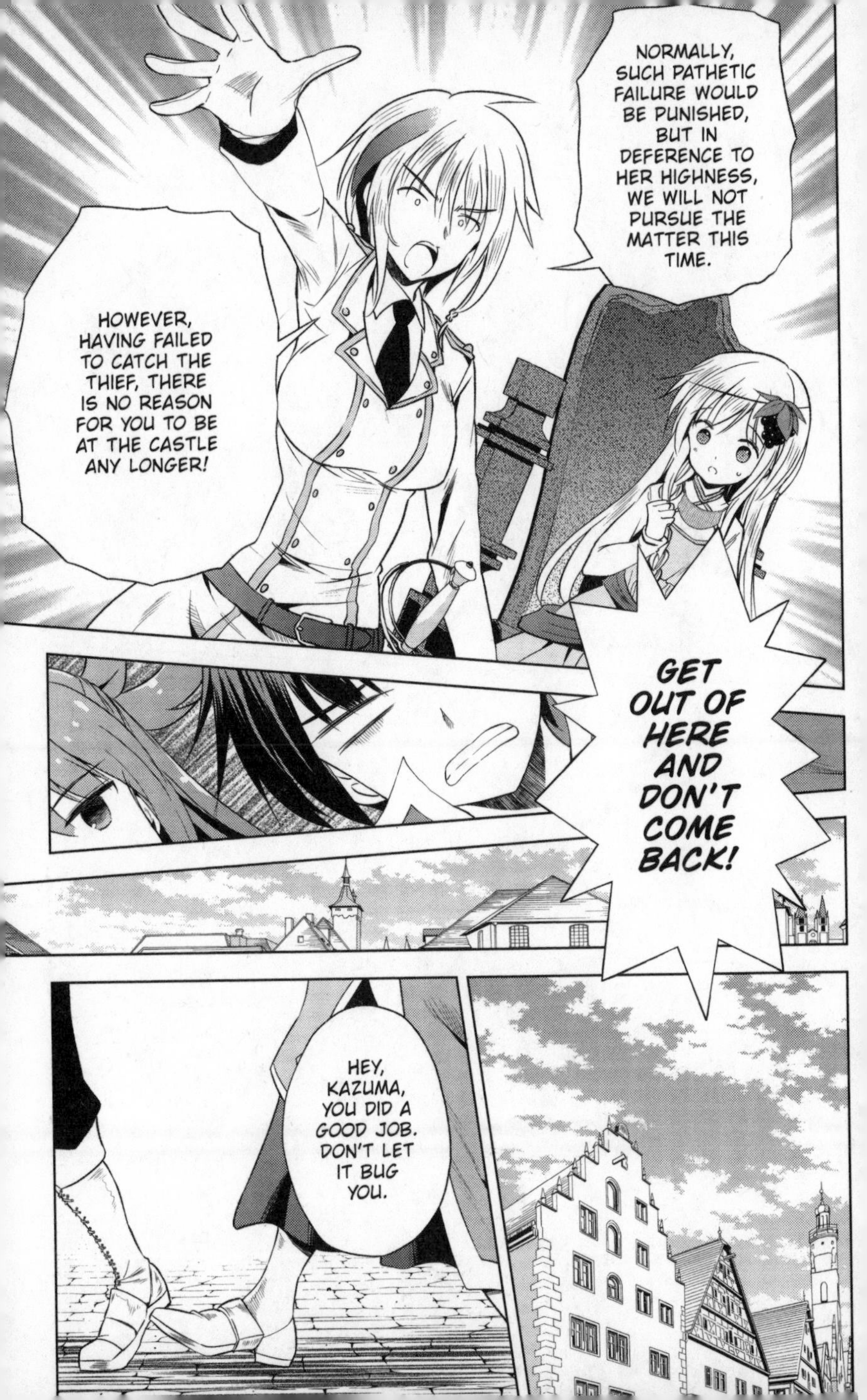
NORMALLY, SUCH PATHETIC FAILURE WOULD BE PUNISHED, BUT IN DEFERENCE TO HER HIGHNESS, WE WILL NOT PURSUE THE MATTER THIS TIME.
HOWEVER, HAVING FAILED TO CATCH THE THIEF, THERE IS NO REASON FOR YOU TO BE AT THE CASTLE ANY LONGER!
GET OUT OF HERE AND DON'T COME BACK!
HEY, KAZUMA, YOU DID A GOOD JOB. DON'T LET IT BUG YOU.

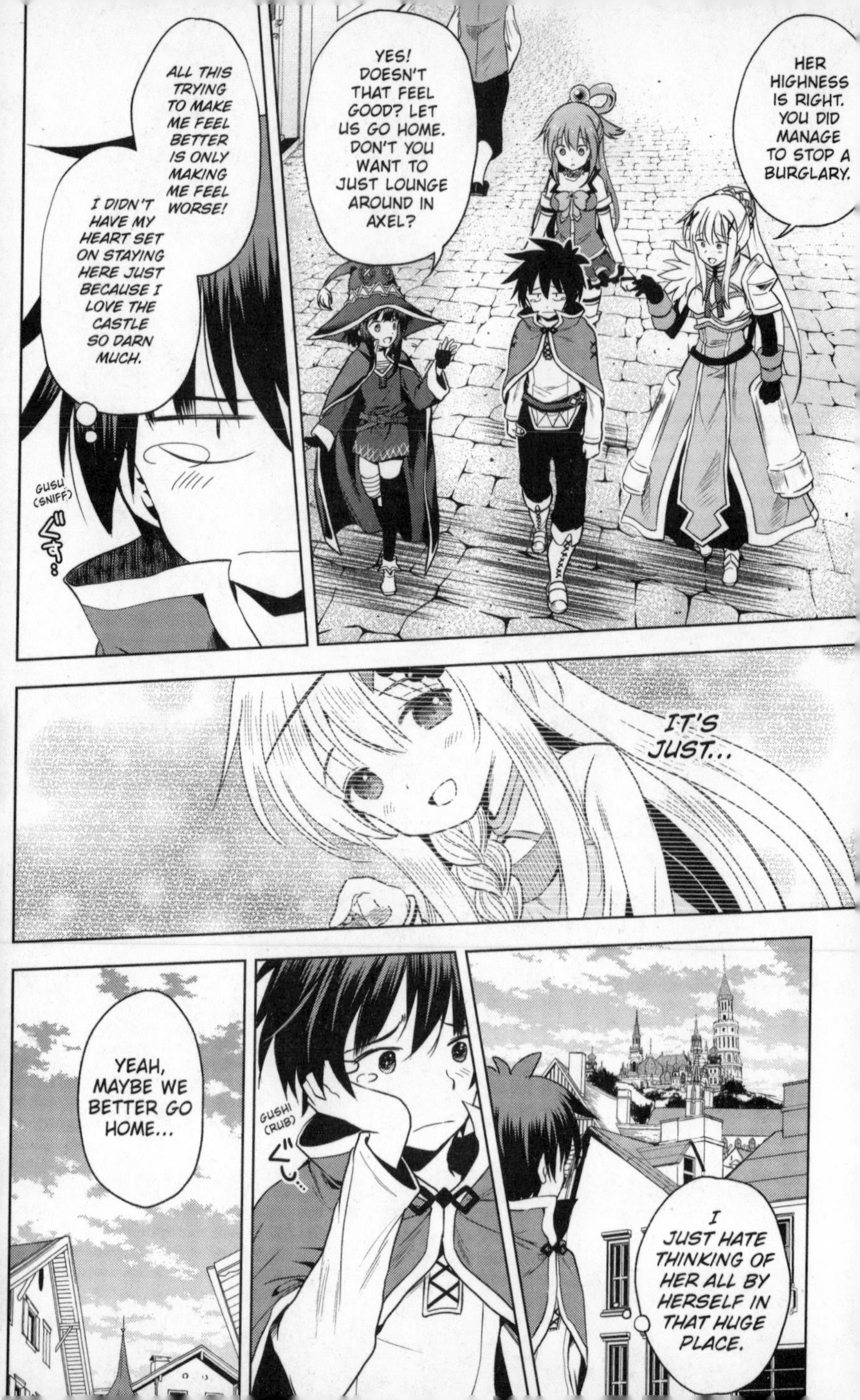
HER HIGHNESS IS RIGHT. YOU DID MANAGE TO STOP A BURGLARY.
YES! DOESN'T THAT FEEL GOOD? LET US GO HOME. DON'T YOU WANT TO JUST LOUNGE AROUND IN AXEL?
ALL THIS TRYING TO MAKE ME FEEL BETTER IS ONLY MAKING ME FEEL WORSE!
I DIDN'T HAVE MY HEART SET ON STAYING HERE JUST BECAUSE I LOVE THE CASTLE SO DARN MUCH.
GUSU (SNIFF)
IT'S JUST...
I JUST HATE THINKING OF HER ALL BY HERSELF IN THAT HUGE PLACE.
GUSHI (RUB)
YEAH, MAYBE WE BETTER GO HOME...

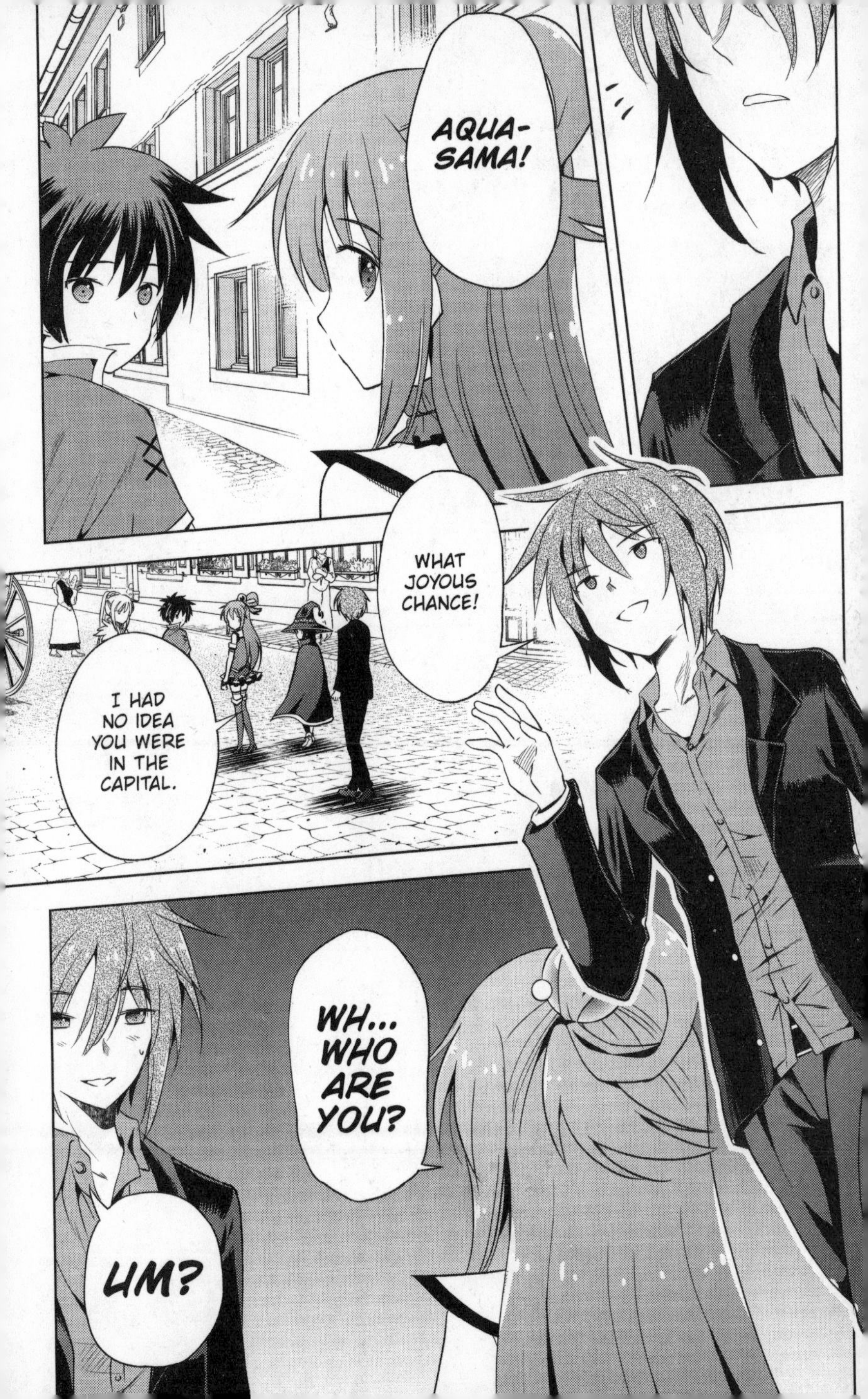
AQUA-SAMA!
WHAT JOYOUS CHANCE!
I HAD NO IDEA YOU WERE IN THE CAPITAL.
WH... WHO ARE YOU?
UM?

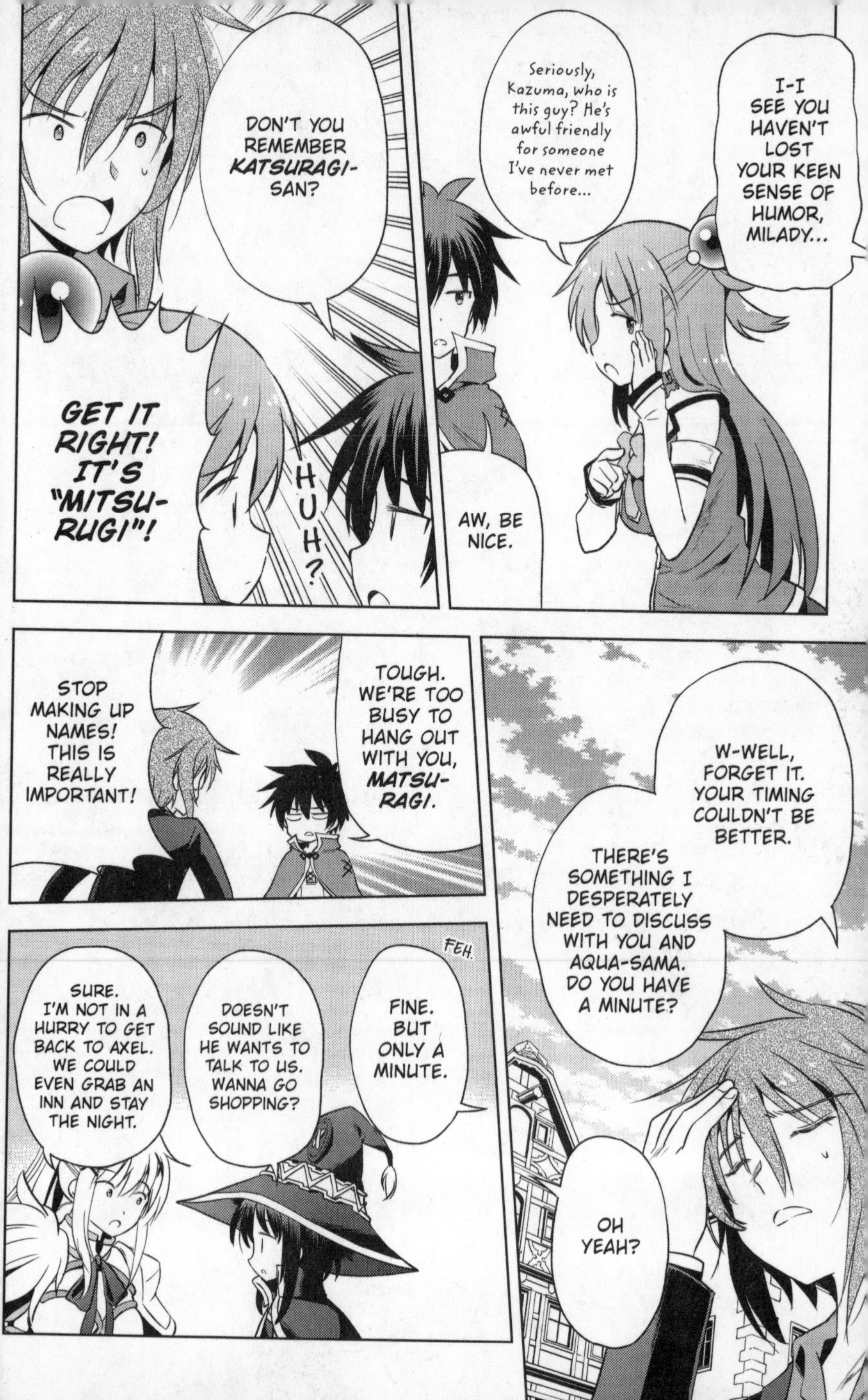
I-I SEE YOU HAVEN'T LOST YOUR KEEN SENSE OF HUMOR, MILADY...
Seriously, Kazuma, who is this guy? He's awful friendly for someone I've never met before...
AW, BE NICE.
DON'T YOU REMEMBER KATSURAGI-SAN?
HUH?
GET IT RIGHT! IT'S "MITSURUGI"!
W-WELL, FORGET IT. YOUR TIMING COULDN'T BE BETTER.
THERE'S SOMETHING I DESPERATELY NEED TO DISCUSS WITH YOU AND AQUA-SAMA. DO YOU HAVE A MINUTE?
OH YEAH?
TOUGH. WE'RE TOO BUSY TO HANG OUT WITH YOU, MATSURAGI.
STOP MAKING UP NAMES! THIS IS REALLY IMPORTANT!
FEH.
FINE. BUT ONLY A MINUTE.
DOESN'T SOUND LIKE HE WANTS TO TALK TO US. WANNA GO SHOPPING?
SURE. I'M NOT IN A HURRY TO GET BACK TO AXEL. WE COULD EVEN GRAB AN INN AND STAY THE NIGHT.

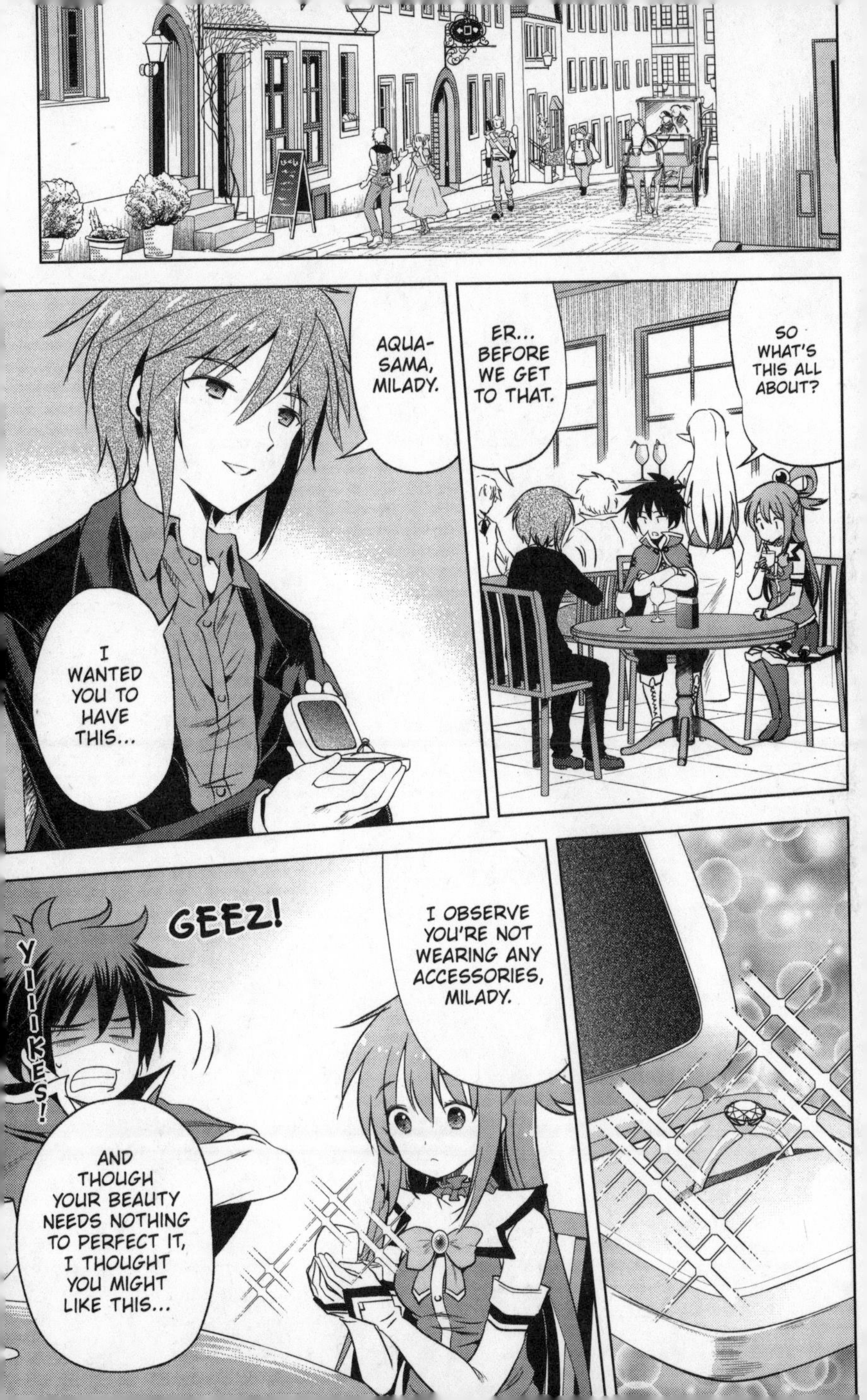
SO WHAT'S THIS ALL ABOUT?
ER... BEFORE WE GET TO THAT.
AQUA-SAMA, MILADY.
I WANTED YOU TO HAVE THIS...
I OBSERVE YOU'RE NOT WEARING ANY ACCESSORIES, MILADY.
GEEZ!
YIIIKES!
AND THOUGH YOUR BEAUTY NEEDS NOTHING TO PERFECT IT, I THOUGHT YOU MIGHT LIKE THIS...

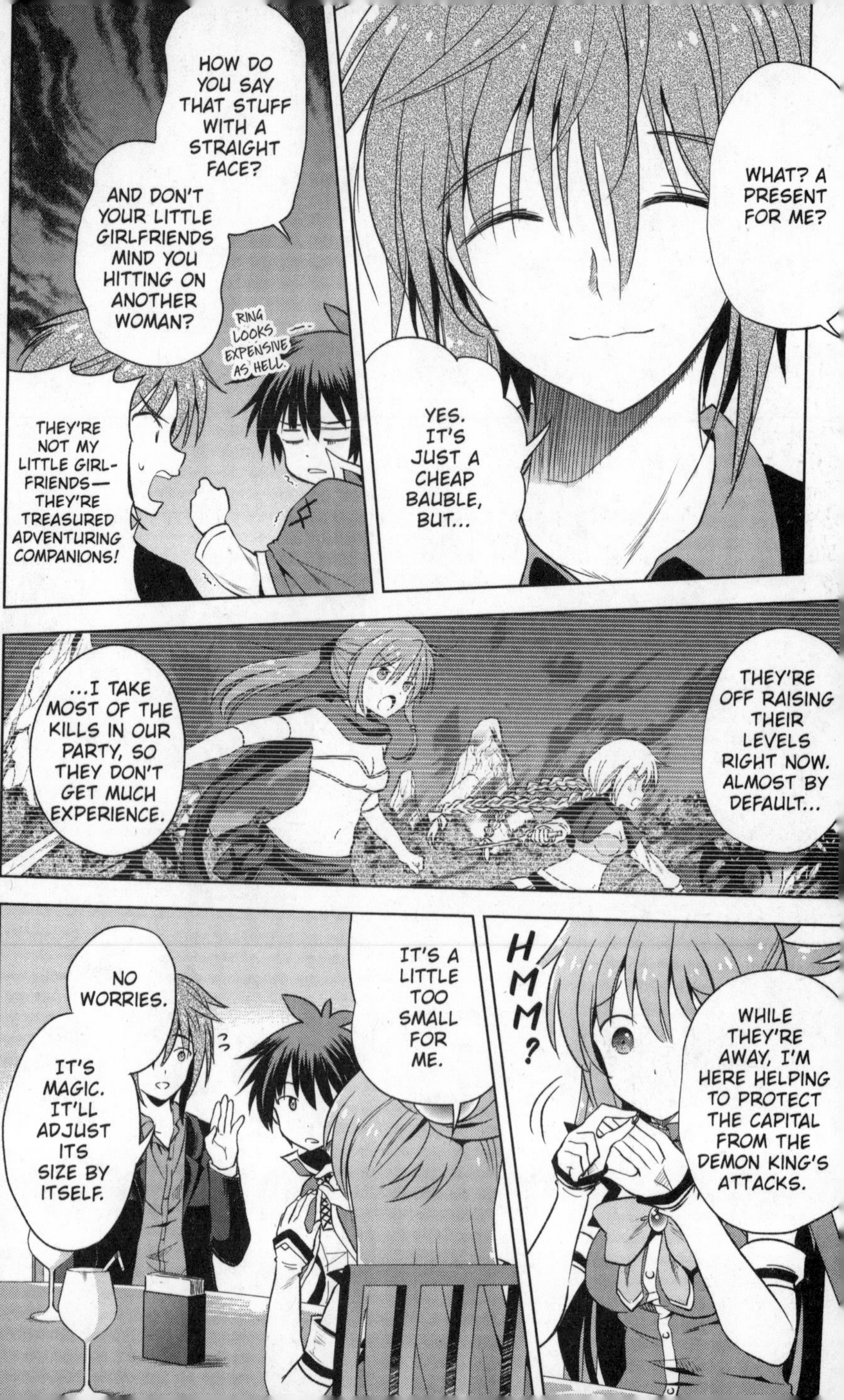
WHAT? A PRESENT FOR ME?
YES. IT'S JUST A CHEAP BAUBLE, BUT...
HOW DO YOU SAY THAT STUFF WITH A STRAIGHT FACE?
AND DON'T YOUR LITTLE GIRLFRIENDS MIND YOU HITTING ON ANOTHER WOMAN?
RING LOOKS EXPENSIVE AS HELL.
THEY'RE NOT MY LITTLE GIRL-FRIENDS—THEY'RE TREASURED ADVENTURING COMPANIONS!
THEY'RE OFF RAISING THEIR LEVELS RIGHT NOW. ALMOST BY DEFAULT...
...I TAKE MOST OF THE KILLS IN OUR PARTY, SO THEY DON'T GET MUCH EXPERIENCE.
HMM?
WHILE THEY'RE AWAY, I'M HERE HELPING TO PROTECT THE CAPITAL FROM THE DEMON KING'S ATTACKS.
IT'S A LITTLE TOO SMALL FOR ME.
NO WORRIES.
IT'S MAGIC. IT'LL ADJUST ITS SIZE BY ITSELF.

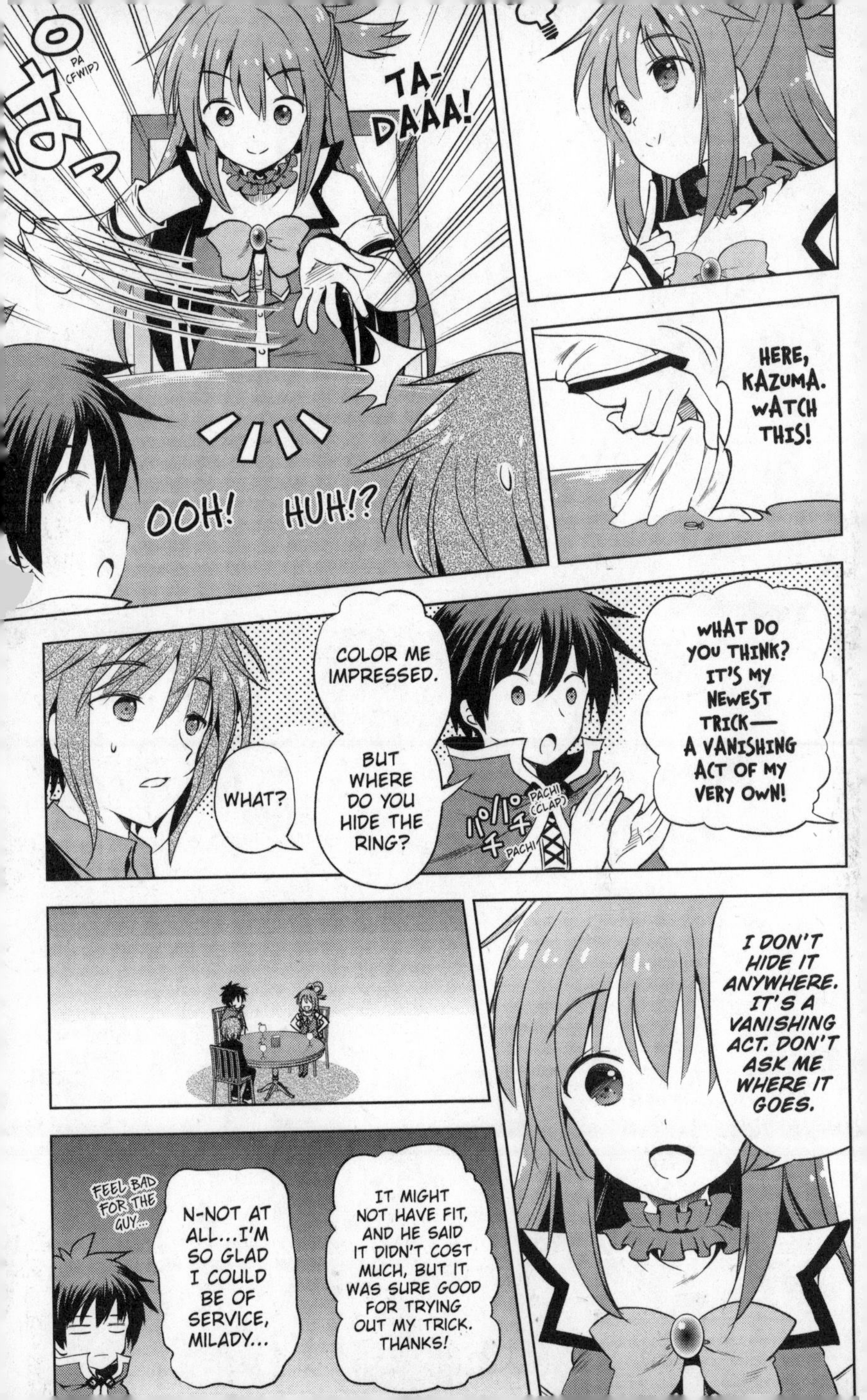
HERE, KAZUMA. WATCH THIS!
PA (FWIP)
TA-DAAA!
HUH!?
OOH!
WHAT DO YOU THINK? IT'S MY NEWEST TRICK—A VANISHING ACT OF MY VERY OWN!
COLOR ME IMPRESSED.
BUT WHERE DO YOU HIDE THE RING?
PACHI (CLAP) PACHI
WHAT?
I DON'T HIDE IT ANYWHERE. IT'S A VANISHING ACT. DON'T ASK ME WHERE IT GOES.
IT MIGHT NOT HAVE FIT, AND HE SAID IT DIDN'T COST MUCH, BUT IT WAS SURE GOOD FOR TRYING OUT MY TRICK. THANKS!
N-NOT AT ALL...I'M SO GLAD I COULD BE OF SERVICE, MILADY...
FEEL BAD FOR THE GUY...

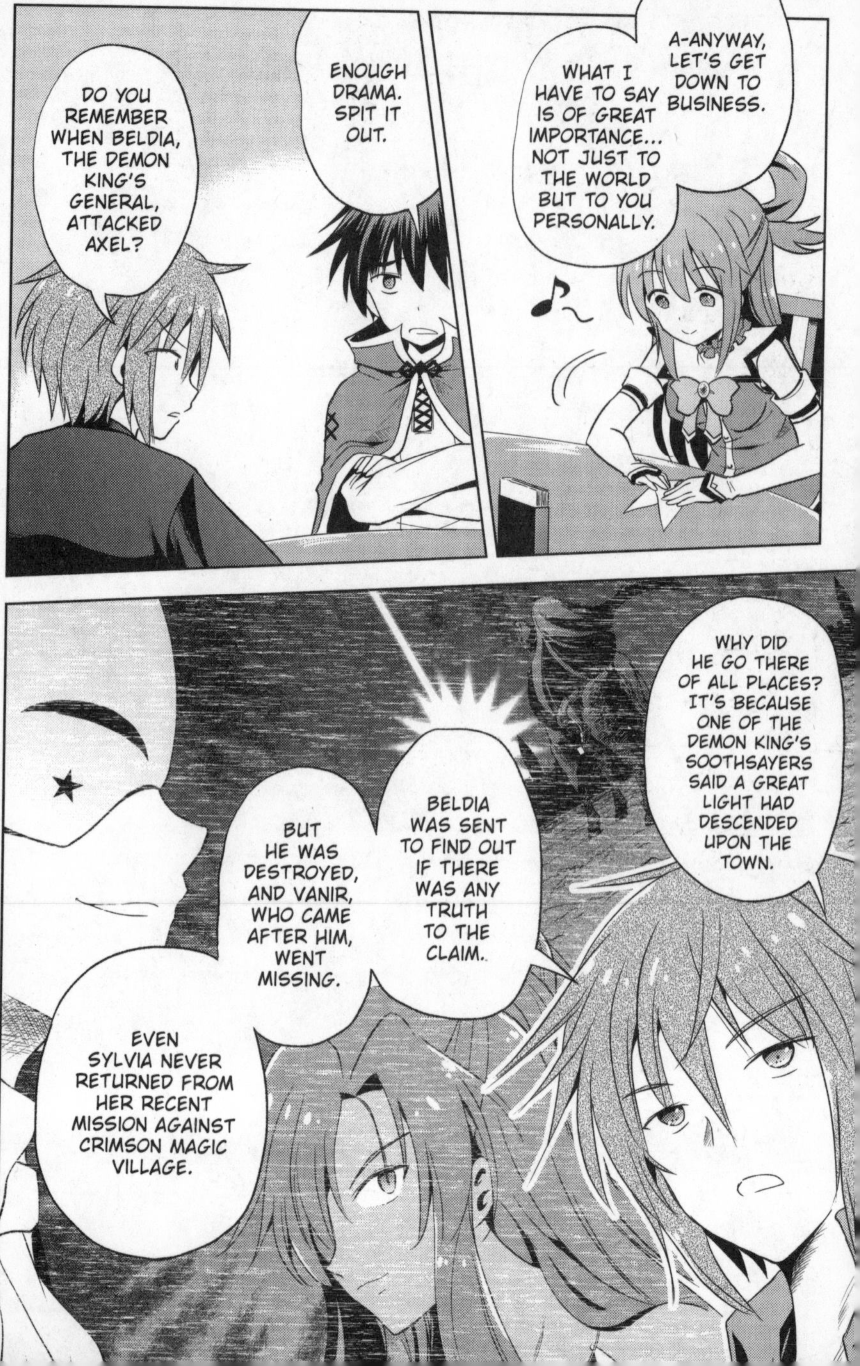
A-ANYWAY, LET'S GET DOWN TO BUSINESS.
WHAT I HAVE TO SAY IS OF GREAT IMPORTANCE... NOT JUST TO THE WORLD BUT TO YOU PERSONALLY.
ENOUGH DRAMA. SPIT IT OUT.
DO YOU REMEMBER WHEN BELDIA, THE DEMON KING'S GENERAL, ATTACKED AXEL?
WHY DID HE GO THERE OF ALL PLACES? IT'S BECAUSE ONE OF THE DEMON KING'S SOOTHSAYERS SAID A GREAT LIGHT HAD DESCENDED UPON THE TOWN.
BELDIA WAS SENT TO FIND OUT IF THERE WAS ANY TRUTH TO THE CLAIM.
BUT HE WAS DESTROYED, AND VANIR, WHO CAME AFTER HIM, WENT MISSING.
EVEN SYLVIA NEVER RETURNED FROM HER RECENT MISSION AGAINST CRIMSON MAGIC VILLAGE.

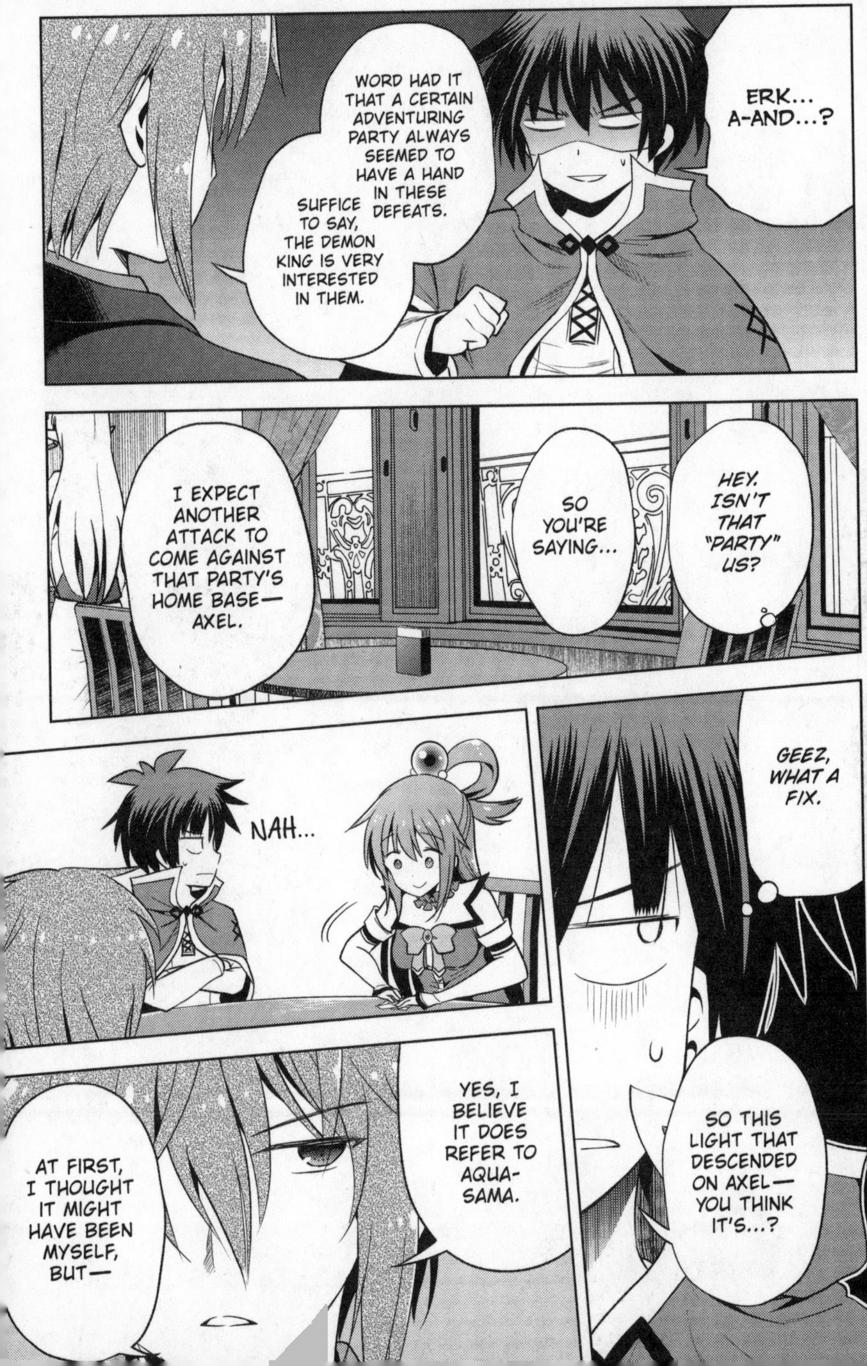

ERK... A-AND...?
WORD HAD IT THAT A CERTAIN ADVENTURING PARTY ALWAYS SEEMED TO HAVE A HAND IN THESE DEFEATS.
SUFFICE TO SAY, THE DEMON KING IS VERY INTERESTED IN THEM.
HEY. ISN'T THAT "PARTY" US?
SO YOU'RE SAYING...
I EXPECT ANOTHER ATTACK TO COME AGAINST THAT PARTY'S HOME BASE— AXEL.
GEEZ, WHAT A FIX.
NAH...
SO THIS LIGHT THAT DESCENDED ON AXEL— YOU THINK IT'S...?
YES, I BELIEVE IT DOES REFER TO AQUA-SAMA.
AT FIRST, I THOUGHT IT MIGHT HAVE BEEN MYSELF, BUT—

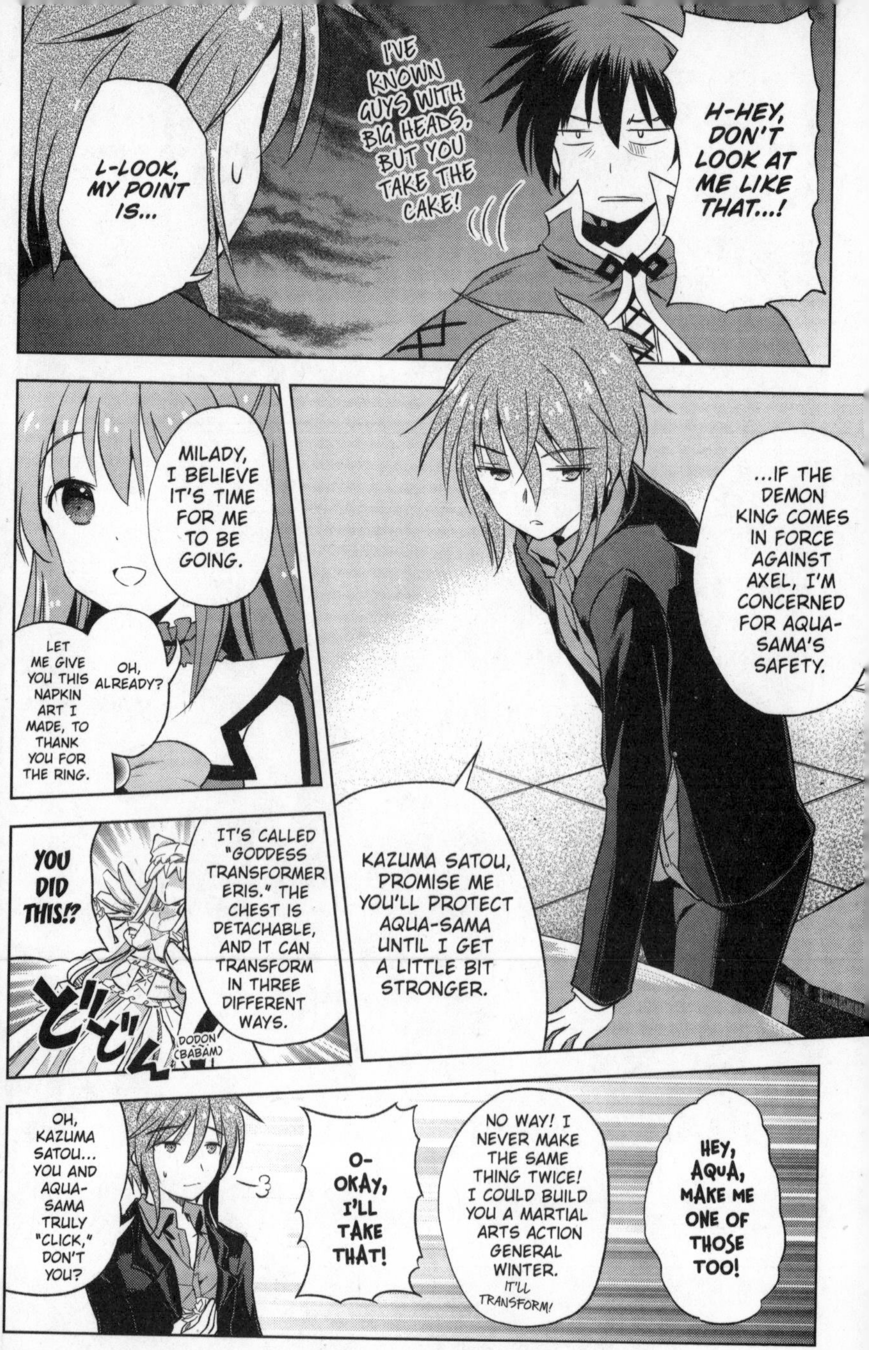
H-HEY, DON'T LOOK AT ME LIKE THAT...!
I'VE KNOWN GUYS WITH BIG HEADS, BUT YOU TAKE THE CAKE!
L-LOOK, MY POINT IS...
...IF THE DEMON KING COMES IN FORCE AGAINST AXEL, I'M CONCERNED FOR AQUA-SAMA'S SAFETY.
KAZUMA SATOU, PROMISE ME YOU'LL PROTECT AQUA-SAMA UNTIL I GET A LITTLE BIT STRONGER.
MILADY, I BELIEVE IT'S TIME FOR ME TO BE GOING.
OH, ALREADY?
LET ME GIVE YOU THIS NAPKIN ART I MADE, TO THANK YOU FOR THE RING.
IT'S CALLED "GODDESS TRANSFORMER ERIS." THE CHEST IS DETACHABLE, AND IT CAN TRANSFORM IN THREE DIFFERENT WAYS.
YOU DID THIS!?
DODON (BABAM)
HEY, AQUA, MAKE ME ONE OF THOSE TOO!
NO WAY! I NEVER MAKE THE SAME THING TWICE! I COULD BUILD YOU A MARTIAL ARTS ACTION GENERAL WINTER.
IT'LL TRANSFORM!
O-OKAY, I'LL TAKE THAT!
OH, KAZUMA SATOU... YOU AND AQUA-SAMA TRULY "CLICK," DON'T YOU?

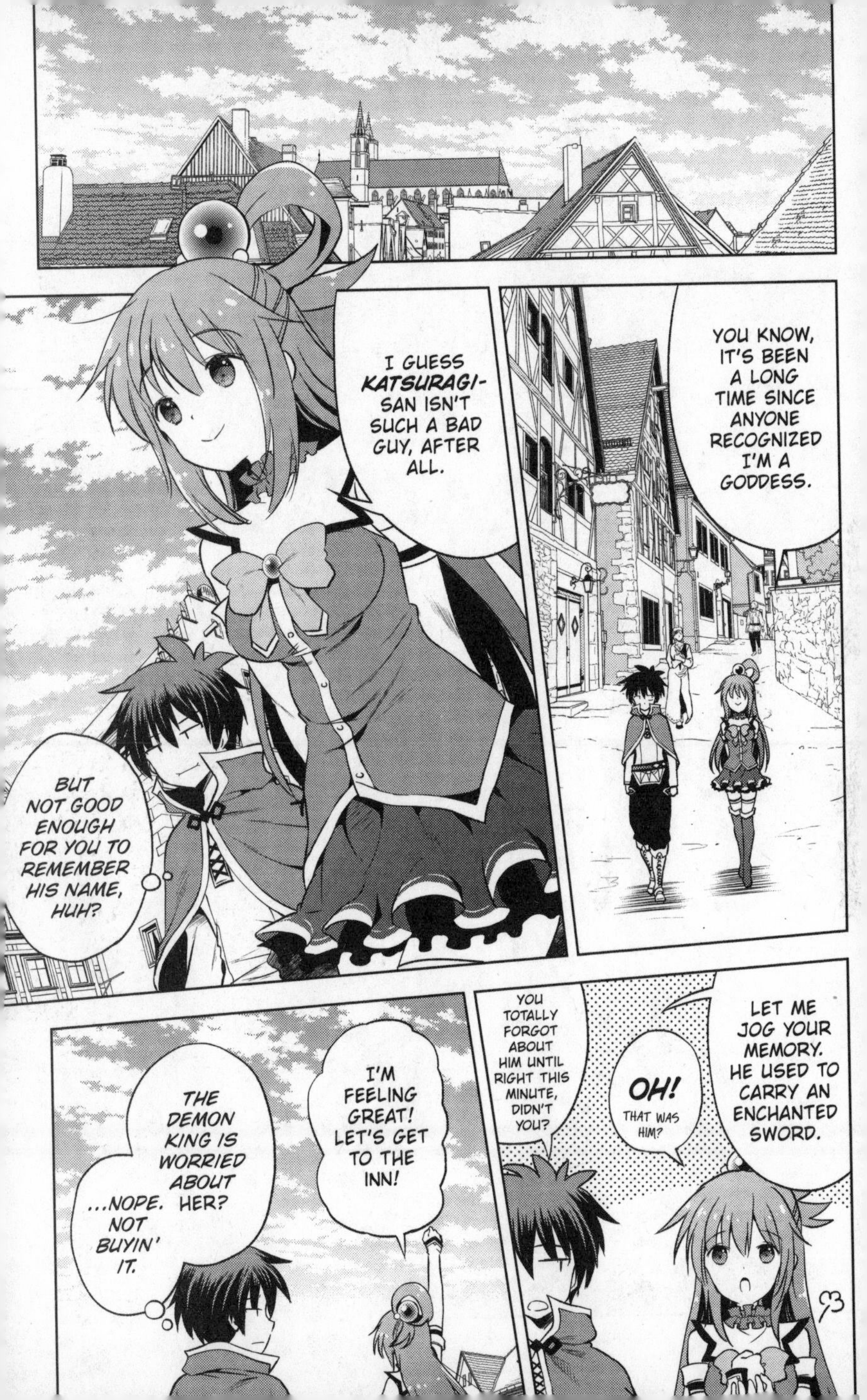
YOU KNOW, IT'S BEEN A LONG TIME SINCE ANYONE RECOGNIZED I'M A GODDESS.
I GUESS KATSURAGI-SAN ISN'T SUCH A BAD GUY, AFTER ALL.
BUT NOT GOOD ENOUGH FOR YOU TO REMEMBER HIS NAME, HUH?
LET ME JOG YOUR MEMORY. HE USED TO CARRY AN ENCHANTED SWORD.
OH! THAT WAS HIM?
YOU TOTALLY FORGOT ABOUT HIM UNTIL RIGHT THIS MINUTE, DIDN'T YOU?
I'M FEELING GREAT! LET'S GET TO THE INN!
THE DEMON KING IS WORRIED ABOUT HER?
...NOPE. NOT BUYIN' IT.

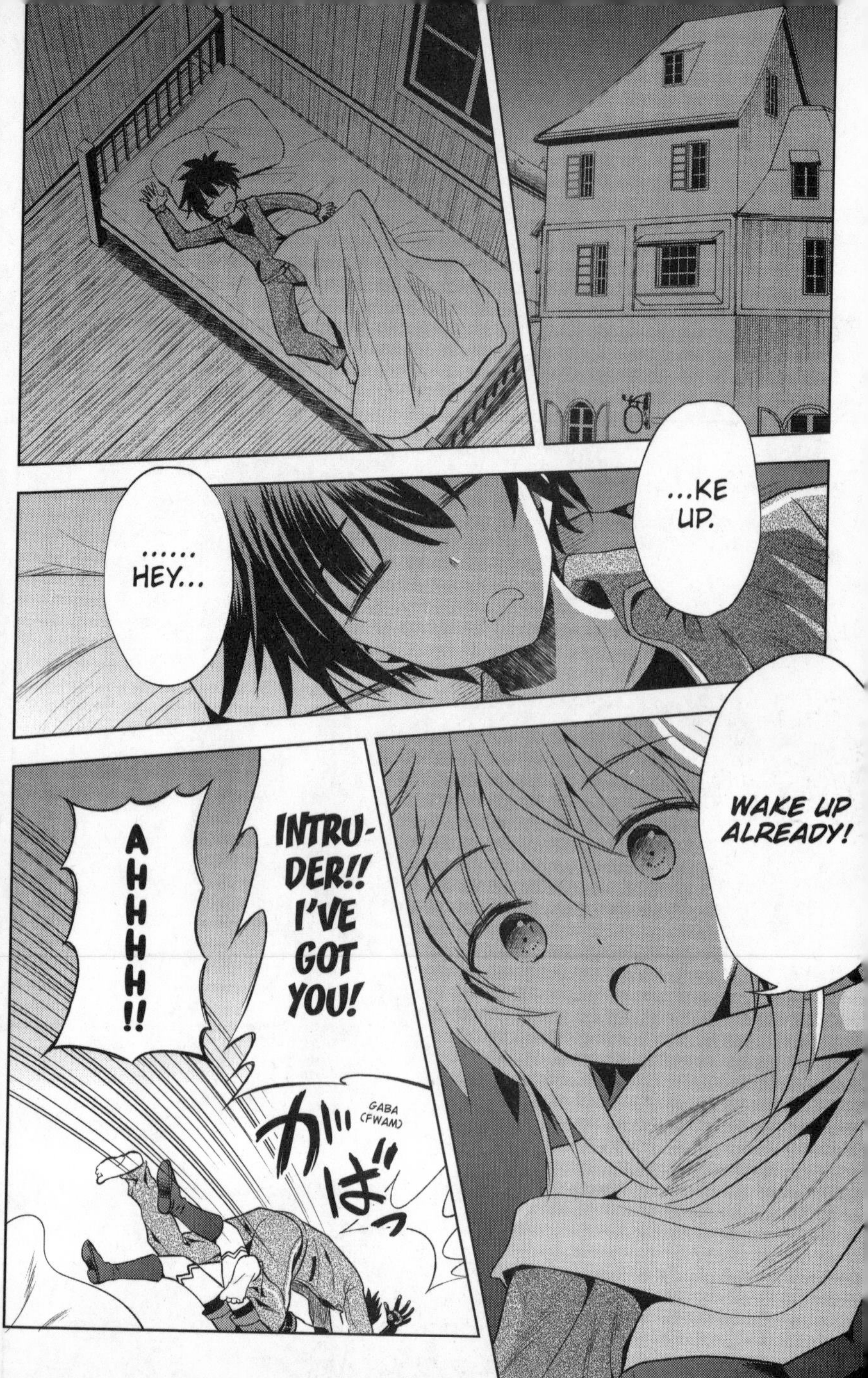
...KE UP.
...... HEY...
WAKE UP ALREADY!
INTRUDER!! I'VE GOT YOU!
AHHHHH!!
がばっ
GABA (FWAM)

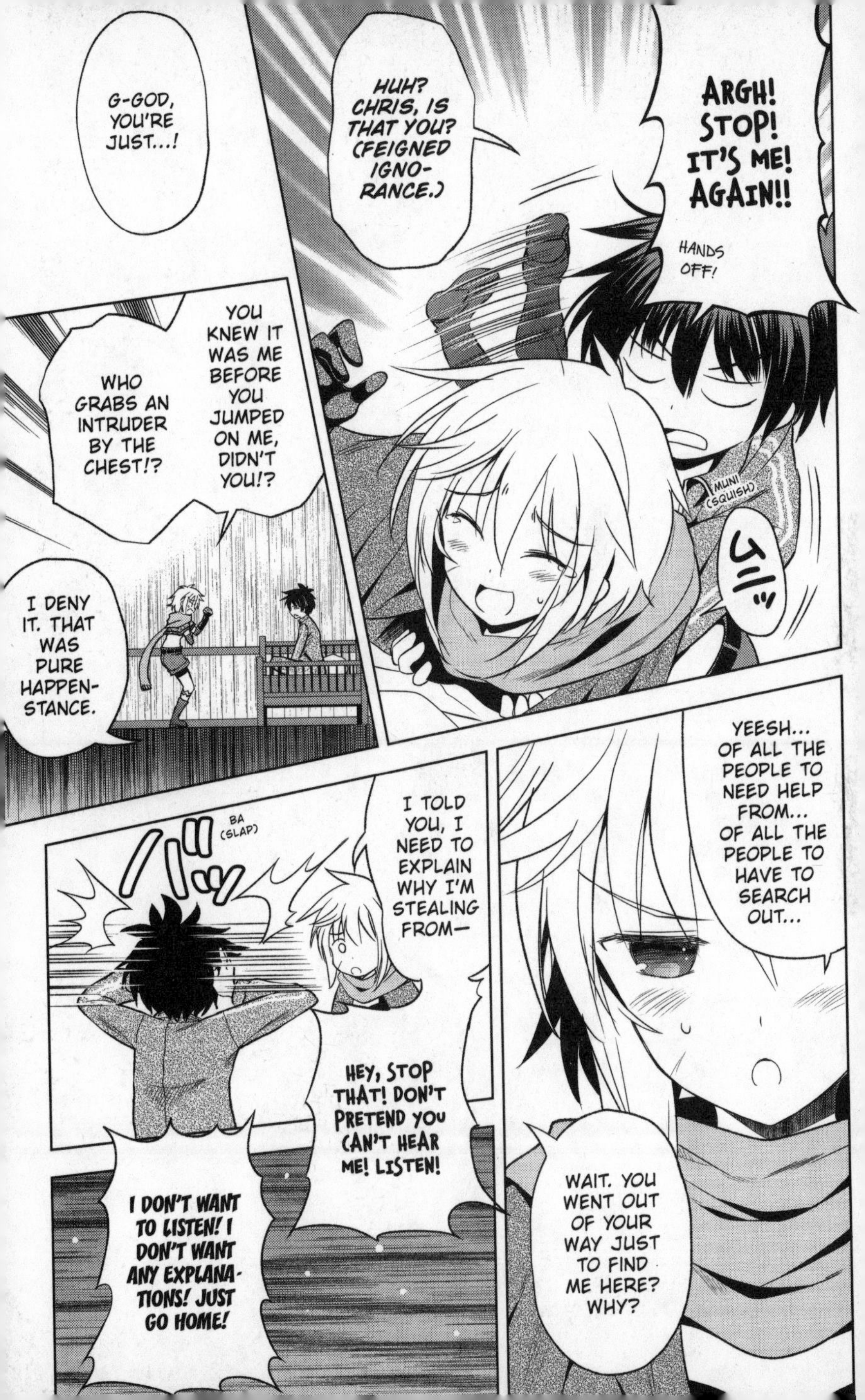
ARGH! STOP! IT'S ME! AGAIN!!
HUH? CHRIS, IS THAT YOU? (FEIGNED IGNO-RANCE.)
HANDS OFF!
MUNI (SQUISH)
ムニッ
G-GOD, YOU'RE JUST...!
YOU KNEW IT WAS ME BEFORE YOU JUMPED ON ME, DIDN'T YOU!?
WHO GRABS AN INTRUDER BY THE CHEST!?
I DENY IT. THAT WAS PURE HAPPEN-STANCE.
YEESH... OF ALL THE PEOPLE TO NEED HELP FROM... OF ALL THE PEOPLE TO HAVE TO SEARCH OUT...
WAIT. YOU WENT OUT OF YOUR WAY JUST TO FIND ME HERE? WHY?
I TOLD YOU, I NEED TO EXPLAIN WHY I'M STEALING FROM—
BA (SLAP)
バッ
HEY, STOP THAT! DON'T PRETEND YOU CAN'T HEAR ME! LISTEN!
I DON'T WANT TO LISTEN! I DON'T WANT ANY EXPLANA-TIONS! JUST GO HOME!

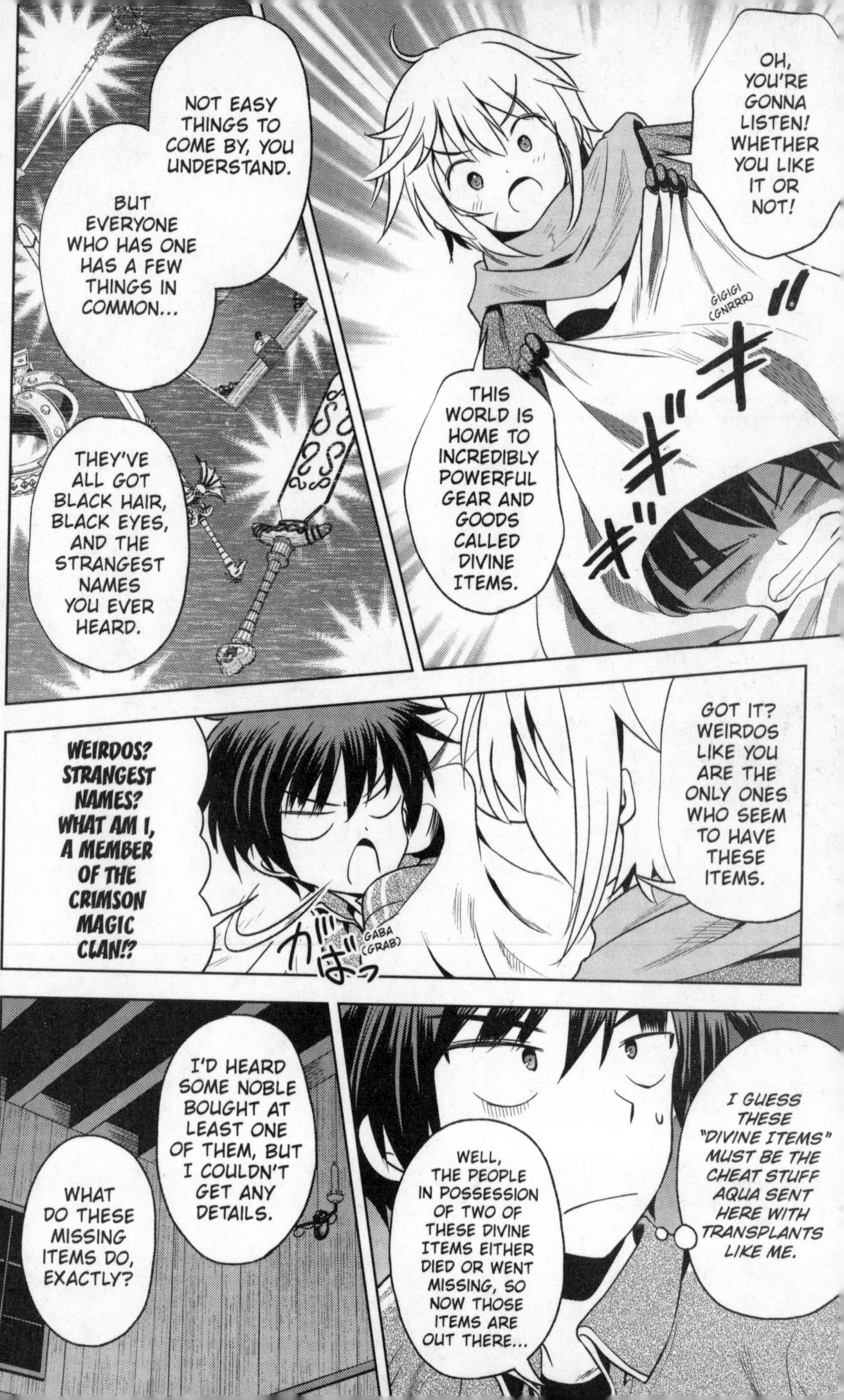
OH, YOU'RE GONNA LISTEN! WHETHER YOU LIKE IT OR NOT!
GIGIGI (GNRRR)
THIS WORLD IS HOME TO INCREDIBLY POWERFUL GEAR AND GOODS CALLED DIVINE ITEMS.
NOT EASY THINGS TO COME BY, YOU UNDERSTAND.
BUT EVERYONE WHO HAS ONE HAS A FEW THINGS IN COMMON...
THEY'VE ALL GOT BLACK HAIR, BLACK EYES, AND THE STRANGEST NAMES YOU EVER HEARD.
GOT IT? WEIRDOS LIKE YOU ARE THE ONLY ONES WHO SEEM TO HAVE THESE ITEMS.
GABA (GRAB)
WEIRDOS? STRANGEST NAMES? WHAT AM I, A MEMBER OF THE CRIMSON MAGIC CLAN!?
I GUESS THESE "DIVINE ITEMS" MUST BE THE CHEAT STUFF AQUA SENT HERE WITH TRANSPLANTS LIKE ME.
WELL, THE PEOPLE IN POSSESSION OF TWO OF THESE DIVINE ITEMS EITHER DIED OR WENT MISSING, SO NOW THOSE ITEMS ARE OUT THERE...
I'D HEARD SOME NOBLE BOUGHT AT LEAST ONE OF THEM, BUT I COULDN'T GET ANY DETAILS.
WHAT DO THESE MISSING ITEMS DO, EXACTLY?

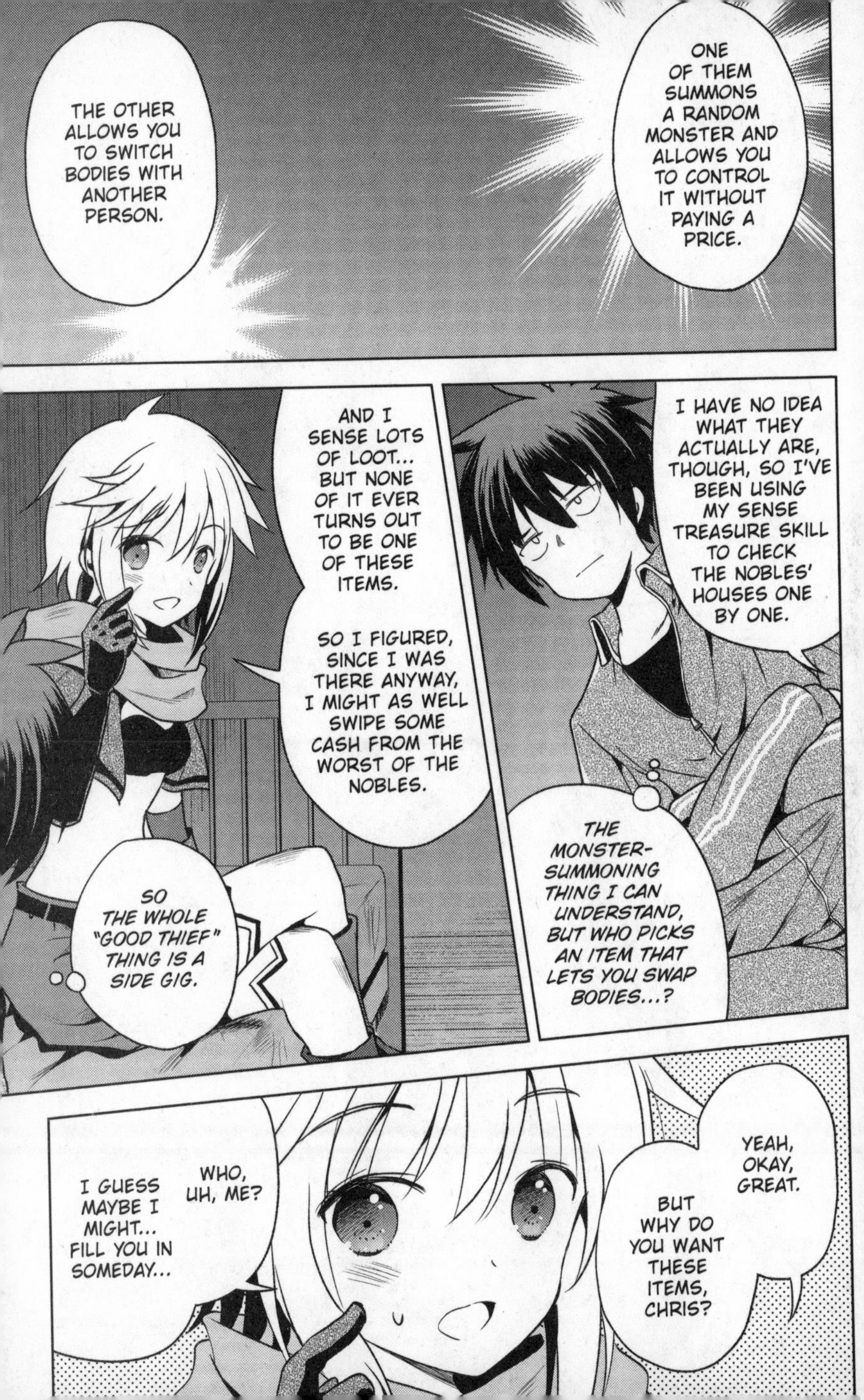
ONE OF THEM SUMMONS A RANDOM MONSTER AND ALLOWS YOU TO CONTROL IT WITHOUT PAYING A PRICE.
THE OTHER ALLOWS YOU TO SWITCH BODIES WITH ANOTHER PERSON.
I HAVE NO IDEA WHAT THEY ACTUALLY ARE, THOUGH, SO I'VE BEEN USING MY SENSE TREASURE SKILL TO CHECK THE NOBLES' HOUSES ONE BY ONE.
THE MONSTER-SUMMONING THING I CAN UNDERSTAND, BUT WHO PICKS AN ITEM THAT LETS YOU SWAP BODIES...?
AND I SENSE LOTS OF LOOT... BUT NONE OF IT EVER TURNS OUT TO BE ONE OF THESE ITEMS.
SO I FIGURED, SINCE I WAS THERE ANYWAY, I MIGHT AS WELL SWIPE SOME CASH FROM THE WORST OF THE NOBLES.
SO THE WHOLE "GOOD THIEF" THING IS A SIDE GIG.
YEAH, OKAY, GREAT.
BUT WHY DO YOU WANT THESE ITEMS, CHRIS?
WHO, UH, ME?
I GUESS MAYBE I MIGHT... FILL YOU IN SOMEDAY...

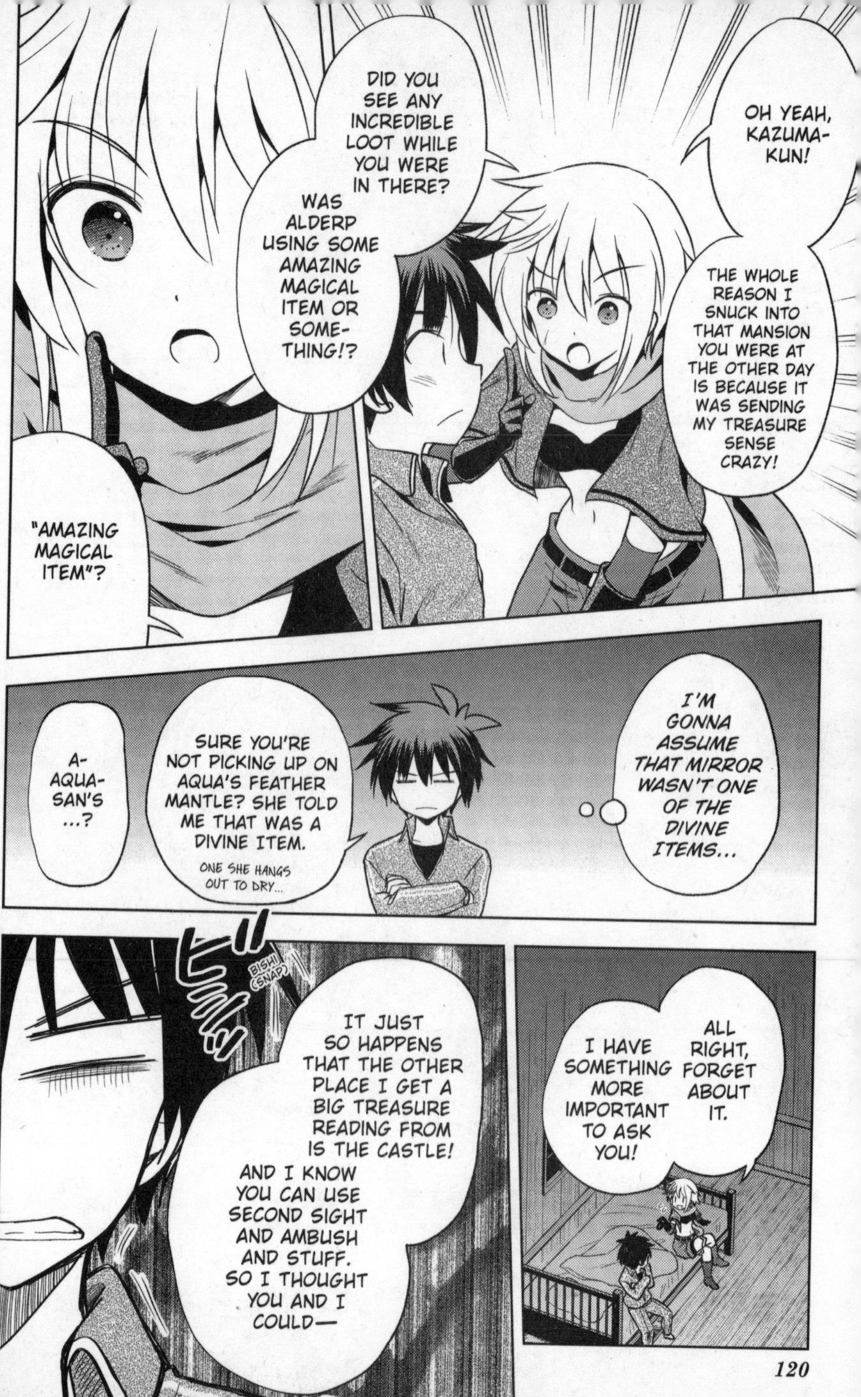
OH YEAH, KAZUMA-KUN!
THE WHOLE REASON I SNUCK INTO THAT MANSION YOU WERE AT THE OTHER DAY IS BECAUSE IT WAS SENDING MY TREASURE SENSE CRAZY!
DID YOU SEE ANY INCREDIBLE LOOT WHILE YOU WERE IN THERE?
WAS ALDERP USING SOME AMAZING MAGICAL ITEM OR SOME-THING!?
"AMAZING MAGICAL ITEM"?
I'M GONNA ASSUME THAT MIRROR WASN'T ONE OF THE DIVINE ITEMS...
SURE YOU'RE NOT PICKING UP ON AQUA'S FEATHER MANTLE? SHE TOLD ME THAT WAS A DIVINE ITEM.
ONE SHE HANGS OUT TO DRY...
A-AQUA-SAN'S ...?
ALL RIGHT, FORGET ABOUT IT.
I HAVE SOMETHING MORE IMPORTANT TO ASK YOU!
BISHI (SNAP)
IT JUST SO HAPPENS THAT THE OTHER PLACE I GET A BIG TREASURE READING FROM IS THE CASTLE!
AND I KNOW YOU CAN USE SECOND SIGHT AND AMBUSH AND STUFF. SO I THOUGHT YOU AND I COULD—

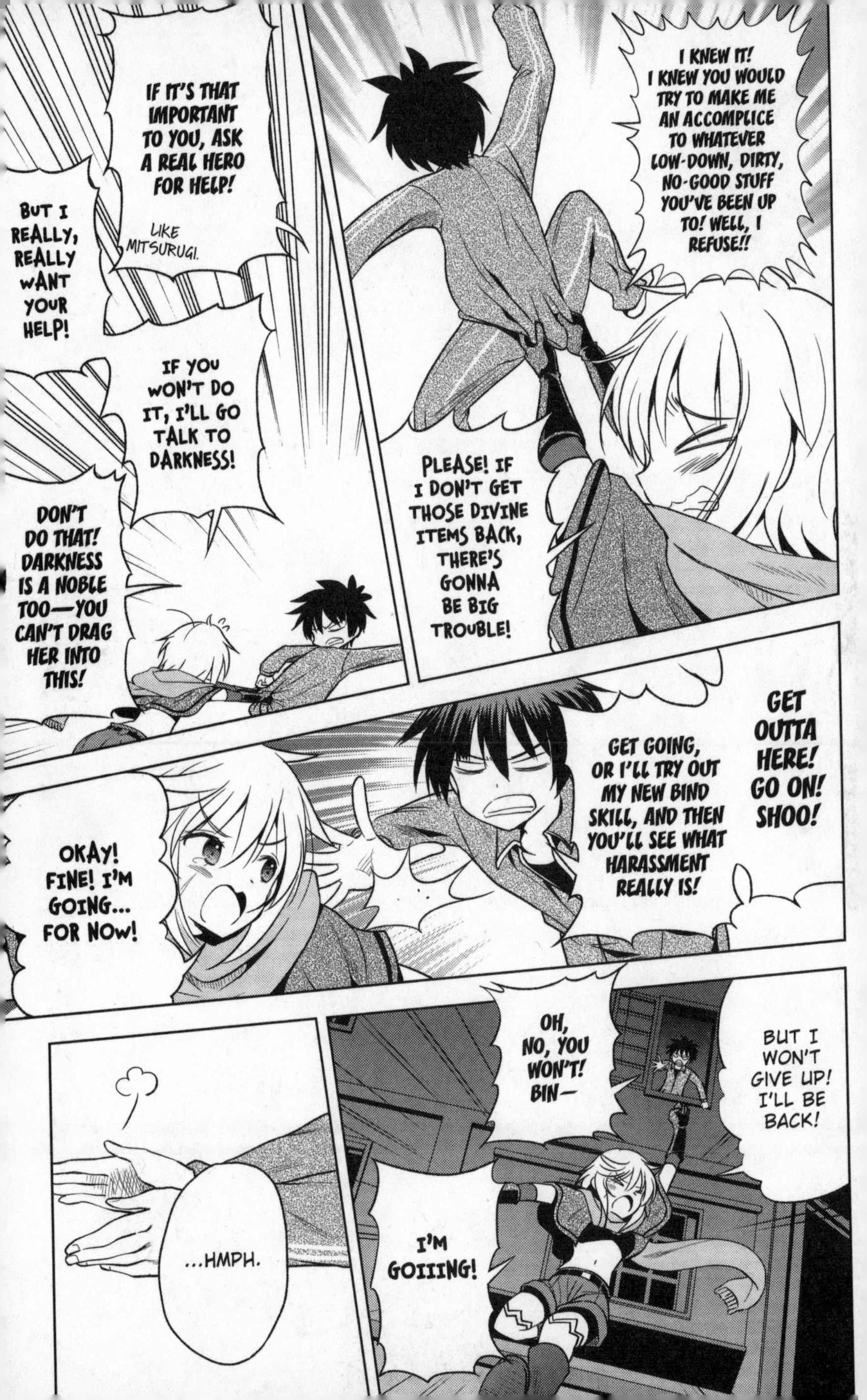
I KNEW IT! I KNEW YOU WOULD TRY TO MAKE ME AN ACCOMPLICE TO WHATEVER LOW-DOWN, DIRTY, NO-GOOD STUFF YOU'VE BEEN UP TO! WELL, I REFUSE!!
PLEASE! IF I DON'T GET THOSE DIVINE ITEMS BACK, THERE'S GONNA BE BIG TROUBLE!
IF IT'S THAT IMPORTANT TO YOU, ASK A REAL HERO FOR HELP!
LIKE MITSURUGI.
BUT I REALLY, REALLY WANT YOUR HELP!
IF YOU WON'T DO IT, I'LL GO TALK TO DARKNESS!
DON'T DO THAT! DARKNESS IS A NOBLE TOO—YOU CAN'T DRAG HER INTO THIS!
GET OUTTA HERE! GO ON! SHOO!
GET GOING, OR I'LL TRY OUT MY NEW BIND SKILL, AND THEN YOU'LL SEE WHAT HARASSMENT REALLY IS!
OKAY! FINE! I'M GOING... FOR NOW!
BUT I WON'T GIVE UP! I'LL BE BACK!
OH, NO, YOU WON'T! BIN—
I'M GOIIING!
...HMPH.

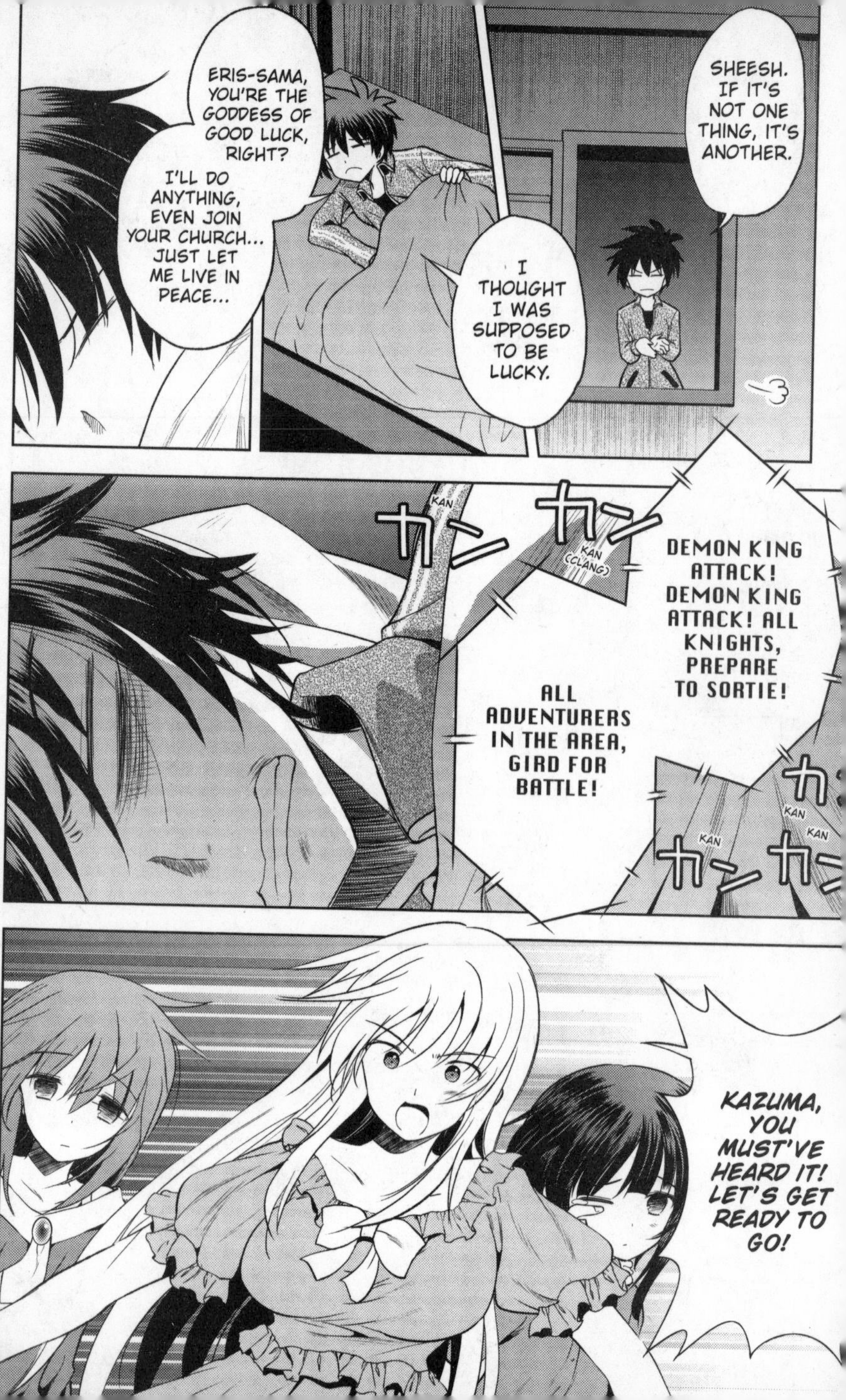
SHEESH. IF IT'S NOT ONE THING, IT'S ANOTHER.
I THOUGHT I WAS SUPPOSED TO BE LUCKY.
ERIS-SAMA, YOU'RE THE GODDESS OF GOOD LUCK, RIGHT?
I'LL DO ANYTHING, EVEN JOIN YOUR CHURCH... JUST LET ME LIVE IN PEACE...
DEMON KING ATTACK! DEMON KING ATTACK! ALL KNIGHTS, PREPARE TO SORTIE!
カン KAN
カン KAN (CLANG)
ALL ADVENTURERS IN THE AREA, GIRD FOR BATTLE!
KAN
KAN
カン KAN
カン
KAZUMA, YOU MUST'VE HEARD IT! LET'S GET READY TO GO!

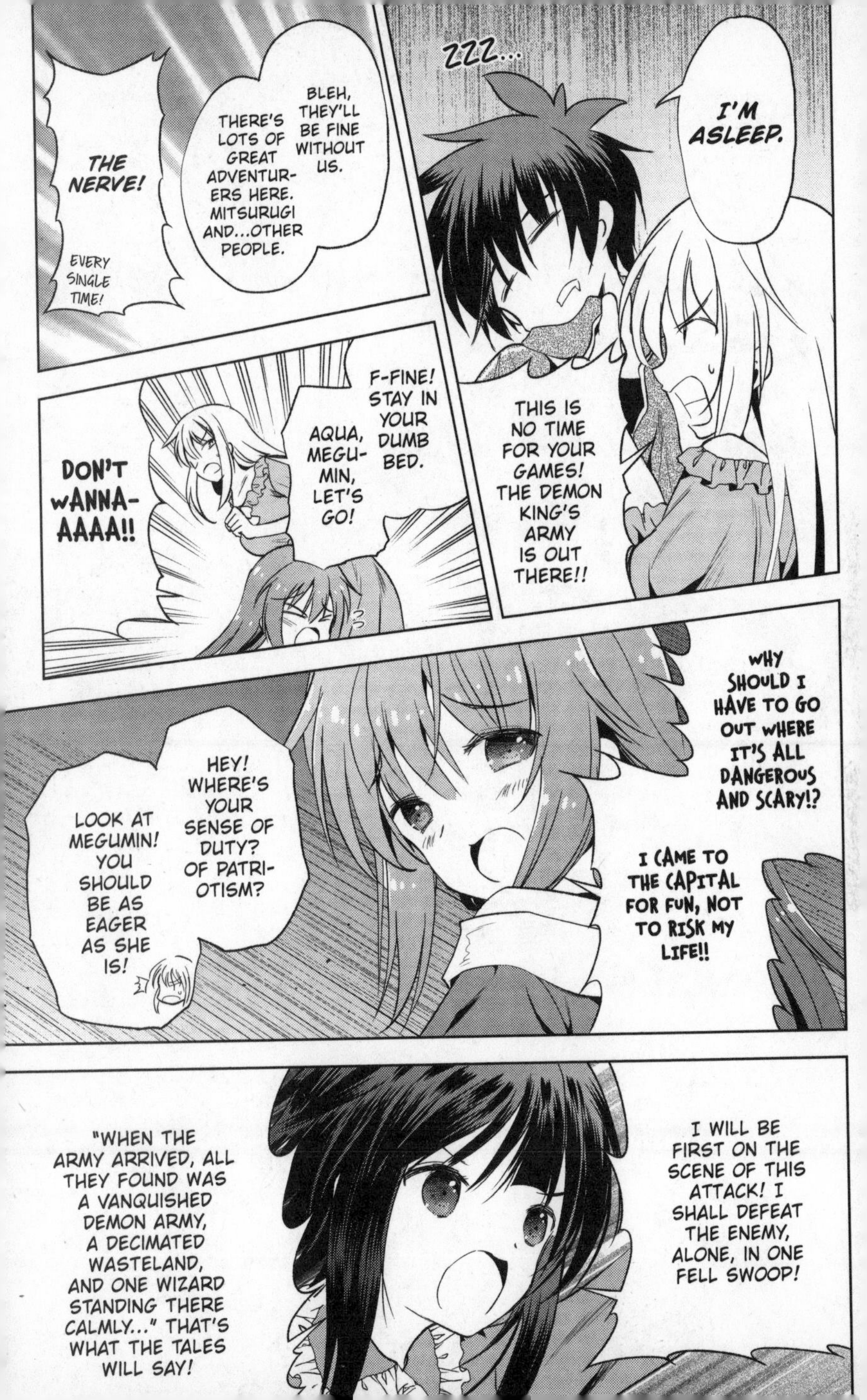
ZZZ...
I'M ASLEEP.
THIS IS NO TIME FOR YOUR GAMES! THE DEMON KING'S ARMY IS OUT THERE!!
BLEH, THEY'LL BE FINE WITHOUT US.
THERE'S LOTS OF GREAT ADVENTURERS HERE. MITSURUGI AND...OTHER PEOPLE.
THE NERVE!
EVERY SINGLE TIME!
F-FINE! STAY IN YOUR DUMB BED.
AQUA, MEGUMIN, LET'S GO!
DON'T wANNA-AAAA!!
WHY SHOULD I HAVE TO GO OUT WHERE IT'S ALL DANGEROUS AND SCARY!?
I CAME TO THE CAPITAL FOR FUN, NOT TO RISK MY LIFE!!
HEY! WHERE'S YOUR SENSE OF DUTY? OF PATRIOTISM?
LOOK AT MEGUMIN! YOU SHOULD BE AS EAGER AS SHE IS!
I WILL BE FIRST ON THE SCENE OF THIS ATTACK! I SHALL DEFEAT THE ENEMY, ALONE, IN ONE FELL SWOOP!
"WHEN THE ARMY ARRIVED, ALL THEY FOUND WAS A VANQUISHED DEMON ARMY, A DECIMATED WASTELAND, AND ONE WIZARD STANDING THERE CALMLY..." THAT'S WHAT THE TALES WILL SAY!

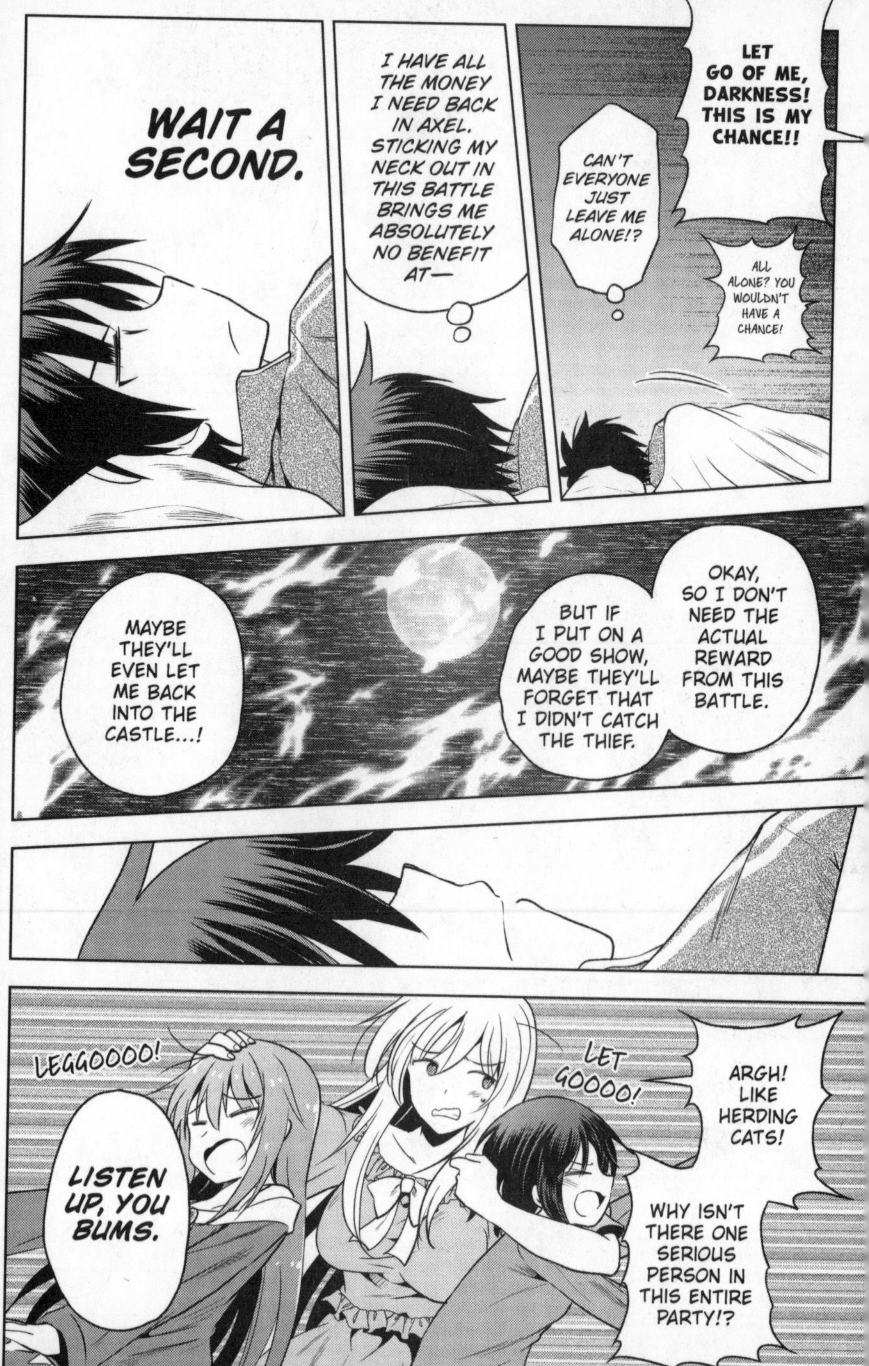
LET GO OF ME, DARKNESS! THIS IS MY CHANCE!!
CAN'T EVERYONE JUST LEAVE ME ALONE!?
ALL ALONE? YOU WOULDN'T HAVE A CHANCE!
I HAVE ALL THE MONEY I NEED BACK IN AXEL. STICKING MY NECK OUT IN THIS BATTLE BRINGS ME ABSOLUTELY NO BENEFIT AT—
WAIT A SECOND.
OKAY, SO I DON'T NEED THE ACTUAL REWARD FROM THIS BATTLE.
BUT IF I PUT ON A GOOD SHOW, MAYBE THEY'LL FORGET THAT I DIDN'T CATCH THE THIEF.
MAYBE THEY'LL EVEN LET ME BACK INTO THE CASTLE...!
ARGH! LIKE HERDING CATS!
LET GOOOO!
WHY ISN'T THERE ONE SERIOUS PERSON IN THIS ENTIRE PARTY!?
LEGGOOOO!
LISTEN UP, YOU BUMS.

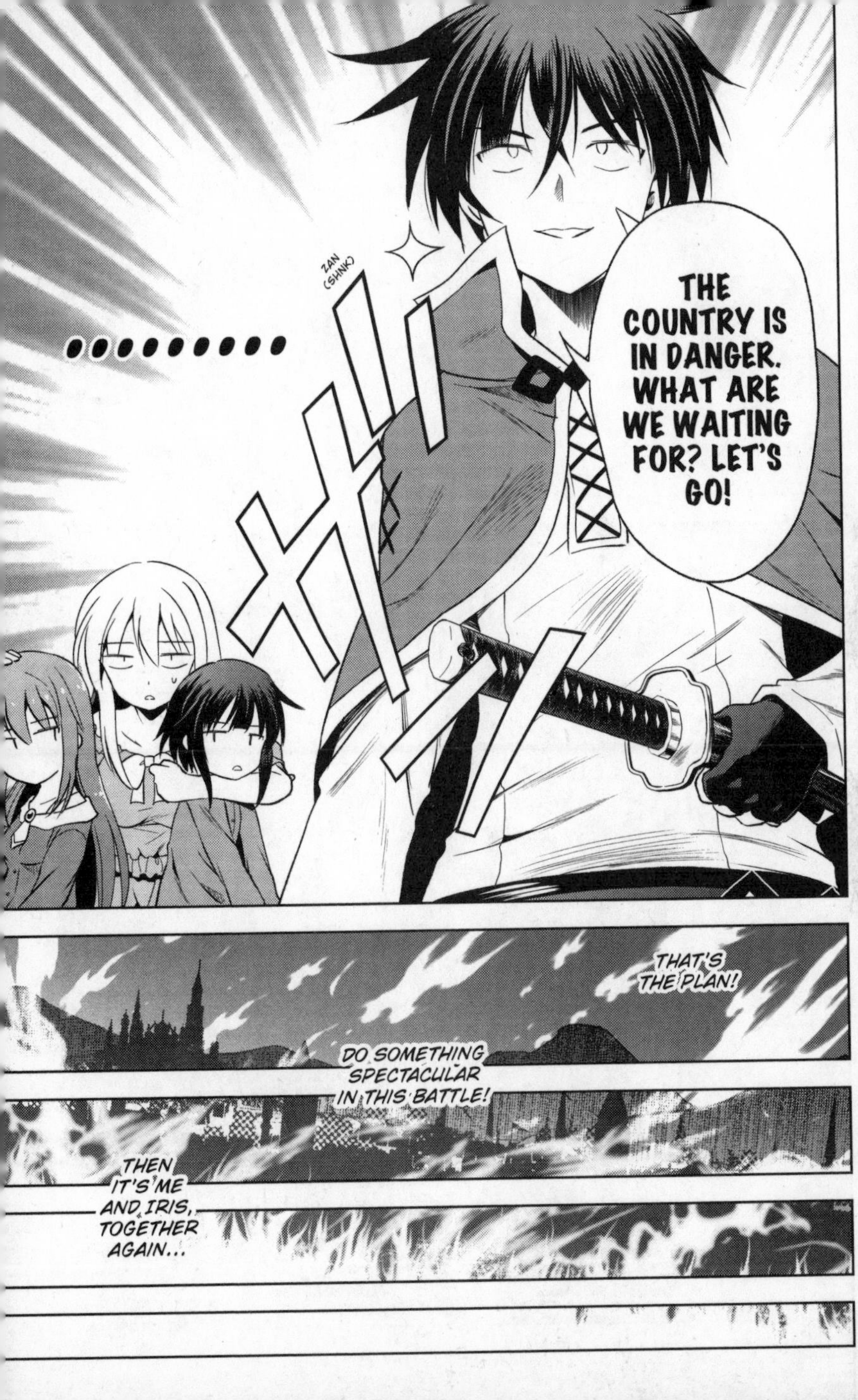
THE COUNTRY IS IN DANGER. WHAT ARE WE WAITING FOR? LET'S GO!
ZAN (SHNK)
....
THAT'S THE PLAN!
DO SOMETHING SPECTACULAR IN THIS BATTLE!
THEN IT'S ME AND IRIS, TOGETHER AGAIN...

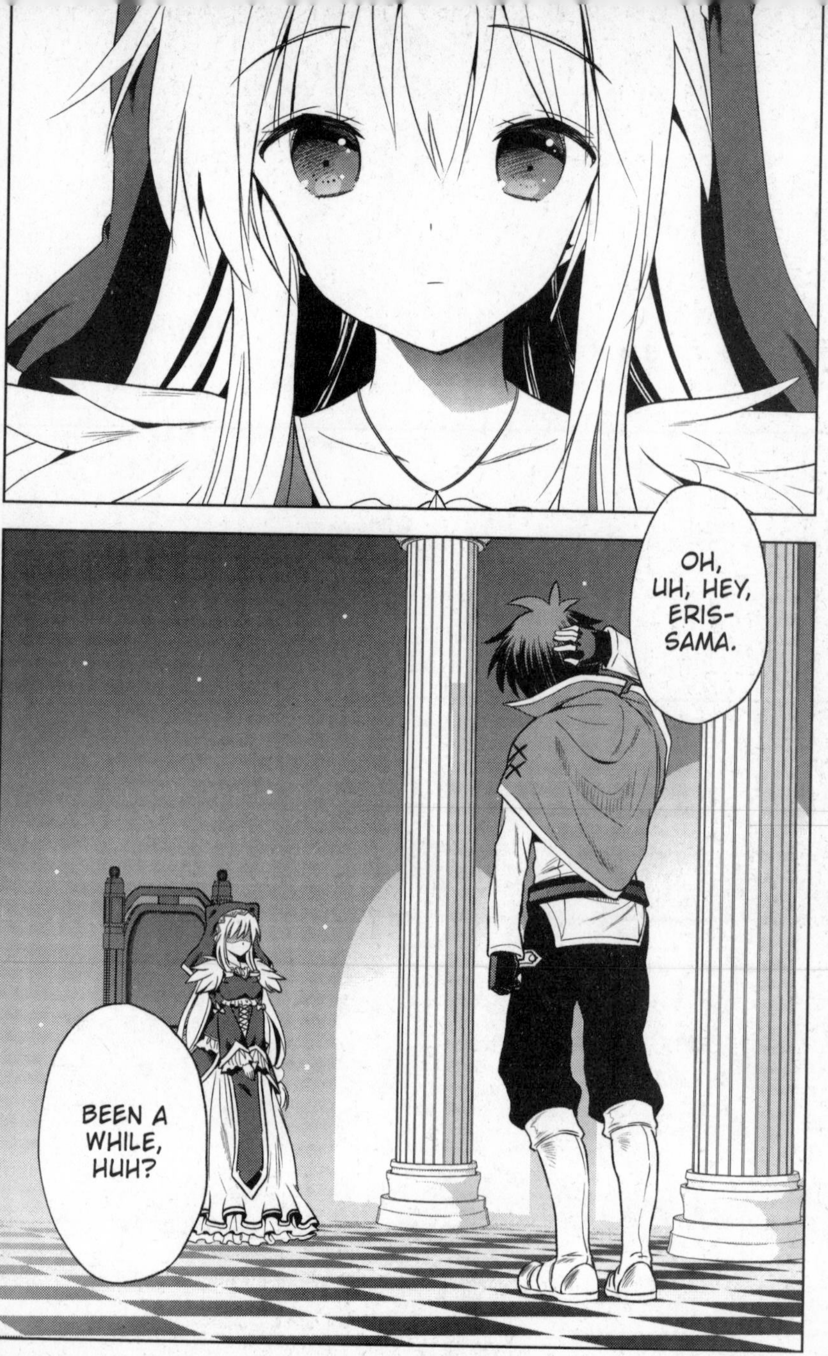
OH, UH, HEY, ERIS-SAMA.
BEEN A WHILE, HUH?

GOD'S
BLESSING
ON THIS
WONDERFUL
WORLD!

10

10

GOD'S
BLESSING
ON THIS
WONDERFUL
WORLD!

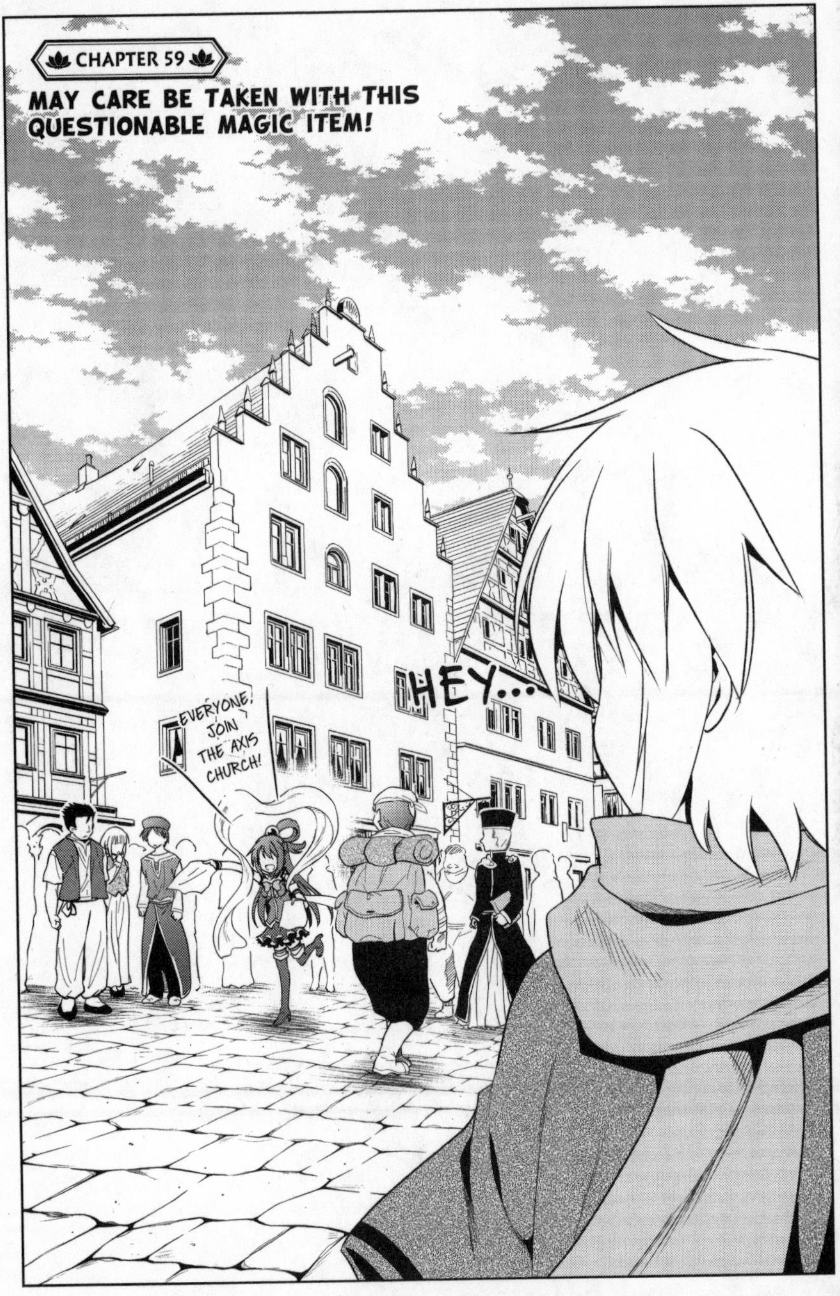
CHAPTER 59
MAY CARE BE TAKEN WITH THIS QUESTIONABLE MAGIC ITEM!
HEY...
EVERYONE! JOIN THE AXIS CHURCH!

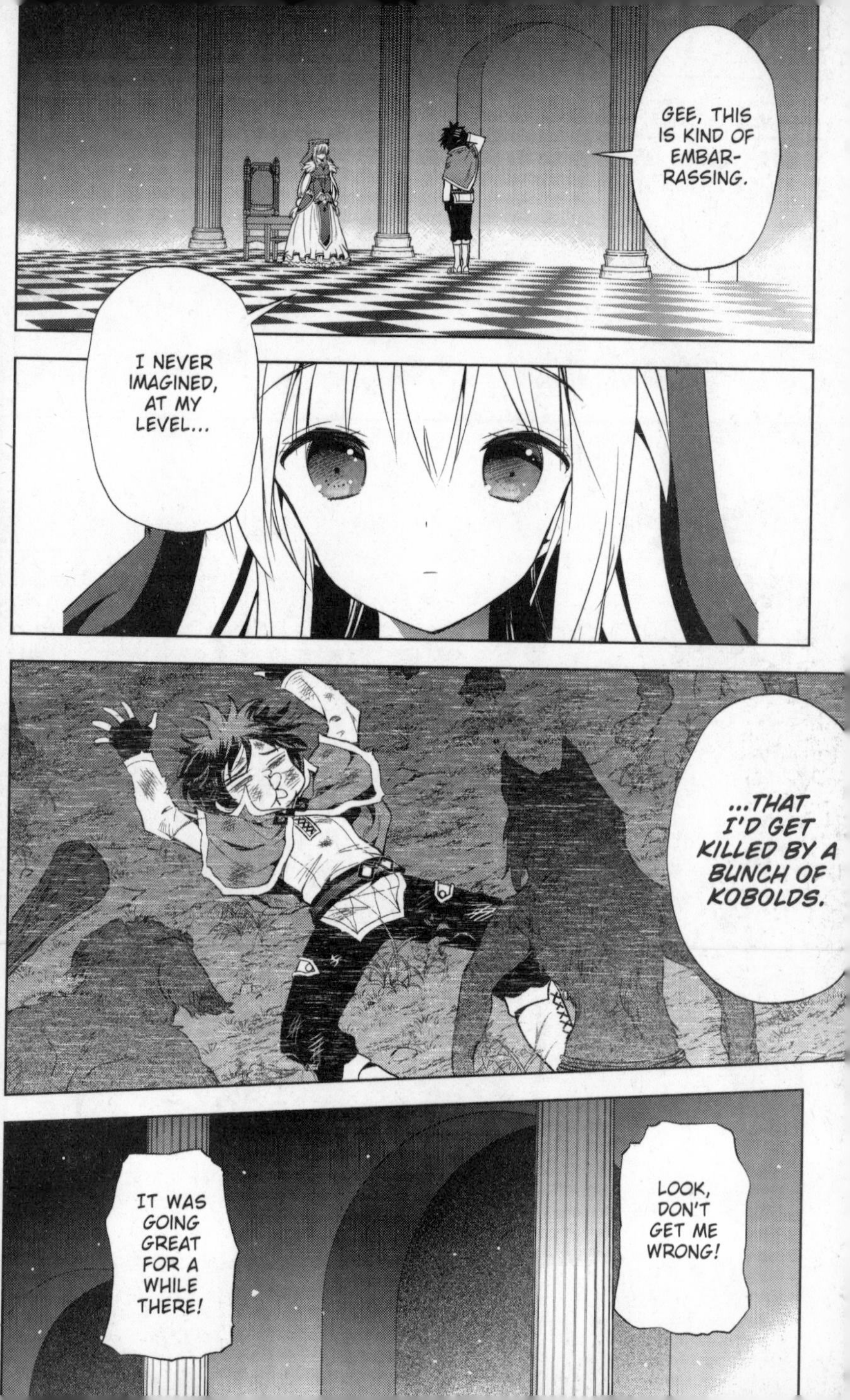
GEE, THIS IS KIND OF EMBARRASSING.
I NEVER IMAGINED, AT MY LEVEL...
...THAT I'D GET KILLED BY A BUNCH OF KOBOLDS.
LOOK, DON'T GET ME WRONG!
IT WAS GOING GREAT FOR A WHILE THERE!

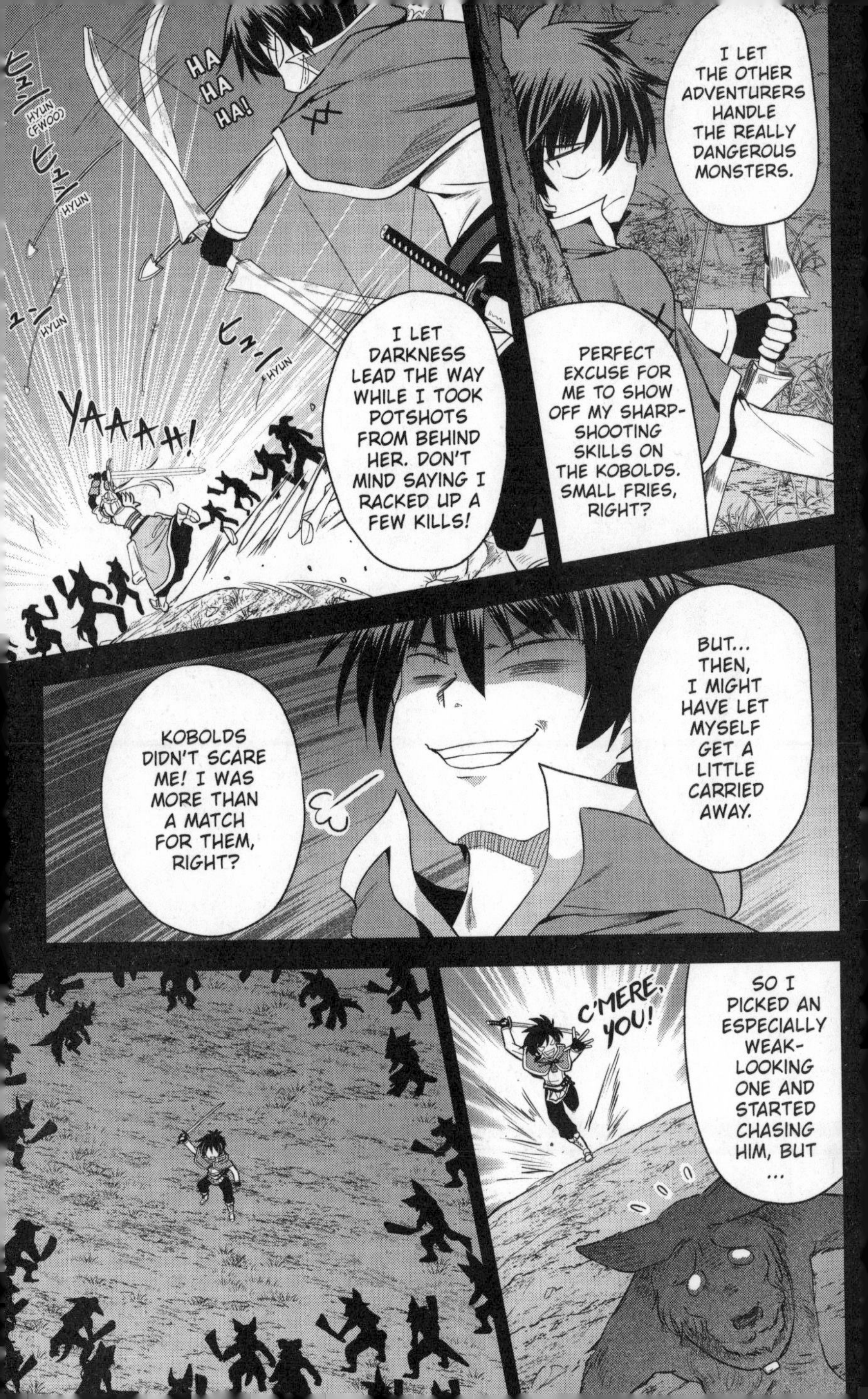
I LET THE OTHER ADVENTURERS HANDLE THE REALLY DANGEROUS MONSTERS.
PERFECT EXCUSE FOR ME TO SHOW OFF MY SHARP-SHOOTING SKILLS ON THE KOBOLDS. SMALL FRIES, RIGHT?
HA HA HA!
HYUN (FWOO)
HYUN
HYUN
HYUN
I LET DARKNESS LEAD THE WAY WHILE I TOOK POTSHOTS FROM BEHIND HER. DON'T MIND SAYING I RACKED UP A FEW KILLS!
YAAAAH!
BUT... THEN, I MIGHT HAVE LET MYSELF GET A LITTLE CARRIED AWAY.
KOBOLDS DIDN'T SCARE ME! I WAS MORE THAN A MATCH FOR THEM, RIGHT?
SO I PICKED AN ESPECIALLY WEAK-LOOKING ONE AND STARTED CHASING HIM, BUT ...
C'MERE, YOU!

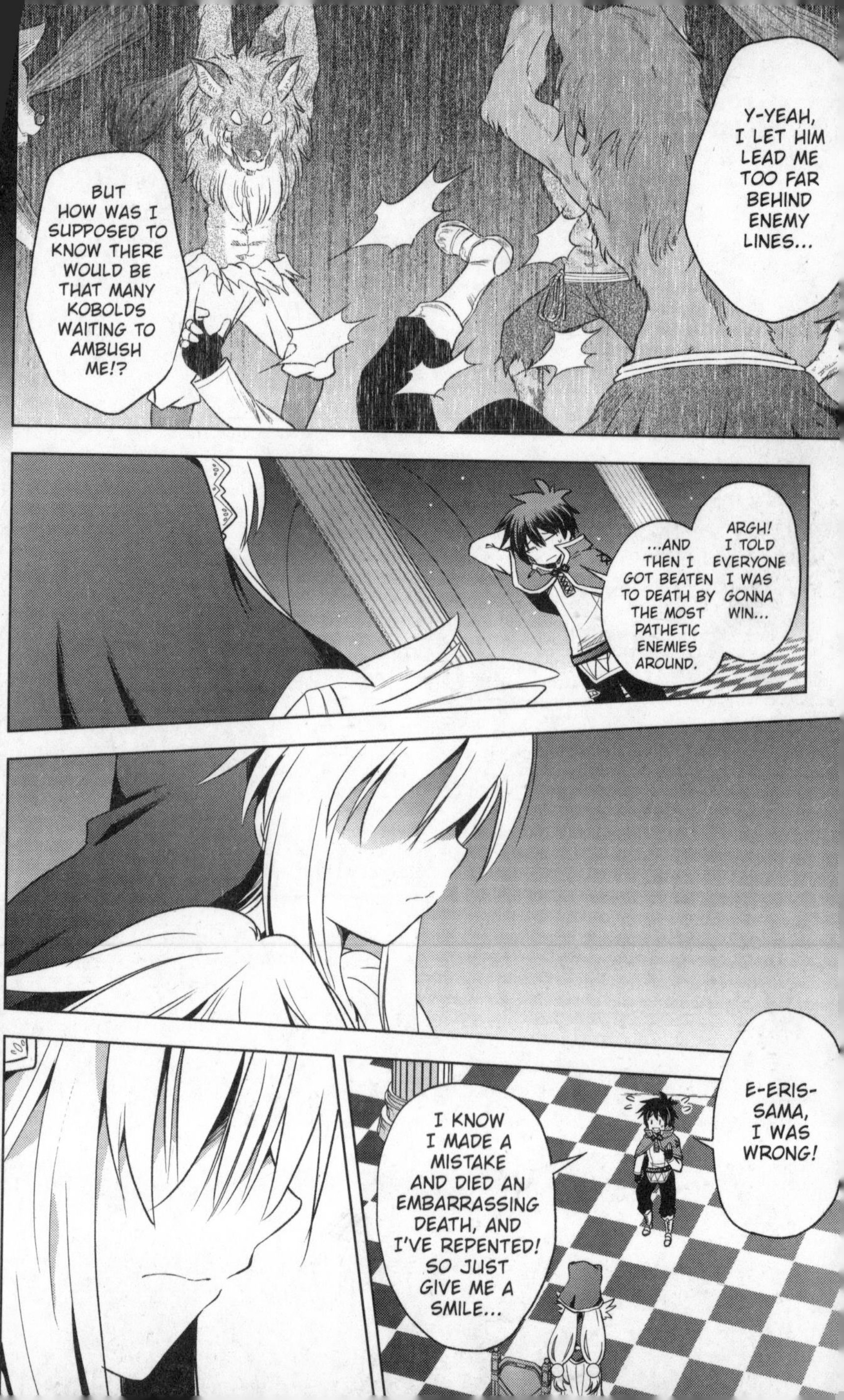
Y-YEAH, I LET HIM LEAD ME TOO FAR BEHIND ENEMY LINES...
BUT HOW WAS I SUPPOSED TO KNOW THERE WOULD BE THAT MANY KOBOLDS WAITING TO AMBUSH ME!?
ARGH! I TOLD EVERYONE I WAS GONNA WIN...
...AND THEN I GOT BEATEN TO DEATH BY THE MOST PATHETIC ENEMIES AROUND.
E-ERIS-SAMA, I WAS WRONG!
I KNOW I MADE A MISTAKE AND DIED AN EMBARRASSING DEATH, AND I'VE REPENTED! SO JUST GIVE ME A SMILE...

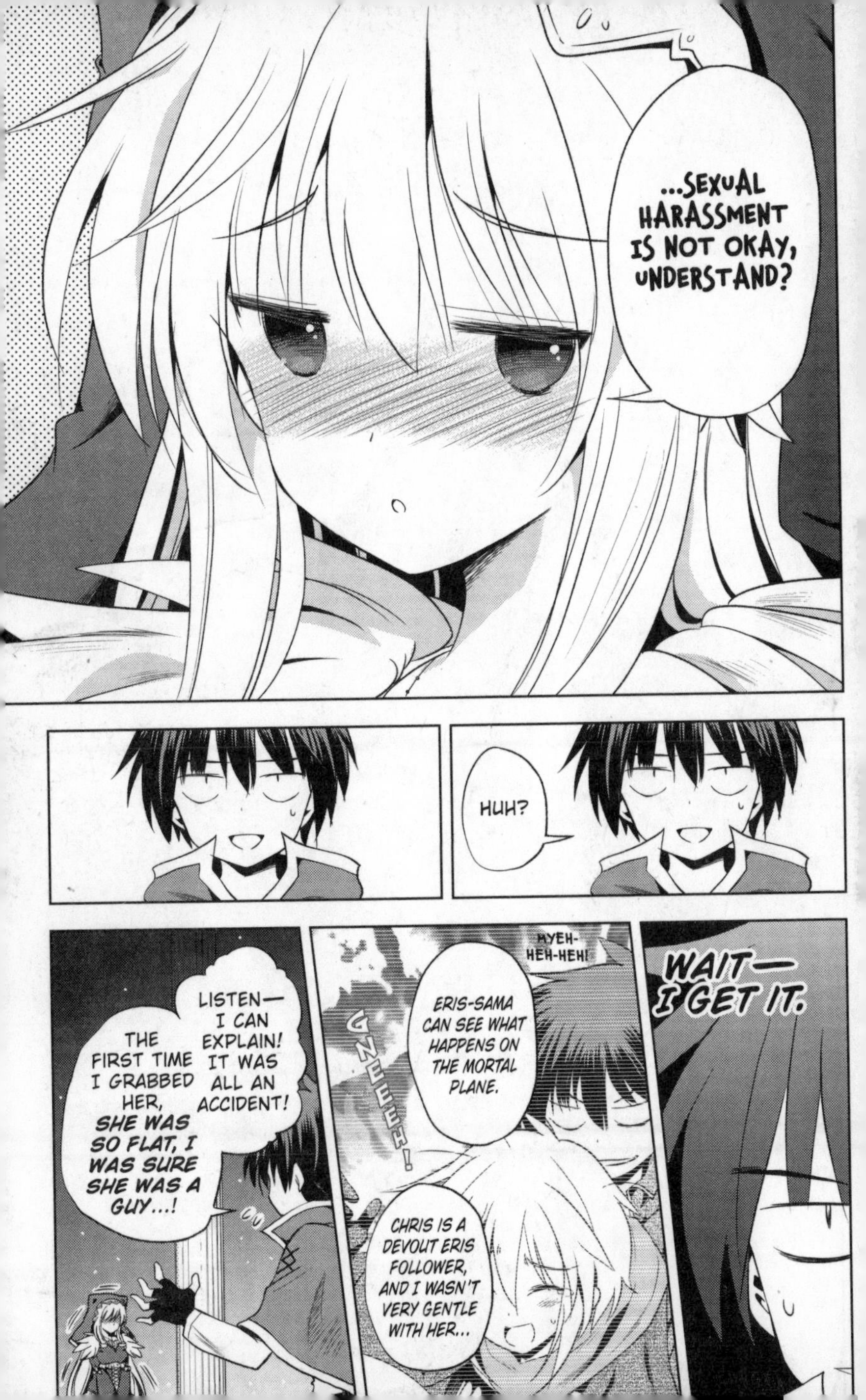
...SEXUAL HARASSMENT IS NOT OKAY, UNDERSTAND?
HUH?
WAIT— I GET IT.
MYEH-HEH-HEH!
ERIS-SAMA CAN SEE WHAT HAPPENS ON THE MORTAL PLANE.
GNEEEEH!
CHRIS IS A DEVOUT ERIS FOLLOWER, AND I WASN'T VERY GENTLE WITH HER...
LISTEN— I CAN EXPLAIN! IT WAS ALL AN ACCIDENT!
THE FIRST TIME I GRABBED HER, SHE WAS SO FLAT, I WAS SURE SHE WAS A GUY...!

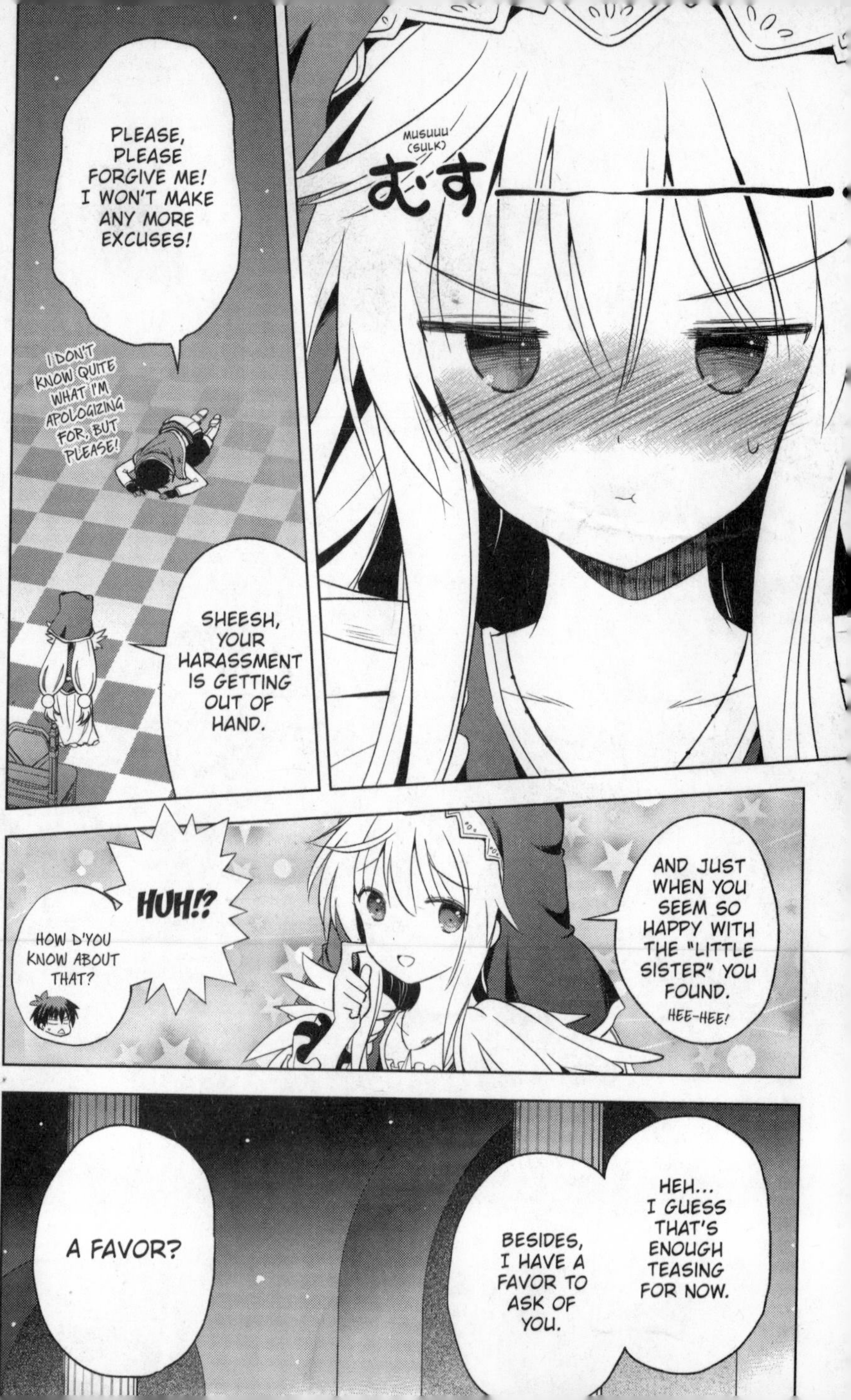
MUSUUU (SULK)
むす
PLEASE, PLEASE FORGIVE ME! I WON'T MAKE ANY MORE EXCUSES!
I DON'T KNOW QUITE WHAT I'M APOLOGIZING FOR, BUT PLEASE!
SHEESH, YOUR HARASSMENT IS GETTING OUT OF HAND.
AND JUST WHEN YOU SEEM SO HAPPY WITH THE "LITTLE SISTER" YOU FOUND.
HEE-HEE!
HUH!?
HOW D'YOU KNOW ABOUT THAT?
HEH... I GUESS THAT'S ENOUGH TEASING FOR NOW.
BESIDES, I HAVE A FAVOR TO ASK OF YOU.
A FAVOR?

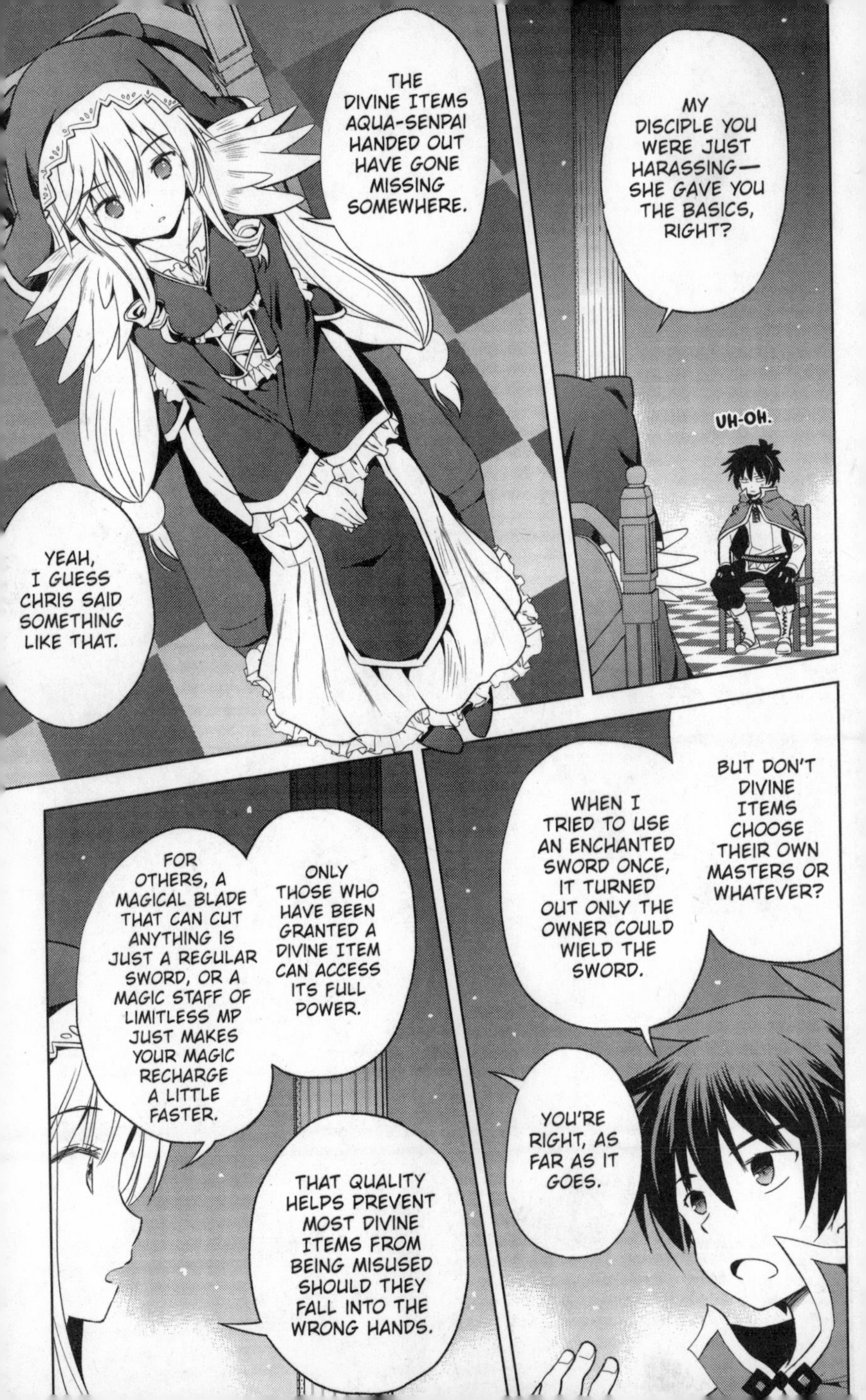
MY DISCIPLE YOU WERE JUST HARASSING— SHE GAVE YOU THE BASICS, RIGHT?
UH-OH.
THE DIVINE ITEMS AQUA-SENPAI HANDED OUT HAVE GONE MISSING SOMEWHERE.
YEAH, I GUESS CHRIS SAID SOMETHING LIKE THAT.
BUT DON'T DIVINE ITEMS CHOOSE THEIR OWN MASTERS OR WHATEVER?
WHEN I TRIED TO USE AN ENCHANTED SWORD ONCE, IT TURNED OUT ONLY THE OWNER COULD WIELD THE SWORD.
YOU'RE RIGHT, AS FAR AS IT GOES.
ONLY THOSE WHO HAVE BEEN GRANTED A DIVINE ITEM CAN ACCESS ITS FULL POWER.
FOR OTHERS, A MAGICAL BLADE THAT CAN CUT ANYTHING IS JUST A REGULAR SWORD, OR A MAGIC STAFF OF LIMITLESS MP JUST MAKES YOUR MAGIC RECHARGE A LITTLE FASTER.
THAT QUALITY HELPS PREVENT MOST DIVINE ITEMS FROM BEING MISUSED SHOULD THEY FALL INTO THE WRONG HANDS.

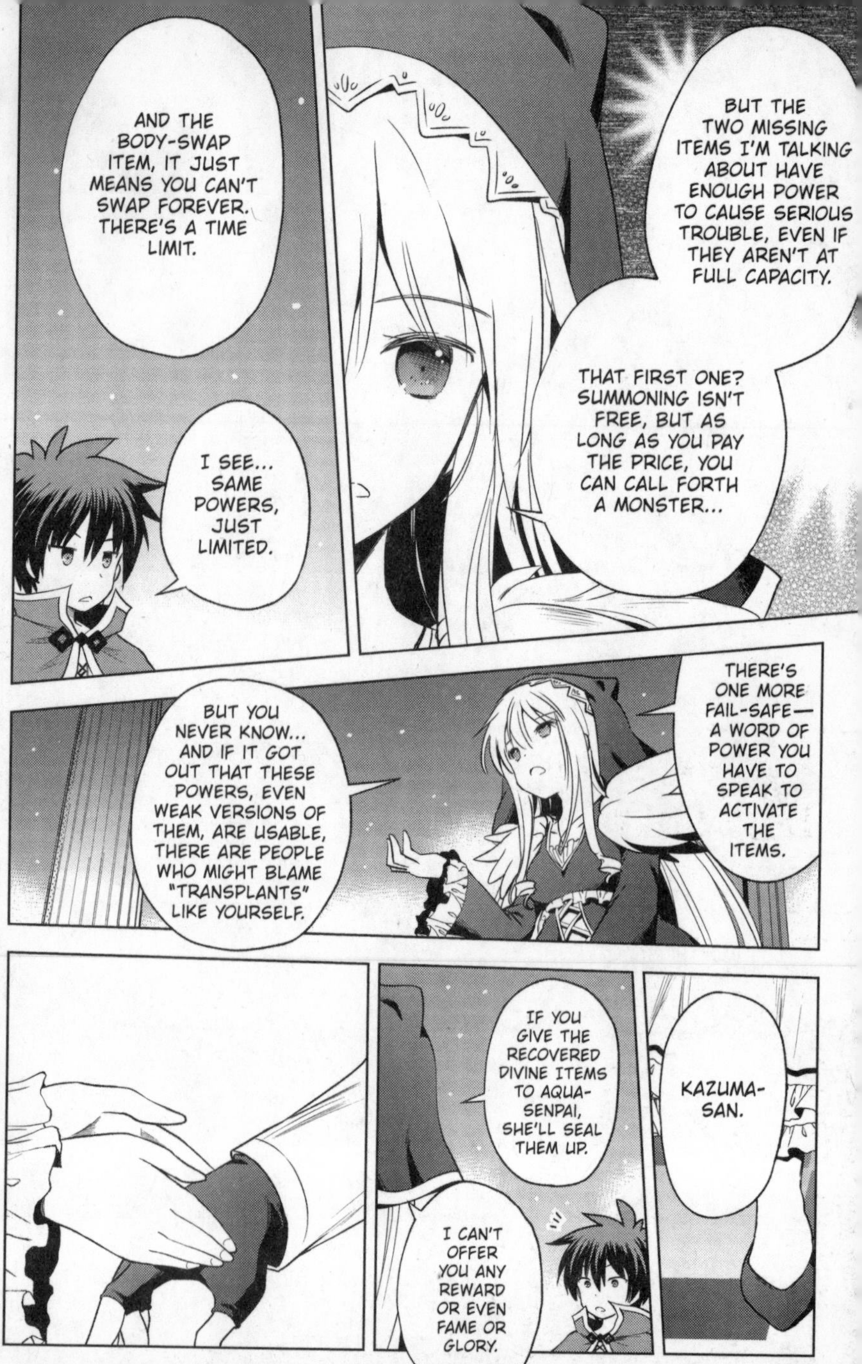
BUT THE TWO MISSING ITEMS I'M TALKING ABOUT HAVE ENOUGH POWER TO CAUSE SERIOUS TROUBLE, EVEN IF THEY AREN'T AT FULL CAPACITY.
THAT FIRST ONE? SUMMONING ISN'T FREE, BUT AS LONG AS YOU PAY THE PRICE, YOU CAN CALL FORTH A MONSTER...
AND THE BODY-SWAP ITEM, IT JUST MEANS YOU CAN'T SWAP FOREVER. THERE'S A TIME LIMIT.
I SEE... SAME POWERS, JUST LIMITED.
THERE'S ONE MORE FAIL-SAFE—A WORD OF POWER YOU HAVE TO SPEAK TO ACTIVATE THE ITEMS.
BUT YOU NEVER KNOW... AND IF IT GOT OUT THAT THESE POWERS, EVEN WEAK VERSIONS OF THEM, ARE USABLE, THERE ARE PEOPLE WHO MIGHT BLAME "TRANSPLANTS" LIKE YOURSELF.
KAZUMA-SAN.
IF YOU GIVE THE RECOVERED DIVINE ITEMS TO AQUA-SENPAI, SHE'LL SEAL THEM UP.
I CAN'T OFFER YOU ANY REWARD OR EVEN FAME OR GLORY.

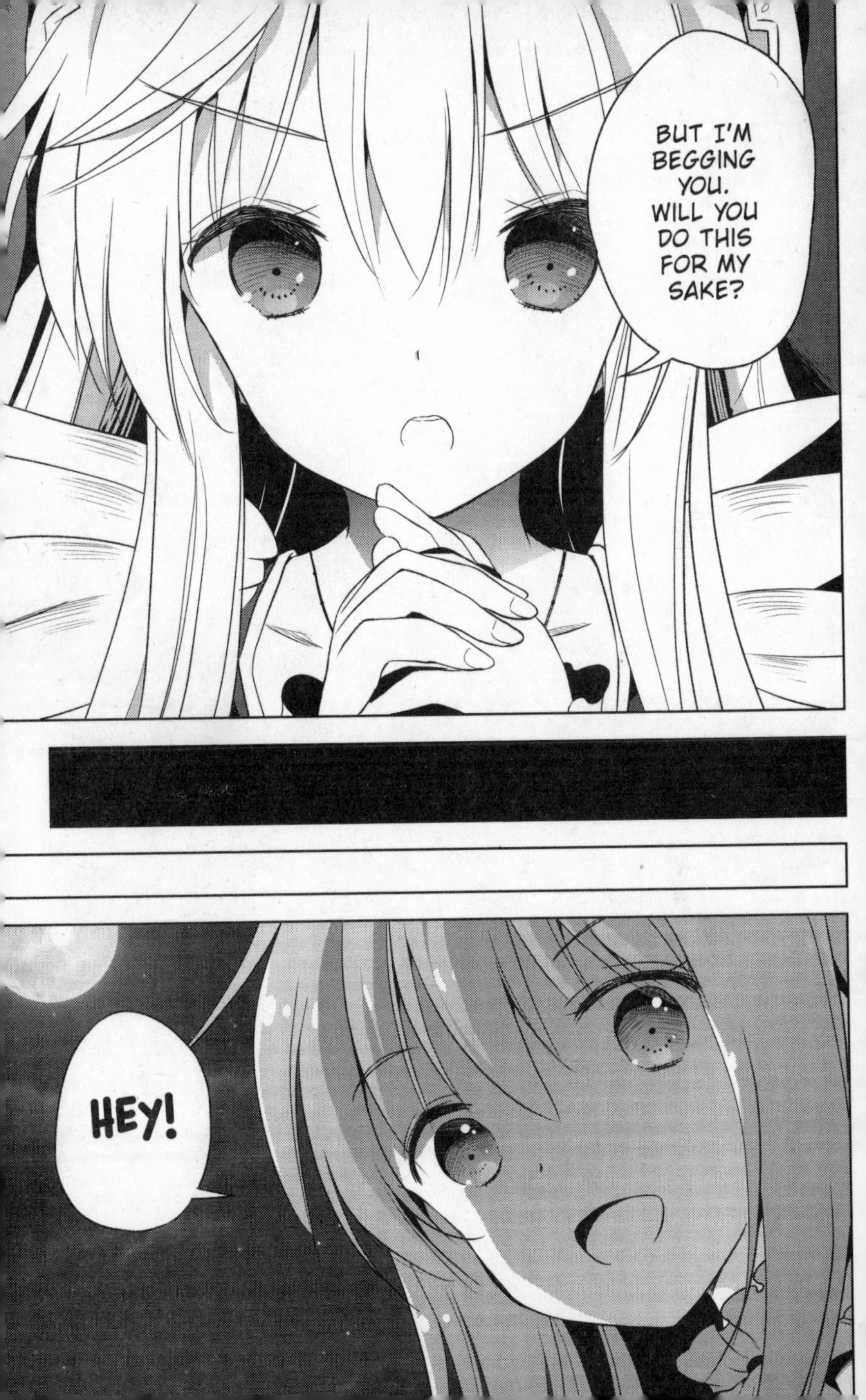
BUT I'M BEGGING YOU. WILL YOU DO THIS FOR MY SAKE?
HEY!

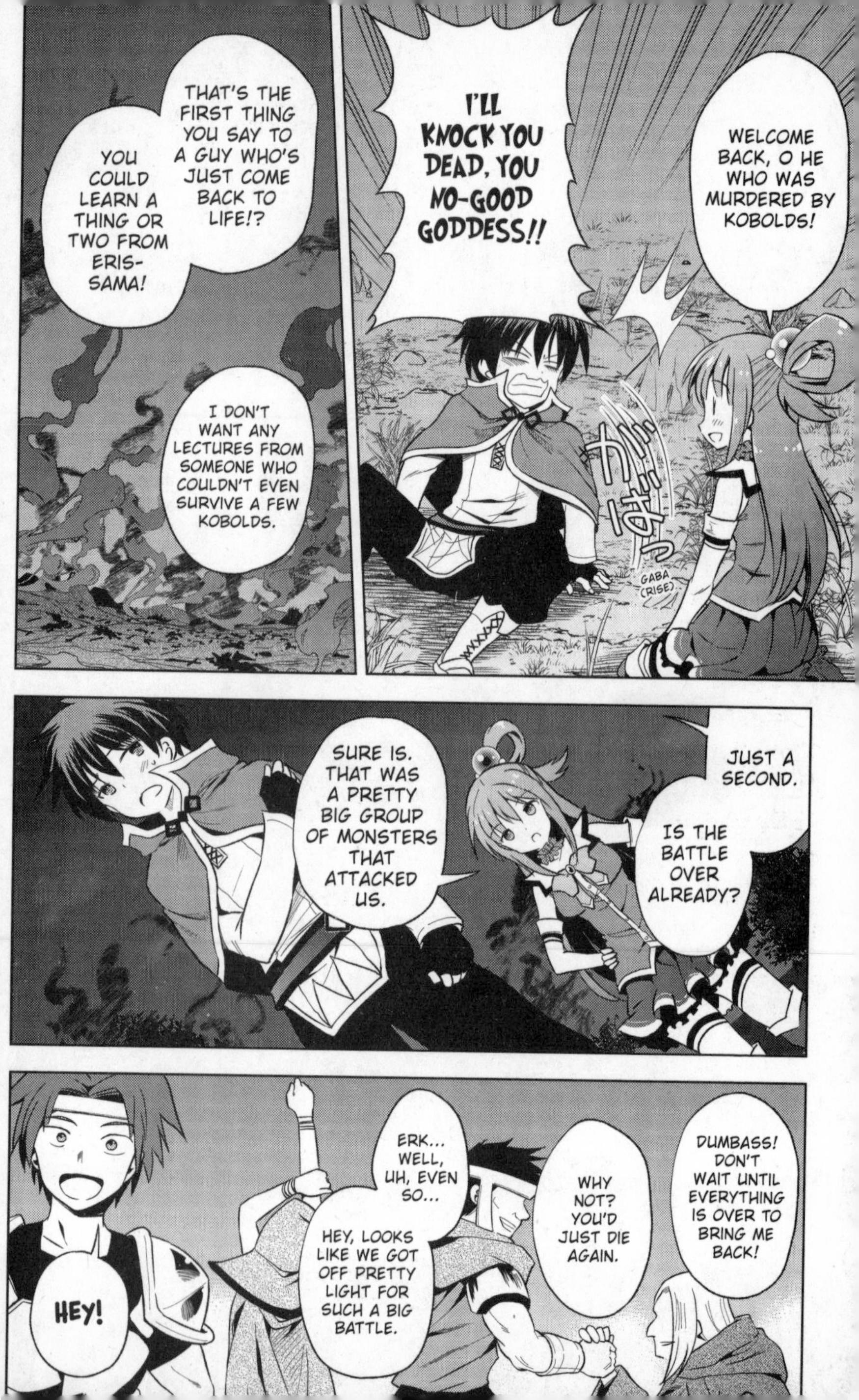
WELCOME BACK, O HE WHO WAS MURDERED BY KOBOLDS!
I'LL KNOCK YOU DEAD, YOU NO-GOOD GODDESS!!
がばっ
GABA (RISE)
THAT'S THE FIRST THING YOU SAY TO A GUY WHO'S JUST COME BACK TO LIFE!?
YOU COULD LEARN A THING OR TWO FROM ERIS-SAMA!
I DON'T WANT ANY LECTURES FROM SOMEONE WHO COULDN'T EVEN SURVIVE A FEW KOBOLDS.
JUST A SECOND.
IS THE BATTLE OVER ALREADY?
SURE IS. THAT WAS A PRETTY BIG GROUP OF MONSTERS THAT ATTACKED US.
DUMBASS! DON'T WAIT UNTIL EVERYTHING IS OVER TO BRING ME BACK!
WHY NOT? YOU'D JUST DIE AGAIN.
ERK... WELL, UH, EVEN SO...
HEY, LOOKS LIKE WE GOT OFF PRETTY LIGHT FOR SUCH A BIG BATTLE.
HEY!

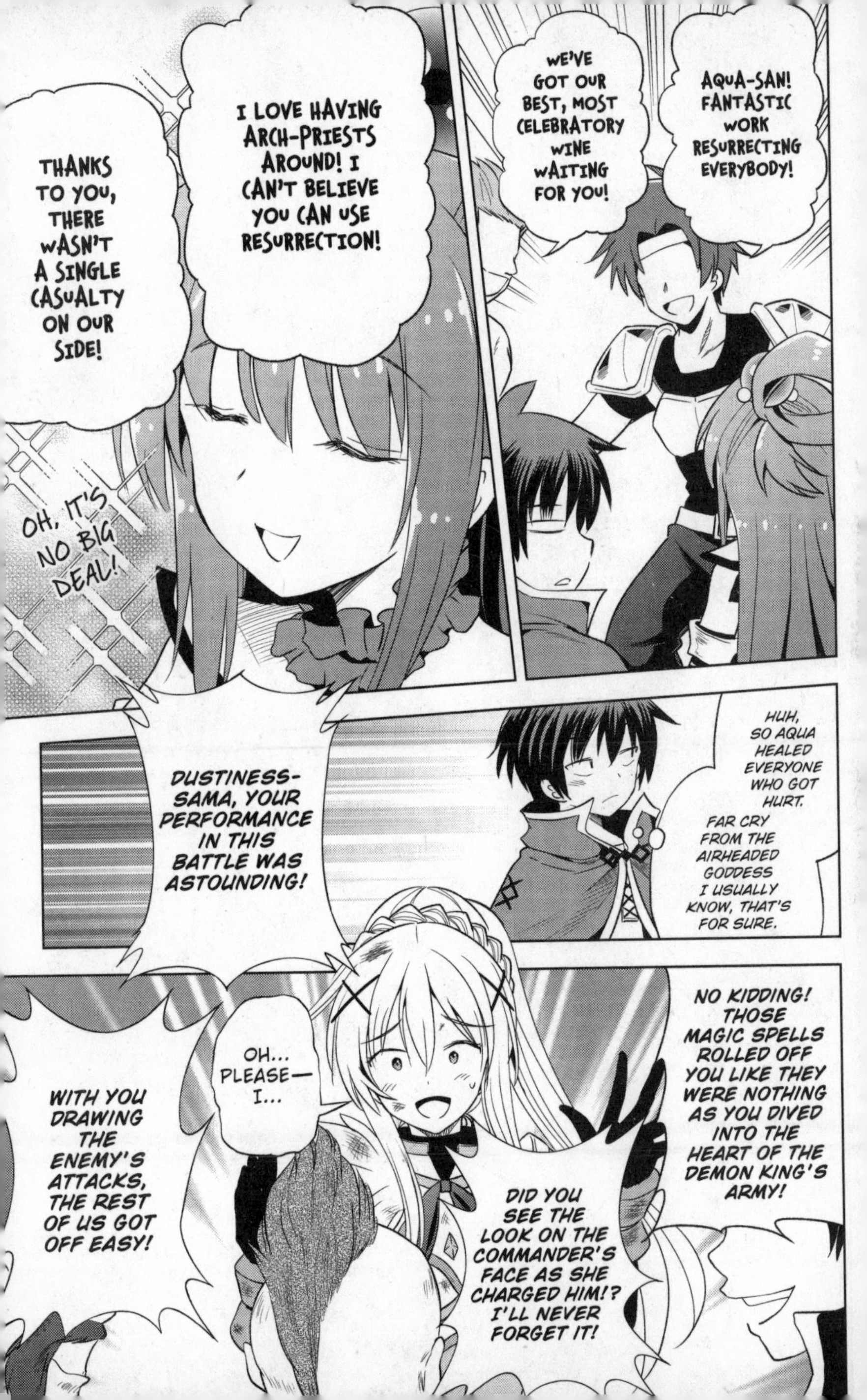
AQUA-SAN! FANTASTIC WORK RESURRECTING EVERYBODY!
WE'VE GOT OUR BEST, MOST CELEBRATORY WINE WAITING FOR YOU!
I LOVE HAVING ARCH-PRIESTS AROUND! I CAN'T BELIEVE YOU CAN USE RESURRECTION!
THANKS TO YOU, THERE WASN'T A SINGLE CASUALTY ON OUR SIDE!
OH, IT'S NO BIG DEAL!
HUH, SO AQUA HEALED EVERYONE WHO GOT HURT.
FAR CRY FROM THE AIRHEADED GODDESS I USUALLY KNOW, THAT'S FOR SURE.
DUSTINESS-SAMA, YOUR PERFORMANCE IN THIS BATTLE WAS ASTOUNDING!
NO KIDDING! THOSE MAGIC SPELLS ROLLED OFF YOU LIKE THEY WERE NOTHING AS YOU DIVED INTO THE HEART OF THE DEMON KING'S ARMY!
OH... PLEASE— I...
WITH YOU DRAWING THE ENEMY'S ATTACKS, THE REST OF US GOT OFF EASY!
DID YOU SEE THE LOOK ON THE COMMANDER'S FACE AS SHE CHARGED HIM!? I'LL NEVER FORGET IT!

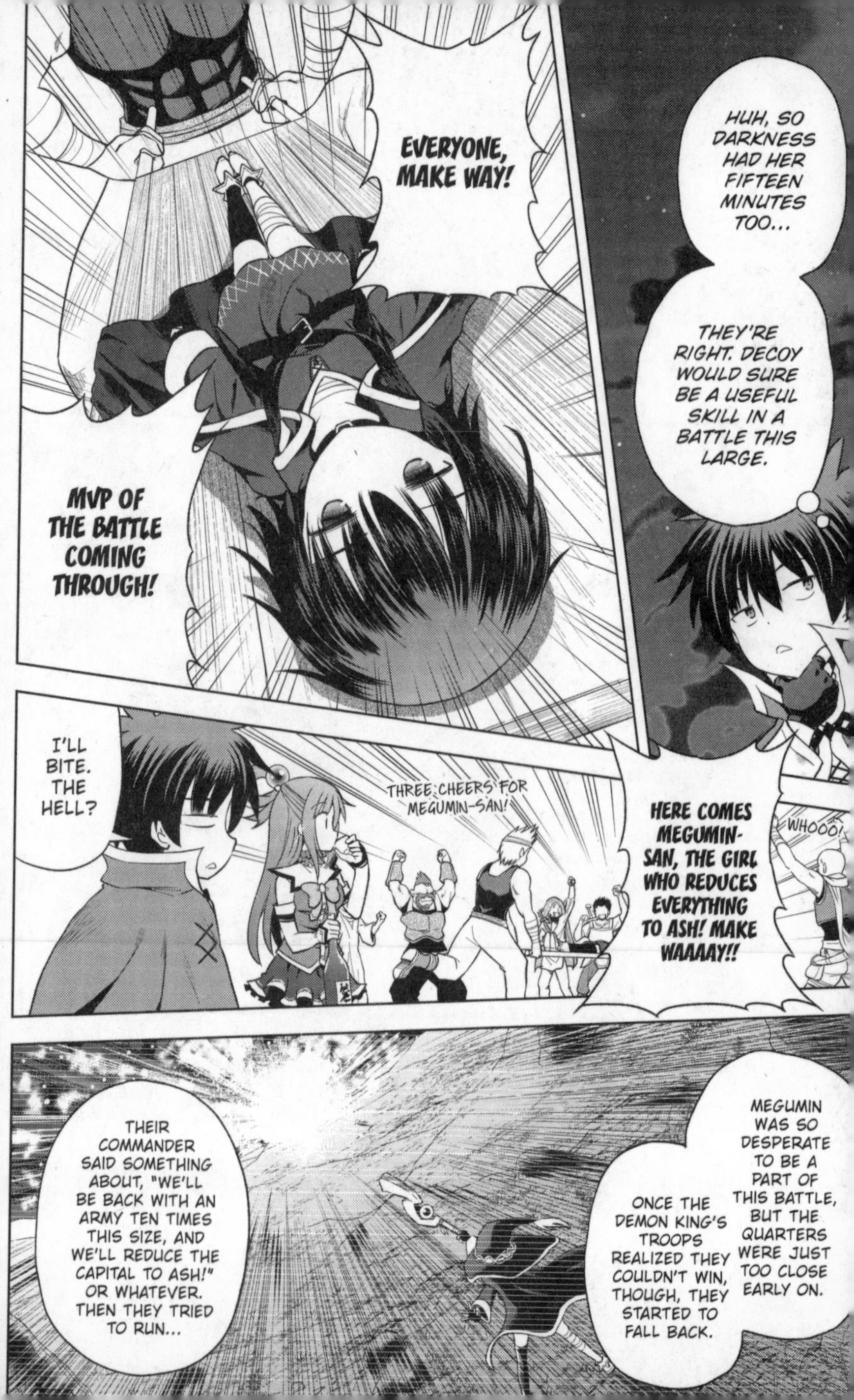
HUH, SO DARKNESS HAD HER FIFTEEN MINUTES TOO...
THEY'RE RIGHT. DECOY WOULD SURE BE A USEFUL SKILL IN A BATTLE THIS LARGE.
EVERYONE, MAKE WAY!
MVP OF THE BATTLE COMING THROUGH!
HERE COMES MEGUMIN-SAN, THE GIRL WHO REDUCES EVERYTHING TO ASH! MAKE WAAAAY!!
WHOOO!
THREE CHEERS FOR MEGUMIN-SAN!
I'LL BITE. THE HELL?
MEGUMIN WAS SO DESPERATE TO BE A PART OF THIS BATTLE, BUT THE QUARTERS WERE JUST TOO CLOSE EARLY ON.
ONCE THE DEMON KING'S TROOPS REALIZED THEY COULDN'T WIN, THOUGH, THEY STARTED TO FALL BACK.
THEIR COMMANDER SAID SOMETHING ABOUT, "WE'LL BE BACK WITH AN ARMY TEN TIMES THIS SIZE, AND WE'LL REDUCE THE CAPITAL TO ASH!" OR WHATEVER. THEN THEY TRIED TO RUN...

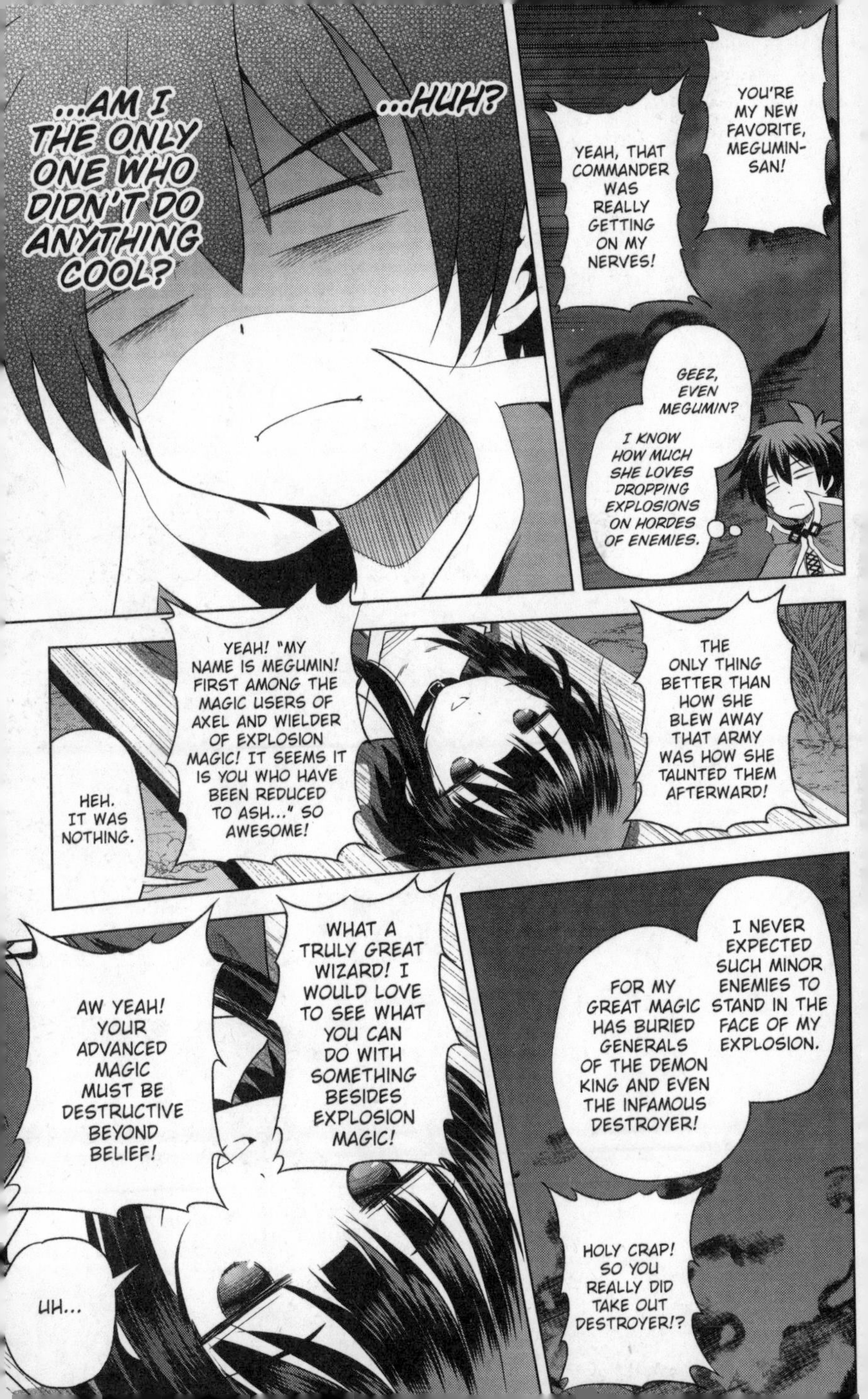
YOU'RE MY NEW FAVORITE, MEGUMIN-SAN!
YEAH, THAT COMMANDER WAS REALLY GETTING ON MY NERVES!
GEEZ, EVEN MEGUMIN?
I KNOW HOW MUCH SHE LOVES DROPPING EXPLOSIONS ON HORDES OF ENEMIES.
...HUH?
...AM I THE ONLY ONE WHO DIDN'T DO ANYTHING COOL?
THE ONLY THING BETTER THAN HOW SHE BLEW AWAY THAT ARMY WAS HOW SHE TAUNTED THEM AFTERWARD!
YEAH! "MY NAME IS MEGUMIN! FIRST AMONG THE MAGIC USERS OF AXEL AND WIELDER OF EXPLOSION MAGIC! IT SEEMS IT IS YOU WHO HAVE BEEN REDUCED TO ASH..." SO AWESOME!
HEH. IT WAS NOTHING.
I NEVER EXPECTED SUCH MINOR ENEMIES TO STAND IN THE FACE OF MY EXPLOSION.
FOR MY GREAT MAGIC HAS BURIED GENERALS OF THE DEMON KING AND EVEN THE INFAMOUS DESTROYER!
HOLY CRAP! SO YOU REALLY DID TAKE OUT DESTROYER!?
WHAT A TRULY GREAT WIZARD! I WOULD LOVE TO SEE WHAT YOU CAN DO WITH SOMETHING BESIDES EXPLOSION MAGIC!
AW YEAH! YOUR ADVANCED MAGIC MUST BE DESTRUCTIVE BEYOND BELIEF!
UH...

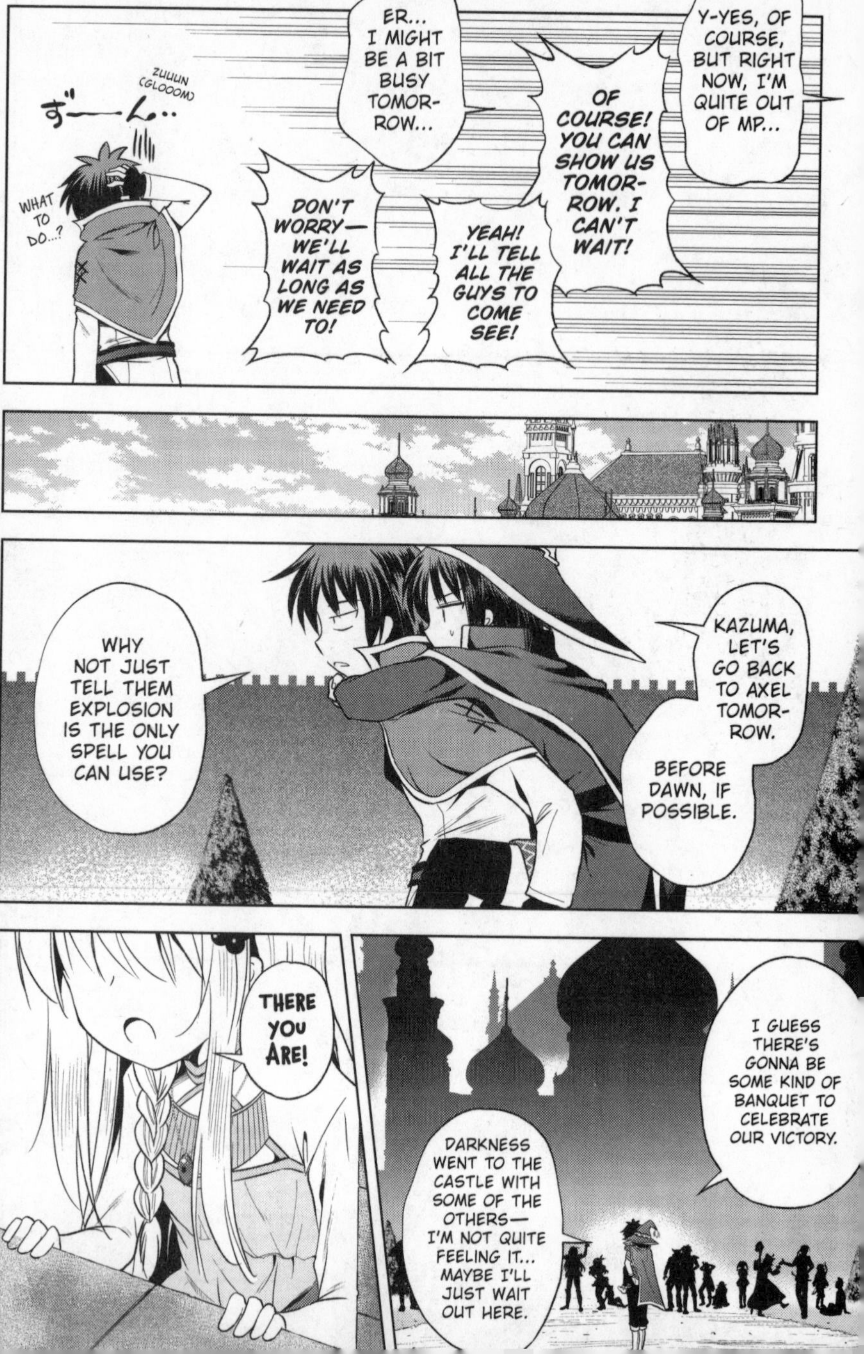
Y-YES, OF COURSE, BUT RIGHT NOW, I'M QUITE OUT OF MP...
OF COURSE! YOU CAN SHOW US TOMORROW. I CAN'T WAIT!
ER... I MIGHT BE A BIT BUSY TOMORROW...
YEAH! I'LL TELL ALL THE GUYS TO COME SEE!
DON'T WORRY—WE'LL WAIT AS LONG AS WE NEED TO!
ずーーん…
ZUUUN (GLOOOM)
WHAT TO DO...?
KAZUMA, LET'S GO BACK TO AXEL TOMORROW.
BEFORE DAWN, IF POSSIBLE.
WHY NOT JUST TELL THEM EXPLOSION IS THE ONLY SPELL YOU CAN USE?
I GUESS THERE'S GONNA BE SOME KIND OF BANQUET TO CELEBRATE OUR VICTORY.
DARKNESS WENT TO THE CASTLE WITH SOME OF THE OTHERS—I'M NOT QUITE FEELING IT... MAYBE I'LL JUST WAIT OUT HERE.
THERE YOU ARE!

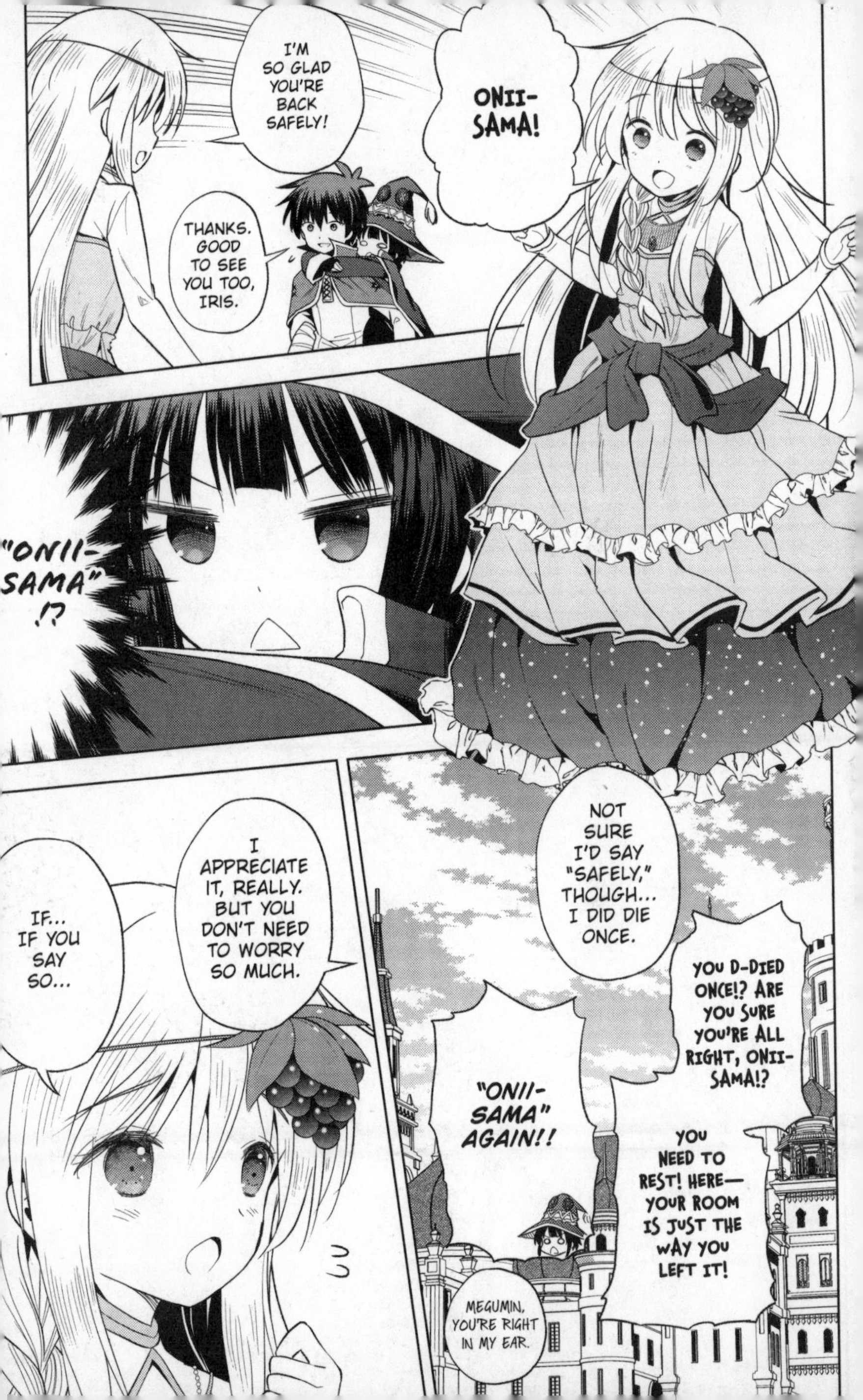
ONII-SAMA!
I'M SO GLAD YOU'RE BACK SAFELY!
THANKS. GOOD TO SEE YOU TOO, IRIS.
"ONII-SAMA" !?
NOT SURE I'D SAY "SAFELY," THOUGH... I DID DIE ONCE.
YOU D-DIED ONCE!? ARE YOU SURE YOU'RE ALL RIGHT, ONII-SAMA!?
YOU NEED TO REST! HERE—YOUR ROOM IS JUST THE WAY YOU LEFT IT!
"ONII-SAMA" AGAIN!!
MEGUMIN, YOU'RE RIGHT IN MY EAR.
I APPRECIATE IT, REALLY. BUT YOU DON'T NEED TO WORRY SO MUCH.
IF... IF YOU SAY SO...

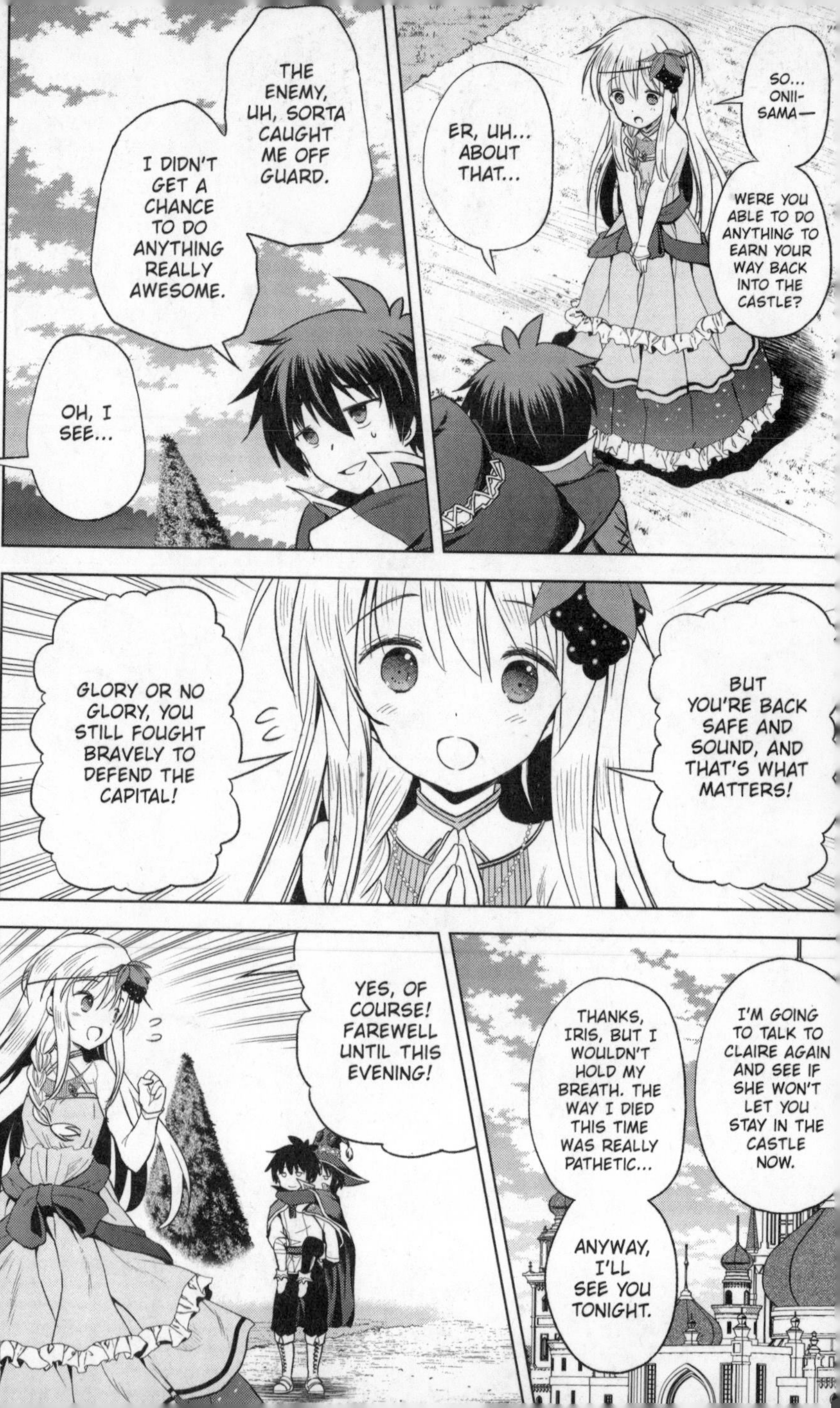
SO... ONII-SAMA—
WERE YOU ABLE TO DO ANYTHING TO EARN YOUR WAY BACK INTO THE CASTLE?
ER, UH... ABOUT THAT...
THE ENEMY, UH, SORTA CAUGHT ME OFF GUARD.
I DIDN'T GET A CHANCE TO DO ANYTHING REALLY AWESOME.
OH, I SEE...
BUT YOU'RE BACK SAFE AND SOUND, AND THAT'S WHAT MATTERS!
GLORY OR NO GLORY, YOU STILL FOUGHT BRAVELY TO DEFEND THE CAPITAL!
I'M GOING TO TALK TO CLAIRE AGAIN AND SEE IF SHE WON'T LET YOU STAY IN THE CASTLE NOW.
THANKS, IRIS, BUT I WOULDN'T HOLD MY BREATH. THE WAY I DIED THIS TIME WAS REALLY PATHETIC...
ANYWAY, I'LL SEE YOU TONIGHT.
YES, OF COURSE! FAREWELL UNTIL THIS EVENING!

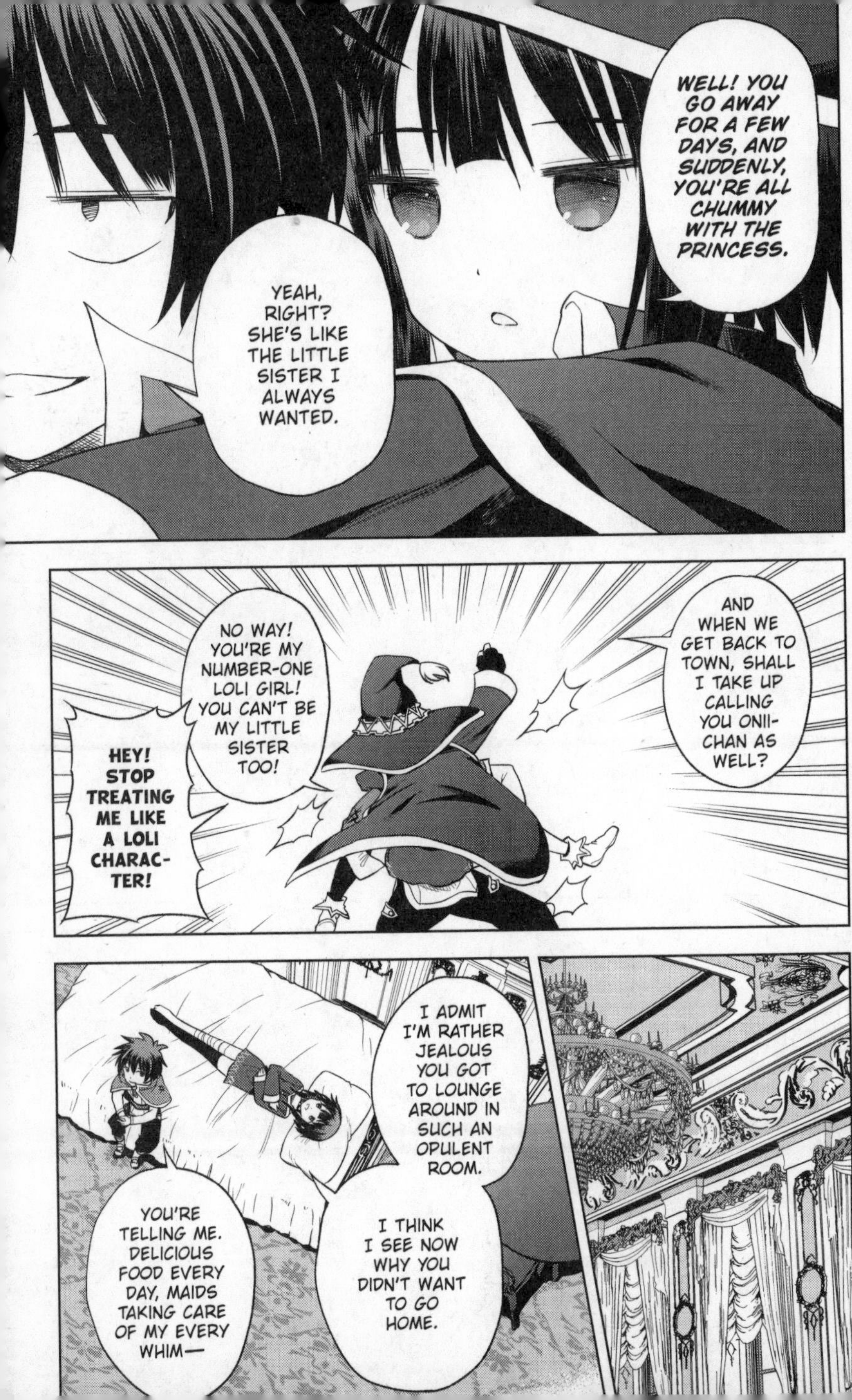
WELL! YOU GO AWAY FOR A FEW DAYS, AND SUDDENLY, YOU'RE ALL CHUMMY WITH THE PRINCESS.
YEAH, RIGHT? SHE'S LIKE THE LITTLE SISTER I ALWAYS WANTED.
AND WHEN WE GET BACK TO TOWN, SHALL I TAKE UP CALLING YOU ONII-CHAN AS WELL?
NO WAY! YOU'RE MY NUMBER-ONE LOLI GIRL! YOU CAN'T BE MY LITTLE SISTER TOO!
HEY! STOP TREATING ME LIKE A LOLI CHARAC-TER!
I ADMIT I'M RATHER JEALOUS YOU GOT TO LOUNGE AROUND IN SUCH AN OPULENT ROOM.
I THINK I SEE NOW WHY YOU DIDN'T WANT TO GO HOME.
YOU'RE TELLING ME. DELICIOUS FOOD EVERY DAY, MAIDS TAKING CARE OF MY EVERY WHIM—

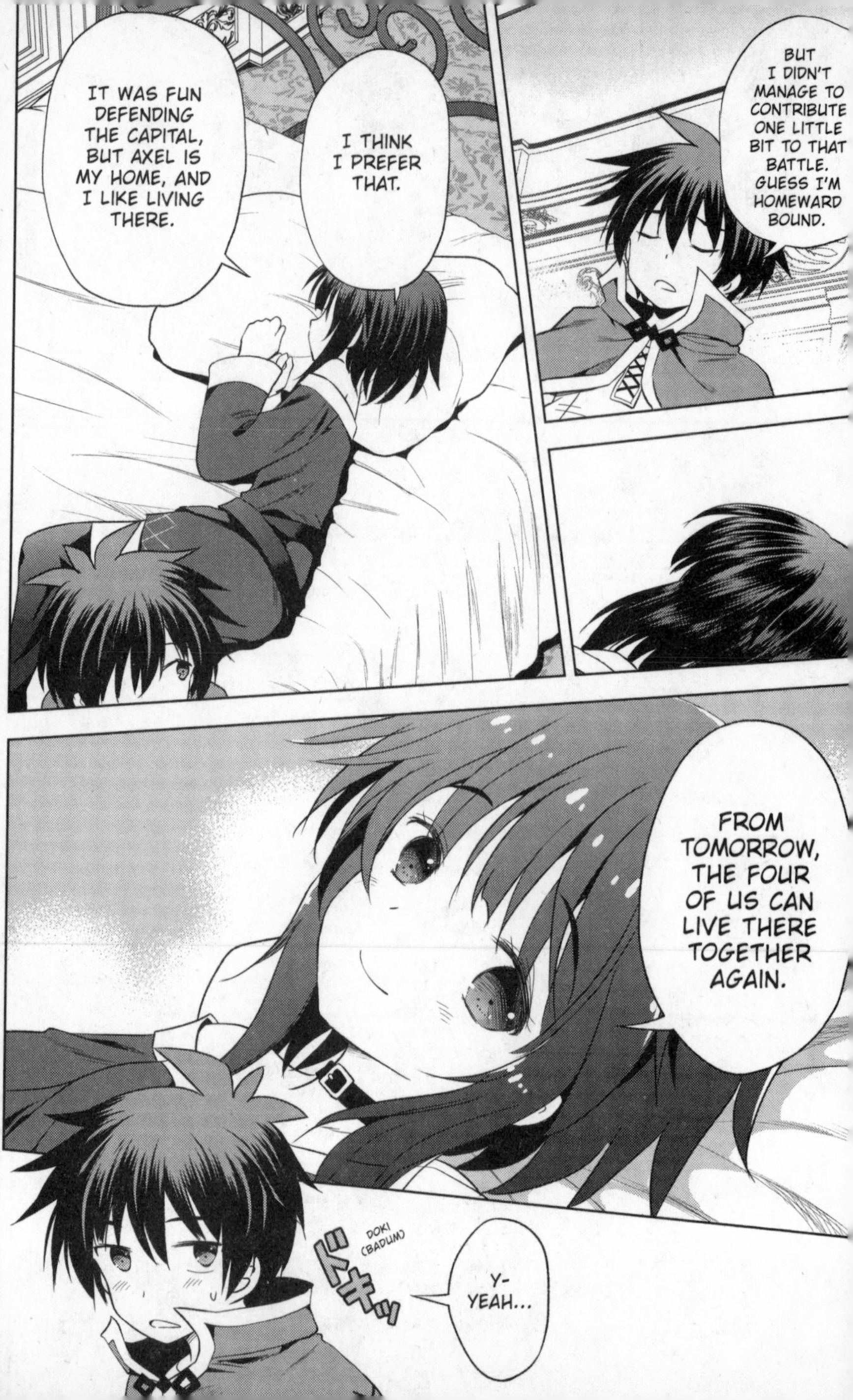
BUT I DIDN'T MANAGE TO CONTRIBUTE ONE LITTLE BIT TO THAT BATTLE. GUESS I'M HOMEWARD BOUND.
IT WAS FUN DEFENDING THE CAPITAL, BUT AXEL IS MY HOME, AND I LIKE LIVING THERE.
I THINK I PREFER THAT.
FROM TOMORROW, THE FOUR OF US CAN LIVE THERE TOGETHER AGAIN.
DOKI (BADUM)
Y- YEAH...

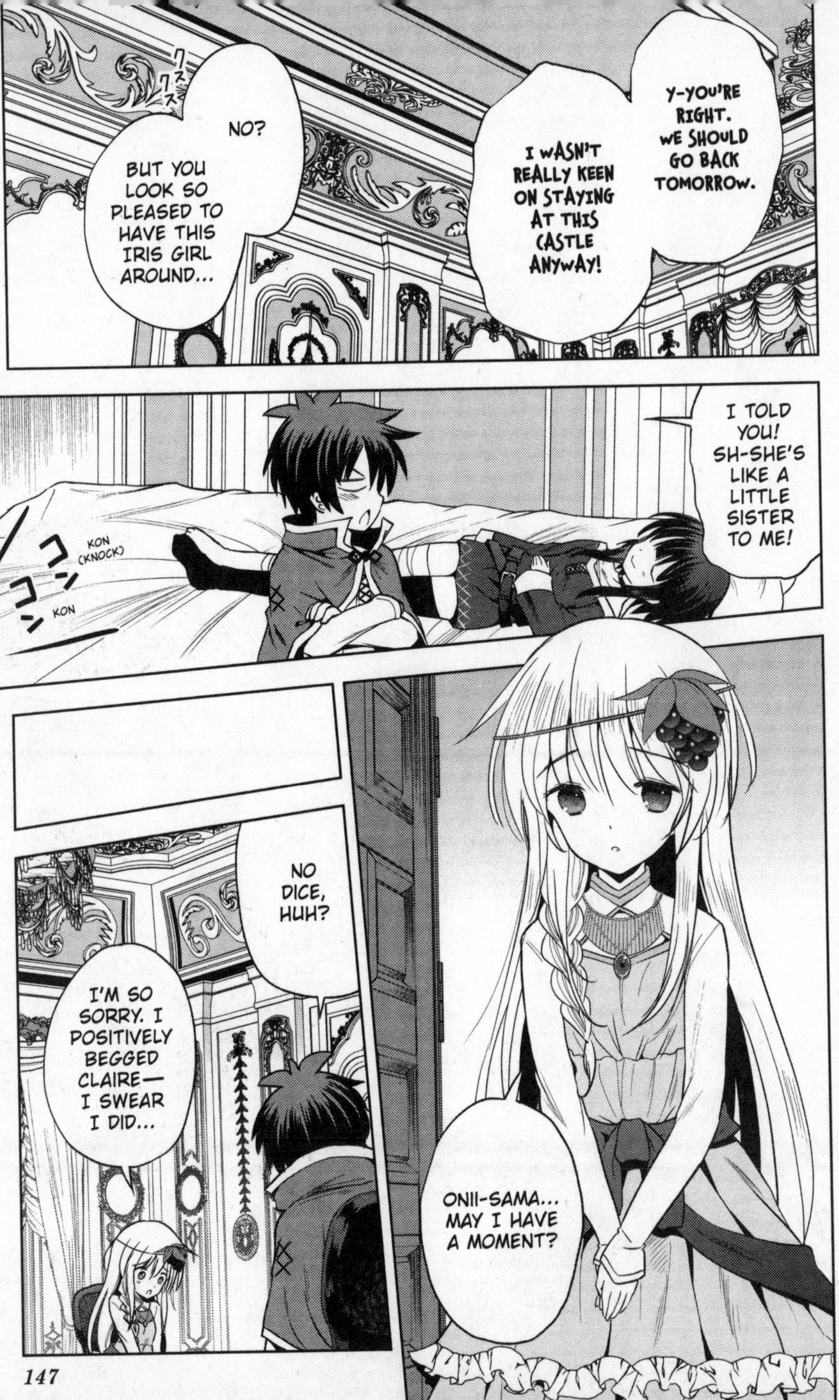
Y-YOU'RE RIGHT. WE SHOULD GO BACK TOMORROW.
I WASN'T REALLY KEEN ON STAYING AT THIS CASTLE ANYWAY!
クスクス
NO?
BUT YOU LOOK SO PLEASED TO HAVE THIS IRIS GIRL AROUND...
I TOLD YOU! SH-SHE'S LIKE A LITTLE SISTER TO ME!
コン KON (KNOCK)
コン KON
ONII-SAMA... MAY I HAVE A MOMENT?
NO DICE, HUH?
I'M SO SORRY. I POSITIVELY BEGGED CLAIRE— I SWEAR I DID...

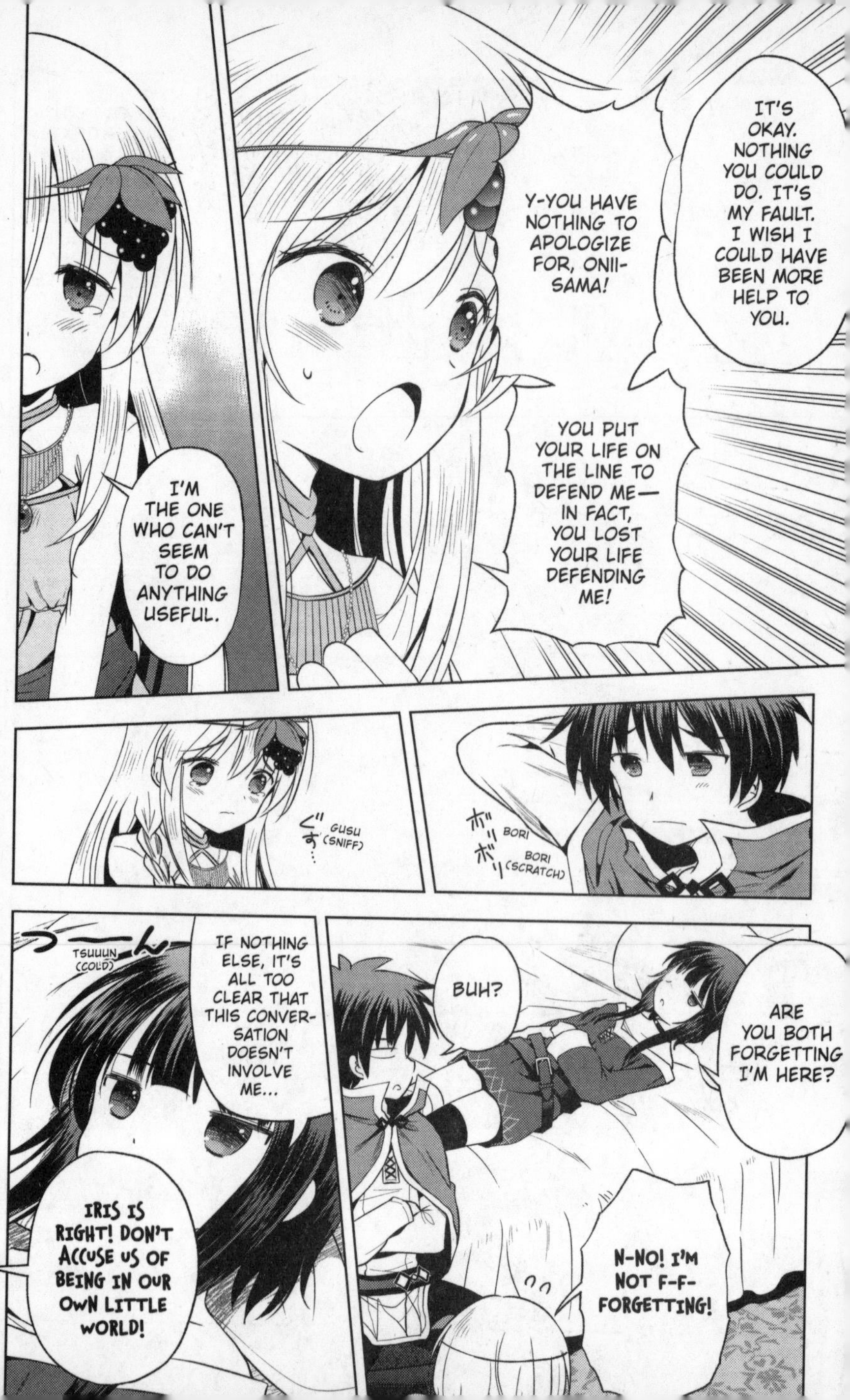
IT'S OKAY. NOTHING YOU COULD DO. IT'S MY FAULT. I WISH I COULD HAVE BEEN MORE HELP TO YOU.
Y-YOU HAVE NOTHING TO APOLOGIZE FOR, ONII-SAMA!
YOU PUT YOUR LIFE ON THE LINE TO DEFEND ME—IN FACT, YOU LOST YOUR LIFE DEFENDING ME!
I'M THE ONE WHO CAN'T SEEM TO DO ANYTHING USEFUL.
ボリボリ
BORI BORI (SCRATCH)
ぐす…
GUSU (SNIFF)
ARE YOU BOTH FORGETTING I'M HERE?
BUH?
N-NO! I'M NOT F-F-FORGETTING!
つーん
TSUUUN (COLD)
IF NOTHING ELSE, IT'S ALL TOO CLEAR THAT THIS CONVER-SATION DOESN'T INVOLVE ME...
IRIS IS RIGHT! DON'T ACCUSE US OF BEING IN OUR OWN LITTLE WORLD!

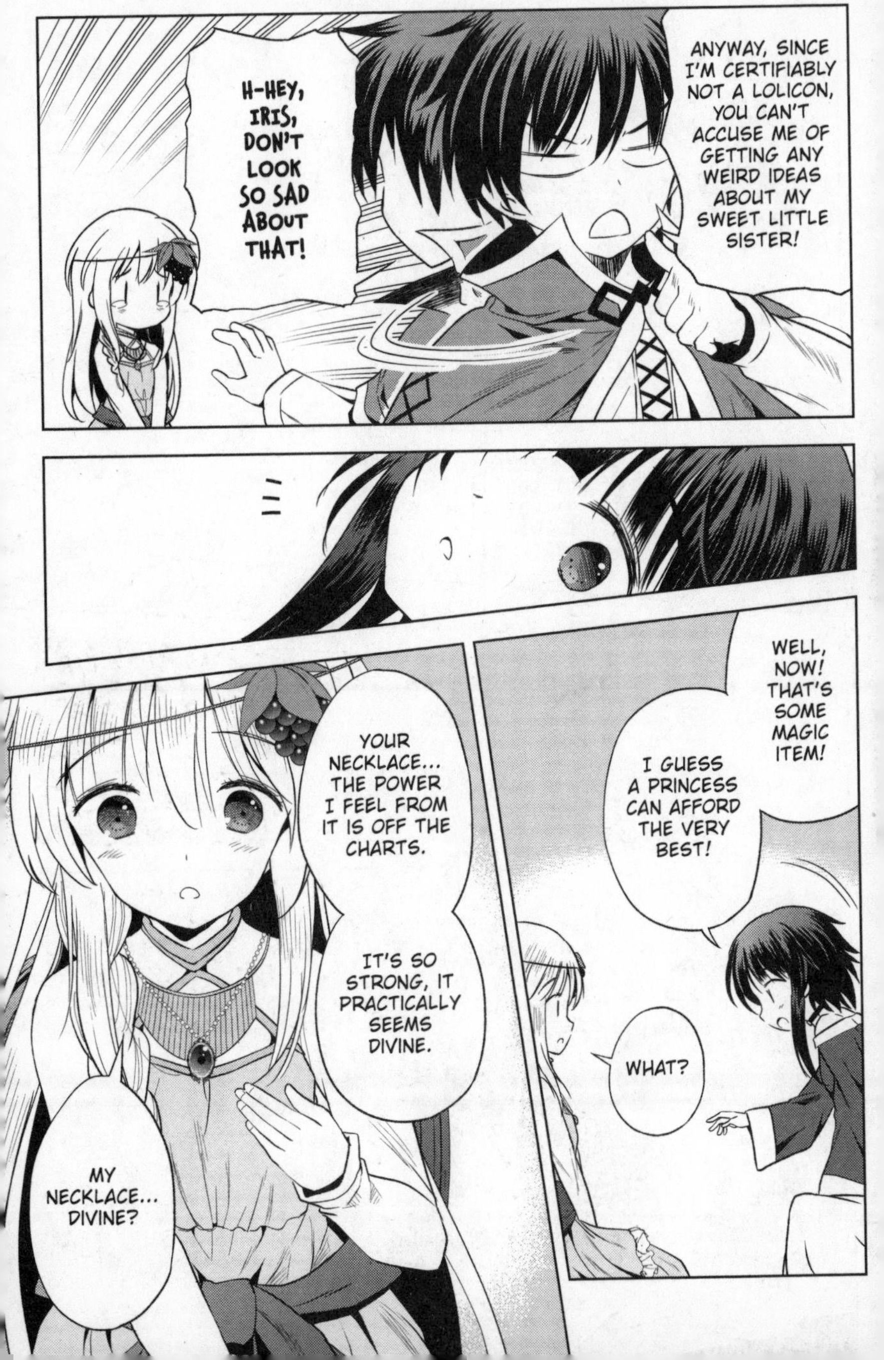
ANYWAY, SINCE I'M CERTIFIABLY NOT A LOLICON, YOU CAN'T ACCUSE ME OF GETTING ANY WEIRD IDEAS ABOUT MY SWEET LITTLE SISTER!
H-HEY, IRIS, DON'T LOOK SO SAD ABOUT THAT!
WELL, NOW! THAT'S SOME MAGIC ITEM!
I GUESS A PRINCESS CAN AFFORD THE VERY BEST!
WHAT?
YOUR NECKLACE... THE POWER I FEEL FROM IT IS OFF THE CHARTS.
IT'S SO STRONG, IT PRACTICALLY SEEMS DIVINE.
MY NECKLACE... DIVINE?

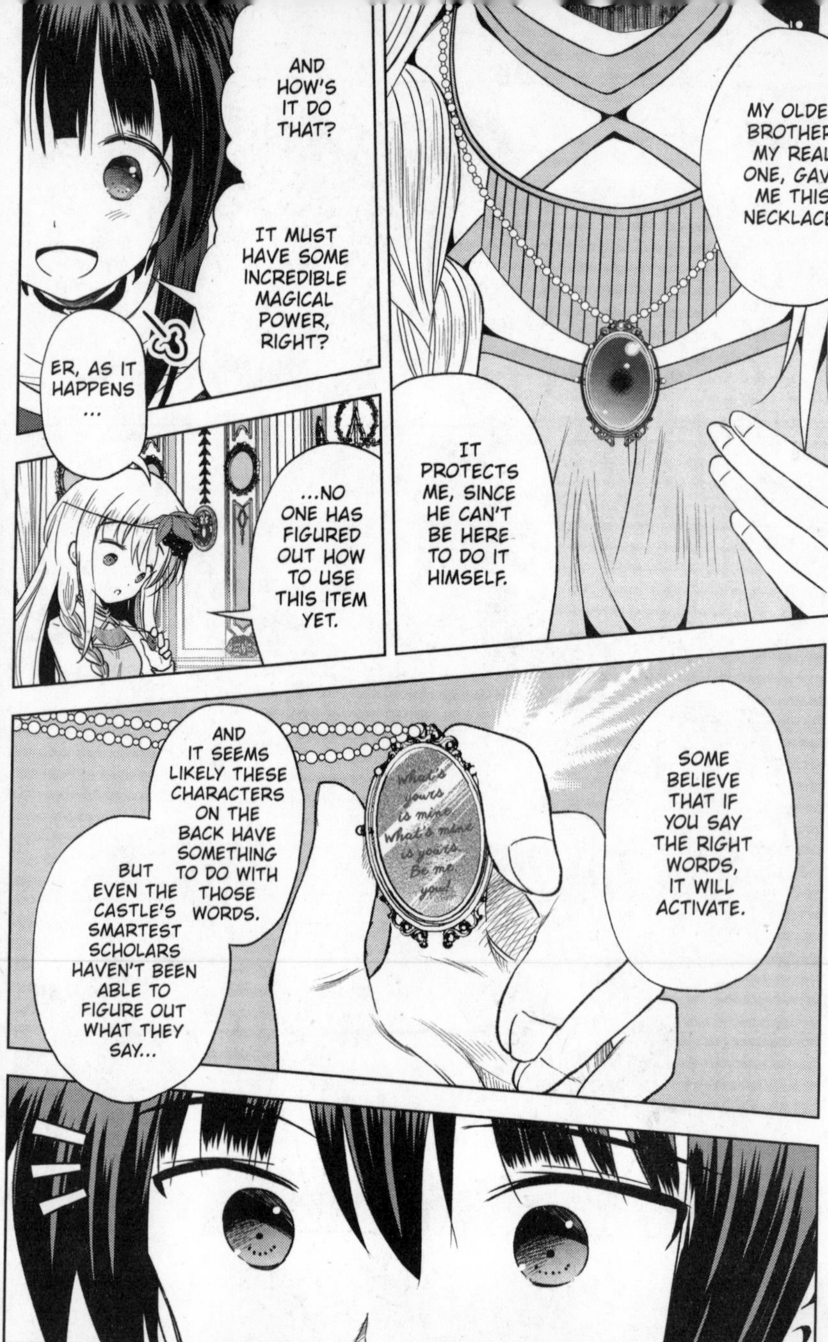

MY OLDER BROTHER, MY REAL ONE, GAVE ME THIS NECKLACE.
IT PROTECTS ME, SINCE HE CAN'T BE HERE TO DO IT HIMSELF.
AND HOW'S IT DO THAT?
IT MUST HAVE SOME INCREDIBLE MAGICAL POWER, RIGHT?
ER, AS IT HAPPENS...
...NO ONE HAS FIGURED OUT HOW TO USE THIS ITEM YET.
SOME BELIEVE THAT IF YOU SAY THE RIGHT WORDS, IT WILL ACTIVATE.
What's yours is mine, what's mine is yours. Be me, you!
AND IT SEEMS LIKELY THESE CHARACTERS ON THE BACK HAVE SOMETHING TO DO WITH THOSE WORDS.
BUT EVEN THE CASTLE'S SMARTEST SCHOLARS HAVEN'T BEEN ABLE TO FIGURE OUT WHAT THEY SAY...

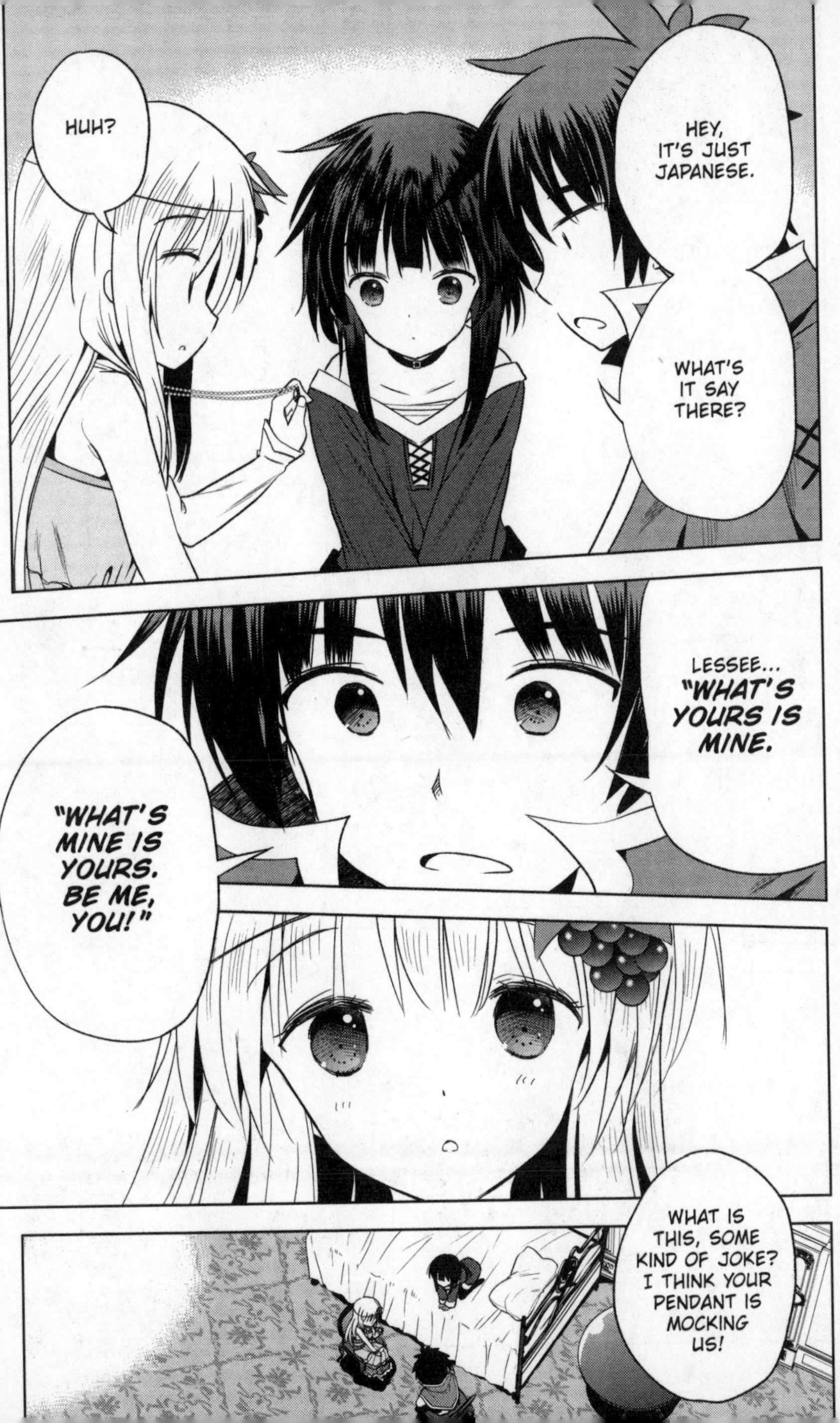
HEY, IT'S JUST JAPANESE.
WHAT'S IT SAY THERE?
HUH?
LESSEE... *"WHAT'S YOURS IS MINE.*
"WHAT'S MINE IS YOURS. BE ME, YOU!"
WHAT IS THIS, SOME KIND OF JOKE? I THINK YOUR PENDANT IS MOCKING US!

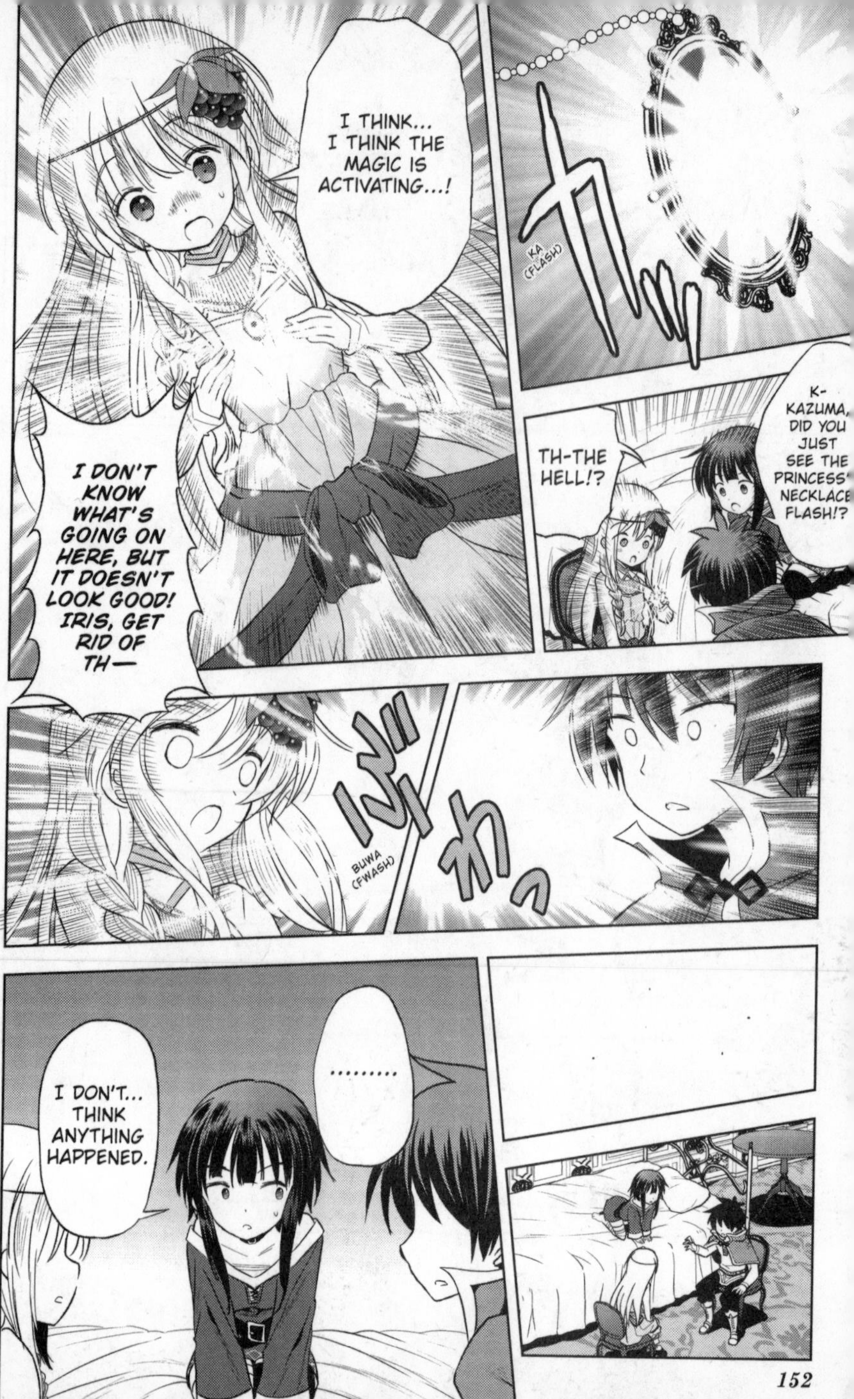
KA (FLASH)
K-KAZUMA, DID YOU JUST SEE THE PRINCESS' NECKLACE FLASH!?
TH-THE HELL!?
I THINK... I THINK THE MAGIC IS ACTIVATING...!
I DON'T KNOW WHAT'S GOING ON HERE, BUT IT DOESN'T LOOK GOOD! IRIS, GET RID OF TH—
BUWA (FWASH)
....
I DON'T... THINK ANYTHING HAPPENED.

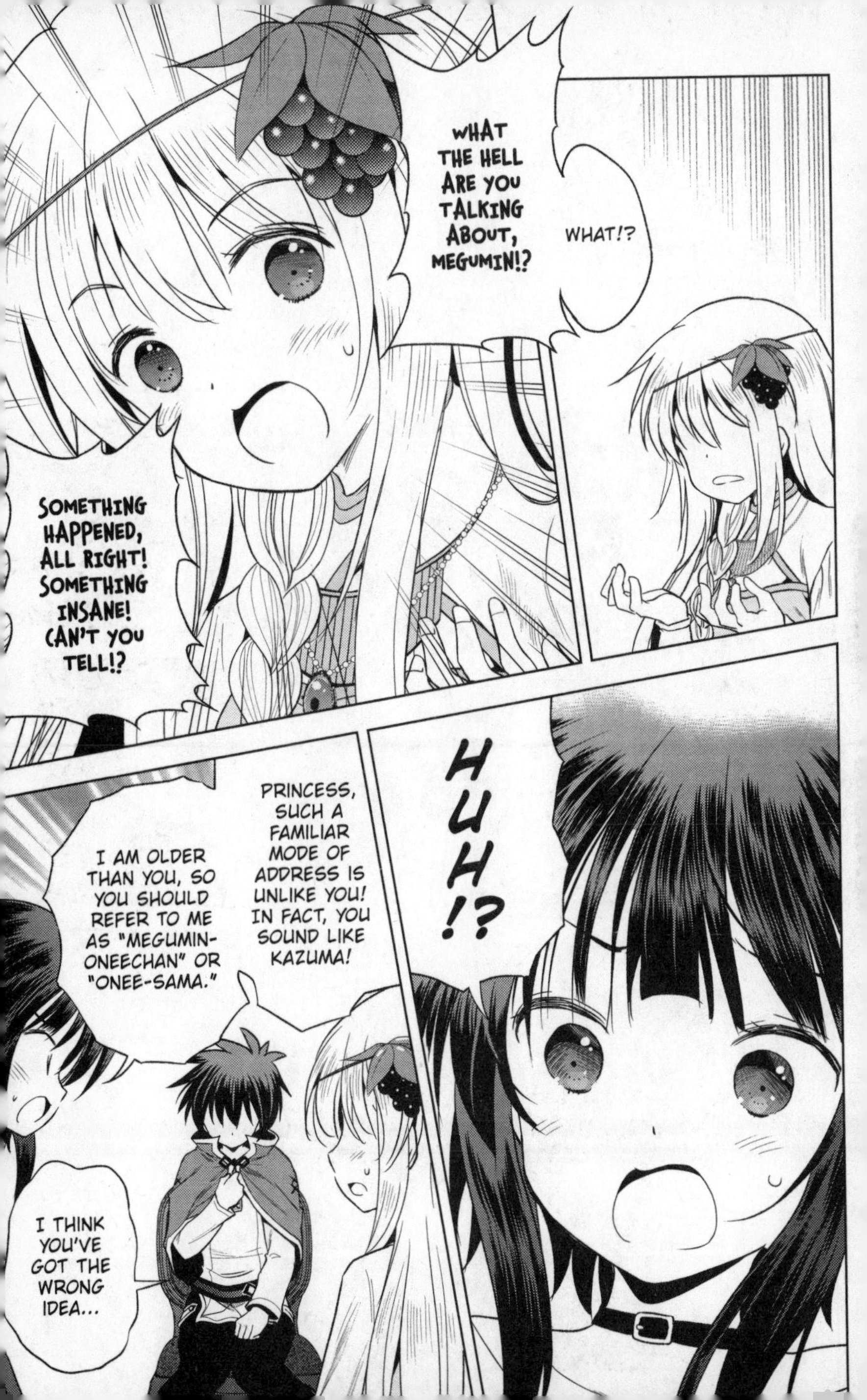
WHAT!?
WHAT THE HELL ARE YOU TALKING ABOUT, MEGUMIN!?
SOMETHING HAPPENED, ALL RIGHT! SOMETHING INSANE! CAN'T YOU TELL!?
HUH!?
PRINCESS, SUCH A FAMILIAR MODE OF ADDRESS IS UNLIKE YOU! IN FACT, YOU SOUND LIKE KAZUMA!
I AM OLDER THAN YOU, SO YOU SHOULD REFER TO ME AS "MEGUMIN-ONEECHAN" OR "ONEE-SAMA."
I THINK YOU'VE GOT THE WRONG IDEA...

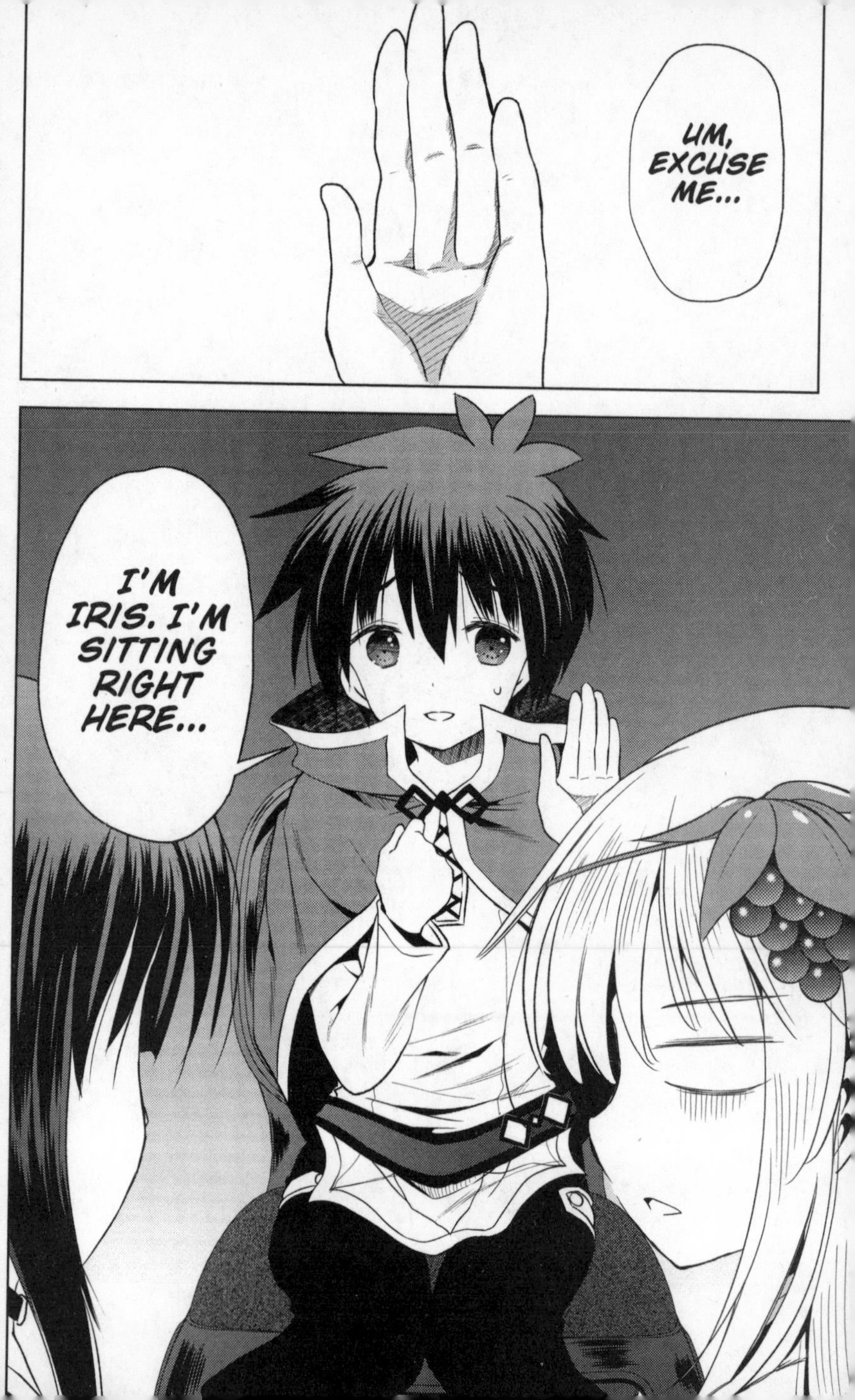
UM, EXCUSE ME...
I'M IRIS. I'M SITTING RIGHT HERE...

TO BE
CONTINUED!

GOD'S
BLESSING
ON THIS
WONDERFUL
WORLD!

10

GOD'S
BLESSING
ON THIS
WONDERFUL
WORLD!

CONGRATULATIONS ON TEN VOLUMES OF THE MANGA VERSION OF *KONOSUBA*! CAN'T BELIEVE THERE'S BEEN THIS MANY ALREADY. AND A MOVIE COMING OUT IN JAPAN THIS YEAR! MAY THE LIGHT NOVEL AND ALL ITS ADAPTATIONS HAVE LONG LIVES!

NATSUME AKATSUKI

VOLUME 10

VOLUME 10 OF THE KONOSUBA MANGA, COMING YOUR WAY!

IT'S THE SUPPORT OF READERS LIKE YOU THAT'S HELPED THIS SERIES GO ON SO LONG. THANK YOU SO MUCH!

THIS TIME, WE EVEN GOT A SPECIAL COMMENT FROM NATSUME AKATSUKI-SENSEI, THE ORIGINAL AUTHOR!
I COULDN'T BE MORE GRATEFUL.

AND THERE'S MUCH MORE OF THIS COMIC TO COME. SEE YOU NEXT VOLUME!

渡真仁

MASAHITO WATARI

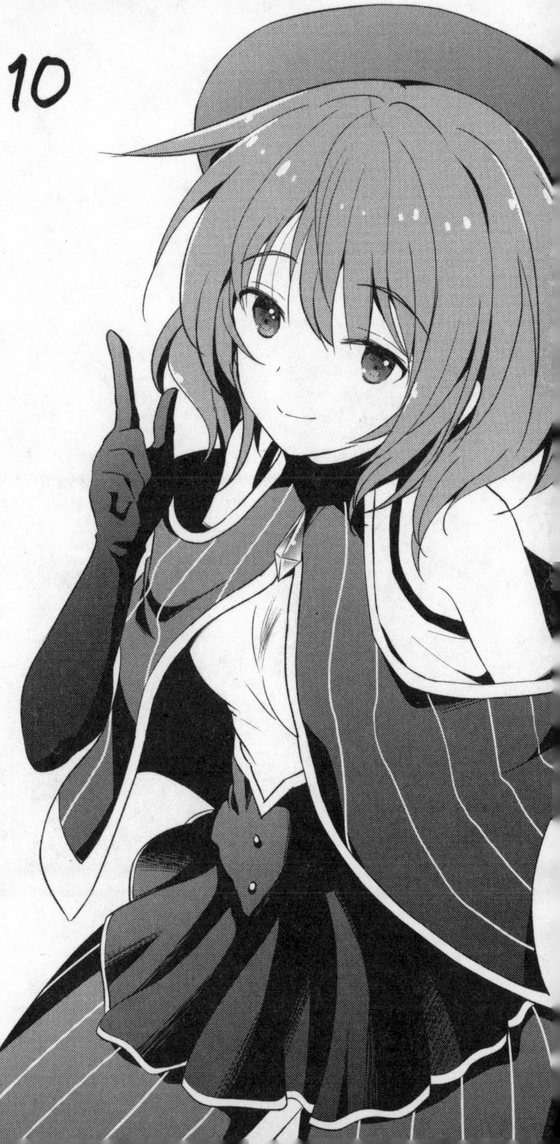

CHARACTER DESIGNS

In honor of the tenth volume of the *Konosuba* manga, we bring you these character design pages! Have a look anytime you're thinking to yourself, **"Wait...What were these guys' skills again?"**

KAZUMA

NAME: **Kazuma Satou**
AGE: **16**
CLASS: **Adventurer**

SKILLS:

- **Ambush**
- **Sense Foe**
- **Steal**
- **One-Handed Sword**
- **Second Sight**
- **Drain Touch**
- **Deadeye**
- **Flee**
- **Bind**
- **Smith**

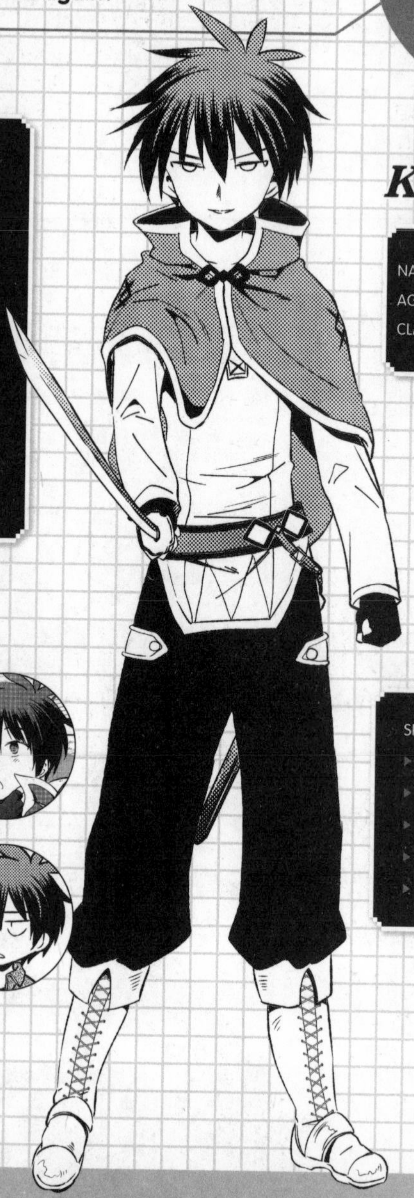

SPELLS:

- **Create Water**
- **Kindle**
- **Create Ice**
- **Wind Breath**
- **Freeze**

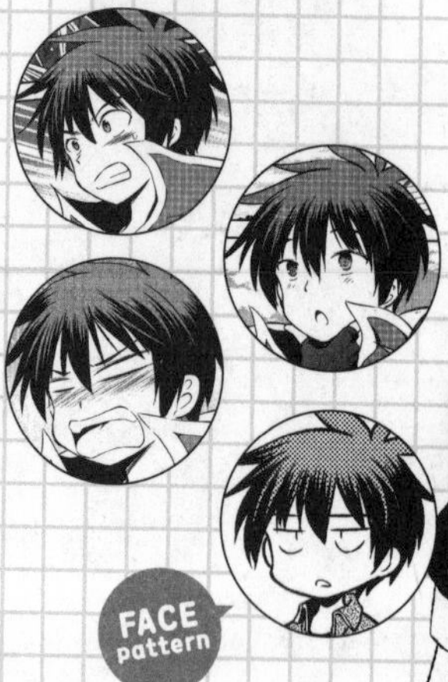

FACE pattern

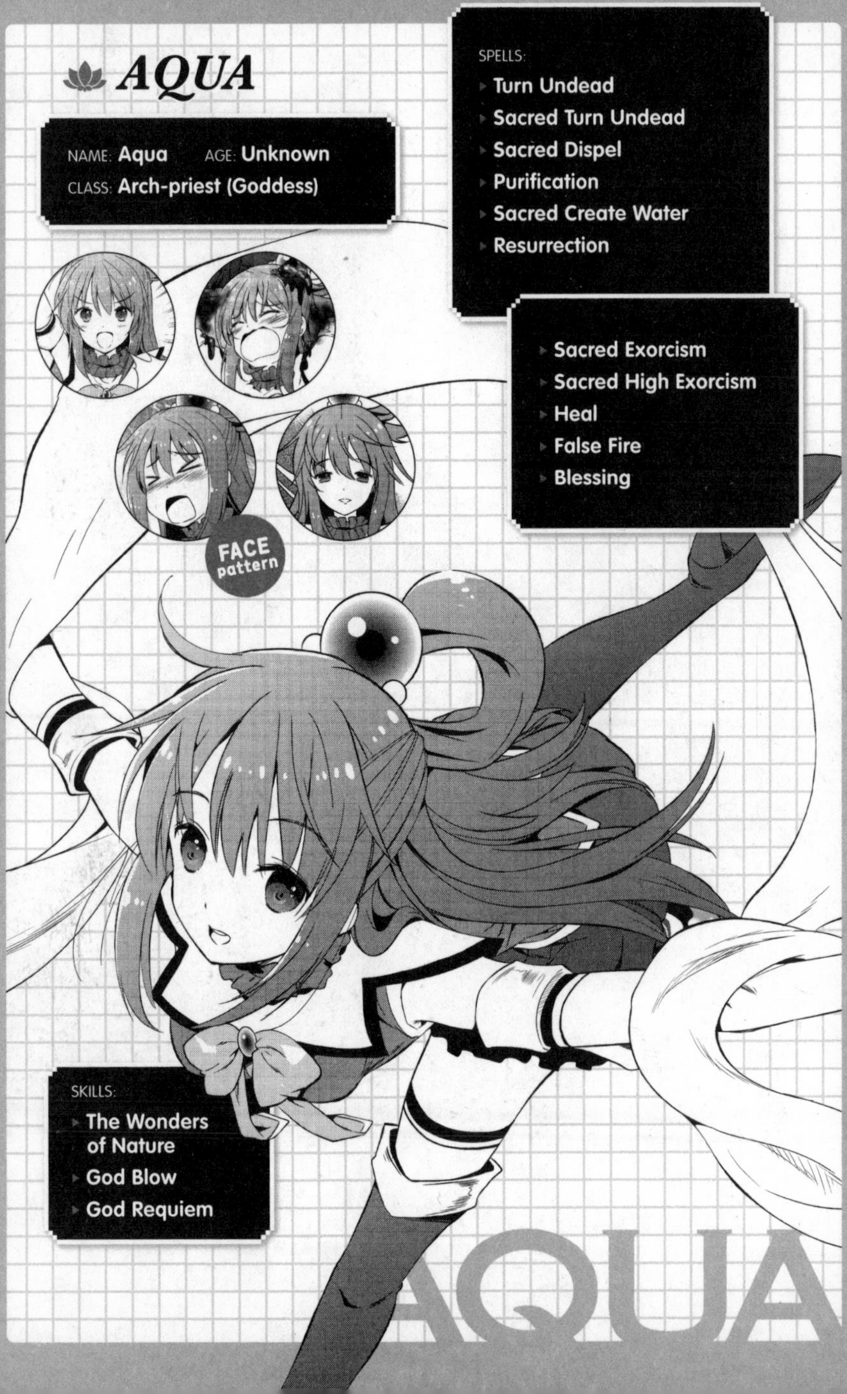
AQUA
NAME: Aqua AGE: Unknown
CLASS: Arch-priest (Goddess)
SPELLS:
Turn Undead
Sacred Turn Undead
Sacred Dispel
Purification
Sacred Create Water
Resurrection
Sacred Exorcism
Sacred High Exorcism
Heal
False Fire
Blessing
FACE pattern
SKILLS:
The Wonders of Nature
God Blow
God Requiem
AQUA

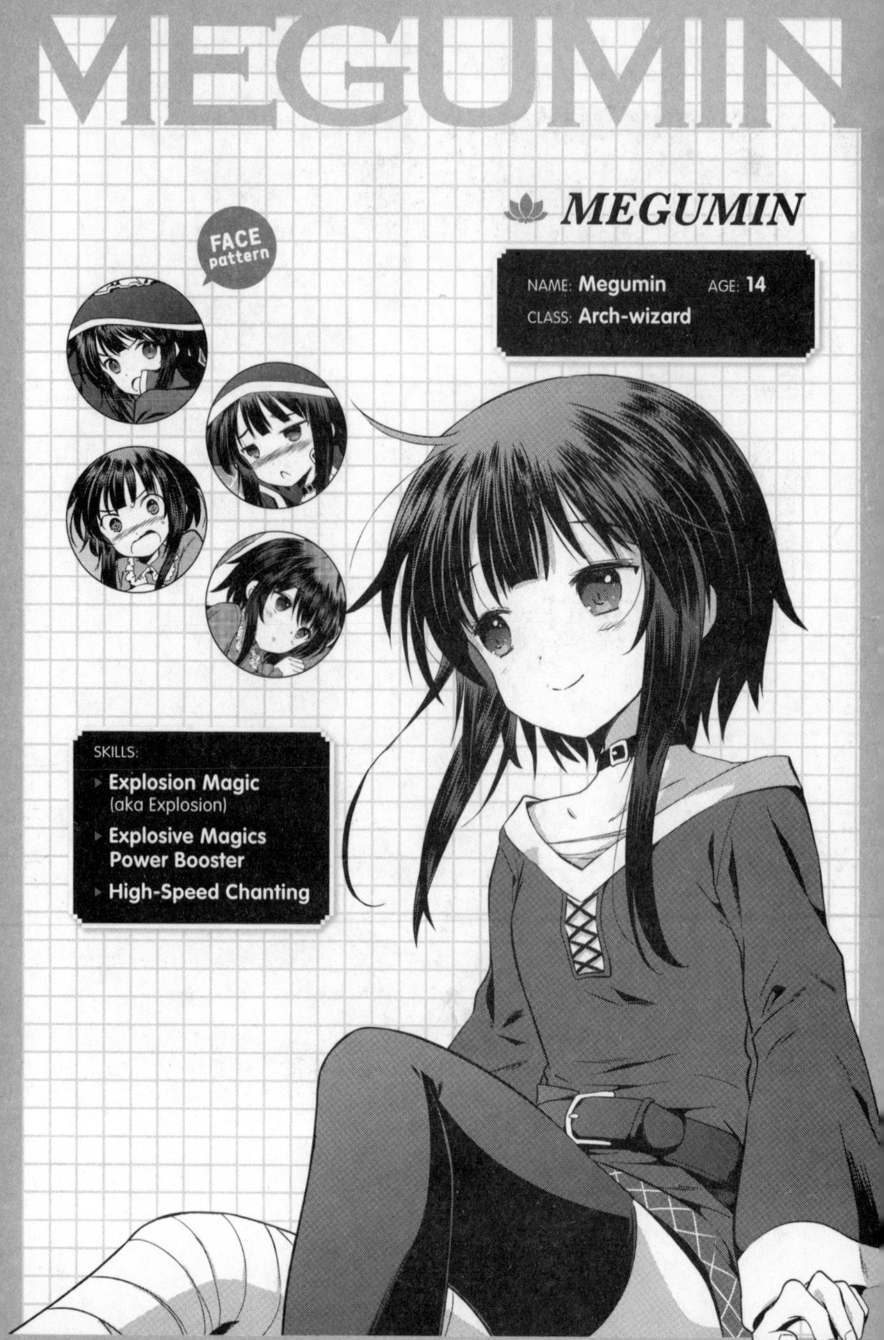

MEGUMIN
MEGUMIN
FACE pattern
NAME: Megumin AGE: 14
CLASS: Arch-wizard
SKILLS:
Explosion Magic (aka Explosion)
Explosive Magics Power Booster
High-Speed Chanting

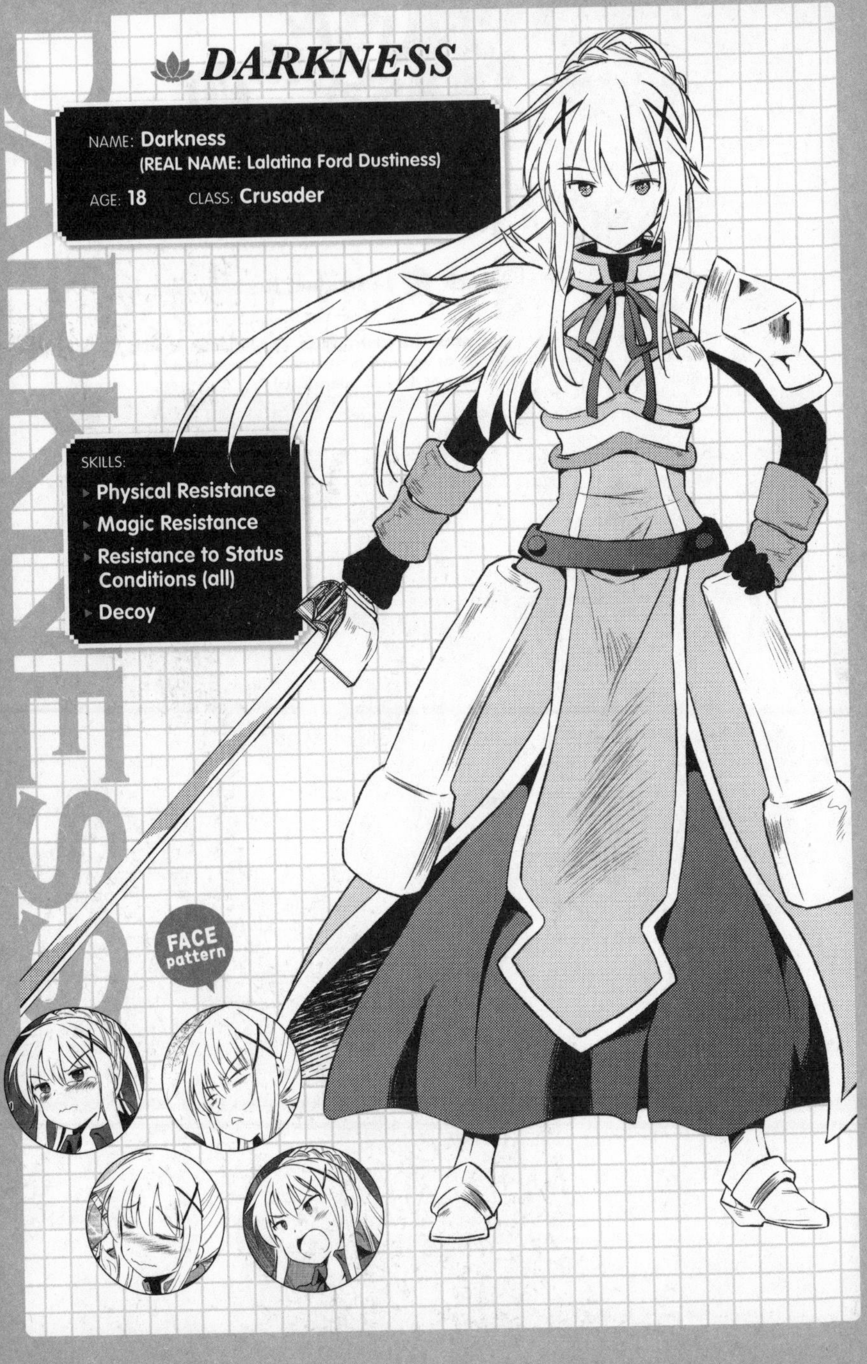
DARKNESS
NAME: Darkness
(REAL NAME: Lalatina Ford Dustiness)
AGE: 18 CLASS: Crusader
SKILLS:
Physical Resistance
Magic Resistance
Resistance to Status Conditions (all)
Decoy
FACE pattern

Translation: Kevin Stei

This book is a work of fiction.
product of the author's imagin
actual events, locales, or persons,

KONO SUBARASHII SEKAI NI SYUKUFUKU WO! Volume 10
©Masahito Watari 2019
©Natsume Akatsuki, Kurone Mishima 2019
First published in Japan in 2019 by Kadokawa Corporation, Tokyo. English
translation rights arranged with KADOKAWA Corporation, Tokyo through
Tuttle-Mori Agency, Inc., Tokyo.

English translation © 2020 by Yen Press, LLC

Yen Press
150 West 30th Street, 19th Floor
New York, NY 10001

Visit us at yenpress.com
facebook.com/yenpress
twitter.com/yenpress
yenpress.tumblr.com
instagram.com/yenpress

First Yen Press Edition: March 2020

Yen Press is an imprint of Yen Press, LLC.
The Yen Press name and logo are trademarks of Yen Press, LLC.

The publisher is not responsible for websites (or their content) that are not owned
by the publisher.

Library of Congress Control Number: 2016946112

ISBNs: 978-1-9753-9947-4 (paperback)
       978-1-9753-1017-2 (ebook)

10 9 8 7 6 5 4 3 2

WOR

Printed in the United States of America